THE NEW
DEADWARDIANS

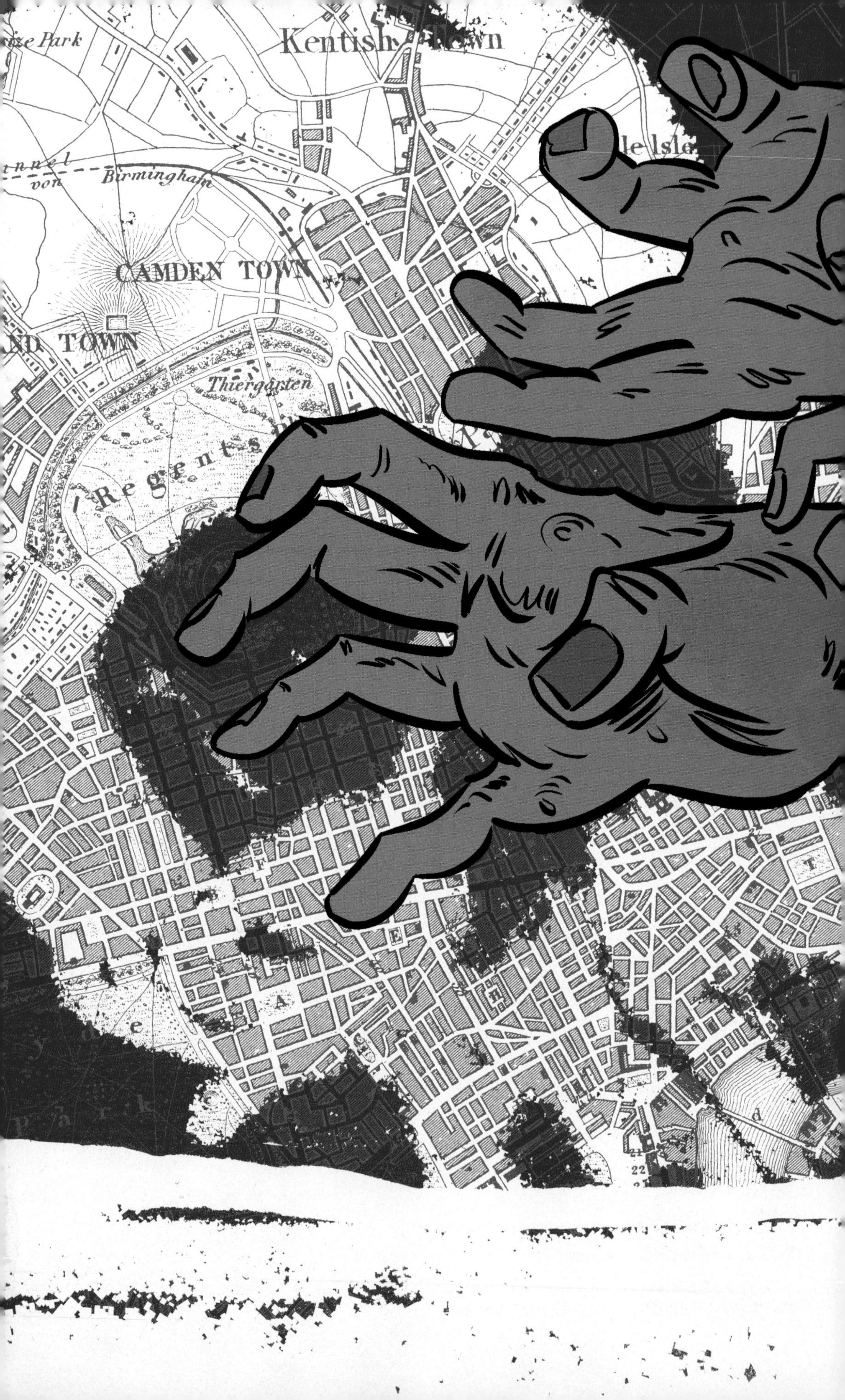
Kentish
Birmingham
CAMDEN TOWN
Thiergarten
Regents

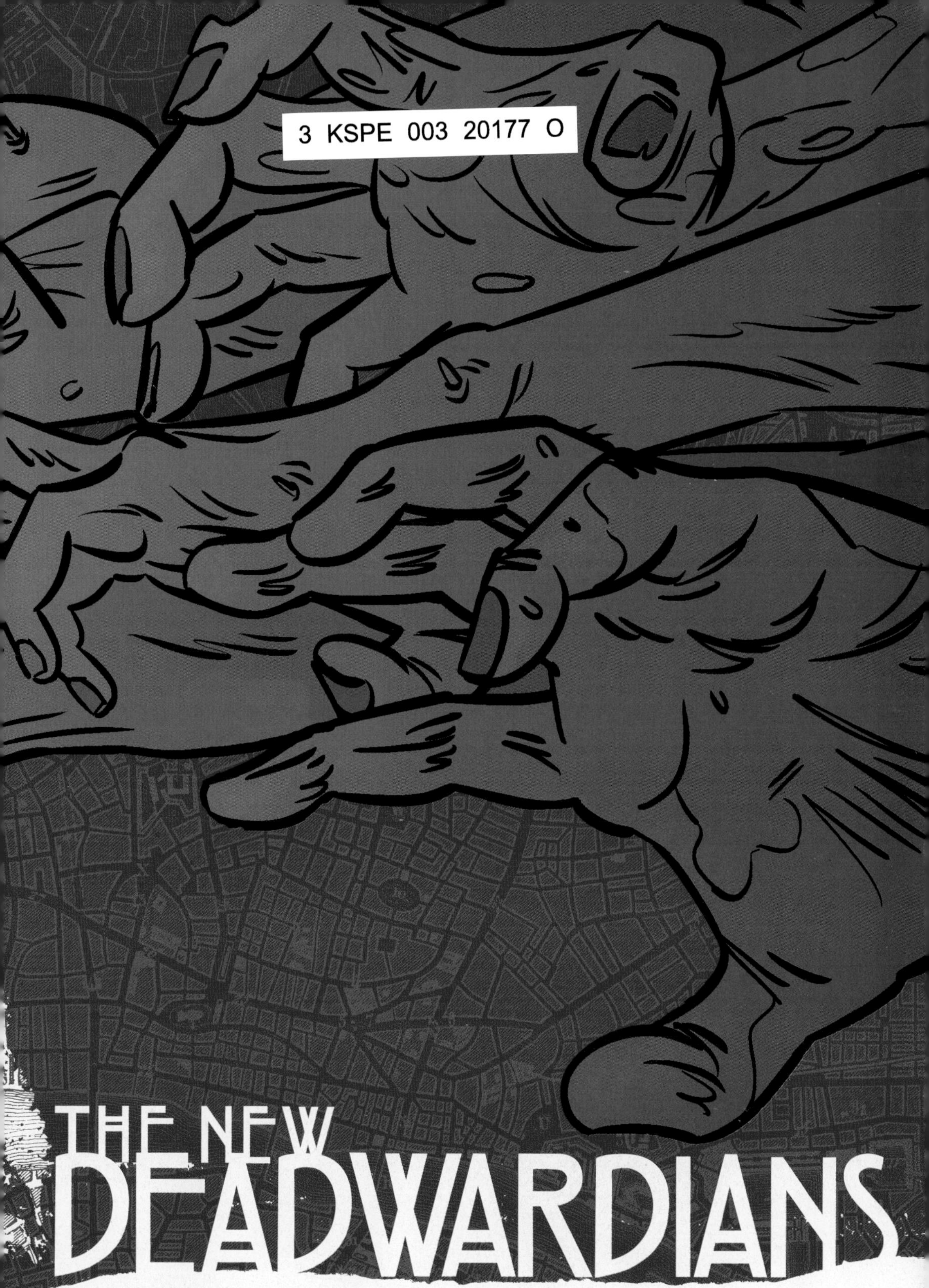

THE NEW DEADWARDIANS

Dan Abnett Writer
I.N.J. Culbard Artist and collection cover artist
Patricia Mulvihill Colorist
Travis Lanham Letterer
New Deadwardians created by Abnett & Culbard

Will Dennis Editor - Original Series
Mark Doyle Associate Editor - Original Series
Rowena Yow Editor
Robbin Brosterman Design Director - Books
Louis Prandi Publication Design

Karen Berger Senior VP - Executive Editor, Vertigo

Bob Harras VP - Editor-in-Chief
Diane Nelson President
Dan DiDio and Jim Lee Co-Publishers
Geoff Johns Chief Creative Officer
John Rood Executive VP - Sales, Marketing and Business Development
Amy Genkins Senior VP - Business and Legal Affairs
Nairi Gardiner Senior VP - Finance
Jeff Boison VP - Publishing Operations
Mark Chiarello VP - Art Direction and Design
John Cunningham VP - Marketing
Terri Cunningham VP - Talent Relations and Services
Alison Gill Senior VP - Manufacturing and Operations
Hank Kanalz Senior VP - Digital
Jay Kogan VP - Business and Legal Affairs, Publishing
Jack Mahan VP - Business Affairs, Talent
Nick Napolitano VP - Manufacturing Administration
Sue Pohja VP - Book Sales
Courtney Simmons Senior VP - Publicity
Bob Wayne Senior VP - Sales

THE NEW DEADWARDIANS
Published by DC Comics.

DC Comics, 1700 Broadway, New York, NY 10019
A Warner Bros. Entertainment Company.
Printed in the USA. 1/4/13. First Printing.
ISBN: 978-1-4012-3763-9

Library of Congress Cataloging-in-Publication Data

Abnett, Dan.
The new Deadwardians / Dan Abnett, Ian Culbard.
p. cm.
"Originally published in single magazine form in The New Deadwardians 1-8."
ISBN 978-1-4012-3763-9
1. Graphic novels. I. Culbard, Ian. II. Title.
PN6727.A257N49 2012
741.5'973--dc23

2012040579

SUSTAINABLE FORESTRY INITIATIVE
Certified Chain of Custody
At Least 20% Certified Forest Content
www.sfiprogram.org
SFI-01042
APPLIES TO TEXT STOCK ONLY

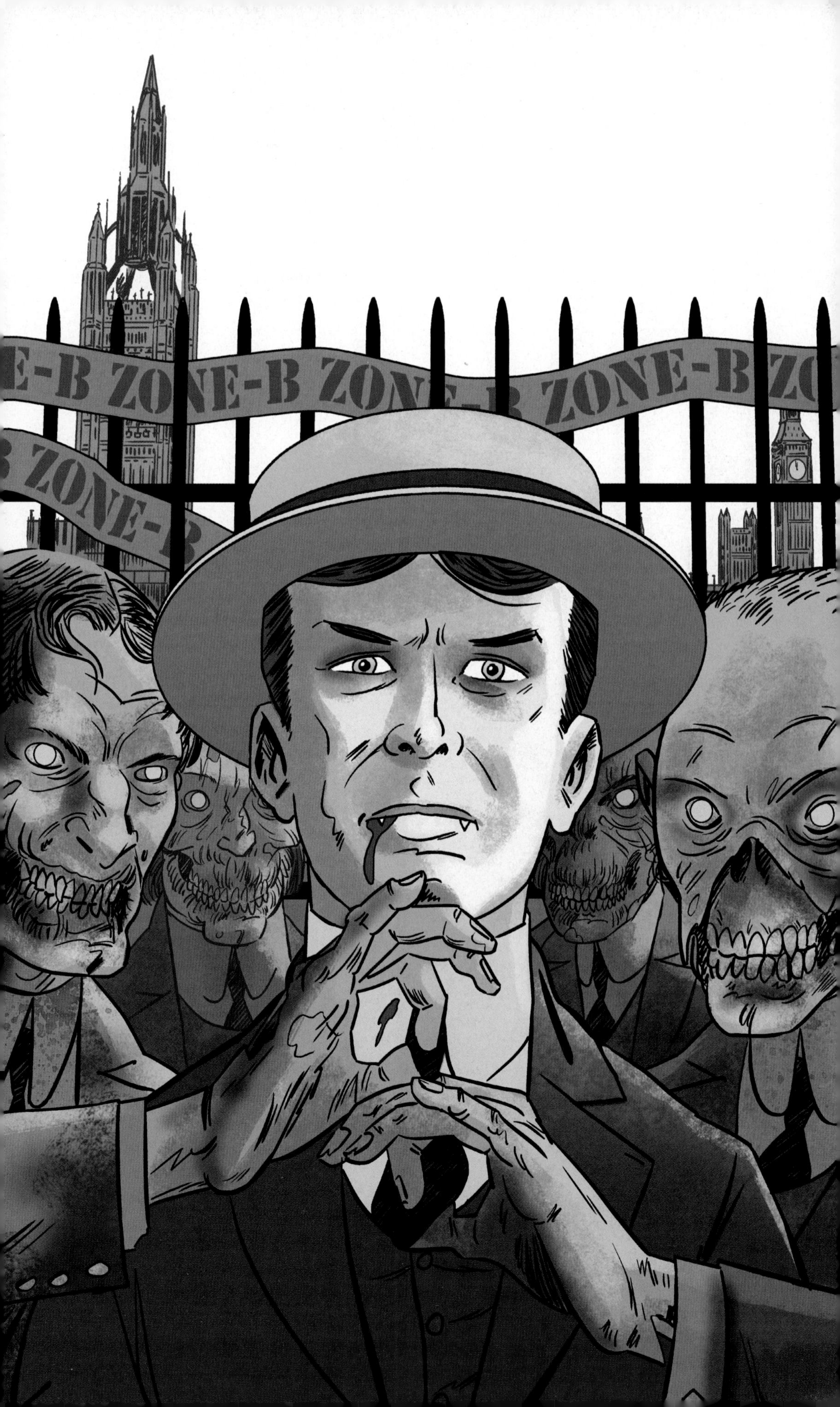
E-B ZONE-B ZONE-B ZONE-B ZO
B ZONE-B

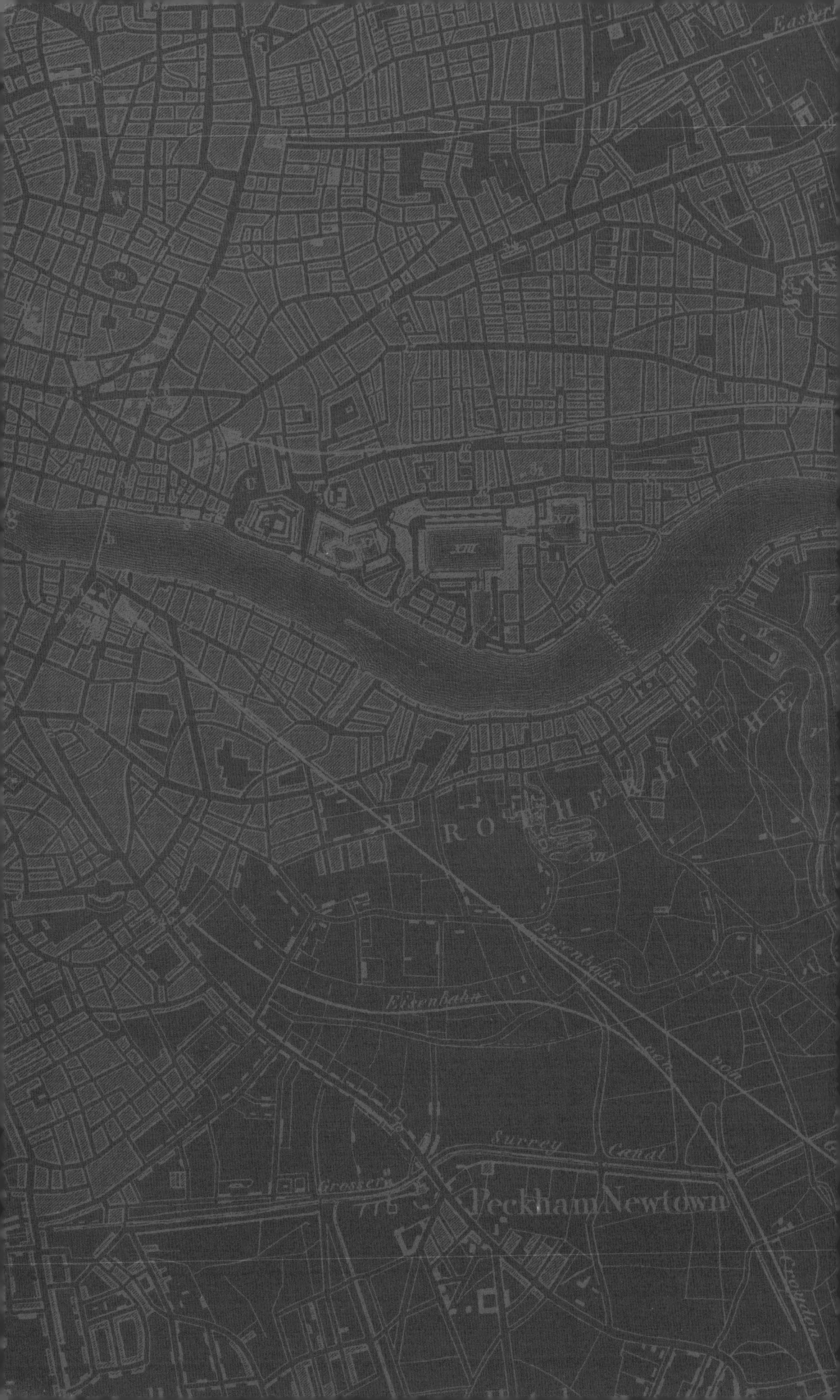
Eisenbahn
Surrey Canal
Peckham Newtown

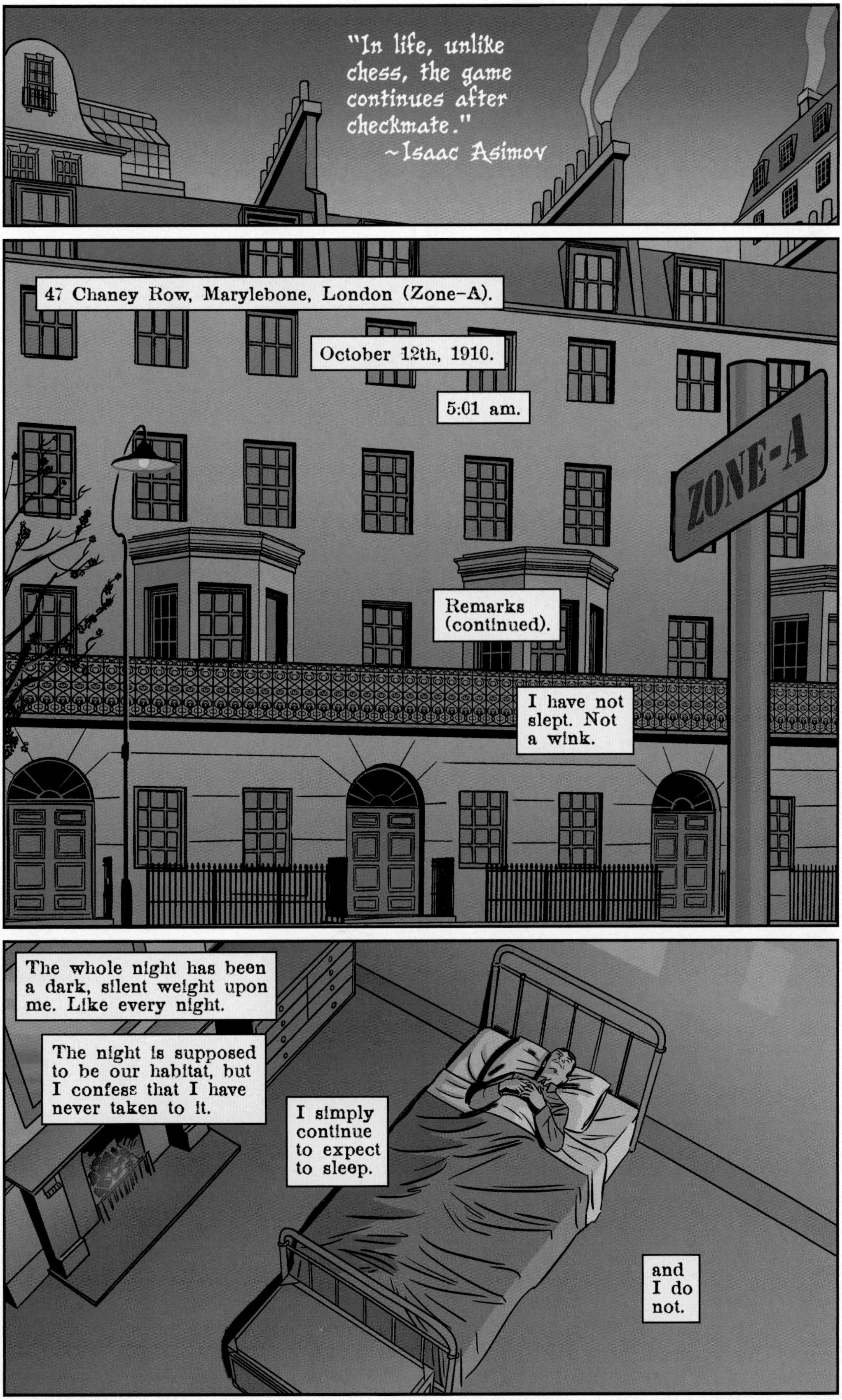
"In life, unlike chess, the game continues after checkmate."
~Isaac Asimov
47 Chaney Row, Marylebone, London (Zone-A).
October 12th, 1910.
5:01 am.
ZONE-A
Remarks (continued).
I have not slept. Not a wink.
The whole night has been a dark, silent weight upon me. Like every night.
The night is supposed to be our habitat, but I confess that I have never taken to it.
I simply continue to expect to sleep.
and I do not.

It is not the sleep that I miss, so much as the dreams.

I do miss dreams very much.

I fail to recall now what my dreams used to be about specifically. I know they were generally about hope. Wishes for the future. that sort of thing.

Now I have **more** future than I could possibly need.

And there is **nothing** I wish to do with it.

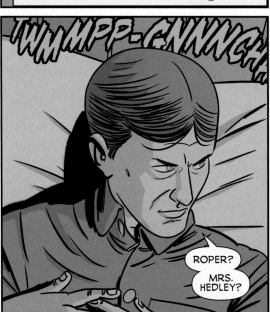

TWMMPP-CNNNCH

ROPER?

MRS. HEDLEY?

FOR GOD'S *SAKE*, ROPER! YOU'LL WAKE THE *WHOLE HOUSE!*

TNNMME

MR. SUTTLE, SIR, WERE YOU CALLING?

DOWNSTAIRS.

SOMETHING *DOWNSTAIRS!*

IS MRS. HEDLEY IN THE *KITCHEN* ALREADY?

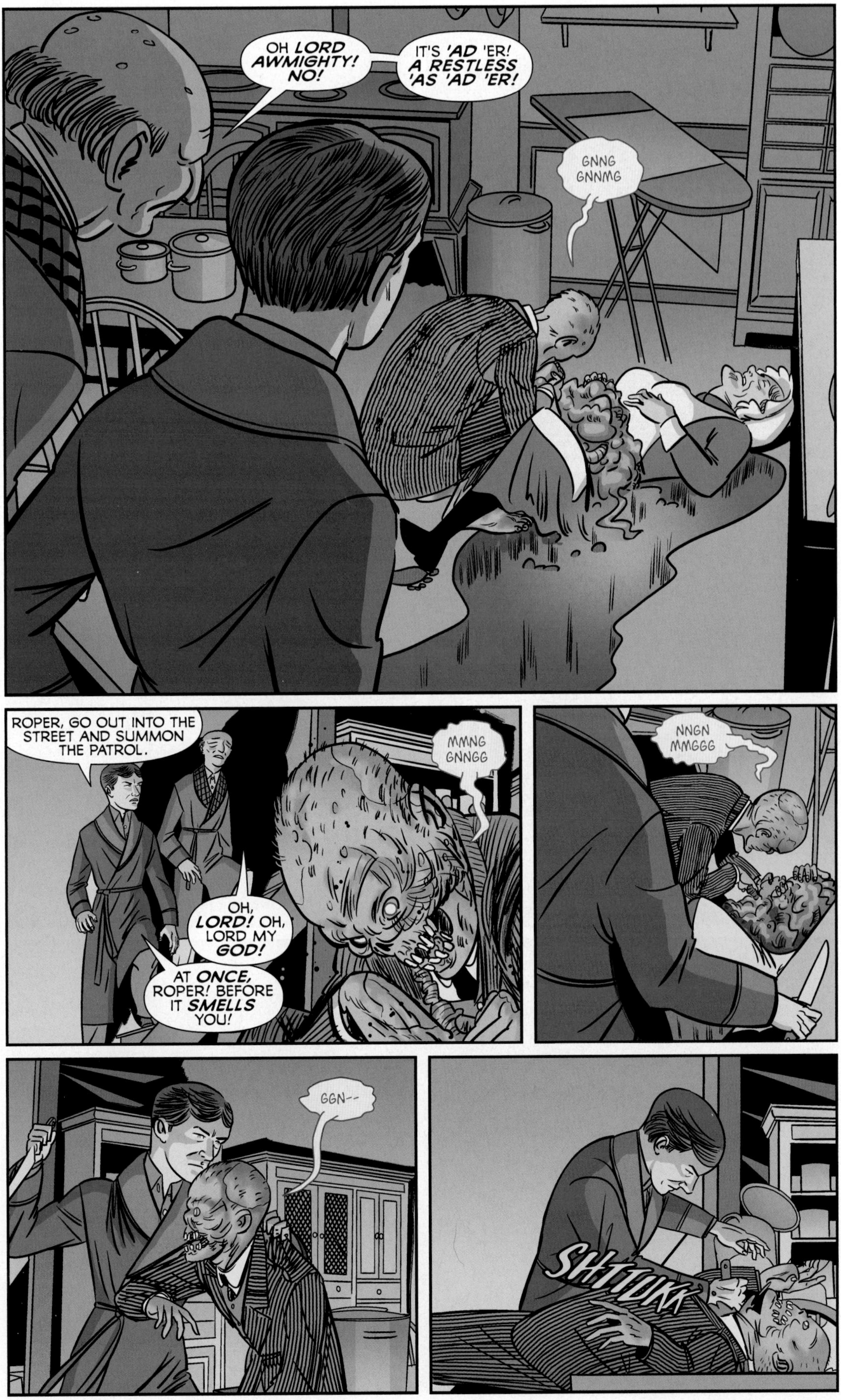
OH LORD AWMIGHTY! NO!
IT'S 'AD 'ER! A RESTLESS 'AS 'AD 'ER!
GNNG GNNMG
ROPER, GO OUT INTO THE STREET AND SUMMON THE PATROL.
MMNG GNNGG
OH, LORD! OH, LORD MY GOD!
AT ONCE, ROPER! BEFORE IT SMELLS YOU!
NNGN MMGGG
GGN--
SHTUKK

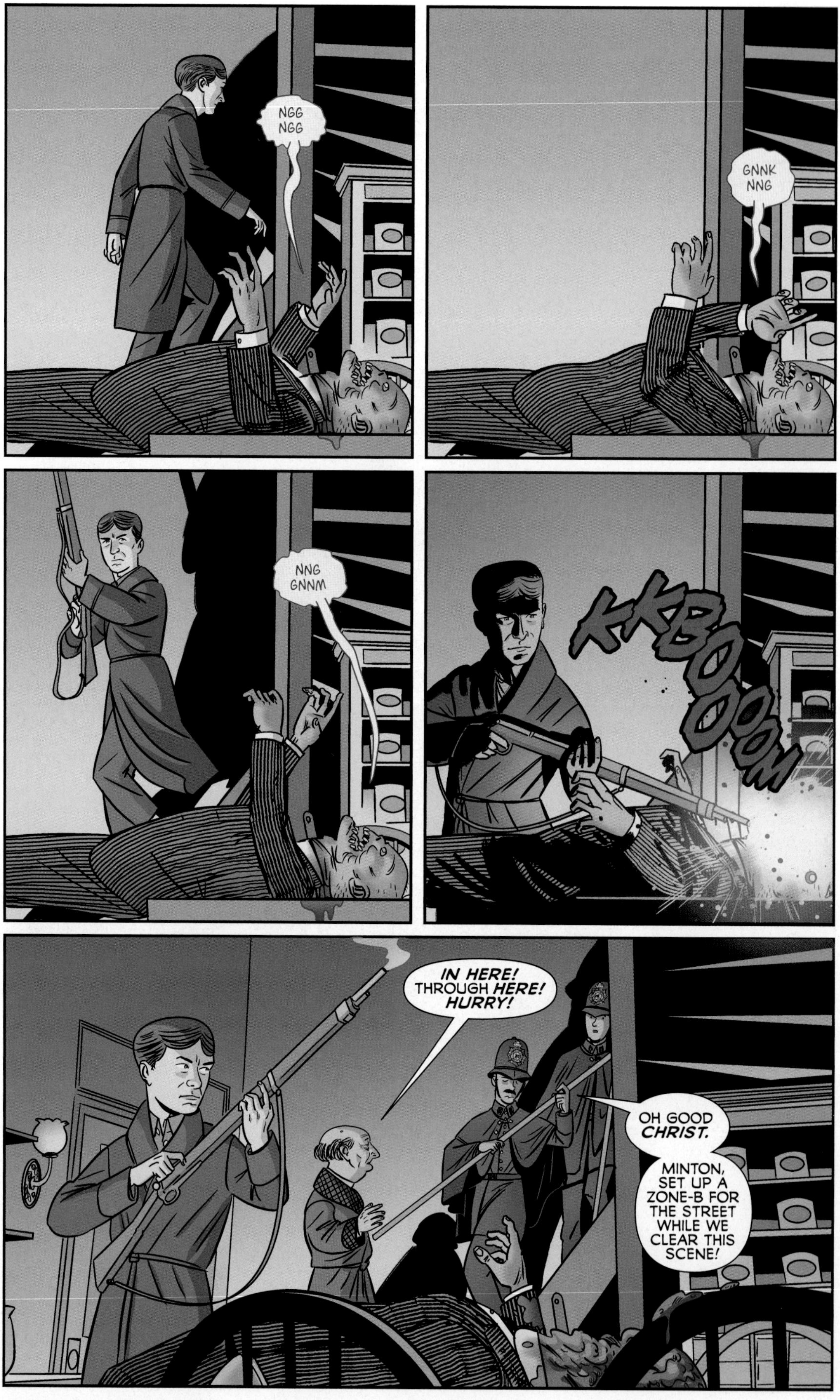
NGG
NGG
GNNK
NNG
NNG
GNNM
KKBOOOOM
IN HERE! THROUGH HERE! HURRY!
OH GOOD CHRIST.
MINTON, SET UP A ZONE-B FOR THE STREET WHILE WE CLEAR THIS SCENE!

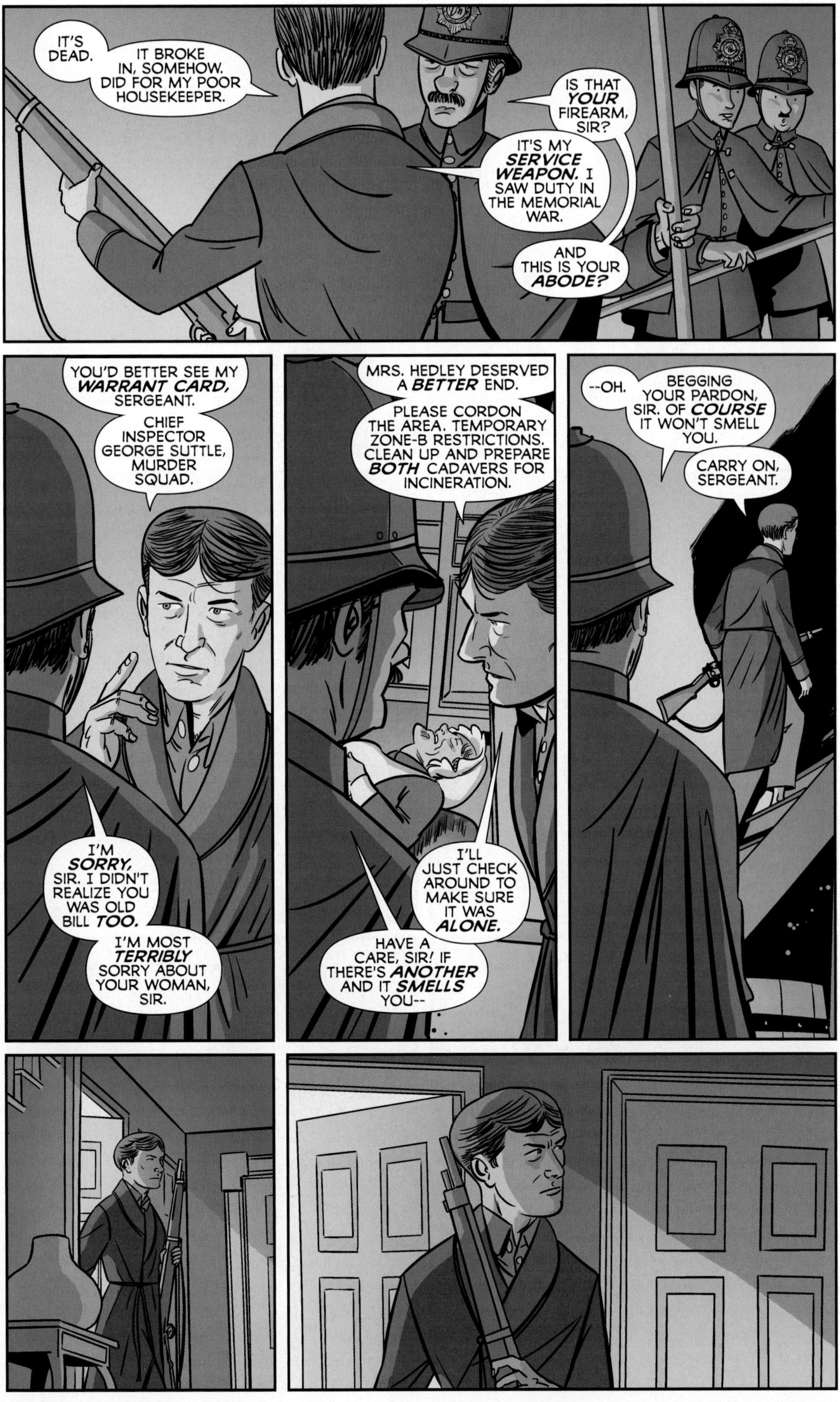
IT'S DEAD.
IT BROKE IN, SOMEHOW. DID FOR MY POOR HOUSEKEEPER.
IS THAT YOUR FIREARM, SIR?
IT'S MY SERVICE WEAPON. I SAW DUTY IN THE MEMORIAL WAR.
AND THIS IS YOUR ABODE?
YOU'D BETTER SEE MY WARRANT CARD, SERGEANT.
CHIEF INSPECTOR GEORGE SUTTLE, MURDER SQUAD.
I'M SORRY, SIR. I DIDN'T REALIZE YOU WAS OLD BILL TOO.
I'M MOST TERRIBLY SORRY ABOUT YOUR WOMAN, SIR.
MRS. HEDLEY DESERVED A BETTER END.
PLEASE CORDON THE AREA. TEMPORARY ZONE-B RESTRICTIONS. CLEAN UP AND PREPARE BOTH CADAVERS FOR INCINERATION.
I'LL JUST CHECK AROUND TO MAKE SURE IT WAS ALONE.
HAVE A CARE, SIR! IF THERE'S ANOTHER AND IT SMELLS YOU--
--OH.
BEGGING YOUR PARDON, SIR. OF COURSE IT WON'T SMELL YOU.
CARRY ON, SERGEANT.

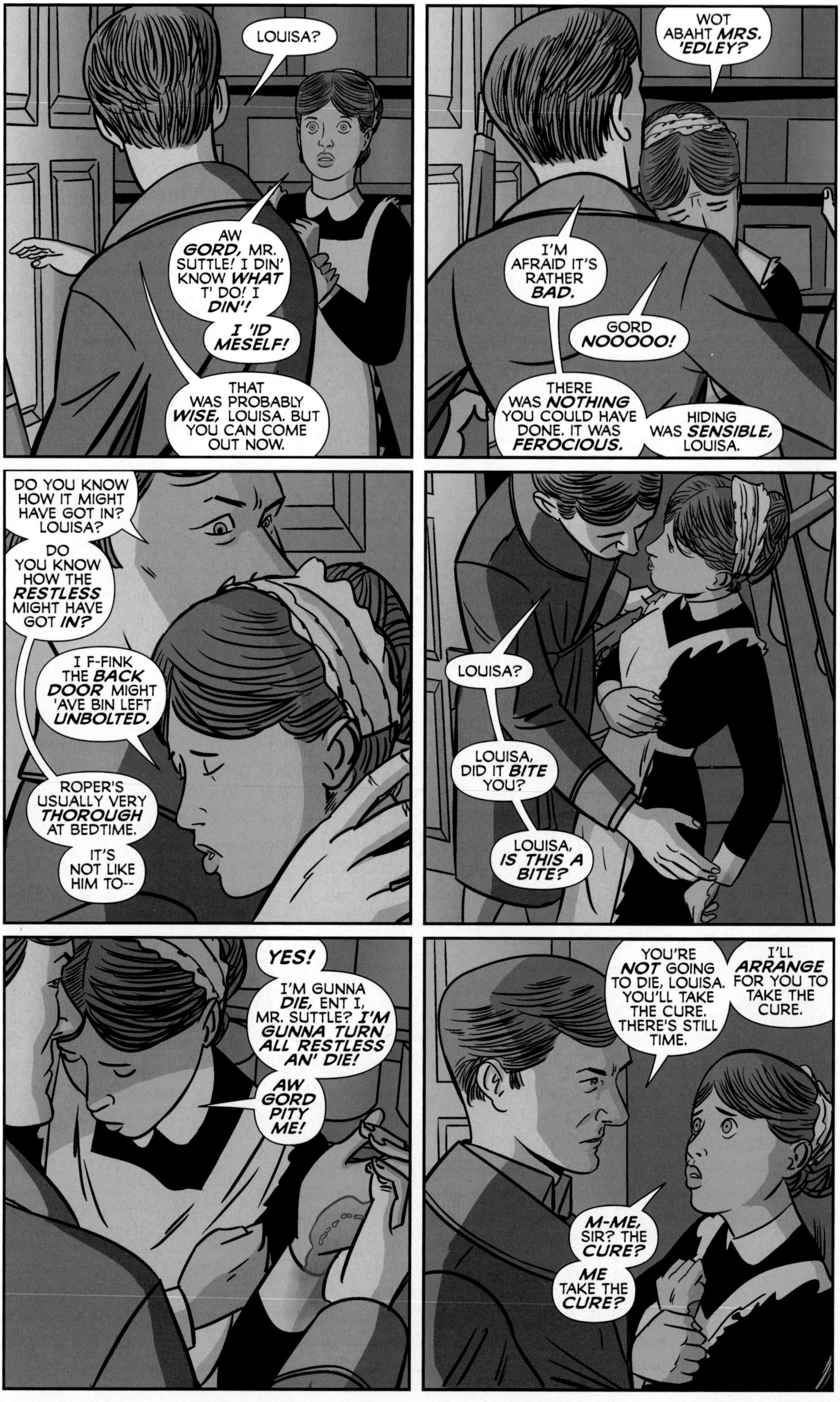
LOUISA?
AW GORD, MR. SUTTLE! I DIN' KNOW WHAT T' DO! I DIN'!
I 'ID MESELF!
THAT WAS PROBABLY WISE, LOUISA. BUT YOU CAN COME OUT NOW.
WOT ABAHT MRS. 'EDLEY?
I'M AFRAID IT'S RATHER BAD.
GORD NOOOOO!
THERE WAS NOTHING YOU COULD HAVE DONE. IT WAS FEROCIOUS.
HIDING WAS SENSIBLE, LOUISA.
DO YOU KNOW HOW IT MIGHT HAVE GOT IN? LOUISA?
DO YOU KNOW HOW THE RESTLESS MIGHT HAVE GOT IN?
I F-FINK THE BACK DOOR MIGHT 'AVE BIN LEFT UNBOLTED.
ROPER'S USUALLY VERY THOROUGH AT BEDTIME.
IT'S NOT LIKE HIM TO--
LOUISA?
LOUISA, DID IT BITE YOU?
LOUISA, IS THIS A BITE?
YES!
I'M GUNNA DIE, ENT I, MR. SUTTLE? I'M GUNNA TURN ALL RESTLESS AN' DIE!
AW GORD PITY ME!
YOU'RE NOT GOING TO DIE, LOUISA. YOU'LL TAKE THE CURE. THERE'S STILL TIME.
I'LL ARRANGE FOR YOU TO TAKE THE CURE.
M-ME, SIR? THE CURE?
ME TAKE THE CURE?

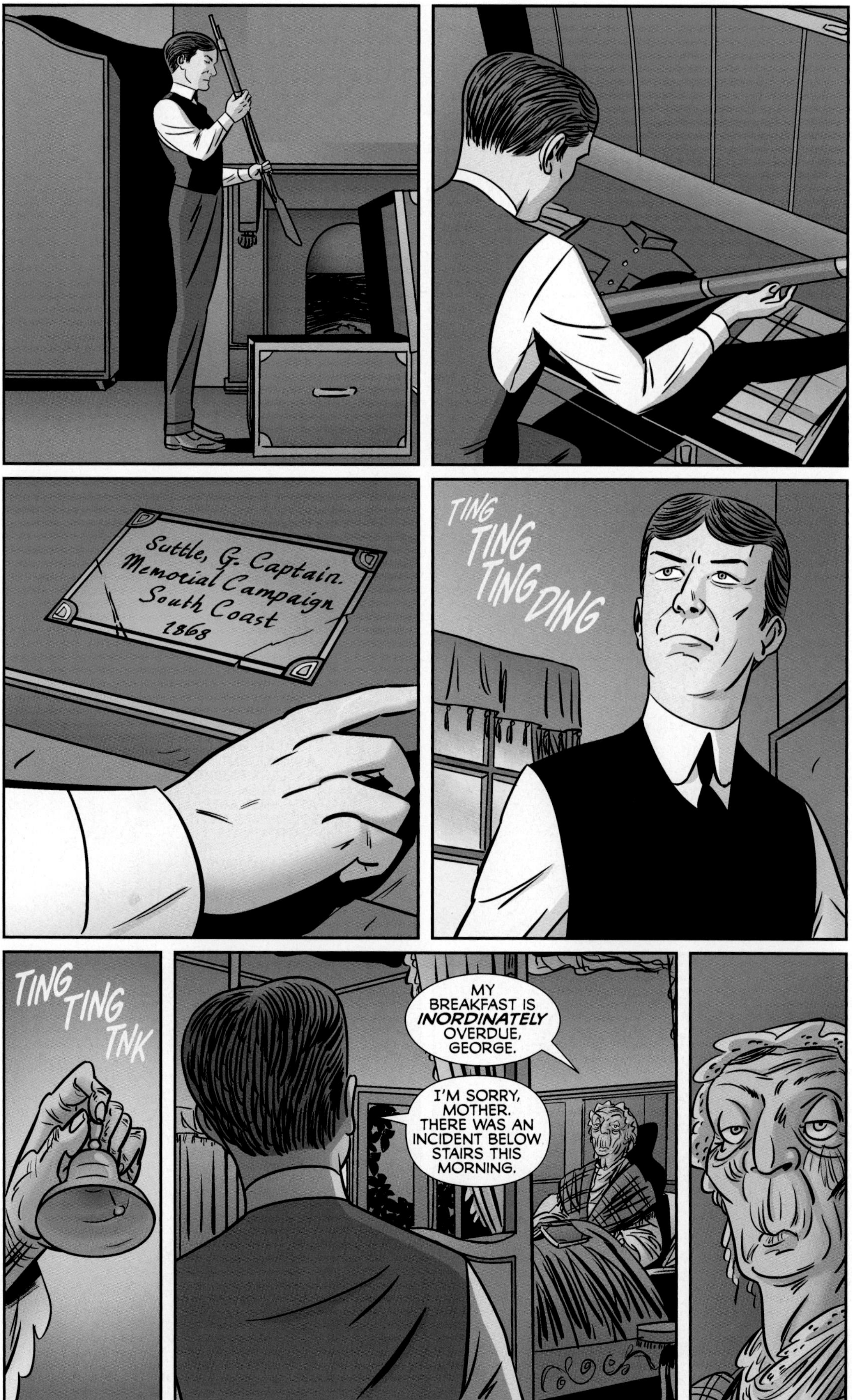
Suttle, G. Captain.
Memorial Campaign
South Coast
1868
TING TING TING DING
TING TING TNK
MY BREAKFAST IS *INORDINATELY* OVERDUE, GEORGE.
I'M SORRY, MOTHER. THERE WAS AN INCIDENT BELOW STAIRS THIS MORNING.

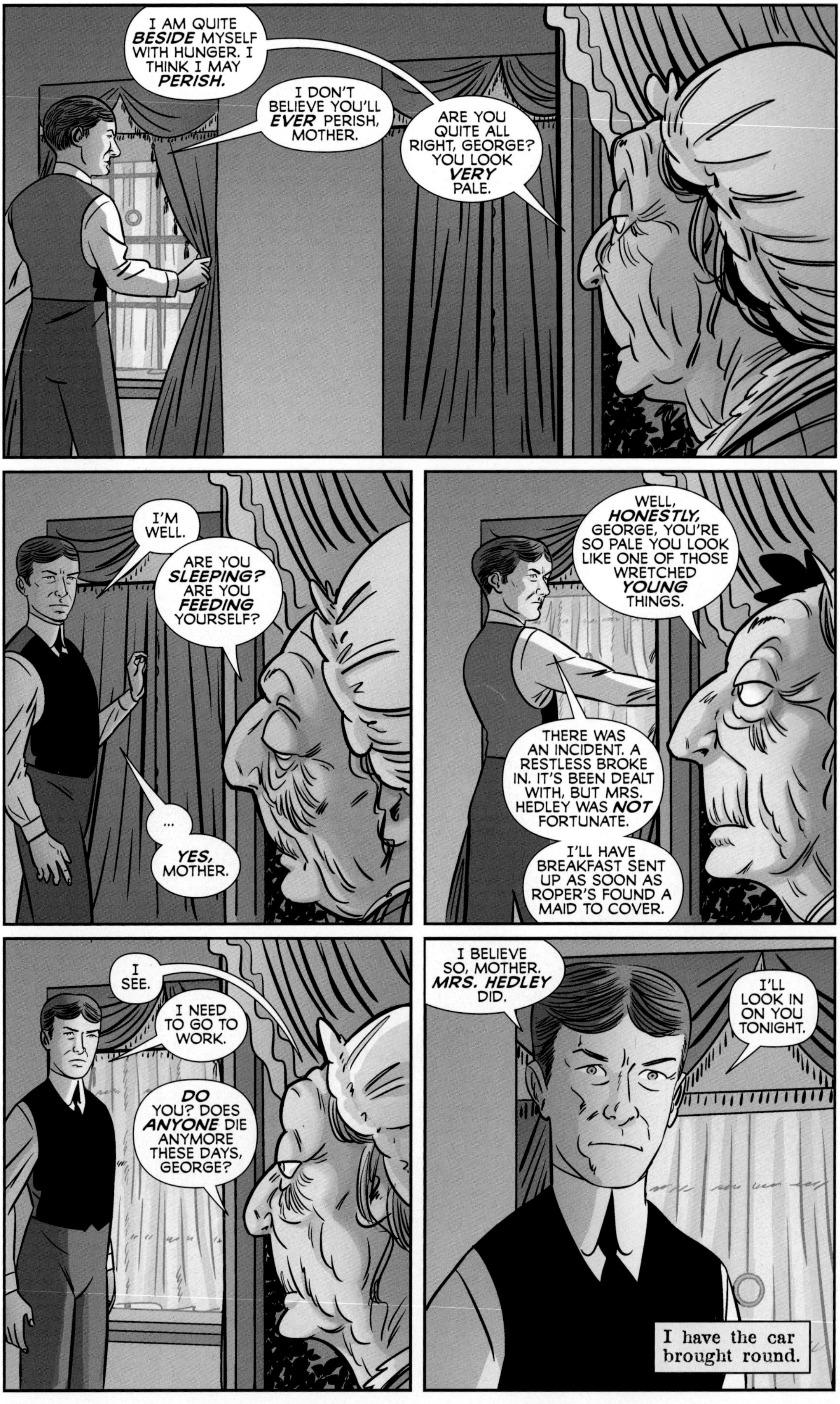
I AM QUITE BESIDE MYSELF WITH HUNGER. I THINK I MAY PERISH.
I DON'T BELIEVE YOU'LL EVER PERISH, MOTHER.
ARE YOU QUITE ALL RIGHT, GEORGE? YOU LOOK VERY PALE.
I'M WELL.
ARE YOU SLEEPING? ARE YOU FEEDING YOURSELF?
...
YES, MOTHER.
WELL, HONESTLY, GEORGE, YOU'RE SO PALE YOU LOOK LIKE ONE OF THOSE WRETCHED YOUNG THINGS.
THERE WAS AN INCIDENT. A RESTLESS BROKE IN. IT'S BEEN DEALT WITH, BUT MRS. HEDLEY WAS NOT FORTUNATE.
I'LL HAVE BREAKFAST SENT UP AS SOON AS ROPER'S FOUND A MAID TO COVER.
I SEE.
I NEED TO GO TO WORK.
DO YOU? DOES ANYONE DIE ANYMORE THESE DAYS, GEORGE?
I BELIEVE SO, MOTHER. MRS. HEDLEY DID.
I'LL LOOK IN ON YOU TONIGHT.
I have the car brought round.

Sunlight is not a problem, provided one uses zinc paste and wears a hat.

And the latter is **only** good breeding, after all.

I don't need breakfast. I merely miss the **notion** of breakfast.

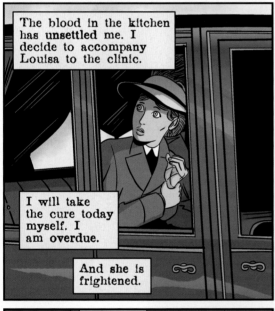

The blood in the kitchen has **unsettled** me. I decide to accompany Louisa to the clinic.

I will take the cure today myself. I am **overdue**.

And she is **frightened**.

WHAT WUZ THE STREETS LIKE, BEFORE THE RESTLESS CURSE COME?

BUSIER. ESPECIALLY HERE IN ZONE-A.

THERE WERE NO *FENCES* TO KEEP THE RESTLESS OUT, OF COURSE.

AND NO PATROLS. AND NO *MOTOR CARS* EITHER.

AND THERE WERE *BIRDS.* WILD BIRDS. SPARROWS AND STARLINGS. YOU KNOW?

WOT 'APPENED TO 'EM?

THEY STAY AWAY. THE RESTLESS *EAT* THEM. AND BIRDS AND ANIMALS TEND TO *AVOID* THE YOUNG.

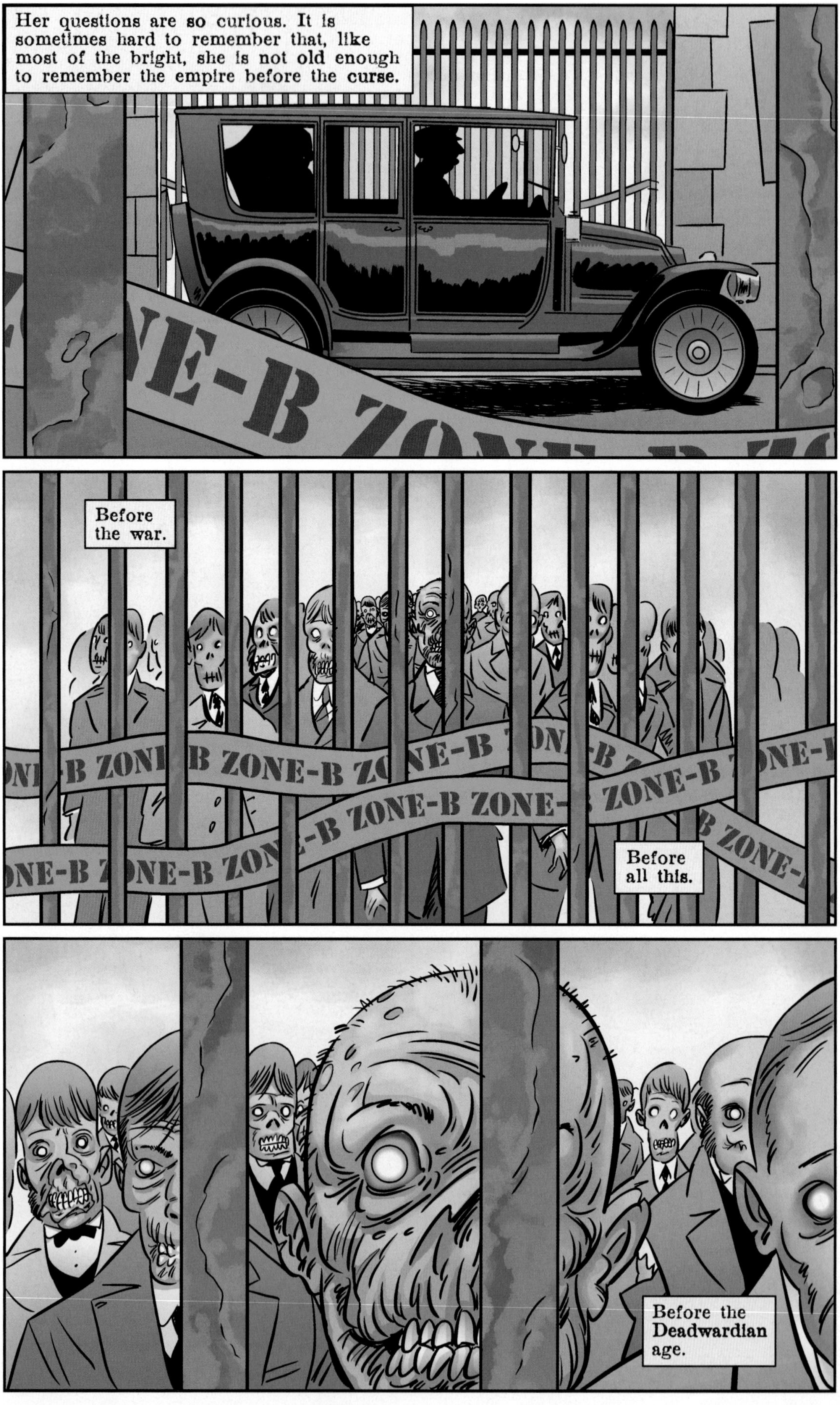
Her questions are so curious. It is sometimes hard to remember that, like most of the bright, she is not old enough to remember the empire before the curse.
ZONE-B
Before the war.
Before all this.
Before the Deadwardian age.

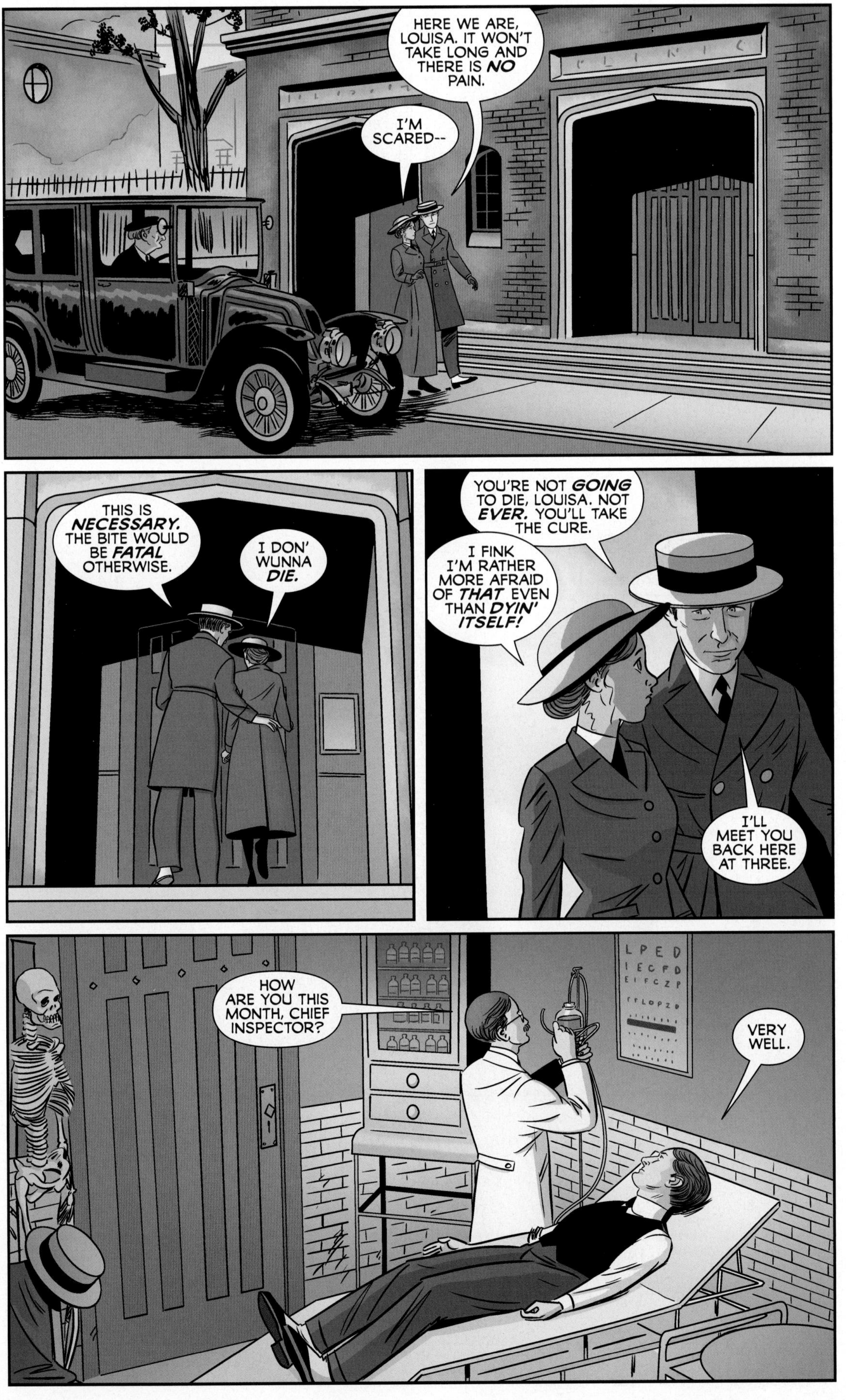
HERE WE ARE, LOUISA. IT WON'T TAKE LONG AND THERE IS NO PAIN.
I'M SCARED--
THIS IS NECESSARY. THE BITE WOULD BE FATAL OTHERWISE.
I DON' WUNNA DIE.
YOU'RE NOT GOING TO DIE, LOUISA. NOT EVER. YOU'LL TAKE THE CURE.
I FINK I'M RATHER MORE AFRAID OF THAT EVEN THAN DYIN' ITSELF!
I'LL MEET YOU BACK HERE AT THREE.
HOW ARE YOU THIS MONTH, CHIEF INSPECTOR?
VERY WELL.

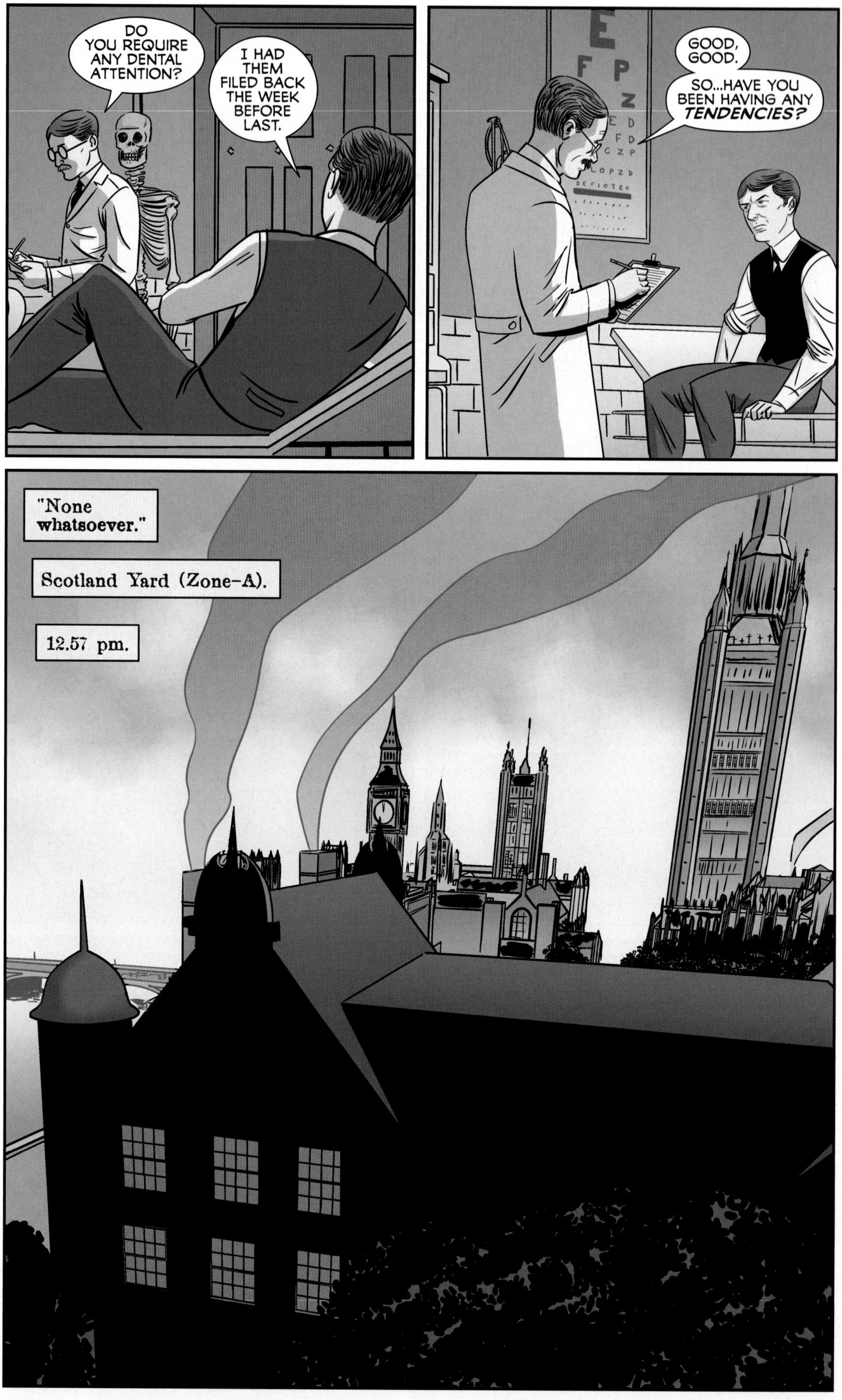
DO YOU REQUIRE ANY DENTAL ATTENTION?
I HAD THEM FILED BACK THE WEEK BEFORE LAST.
GOOD, GOOD.
SO...HAVE YOU BEEN HAVING ANY *TENDENCIES?*
"None whatsoever."
Scotland Yard (Zone-A).
12.57 pm.

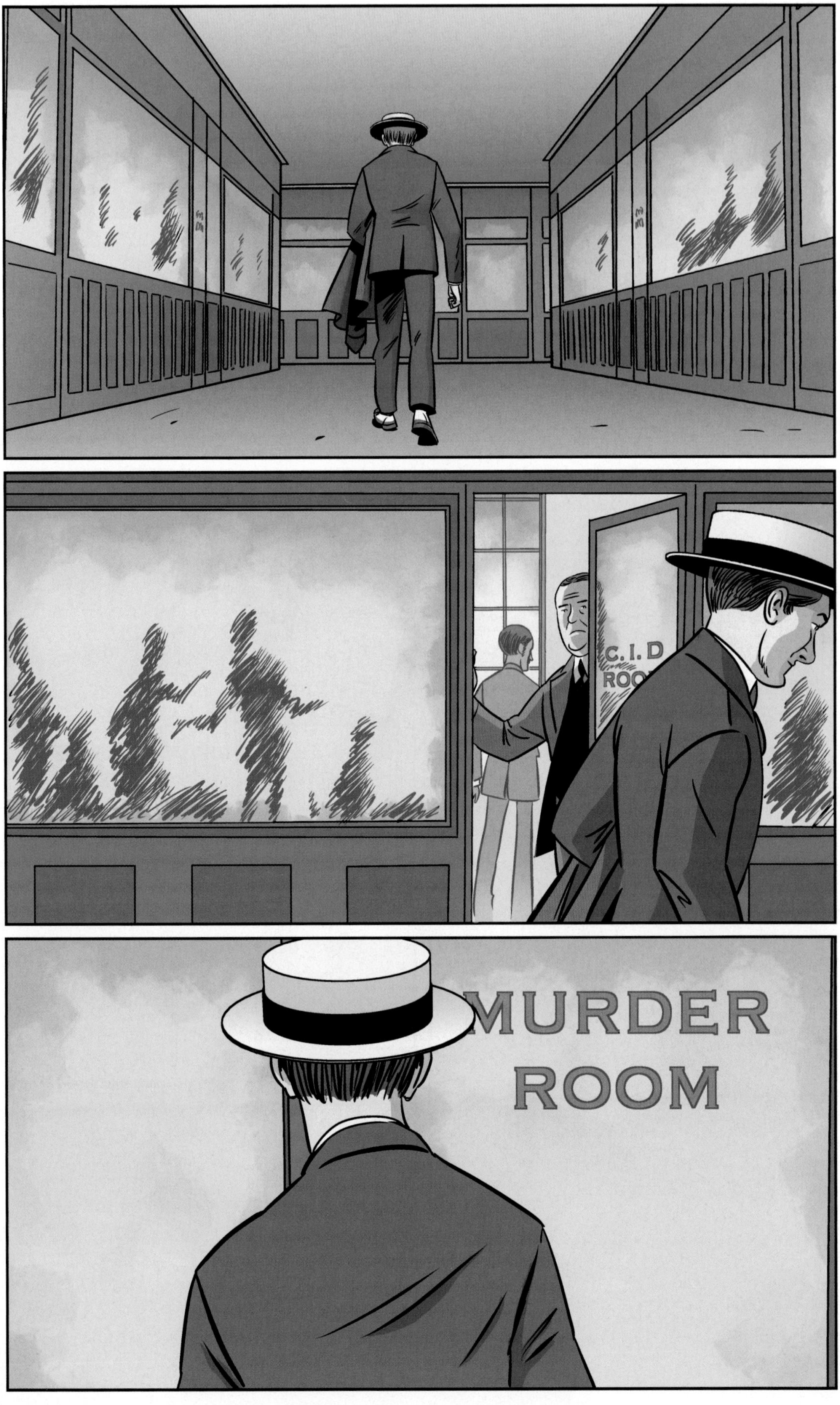
C. I. D
MURDER
ROOM

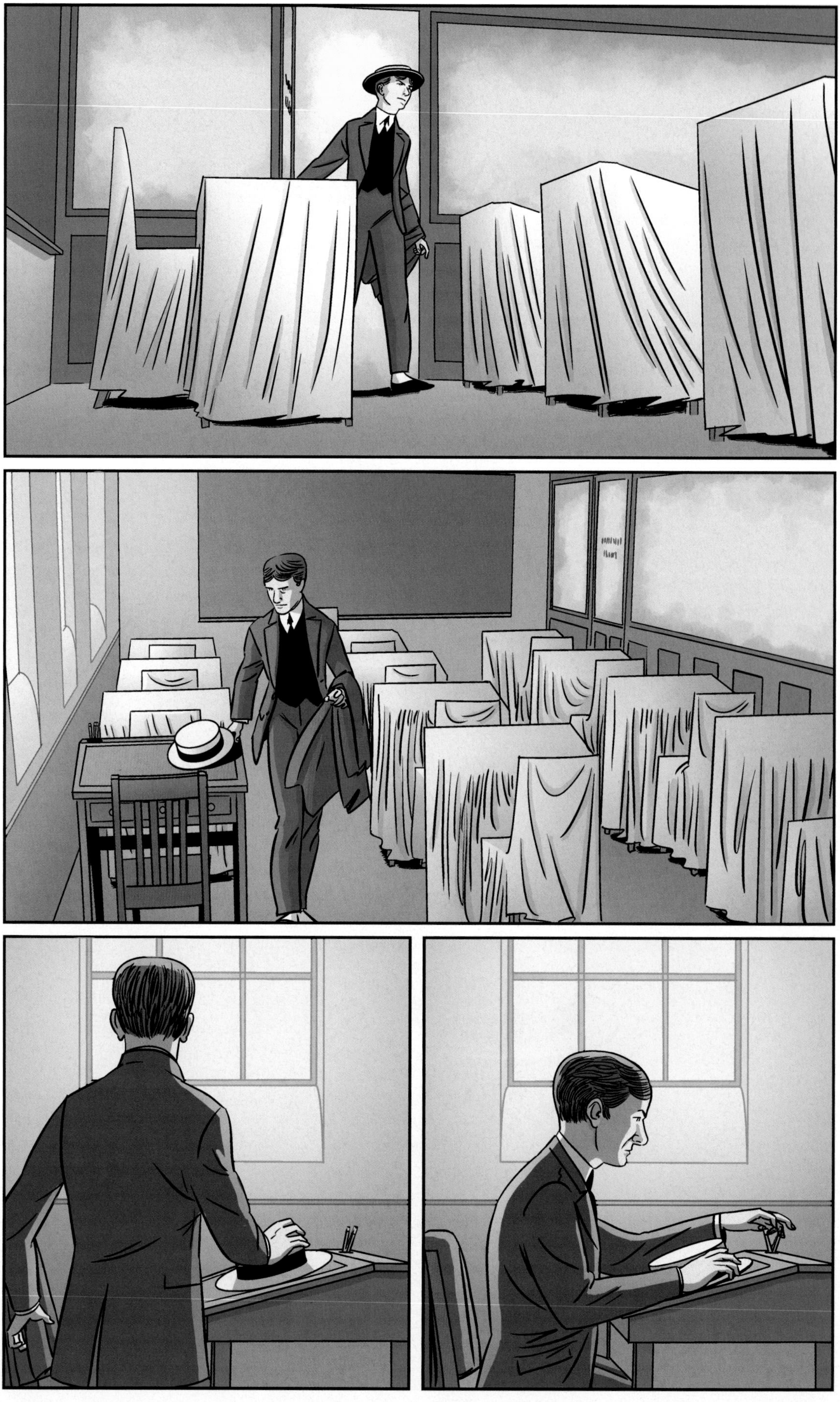

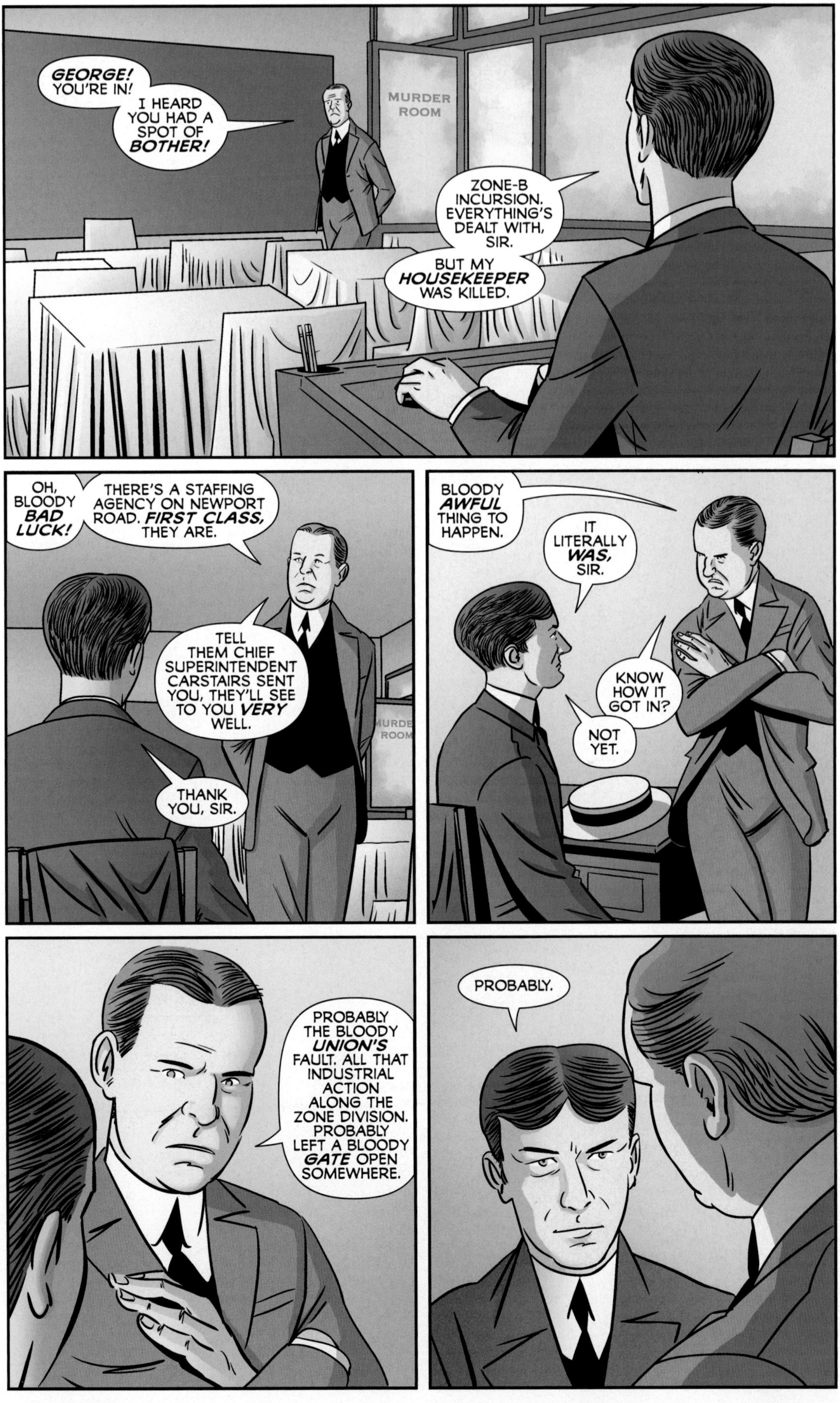
MURDER ROOM
GEORGE! YOU'RE IN!
I HEARD YOU HAD A SPOT OF BOTHER!
ZONE-B INCURSION. EVERYTHING'S DEALT WITH, SIR.
BUT MY HOUSEKEEPER WAS KILLED.
OH, BLOODY BAD LUCK!
THERE'S A STAFFING AGENCY ON NEWPORT ROAD. FIRST CLASS, THEY ARE.
TELL THEM CHIEF SUPERINTENDENT CARSTAIRS SENT YOU, THEY'LL SEE TO YOU VERY WELL.
THANK YOU, SIR.
BLOODY AWFUL THING TO HAPPEN.
IT LITERALLY WAS, SIR.
KNOW HOW IT GOT IN?
NOT YET.
PROBABLY THE BLOODY UNION'S FAULT. ALL THAT INDUSTRIAL ACTION ALONG THE ZONE DIVISION. PROBABLY LEFT A BLOODY GATE OPEN SOMEWHERE.
PROBABLY.

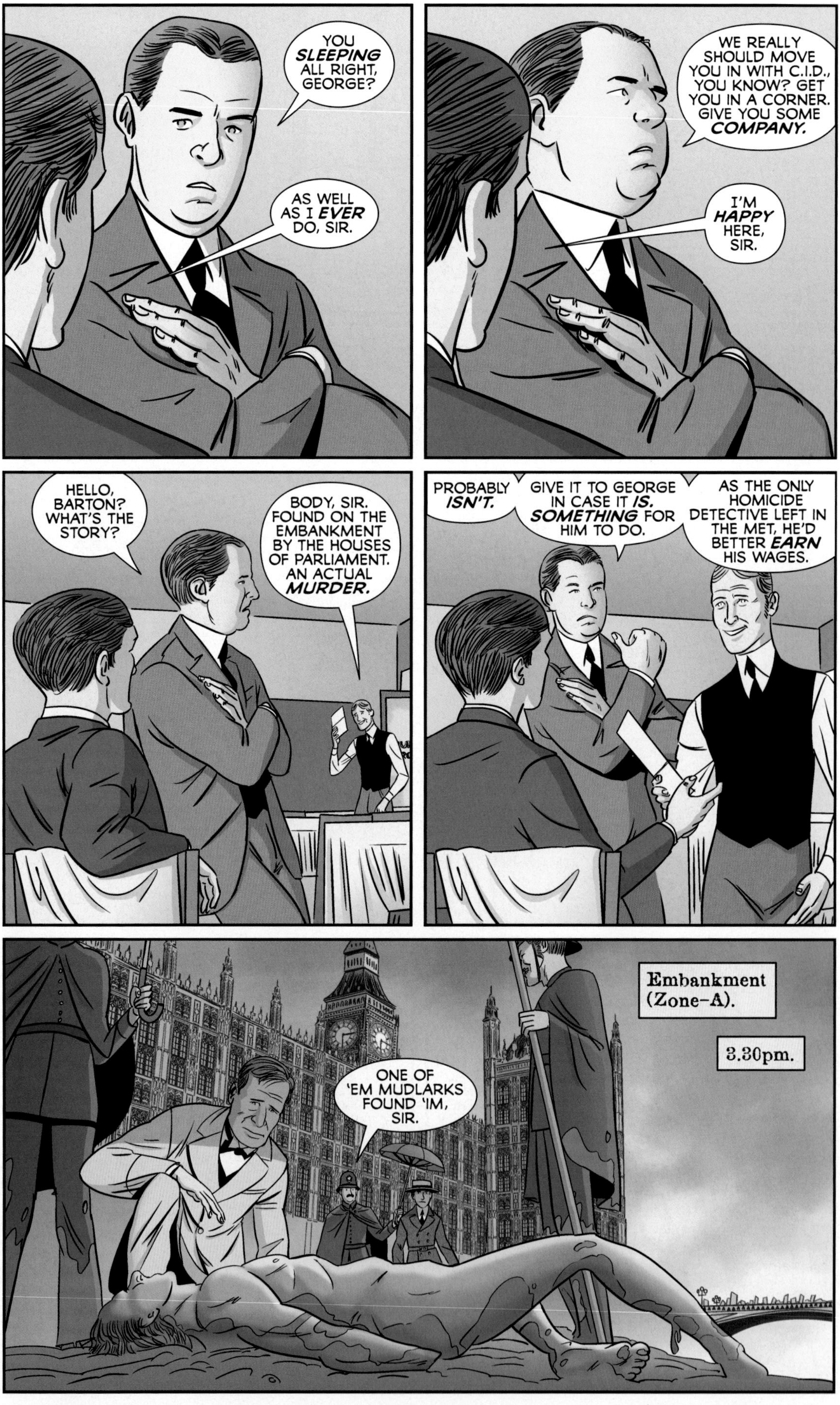
YOU *SLEEPING* ALL RIGHT, GEORGE?
AS WELL AS I *EVER* DO, SIR.
WE REALLY SHOULD MOVE YOU IN WITH C.I.D., YOU KNOW? GET YOU IN A CORNER. GIVE YOU SOME *COMPANY.*
I'M *HAPPY* HERE, SIR.
HELLO, BARTON? WHAT'S THE STORY?
BODY, SIR. FOUND ON THE EMBANKMENT BY THE HOUSES OF PARLIAMENT. AN ACTUAL *MURDER.*
PROBABLY *ISN'T.*
GIVE IT TO GEORGE IN CASE IT *IS. SOMETHING* FOR HIM TO DO.
AS THE ONLY HOMICIDE DETECTIVE LEFT IN THE MET, HE'D BETTER *EARN* HIS WAGES.
Embankment (Zone-A).
3.30pm.
ONE OF 'EM MUDLARKS FOUND 'IM, SIR.

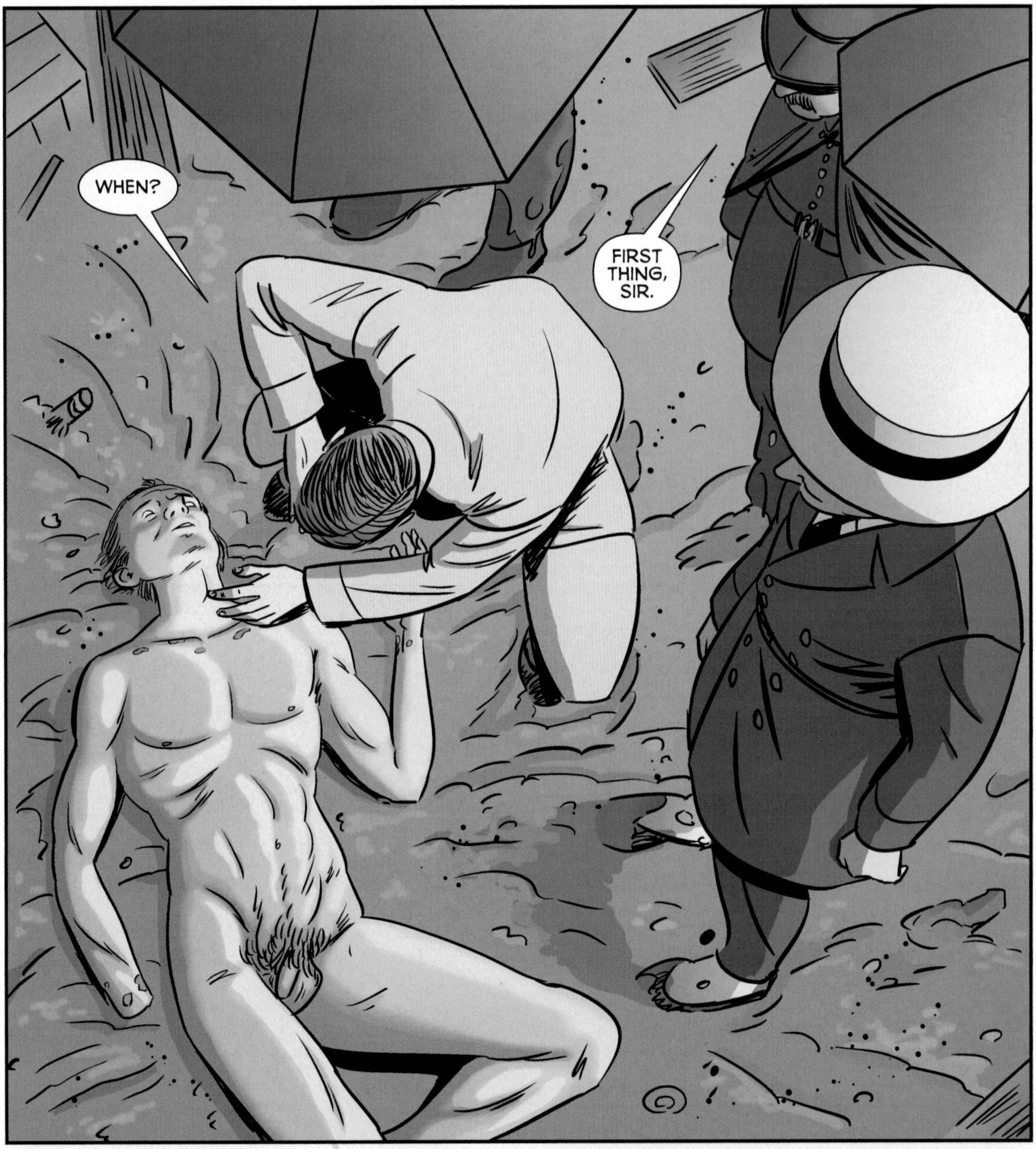
WHEN?
FIRST THING, SIR.

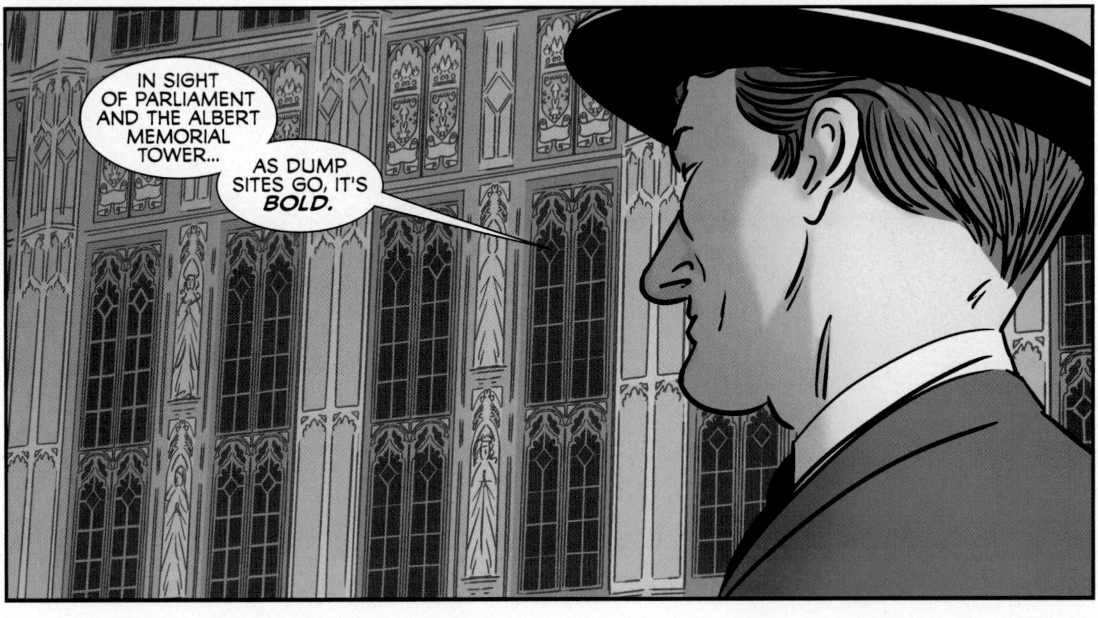
IN SIGHT OF PARLIAMENT AND THE ALBERT MEMORIAL TOWER...
AS DUMP SITES GO, IT'S *BOLD.*

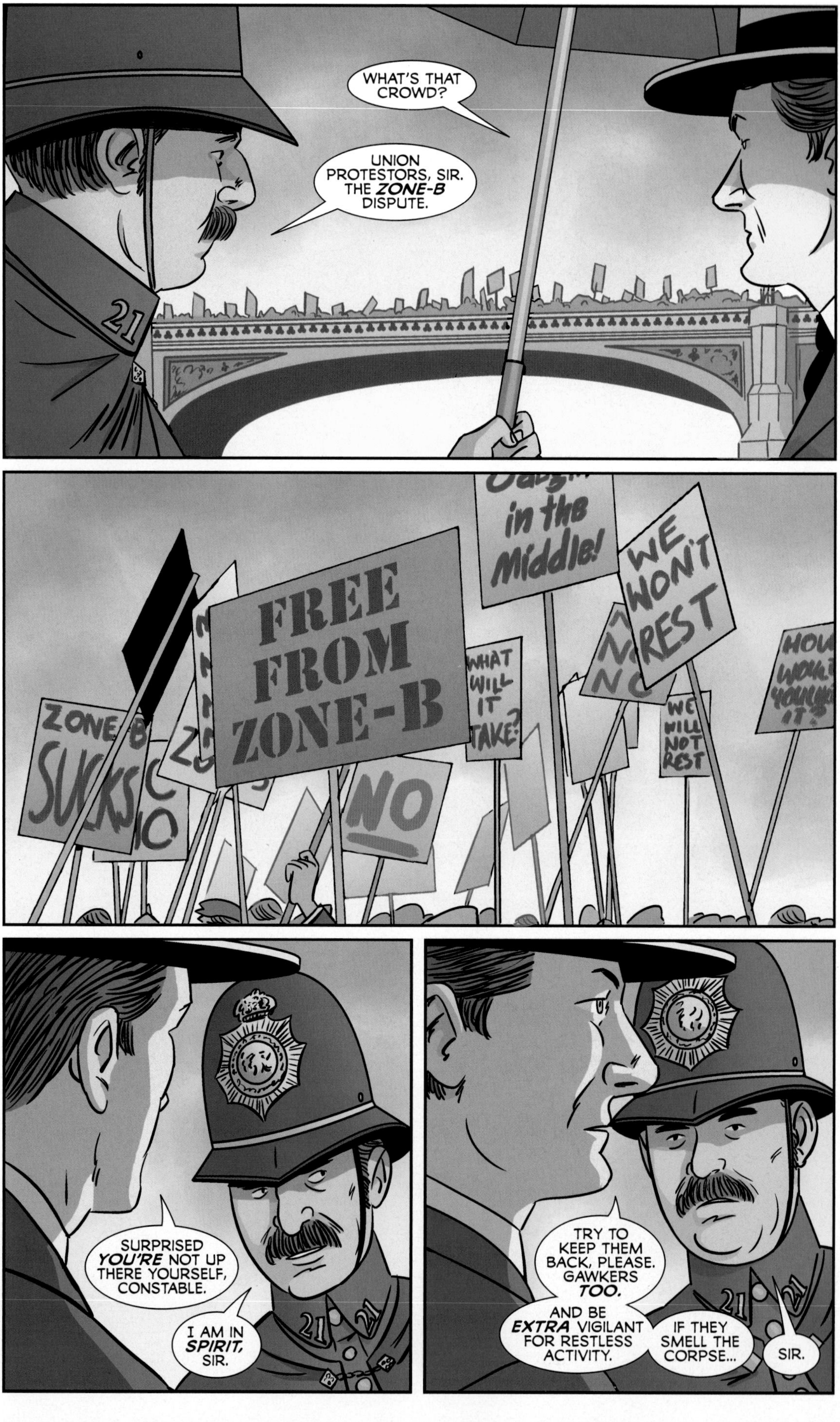
WHAT'S THAT CROWD?
UNION PROTESTORS, SIR. THE *ZONE-B* DISPUTE.
FREE FROM ZONE-B
in the Middle!
WE WON'T REST
ZONE-B SUCKS
WHAT WILL IT TAKE?
WE WILL NOT REST
NO
SURPRISED *YOU'RE* NOT UP THERE YOURSELF, CONSTABLE.
I AM IN *SPIRIT,* SIR.
TRY TO KEEP THEM BACK, PLEASE. GAWKERS *TOO.*
AND BE *EXTRA* VIGILANT FOR RESTLESS ACTIVITY.
IF THEY SMELL THE CORPSE...
SIR.

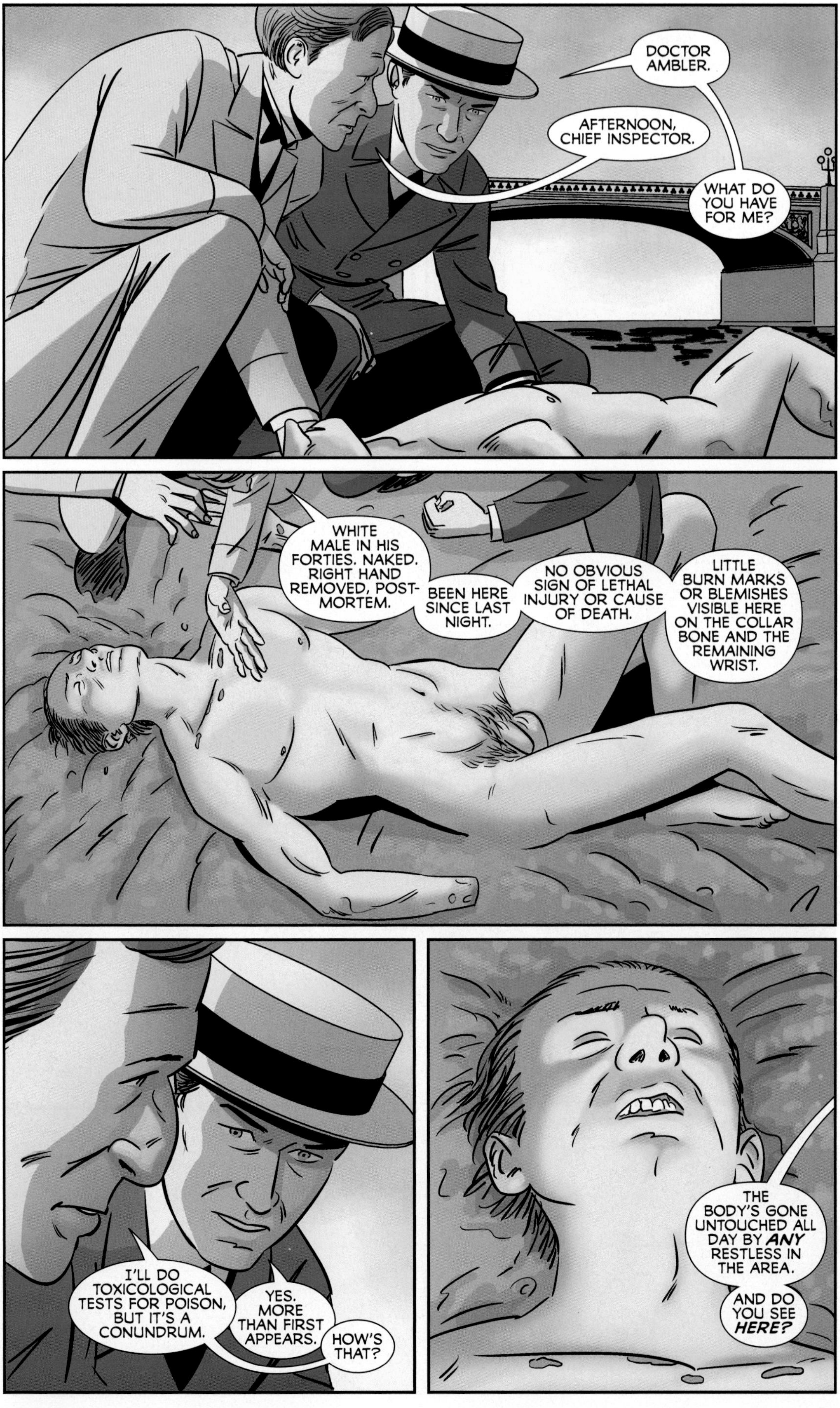
DOCTOR AMBLER.
AFTERNOON, CHIEF INSPECTOR.
WHAT DO YOU HAVE FOR ME?
WHITE MALE IN HIS FORTIES. NAKED. RIGHT HAND REMOVED, POST-MORTEM.
BEEN HERE SINCE LAST NIGHT.
NO OBVIOUS SIGN OF LETHAL INJURY OR CAUSE OF DEATH.
LITTLE BURN MARKS OR BLEMISHES VISIBLE HERE ON THE COLLAR BONE AND THE REMAINING WRIST.
I'LL DO TOXICOLOGICAL TESTS FOR POISON, BUT IT'S A CONUNDRUM.
YES. MORE THAN FIRST APPEARS.
HOW'S THAT?
THE BODY'S GONE UNTOUCHED ALL DAY BY *ANY* RESTLESS IN THE AREA.
AND DO YOU SEE ***HERE?***

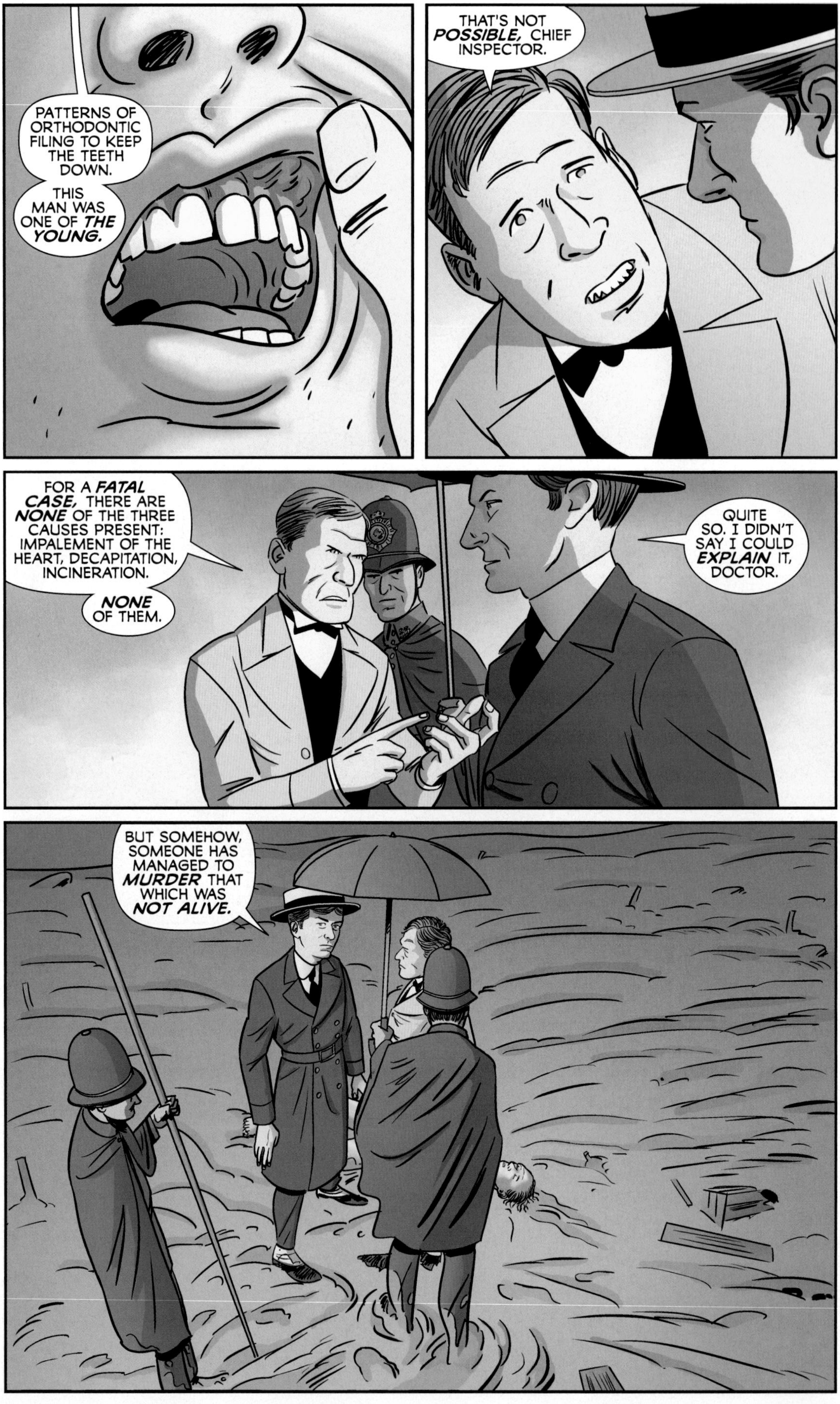
PATTERNS OF ORTHODONTIC FILING TO KEEP THE TEETH DOWN.
THIS MAN WAS ONE OF *THE YOUNG.*
THAT'S NOT *POSSIBLE,* CHIEF INSPECTOR.
FOR A *FATAL CASE,* THERE ARE *NONE* OF THE THREE CAUSES PRESENT: IMPALEMENT OF THE HEART, DECAPITATION, INCINERATION.
NONE OF THEM.
QUITE SO. I DIDN'T SAY I COULD *EXPLAIN* IT, DOCTOR.
BUT SOMEHOW, SOMEONE HAS MANAGED TO *MURDER* THAT WHICH WAS *NOT ALIVE.*

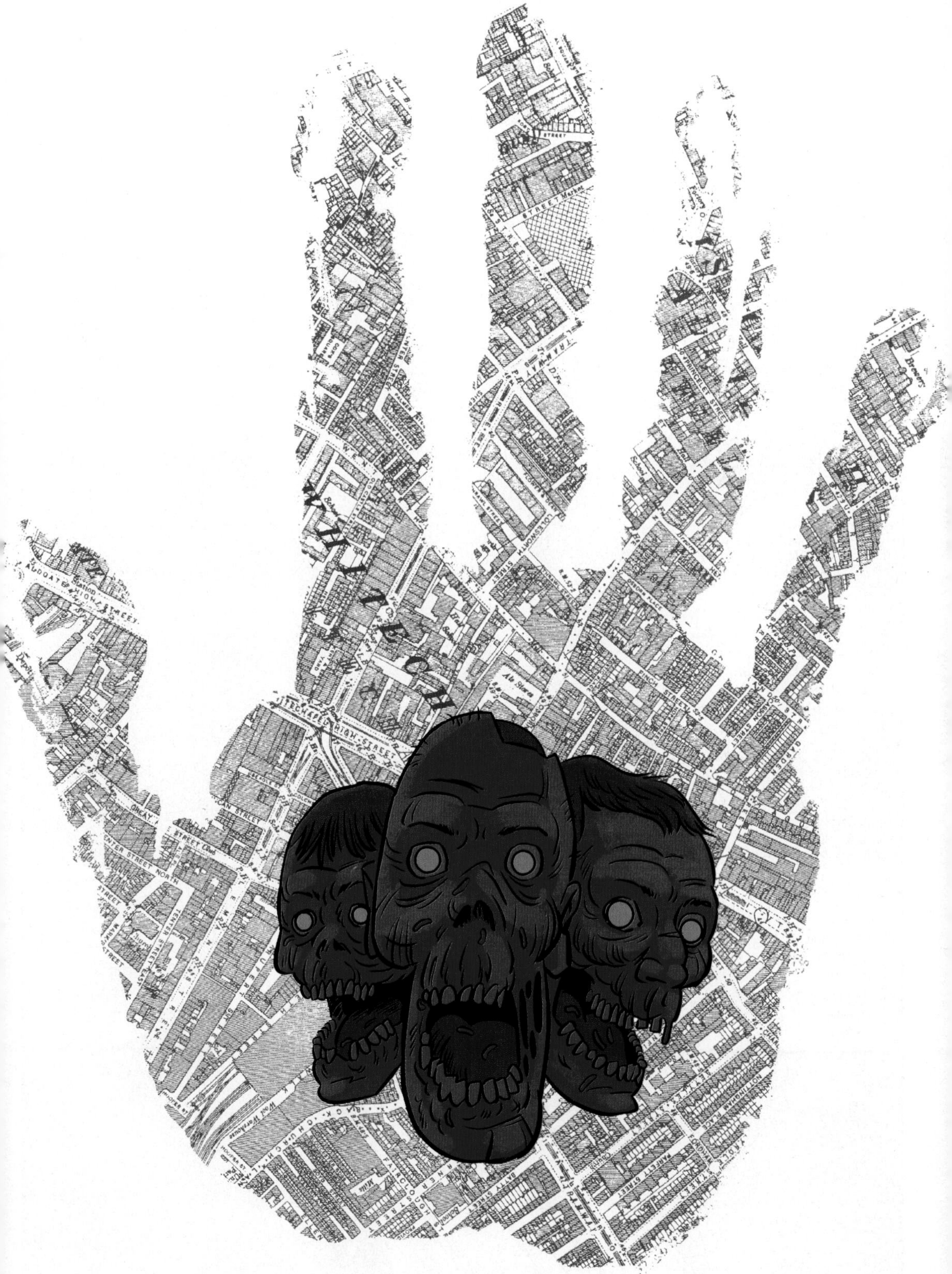

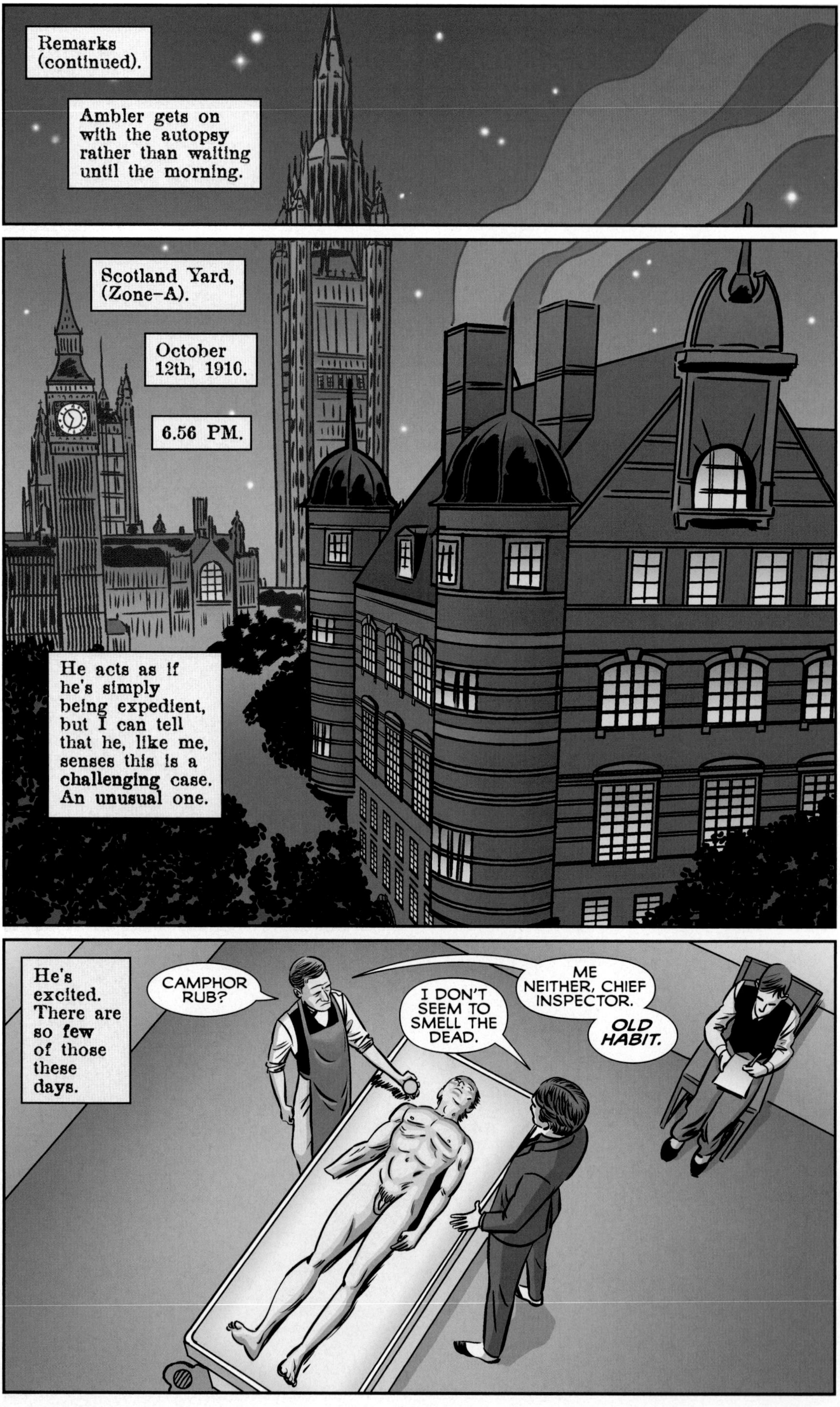
Remarks (continued).
Ambler gets on with the autopsy rather than waiting until the morning.
Scotland Yard, (Zone-A).
October 12th, 1910.
6.56 PM.
He acts as if he's simply being expedient, but I can tell that he, like me, senses this is a challenging case. An unusual one.
He's excited. There are so few of those these days.
CAMPHOR RUB?
I DON'T SEEM TO SMELL THE DEAD.
ME NEITHER, CHIEF INSPECTOR.
OLD HABIT.

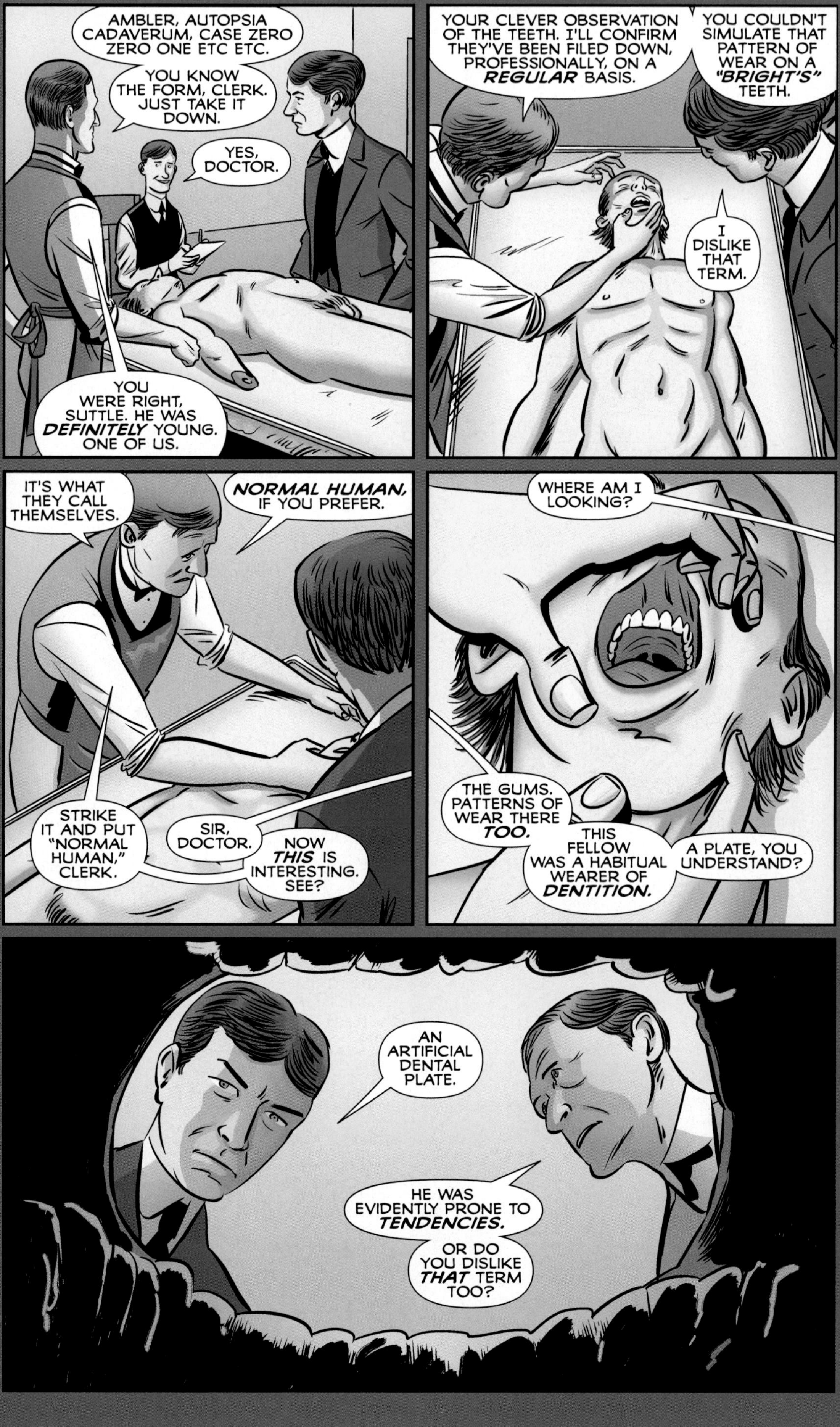
AMBLER, AUTOPSIA CADAVERUM, CASE ZERO ZERO ONE ETC ETC.
YOU KNOW THE FORM, CLERK. JUST TAKE IT DOWN.
YES, DOCTOR.
YOU WERE RIGHT, SUTTLE. HE WAS ***DEFINITELY*** YOUNG. ONE OF US.
YOUR CLEVER OBSERVATION OF THE TEETH. I'LL CONFIRM THEY'VE BEEN FILED DOWN, PROFESSIONALLY, ON A ***REGULAR*** BASIS.
YOU COULDN'T SIMULATE THAT PATTERN OF WEAR ON A ***"BRIGHT'S"*** TEETH.
I DISLIKE THAT TERM.
IT'S WHAT THEY CALL THEMSELVES.
NORMAL HUMAN, IF YOU PREFER.
STRIKE IT AND PUT "NORMAL HUMAN," CLERK.
SIR, DOCTOR.
NOW ***THIS*** IS INTERESTING. SEE?
WHERE AM I LOOKING?
THE GUMS. PATTERNS OF WEAR THERE ***TOO.***
THIS FELLOW WAS A HABITUAL WEARER OF ***DENTITION.***
A PLATE, YOU UNDERSTAND?
AN ARTIFICIAL DENTAL PLATE.
HE WAS EVIDENTLY PRONE TO ***TENDENCIES.***
OR DO YOU DISLIKE ***THAT*** TERM TOO?

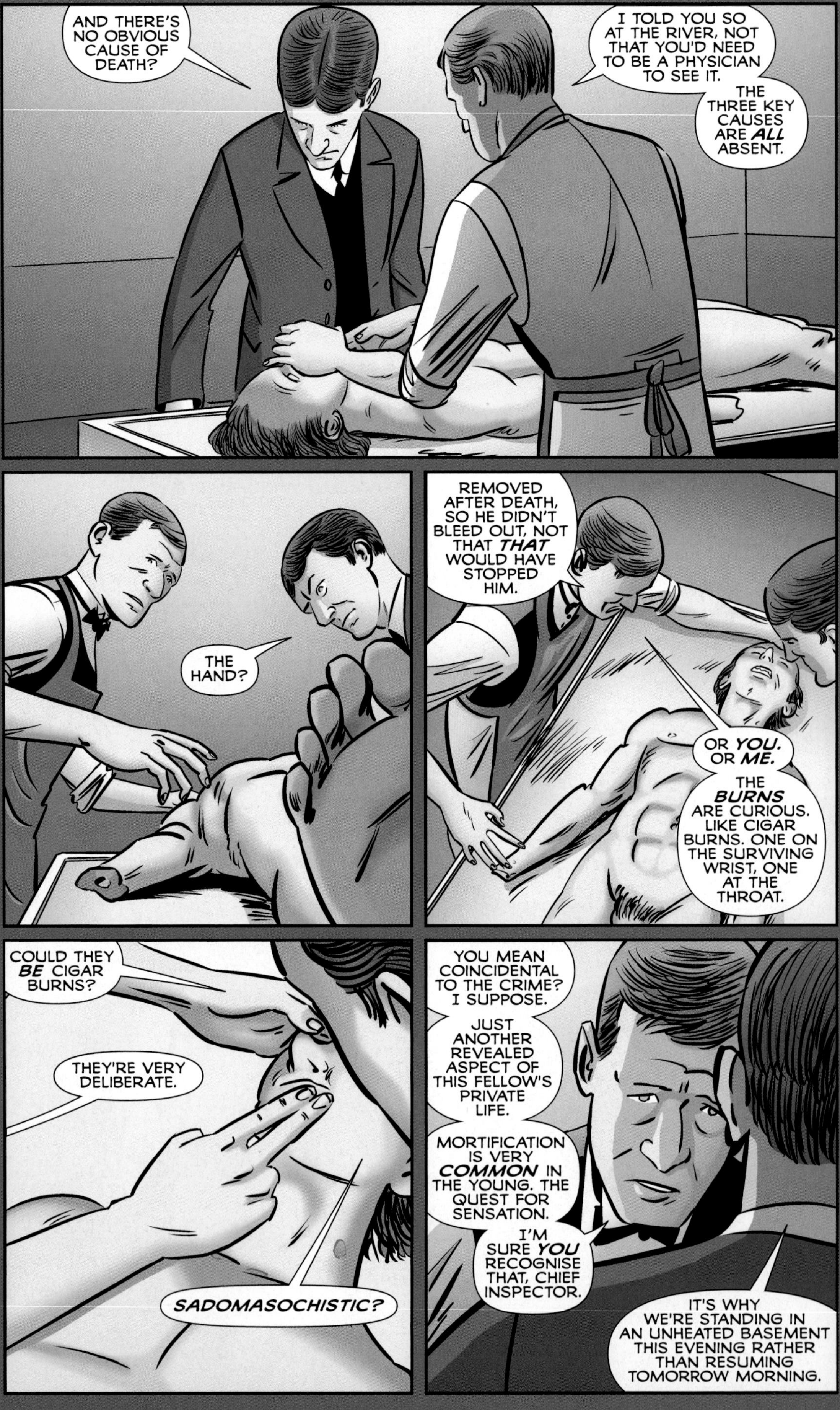
AND THERE'S NO OBVIOUS CAUSE OF DEATH?
I TOLD YOU SO AT THE RIVER, NOT THAT YOU'D NEED TO BE A PHYSICIAN TO SEE IT.
THE THREE KEY CAUSES ARE *ALL* ABSENT.
THE HAND?
REMOVED AFTER DEATH, SO HE DIDN'T BLEED OUT, NOT THAT *THAT* WOULD HAVE STOPPED HIM.
OR *YOU.* OR *ME.*
THE *BURNS* ARE CURIOUS. LIKE CIGAR BURNS. ONE ON THE SURVIVING WRIST, ONE AT THE THROAT.
COULD THEY *BE* CIGAR BURNS?
THEY'RE VERY DELIBERATE.
SADOMASOCHISTIC?
YOU MEAN COINCIDENTAL TO THE CRIME? I SUPPOSE.
JUST ANOTHER REVEALED ASPECT OF THIS FELLOW'S PRIVATE LIFE.
MORTIFICATION IS VERY *COMMON* IN THE YOUNG. THE QUEST FOR SENSATION.
I'M SURE *YOU* RECOGNISE THAT, CHIEF INSPECTOR.
IT'S WHY WE'RE STANDING IN AN UNHEATED BASEMENT THIS EVENING RATHER THAN RESUMING TOMORROW MORNING.

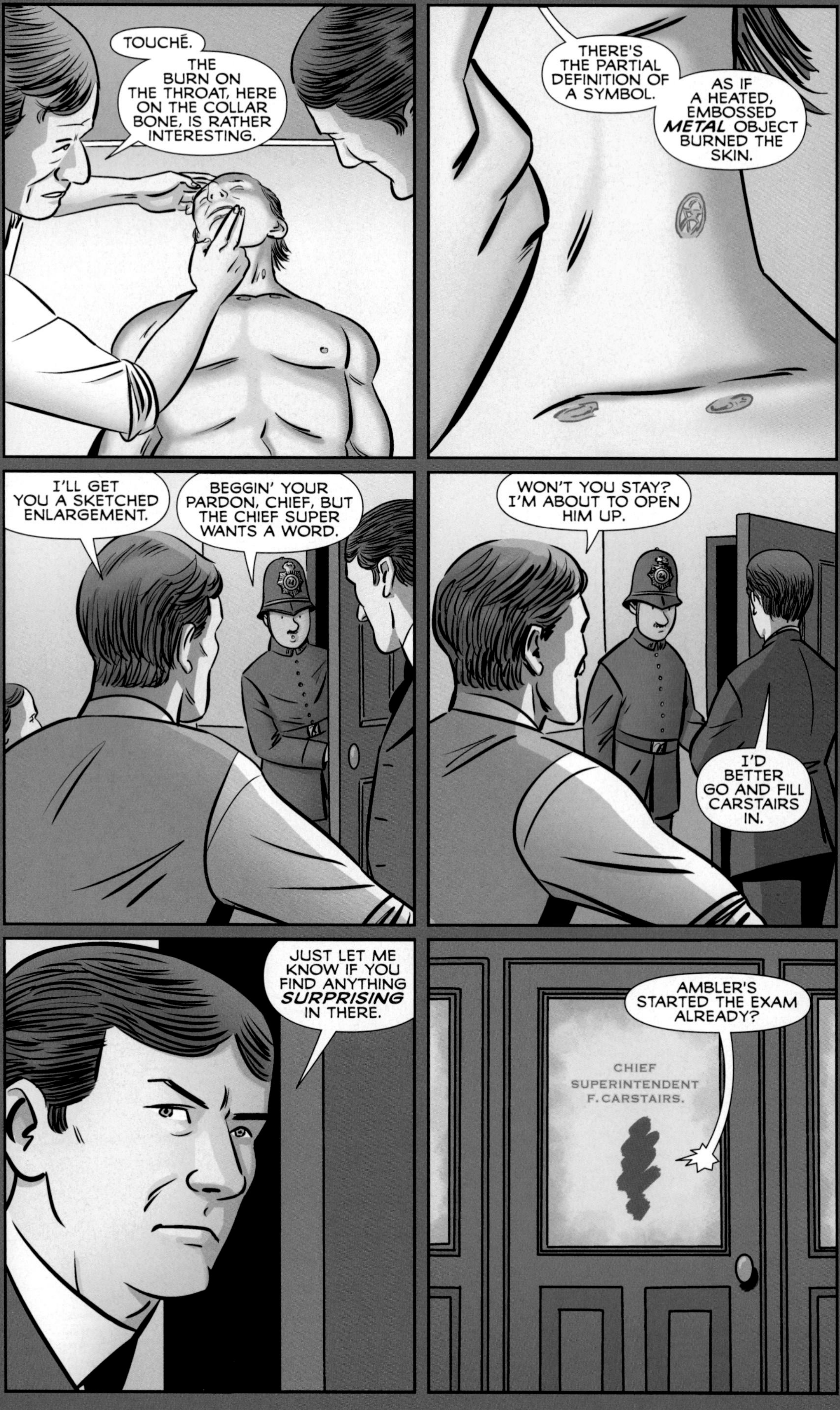
TOUCHÉ.
THE BURN ON THE THROAT, HERE ON THE COLLAR BONE, IS RATHER INTERESTING.
THERE'S THE PARTIAL DEFINITION OF A SYMBOL.
AS IF A HEATED, EMBOSSED *METAL* OBJECT BURNED THE SKIN.
I'LL GET YOU A SKETCHED ENLARGEMENT.
BEGGIN' YOUR PARDON, CHIEF, BUT THE CHIEF SUPER WANTS A WORD.
WON'T YOU STAY? I'M ABOUT TO OPEN HIM UP.
I'D BETTER GO AND FILL CARSTAIRS IN.
JUST LET ME KNOW IF YOU FIND ANYTHING *SURPRISING* IN THERE.
AMBLER'S STARTED THE EXAM ALREADY?
CHIEF SUPERINTENDENT F. CARSTAIRS.

GOD, I REMEMBER WHEN THE EXAMINERS USED TO PUT OFF P.M.S AS *LONG* AS POSSIBLE.

URGENCY WAS *WASTED* ON THE DEAD. THEY WEREN'T GOING ANYWHERE.

THAT HASN'T BEEN THE CASE FOR A RATHER *LONG* TIME, SIR, HAS IT?

OH HA BLOODY HA, GEORGE.

IS IT TRUE WHAT THEY'RE SAYING? HE WAS ONE OF *US?*

THE VICTIM *WAS* YOUNG, SIR.

AND NONE OF THE THREE--

NO *STANDARD CAUSE,* NO SIR.

BLOODY HELL. BLOODY *HELL.*

GEORGE, I NEED YOU TO CLOSE THIS SWIFTLY AND WITH THE *UTMOST* DISCRETION.

THE BLOODY UNION ACTION IS CAUSING *ENOUGH* DISRUPTION AS IT IS.

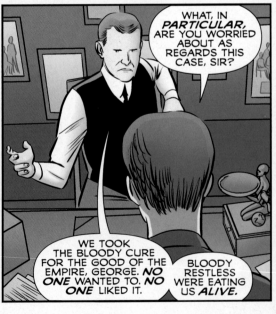

WHAT, IN *PARTICULAR,* ARE YOU WORRIED ABOUT AS REGARDS THIS CASE, SIR?

WE TOOK THE BLOODY CURE FOR THE GOOD OF THE EMPIRE, GEORGE. *NO ONE* WANTED TO. *NO ONE* LIKED IT.

BLOODY RESTLESS WERE EATING US *ALIVE.*

WE GOT ON WITH IT TO KEEP THIS COUNTRY TOGETHER. FOR *KING* AND *COUNTRY*, GEORGE.

THE ONLY SOLACE WE TOOK WAS THE REWARD OF *NOT DYING*.

YES, SIR.

Carstairs is so typical of our kind. He talks about the Cure like it was an inconvenient war effort.

Like collecting ironmongery or rationing bathwater.

He seems to forget that it was as **much** of a curse as the curse we were fighting.

He seems to forget...or to prefer not to remember.

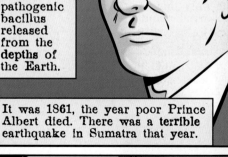

We don't know where the Restless Curse came from. A plague, of a form unknown to science. Perhaps an ancient pathogenic bacillus released from the **depths** of the Earth.

It was 1861, the year poor Prince Albert died. There was a terrible earthquake in Sumatra that year.

Or was it just a *gypsy curse?* A witch's hex? No less likely than a bacillus.

When the stratagem of warfare didn't stop the Restless, the ruling classes took the Cure instead.

Allowing ourselves to become technically dead rendered us **invisible** to the Cursed.

It was superlative pragmatism.

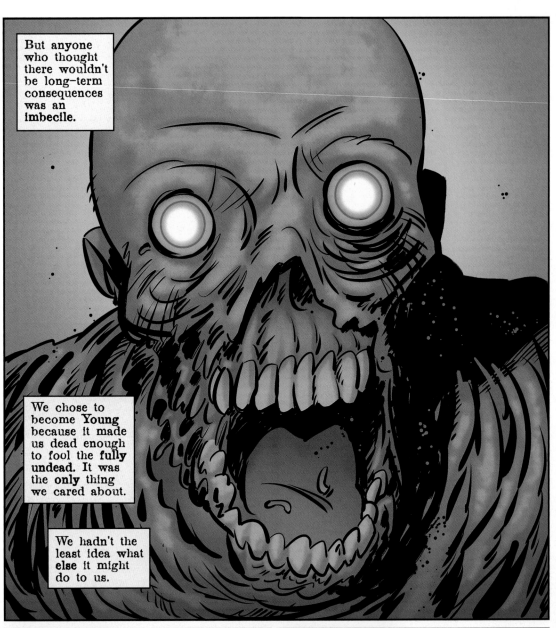

But anyone who thought there wouldn't be long-term consequences was an imbecile.

We chose to become **Young** because it made us dead enough to fool the **fully** undead. It was the **only** thing we cared about.

We hadn't the least idea what **else** it might do to us.

ARE YOU *LISTENING*, GEORGE?

IF WE'RE BLOODY *DYING* NOW...IF THE CURE IS SOMEHOW *FAILING*...

DAMMIT, GEORGE, IT WOULD SHOOT A *SHOCK WAVE* THROUGH THE YOUNG CLASSES.

NOT TO *MENTION* THE BRIGHT.

FORGOT. YOU DON'T LIKE THAT TERM, DO YOU?

THE *COMMON BLOODY FOLK.* WE WON'T SEEM SO BLOODY *SUPERHUMAN* AND *IMMORTAL* AFTER ALL, WILL WE?

I IMAGINE NOT.

GET IT CLOSED, GEORGE.

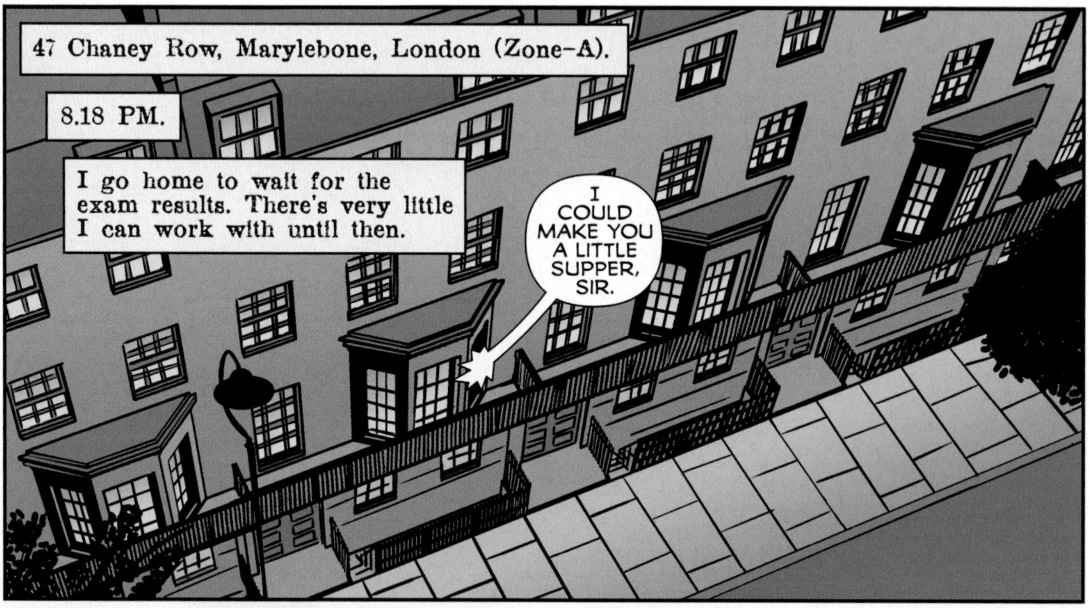
47 Chaney Row, Marylebone, London (Zone-A).
8.18 PM.
I go home to wait for the exam results. There's very little I can work with until then.
I COULD MAKE YOU A LITTLE SUPPER, SIR.

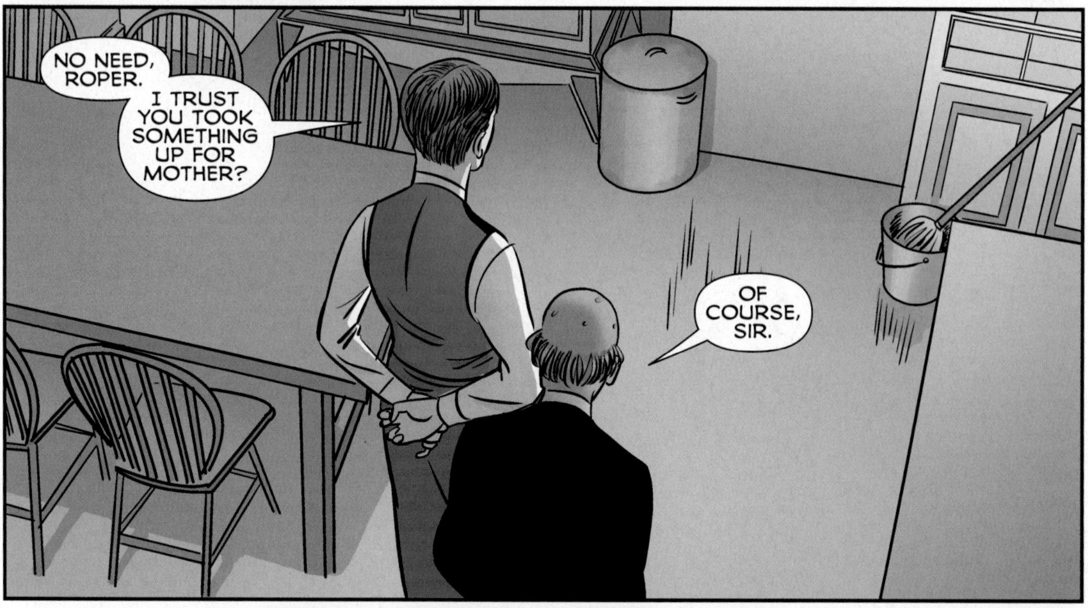
NO NEED, ROPER.
I TRUST YOU TOOK SOMETHING UP FOR MOTHER?
OF COURSE, SIR.

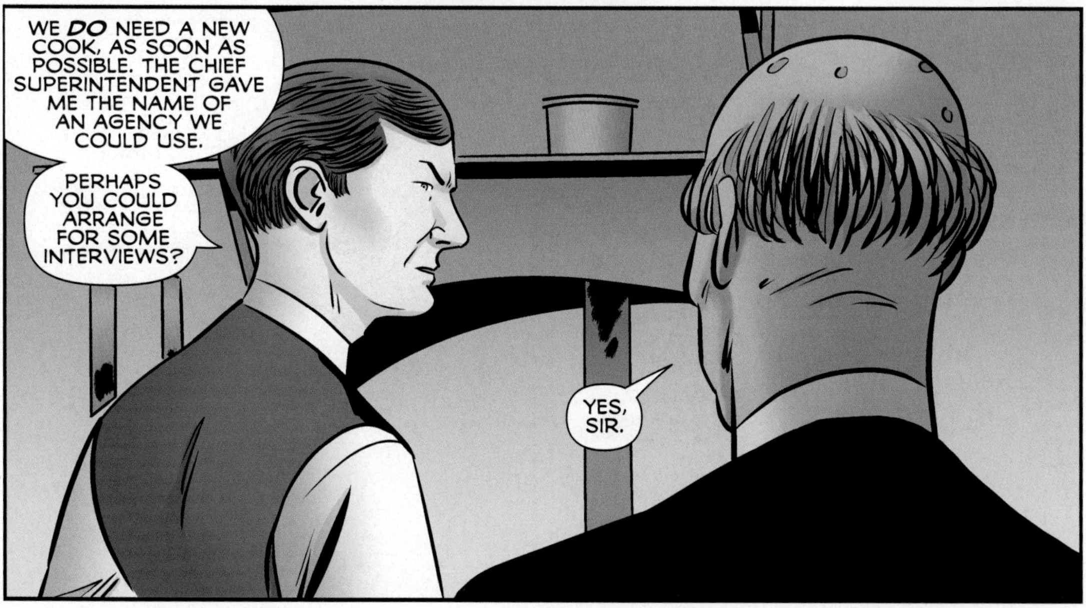
WE *DO* NEED A NEW COOK, AS SOON AS POSSIBLE. THE CHIEF SUPERINTENDENT GAVE ME THE NAME OF AN AGENCY WE COULD USE.
PERHAPS YOU COULD ARRANGE FOR SOME INTERVIEWS?
YES, SIR.

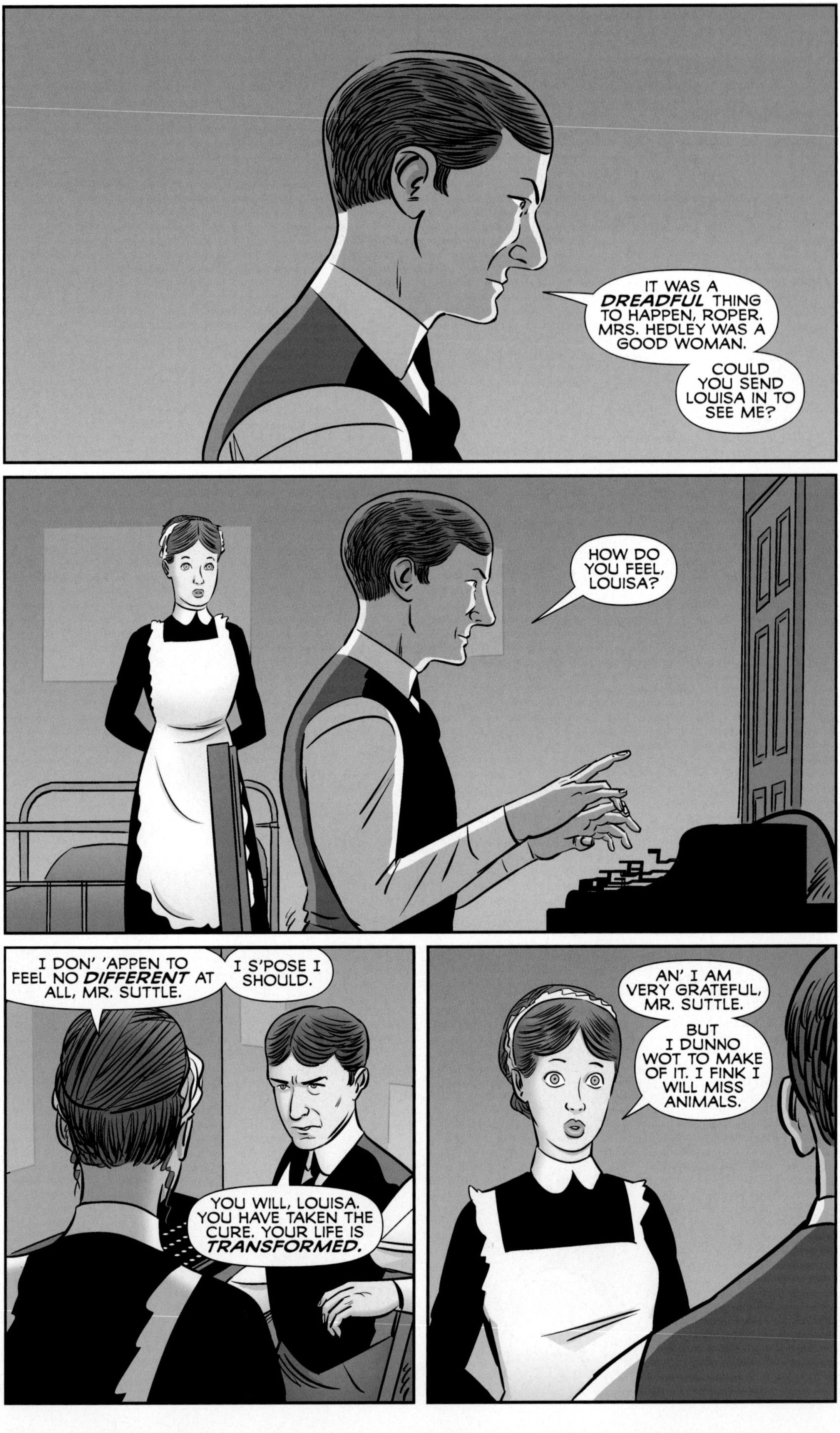
IT WAS A DREADFUL THING TO HAPPEN, ROPER. MRS. HEDLEY WAS A GOOD WOMAN.
COULD YOU SEND LOUISA IN TO SEE ME?
HOW DO YOU FEEL, LOUISA?
I DON' 'APPEN TO FEEL NO DIFFERENT AT ALL, MR. SUTTLE.
I S'POSE I SHOULD.
YOU WILL, LOUISA. YOU HAVE TAKEN THE CURE. YOUR LIFE IS TRANSFORMED.
AN' I AM VERY GRATEFUL, MR. SUTTLE.
BUT I DUNNO WOT TO MAKE OF IT. I FINK I WILL MISS ANIMALS.

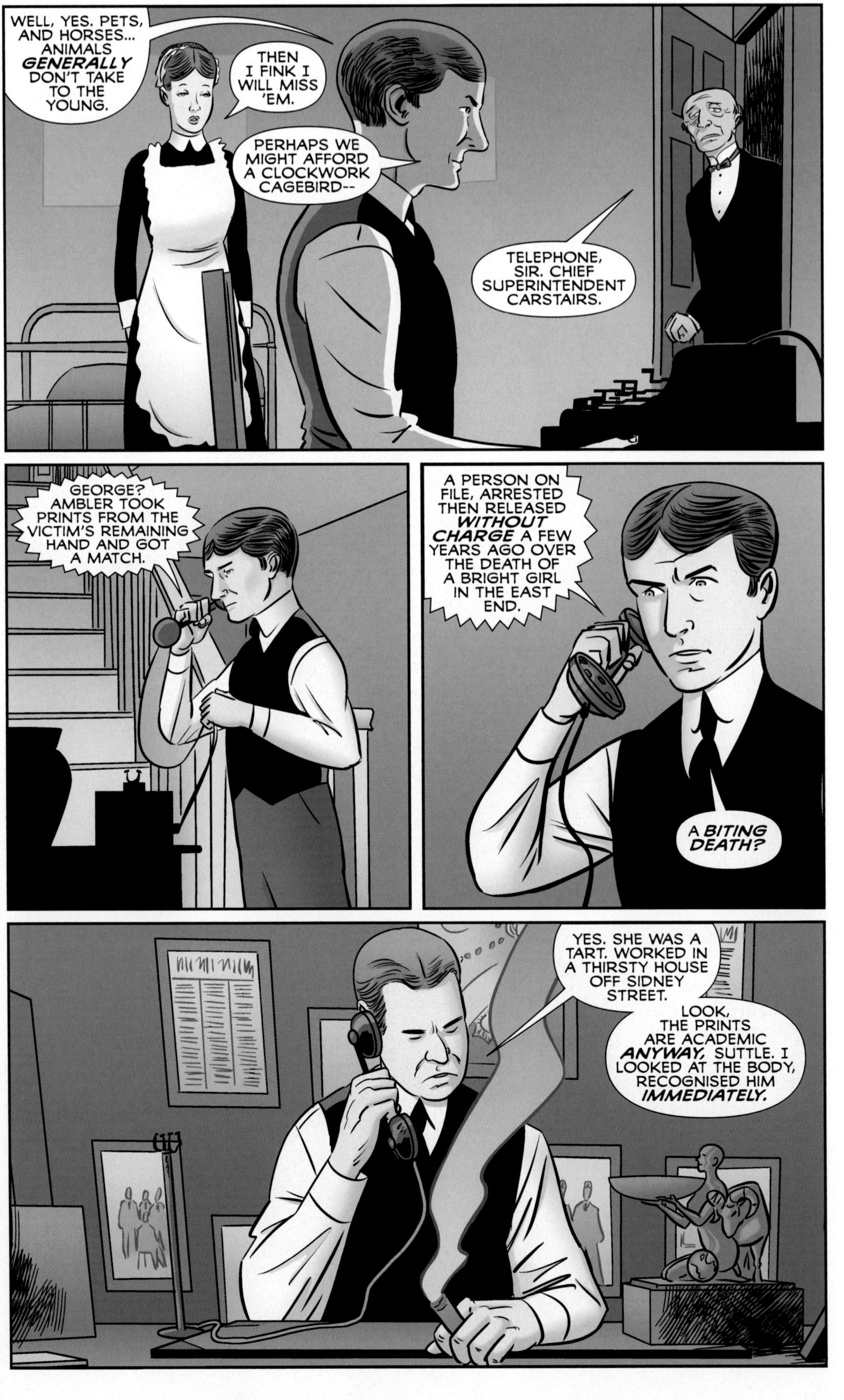

WELL, YES. PETS, AND HORSES... ANIMALS GENERALLY DON'T TAKE TO THE YOUNG.
THEN I FINK I WILL MISS 'EM.
PERHAPS WE MIGHT AFFORD A CLOCKWORK CAGEBIRD--
TELEPHONE, SIR. CHIEF SUPERINTENDENT CARSTAIRS.
GEORGE? AMBLER TOOK PRINTS FROM THE VICTIM'S REMAINING HAND AND GOT A MATCH.
A PERSON ON FILE, ARRESTED THEN RELEASED WITHOUT CHARGE A FEW YEARS AGO OVER THE DEATH OF A BRIGHT GIRL IN THE EAST END.
A BITING DEATH?
YES. SHE WAS A TART. WORKED IN A THIRSTY HOUSE OFF SIDNEY STREET.
LOOK, THE PRINTS ARE ACADEMIC ANYWAY, SUTTLE. I LOOKED AT THE BODY, RECOGNISED HIM IMMEDIATELY.

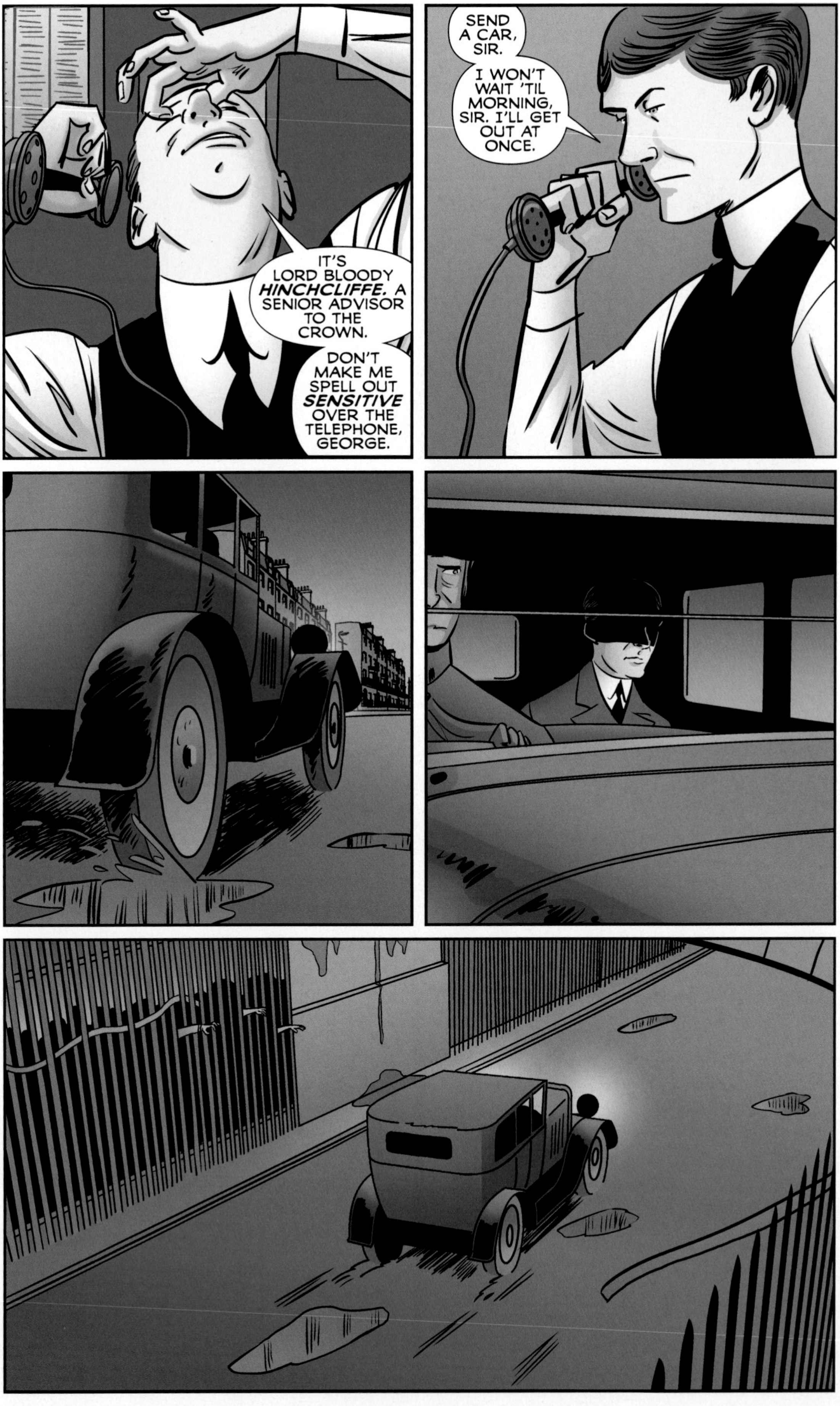
IT'S LORD BLOODY HINCHCLIFFE. A SENIOR ADVISOR TO THE CROWN.
DON'T MAKE ME SPELL OUT SENSITIVE OVER THE TELEPHONE, GEORGE.
SEND A CAR, SIR.
I WON'T WAIT 'TIL MORNING, SIR. I'LL GET OUT AT ONCE.

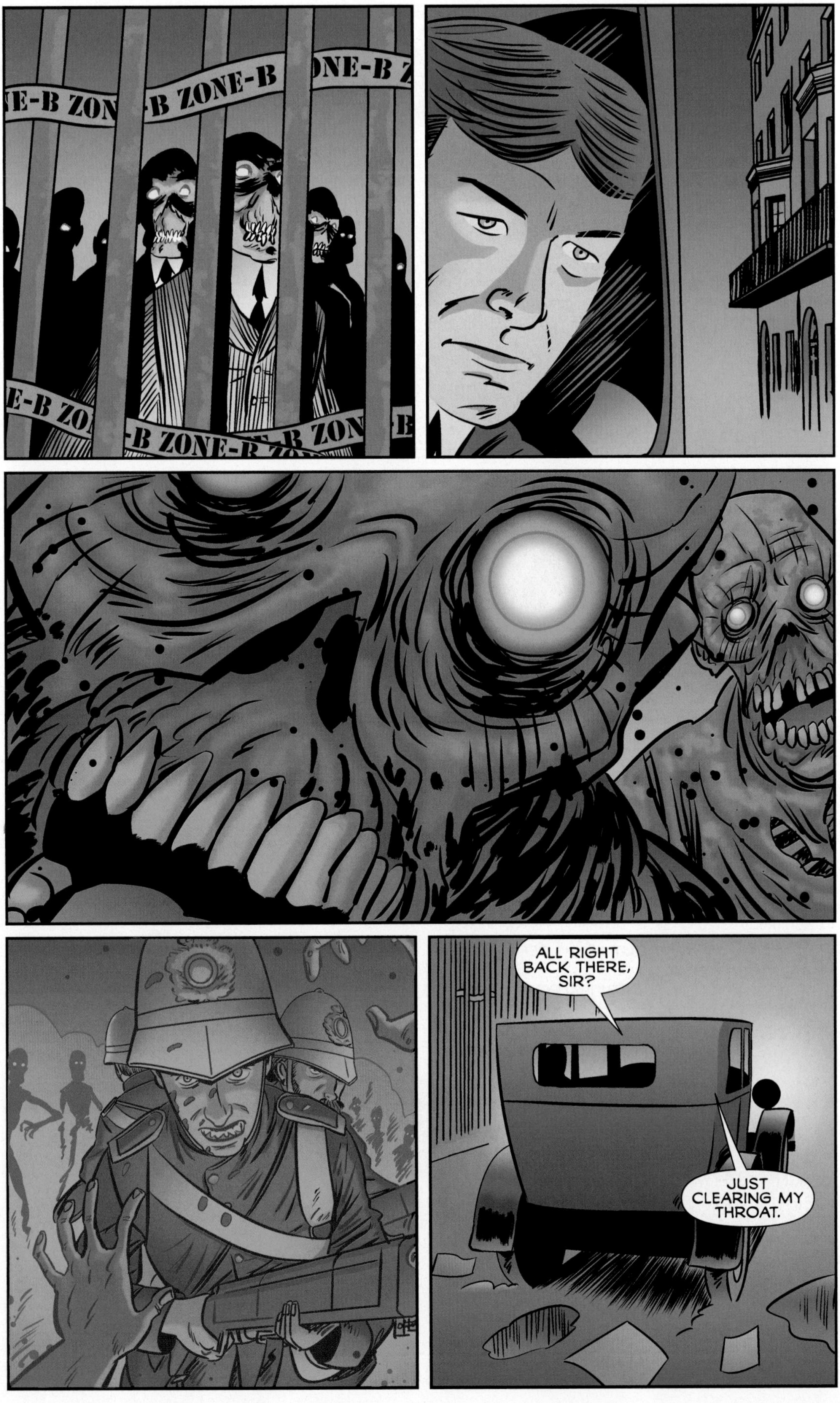
NE-B ZONE-B ZONE-B ZONE-B Z
E-B ZON -B ZONE-B ZON -B
ALL RIGHT BACK THERE, SIR?
JUST CLEARING MY THROAT.

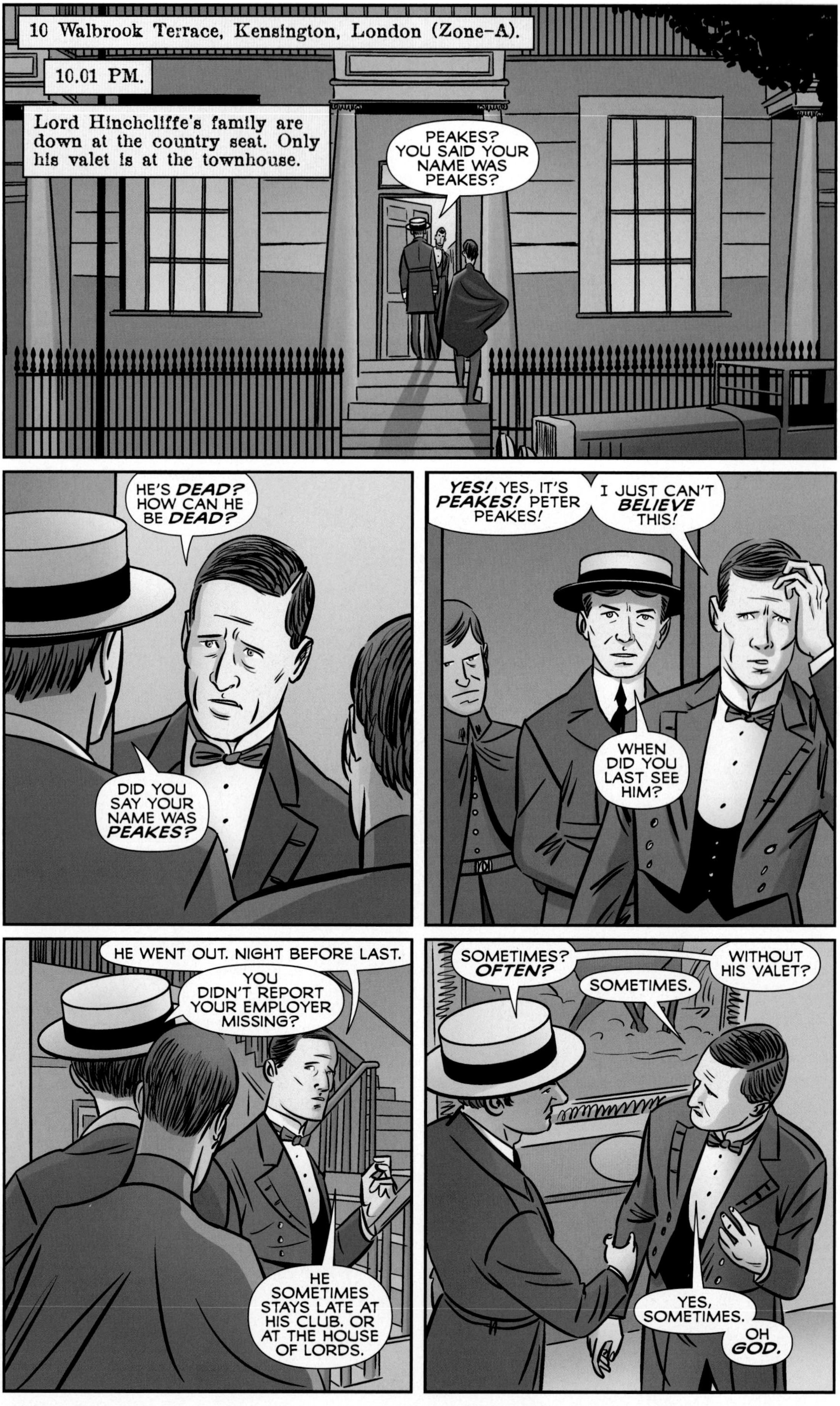
10 Walbrook Terrace, Kensington, London (Zone-A).
10.01 PM.
Lord Hinchcliffe's family are down at the country seat. Only his valet is at the townhouse.
PEAKES? YOU SAID YOUR NAME WAS PEAKES?
HE'S DEAD? HOW CAN HE BE DEAD?
DID YOU SAY YOUR NAME WAS PEAKES?
YES! YES, IT'S PEAKES! PETER PEAKES!
I JUST CAN'T BELIEVE THIS!
WHEN DID YOU LAST SEE HIM?
HE WENT OUT. NIGHT BEFORE LAST.
YOU DIDN'T REPORT YOUR EMPLOYER MISSING?
HE SOMETIMES STAYS LATE AT HIS CLUB. OR AT THE HOUSE OF LORDS.
SOMETIMES? OFTEN?
WITHOUT HIS VALET?
SOMETIMES.
YES, SOMETIMES.
OH GOD.

The house is most interesting for what is **not** there.

Evening attire is absent. Hinchcliffe left dressed for dinner.

Cases for cufflinks, and perhaps a matching medallion. Empty.

I CAN'T *BELIEVE* THIS HAS HAPPENED.

WHAT THE *DEVIL* WILL BECOME OF ME?

Ziegler and Sons. Hatton Garden.

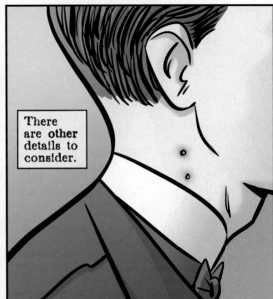

There are other details to consider.

YOU'RE YOUNG, PEAKES.

WHAT OF IT, SIR?

WHEN DID YOU TAKE THE CURE?

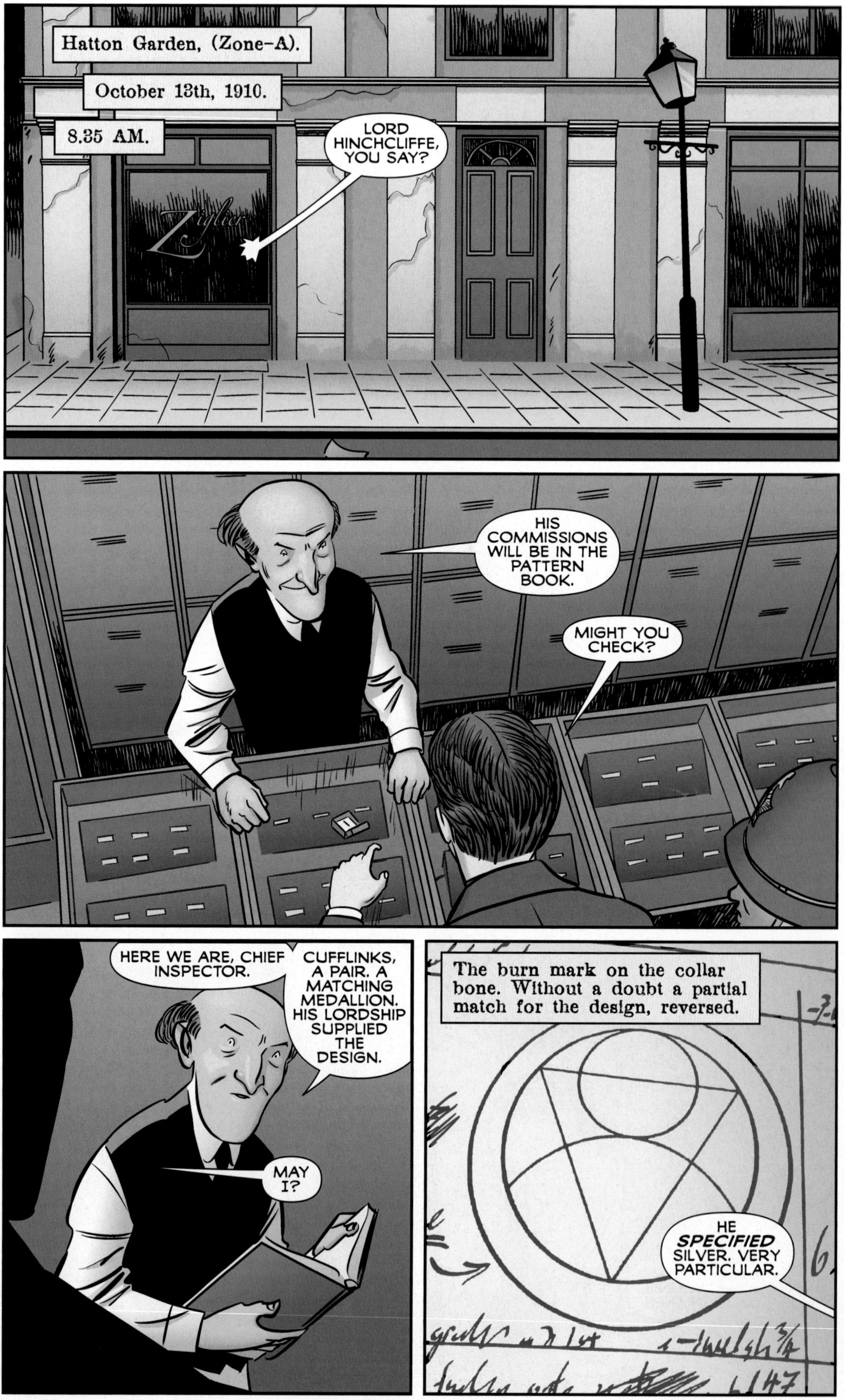

Hatton Garden, (Zone-A).
October 13th, 1910.
8.35 AM.
LORD HINCHCLIFFE, YOU SAY?
HIS COMMISSIONS WILL BE IN THE PATTERN BOOK.
MIGHT YOU CHECK?
HERE WE ARE, CHIEF INSPECTOR.
CUFFLINKS, A PAIR. A MATCHING MEDALLION. HIS LORDSHIP SUPPLIED THE DESIGN.
MAY I?
The burn mark on the collar bone. Without a doubt a partial match for the design, reversed.
HE *SPECIFIED* SILVER. VERY PARTICULAR.

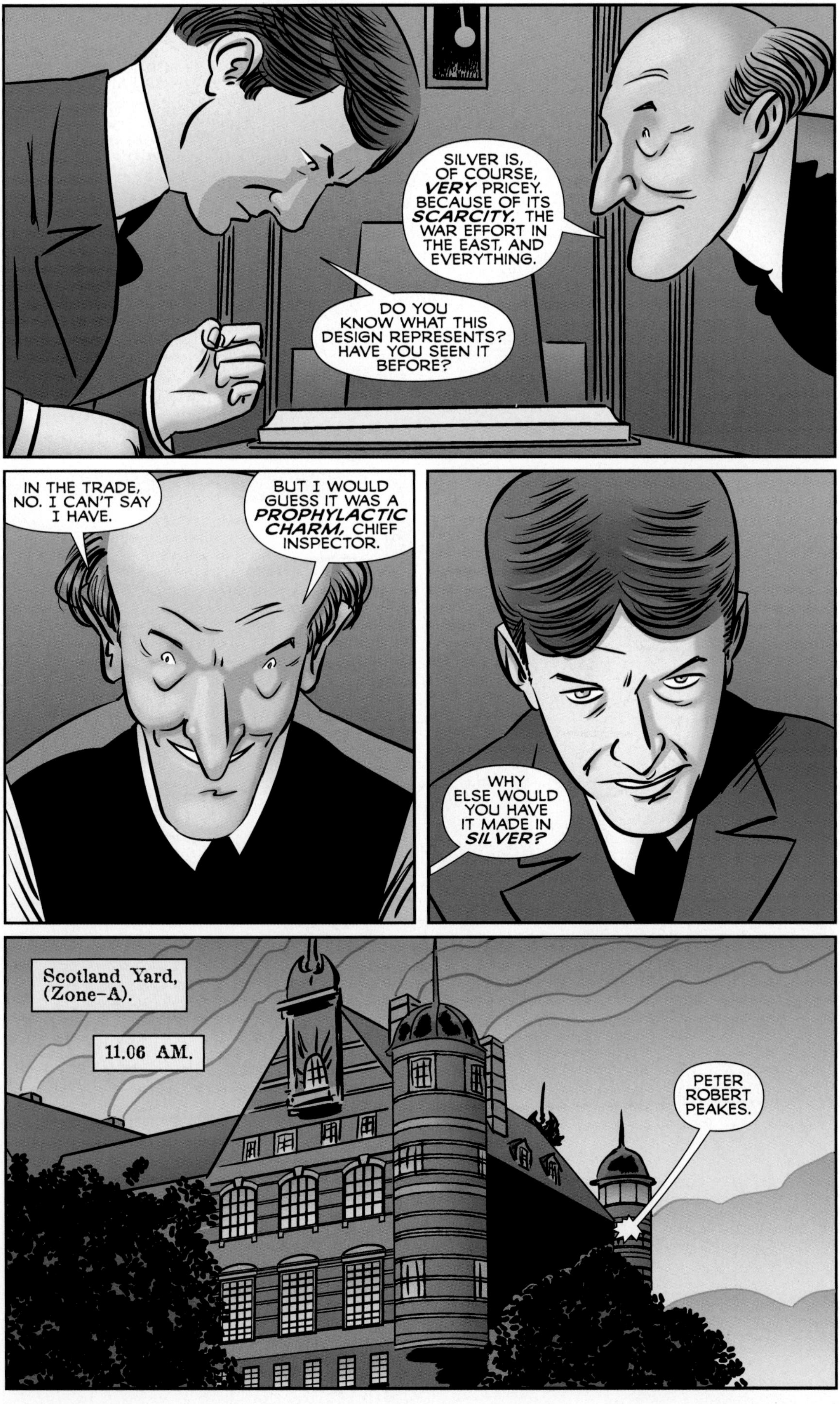
SILVER IS, OF COURSE, VERY PRICEY. BECAUSE OF ITS SCARCITY. THE WAR EFFORT IN THE EAST, AND EVERYTHING.
DO YOU KNOW WHAT THIS DESIGN REPRESENTS? HAVE YOU SEEN IT BEFORE?
IN THE TRADE, NO. I CAN'T SAY I HAVE.
BUT I WOULD GUESS IT WAS A PROPHYLACTIC CHARM, CHIEF INSPECTOR.
WHY ELSE WOULD YOU HAVE IT MADE IN SILVER?
Scotland Yard, (Zone-A).
11.06 AM.
PETER ROBERT PEAKES.

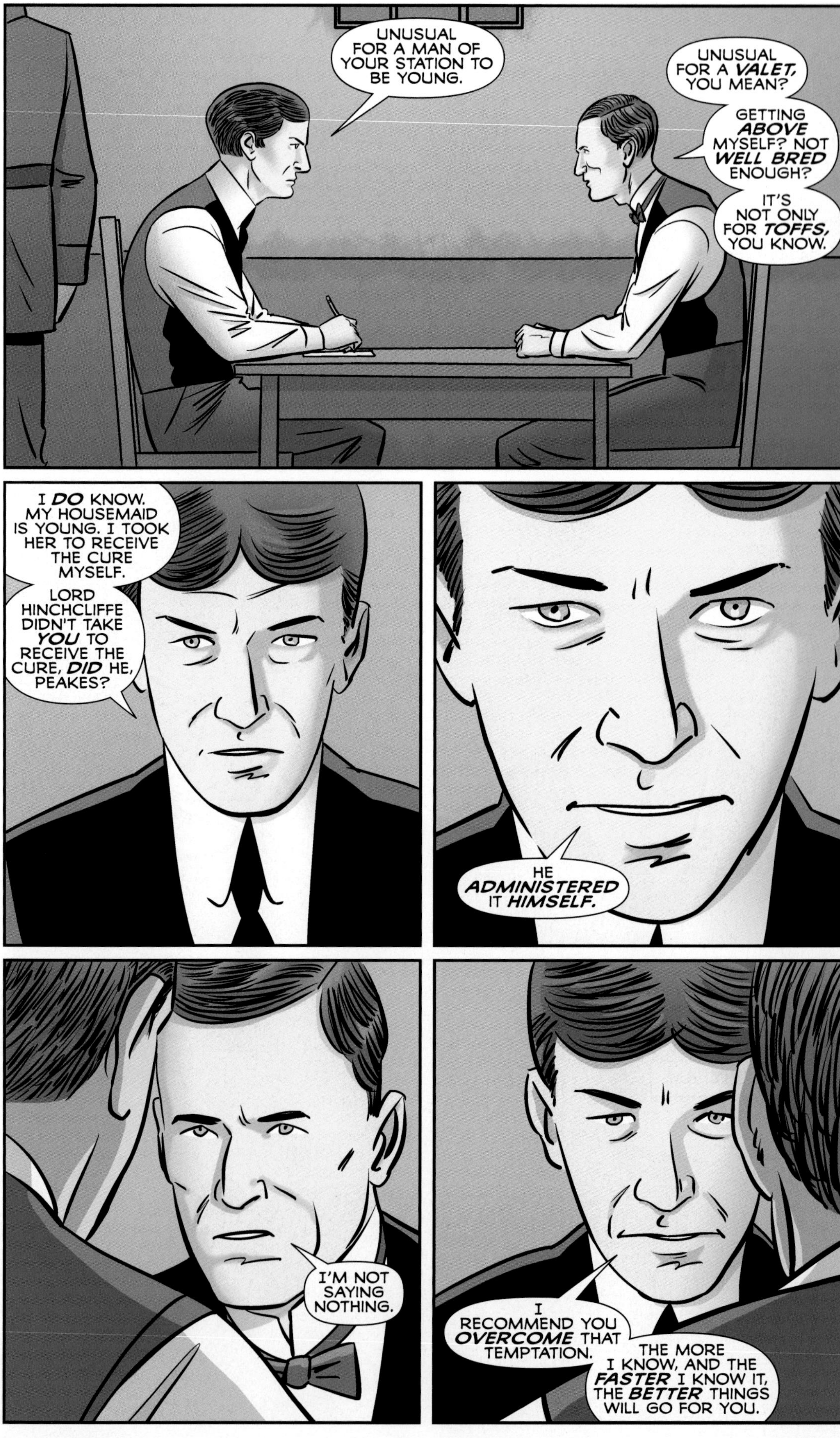
UNUSUAL FOR A MAN OF YOUR STATION TO BE YOUNG.
UNUSUAL FOR A *VALET,* YOU MEAN?
GETTING *ABOVE* MYSELF? NOT *WELL BRED* ENOUGH?
IT'S NOT ONLY FOR *TOFFS,* YOU KNOW.
I *DO* KNOW. MY HOUSEMAID IS YOUNG. I TOOK HER TO RECEIVE THE CURE MYSELF.
LORD HINCHCLIFFE DIDN'T TAKE *YOU* TO RECEIVE THE CURE, *DID* HE, PEAKES?
HE *ADMINISTERED* IT *HIMSELF.*
I'M NOT SAYING NOTHING.
I RECOMMEND YOU *OVERCOME* THAT TEMPTATION.
THE MORE I KNOW, AND THE *FASTER* I KNOW IT, THE *BETTER* THINGS WILL GO FOR YOU.

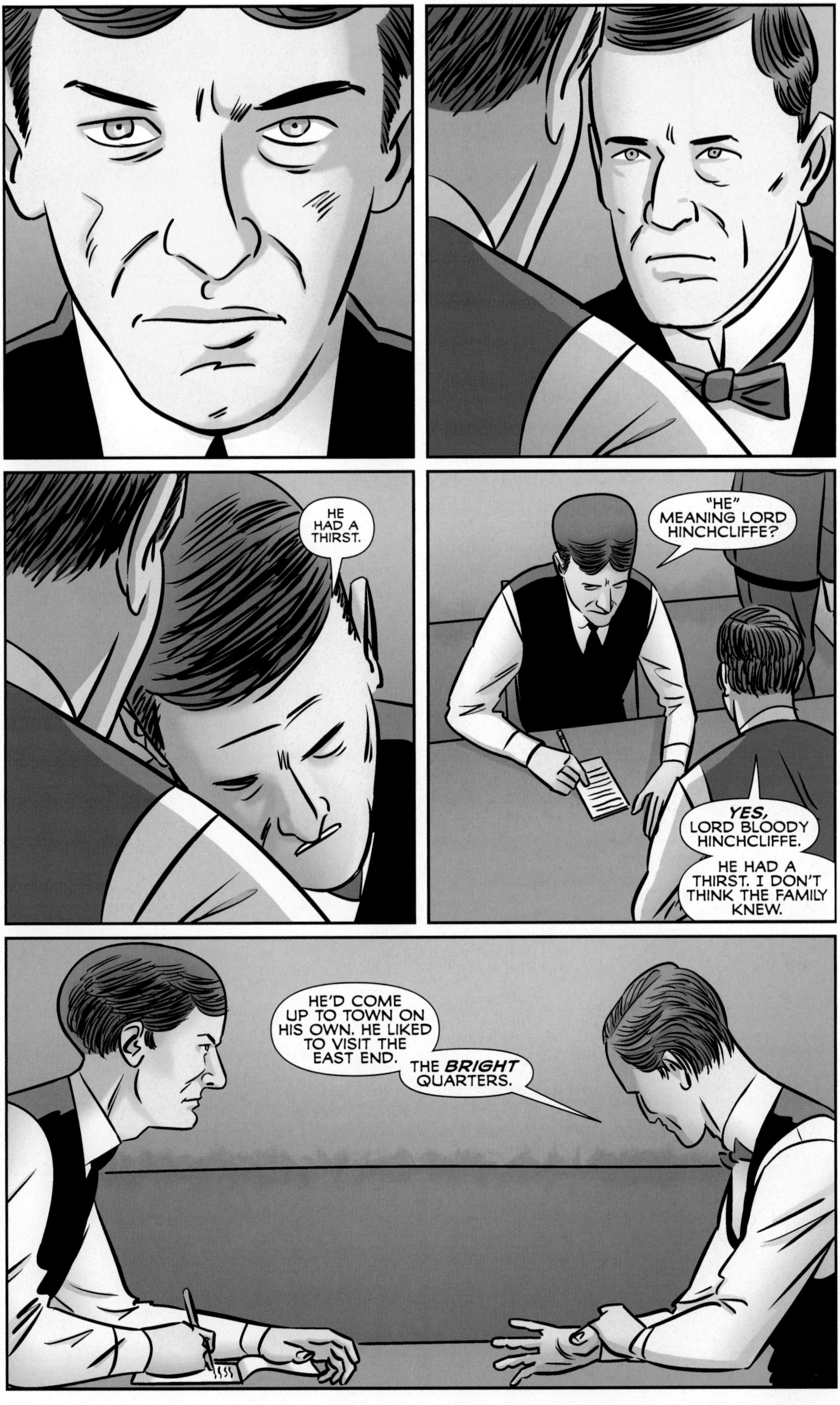
HE HAD A THIRST.
"HE" MEANING LORD HINCHCLIFFE?
YES, LORD BLOODY HINCHCLIFFE.
HE HAD A THIRST. I DON'T THINK THE FAMILY KNEW.
HE'D COME UP TO TOWN ON HIS OWN. HE LIKED TO VISIT THE EAST END.
THE *BRIGHT* QUARTERS.

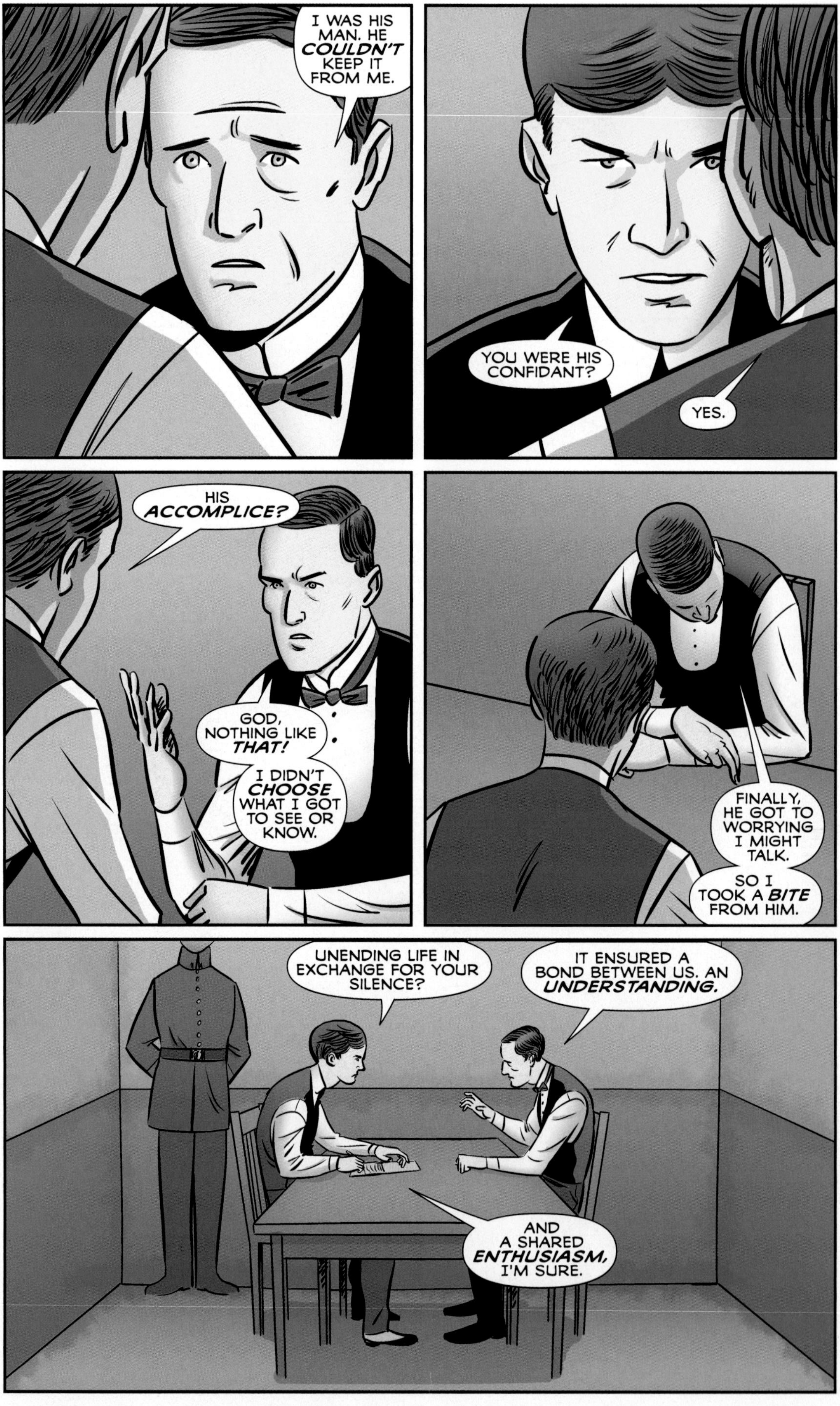
I WAS HIS MAN. HE *COULDN'T* KEEP IT FROM ME.
YOU WERE HIS CONFIDANT?
YES.
HIS *ACCOMPLICE?*
GOD, NOTHING LIKE *THAT!*
I DIDN'T *CHOOSE* WHAT I GOT TO SEE OR KNOW.
FINALLY, HE GOT TO WORRYING I MIGHT TALK.
SO I TOOK A *BITE* FROM HIM.
UNENDING LIFE IN EXCHANGE FOR YOUR SILENCE?
IT ENSURED A BOND BETWEEN US. AN *UNDERSTANDING.*
AND A SHARED *ENTHUSIASM,* I'M SURE.

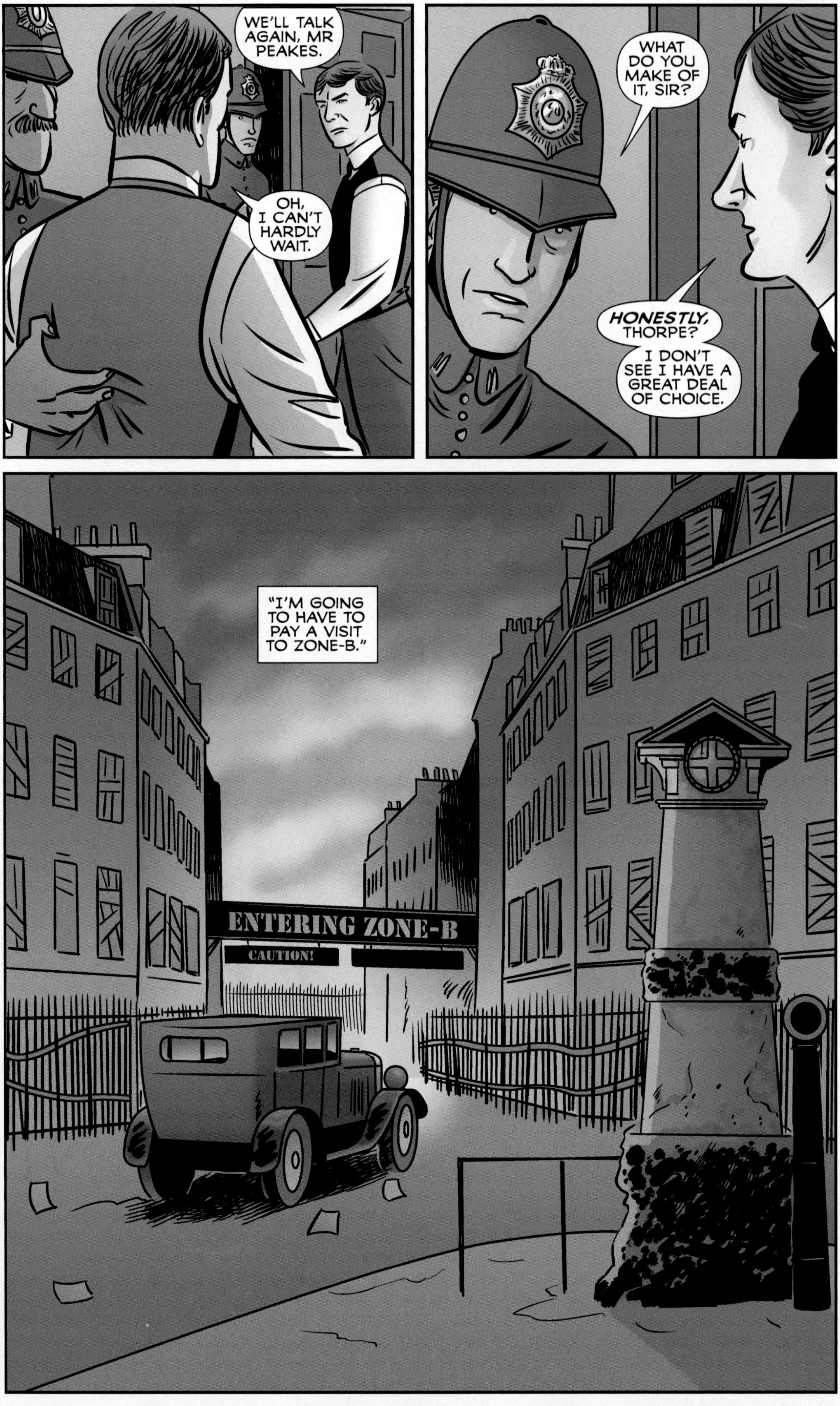
WE'LL TALK AGAIN, MR PEAKES.
OH, I CAN'T HARDLY WAIT.
WHAT DO YOU MAKE OF IT, SIR?
HONESTLY, THORPE?
I DON'T SEE I HAVE A GREAT DEAL OF CHOICE.
"I'M GOING TO HAVE TO PAY A VISIT TO ZONE-B."
ENTERING ZONE-B
CAUTION!

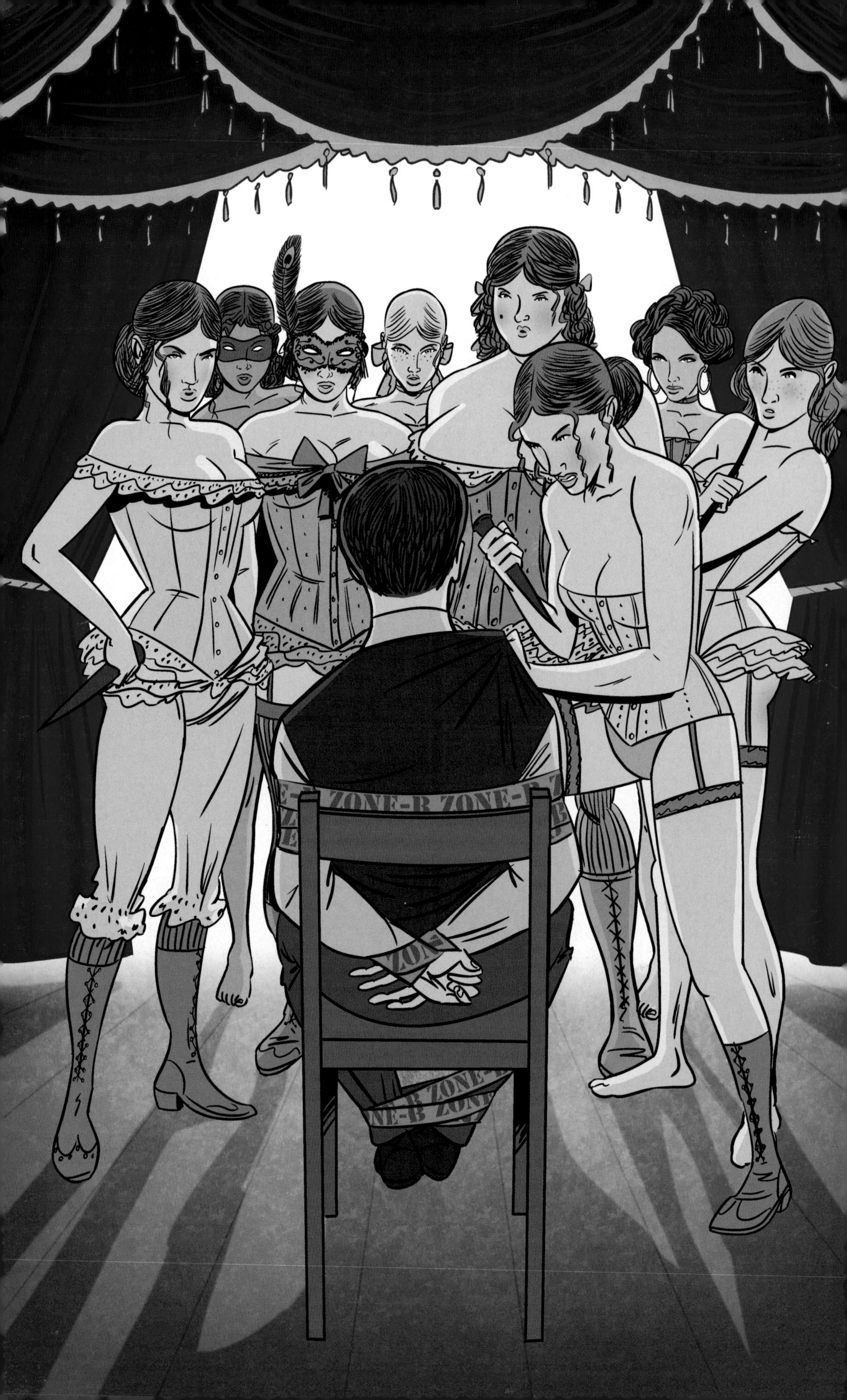
ZONE-B
ZONE-B

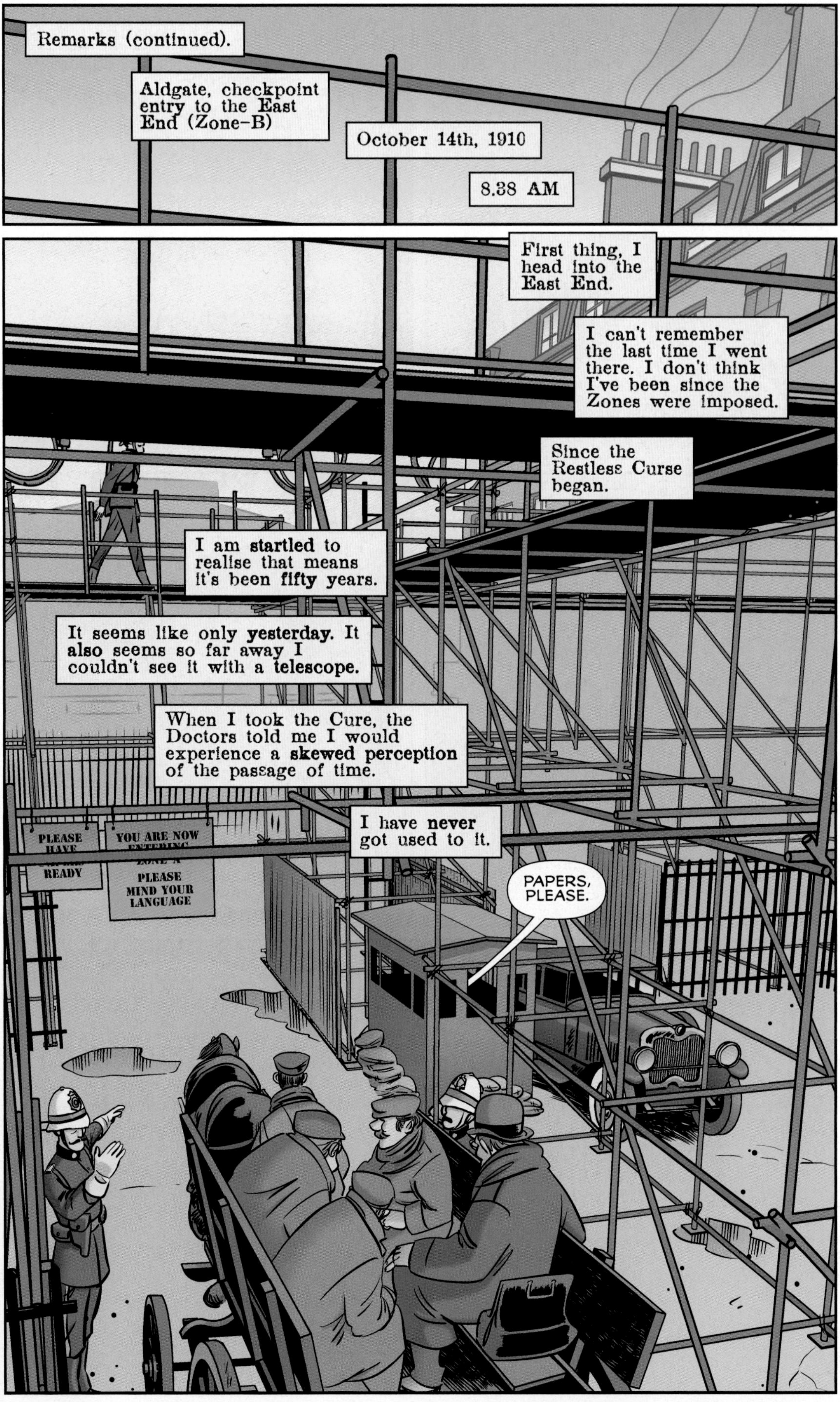

Remarks (continued).
Aldgate, checkpoint entry to the East End (Zone-B)
October 14th, 1910
8.38 AM
First thing, I head into the East End.
I can't remember the last time I went there. I don't think I've been since the Zones were imposed.
Since the Restless Curse began.
I am **startled** to realise that means it's been **fifty** years.
It seems like only **yesterday.** It **also** seems so far away I couldn't see it with a **telescope.**
When I took the Cure, the Doctors told me I would experience a **skewed perception** of the passage of time.
I have **never** got used to it.
PLEASE
READY
YOU ARE NOW
PLEASE MIND YOUR LANGUAGE
PAPERS, PLEASE.

CHIEF INSPECTOR GEORGE SUTTLE. VISITING ZONE-B PURSUANT TO A CASE.

RIGHT-HO, SIR.

YOU'LL BE *AGAINST* THE TRAFFIC THIS TIME OF DAY. MOST OF IT'S BRIGHT WORKERS COMING IN TO ZONE-A FOR THE DAY SHIFT.

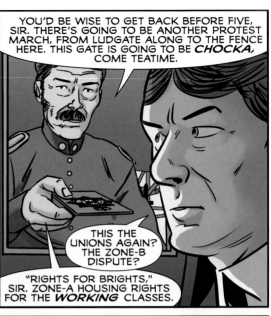

YOU'D BE WISE TO GET BACK BEFORE FIVE, SIR. THERE'S GOING TO BE ANOTHER PROTEST MARCH, FROM LUDGATE ALONG TO THE FENCE HERE. THIS GATE IS GOING TO BE *CHOCKA*, COME TEATIME.

THIS THE UNIONS AGAIN? THE ZONE-B DISPUTE?

"RIGHTS FOR BRIGHTS," SIR. ZONE-A HOUSING RIGHTS FOR THE *WORKING* CLASSES.

I TAKE IT YOU'RE SYMPATHETIC?

NOT MY PLACE TO SAY.

YOU MIND HOW YOU GO, SIR.

WHAT DID HE MEAN? "MIND HOW I GO"?

JUST A FRIENDLY WARNING, I'M SURE, SIR.

My driver's name is Bowes. He's Bright-- that is, **normal human**. I sense a tone.

A WARNING?

WELL, SIR... THE EAST END? ZONE-B? THE BRIGHT QUARTERS?

IT'S HARDLY *SAFE*, THIS SIDE OF THE FENCE. AND THE LIKES OF YOU WILL *STAND OUT*, EXCUSE ME FOR SAYING SO.

YOU ARE NOW ENTERING ZONE-B

PLEASE MIND YOUR BELONGINGS

ABANDON ALL HOPE

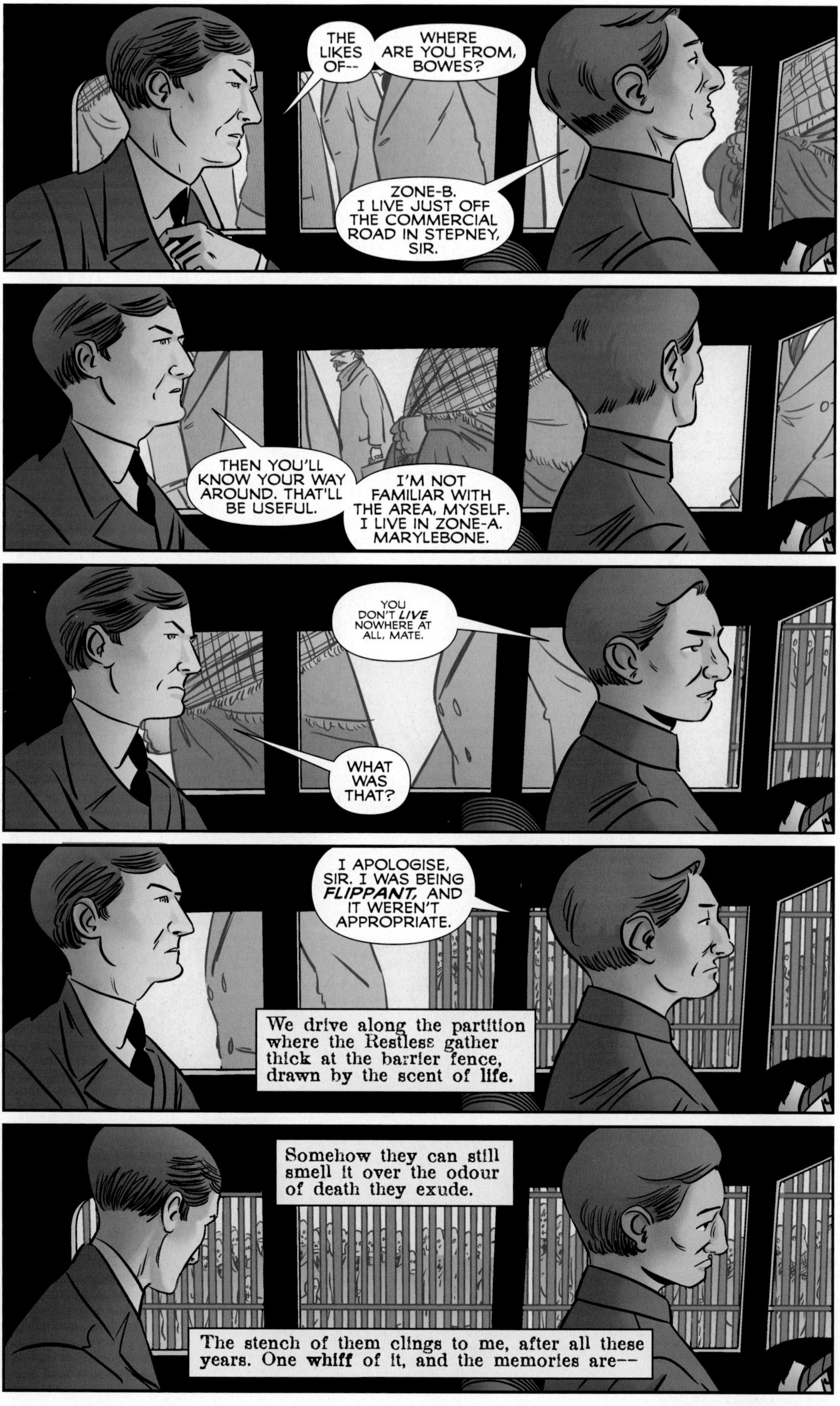
THE LIKES OF--
WHERE ARE YOU FROM, BOWES?
ZONE-B. I LIVE JUST OFF THE COMMERCIAL ROAD IN STEPNEY, SIR.
THEN YOU'LL KNOW YOUR WAY AROUND. THAT'LL BE USEFUL.
I'M NOT FAMILIAR WITH THE AREA, MYSELF. I LIVE IN ZONE-A. MARYLEBONE.
YOU DON'T *LIVE* NOWHERE AT ALL, MATE.
WHAT WAS THAT?
I APOLOGISE, SIR. I WAS BEING *FLIPPANT,* AND IT WEREN'T APPROPRIATE.
We drive along the partition where the Restless gather thick at the barrier fence, drawn by the scent of life.
Somehow they can still smell it over the odour of death they exude.
The stench of them clings to me, after all these years. One whiff of it, and the memories are--

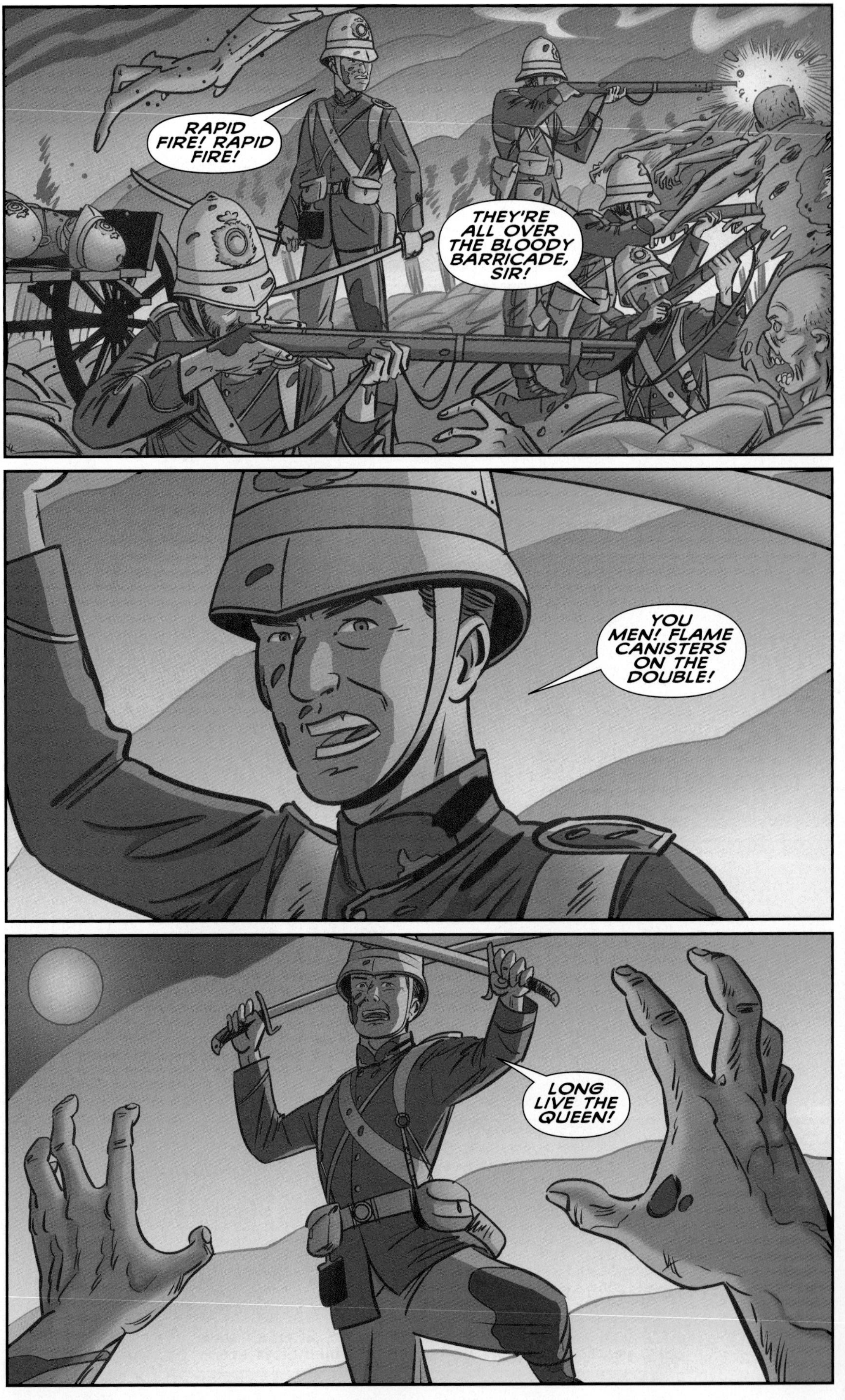
RAPID FIRE! RAPID FIRE!
THEY'RE ALL OVER THE BLOODY BARRICADE, SIR!
YOU MEN! FLAME CANISTERS ON THE DOUBLE!
LONG LIVE THE QUEEN!

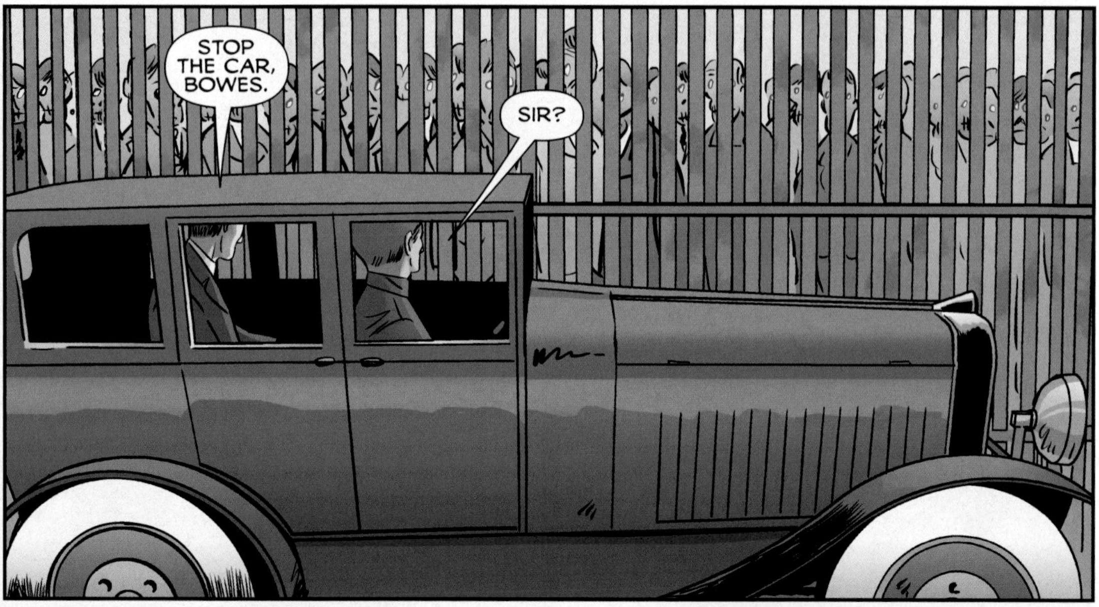
STOP THE CAR, BOWES.
SIR?

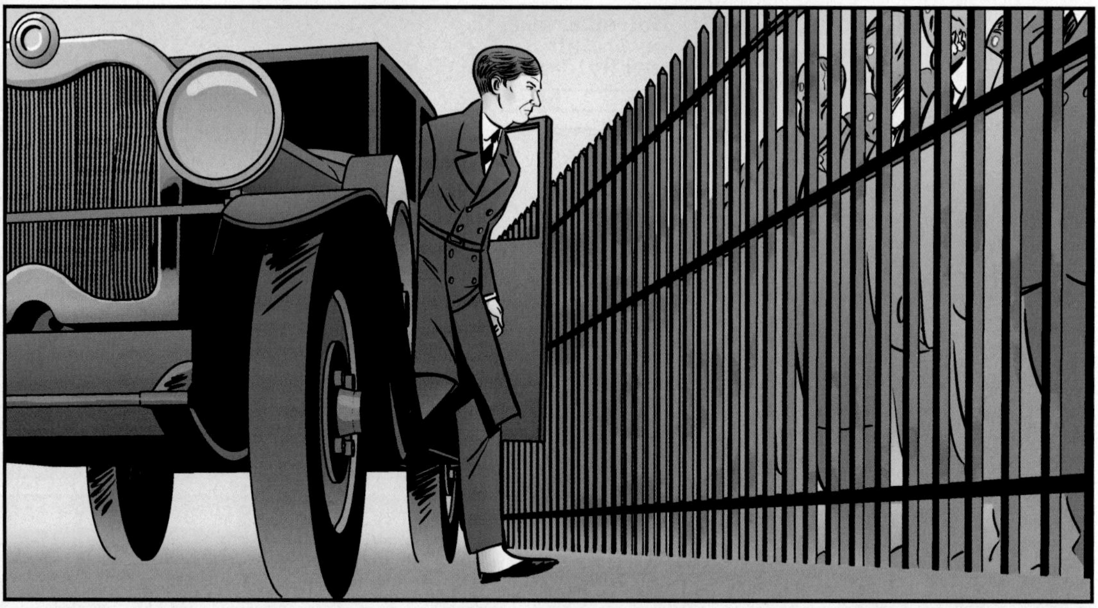

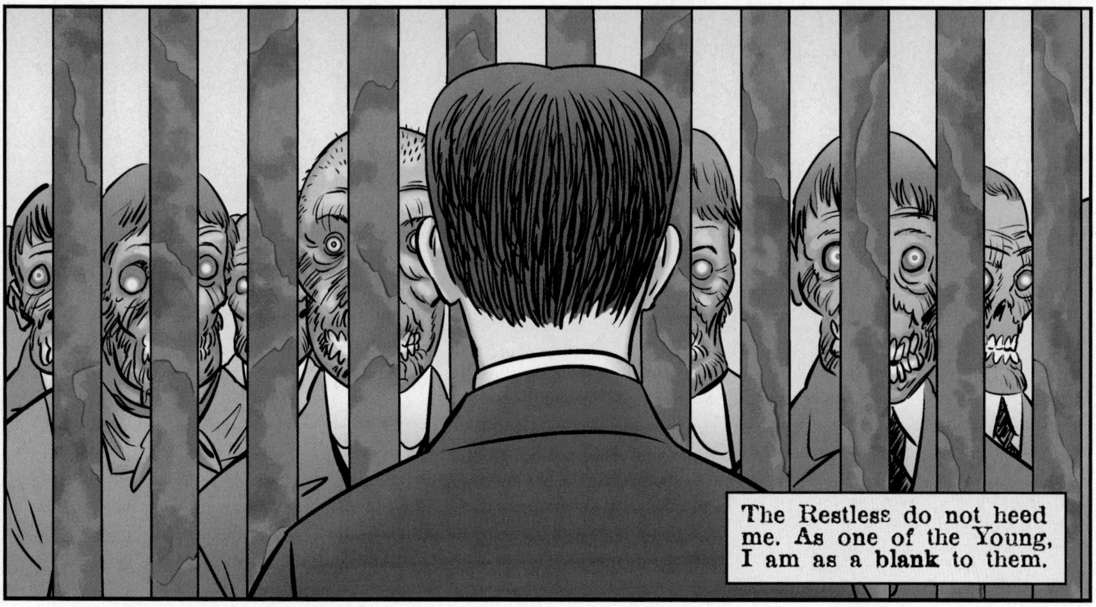
The Restless do not heed me. As one of the Young, I am as a blank to them.

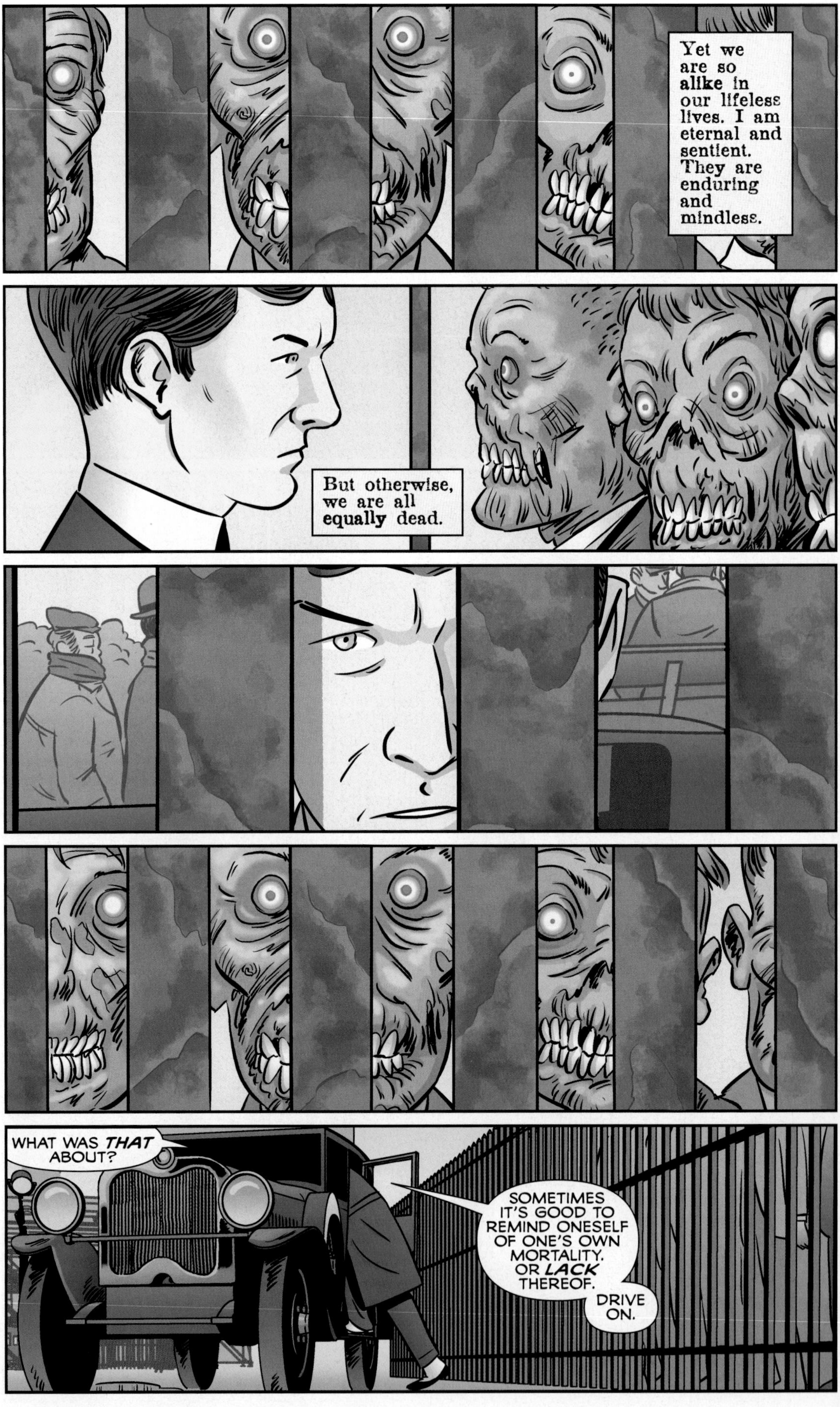
Yet we are so **alike** in our lifeless lives. I am eternal and sentient. They are enduring and mindless.
But otherwise, we are all **equally** dead.
WHAT WAS *THAT* ABOUT?
SOMETIMES IT'S GOOD TO REMIND ONESELF OF ONE'S OWN MORTALITY. OR *LACK* THEREOF.
DRIVE ON.

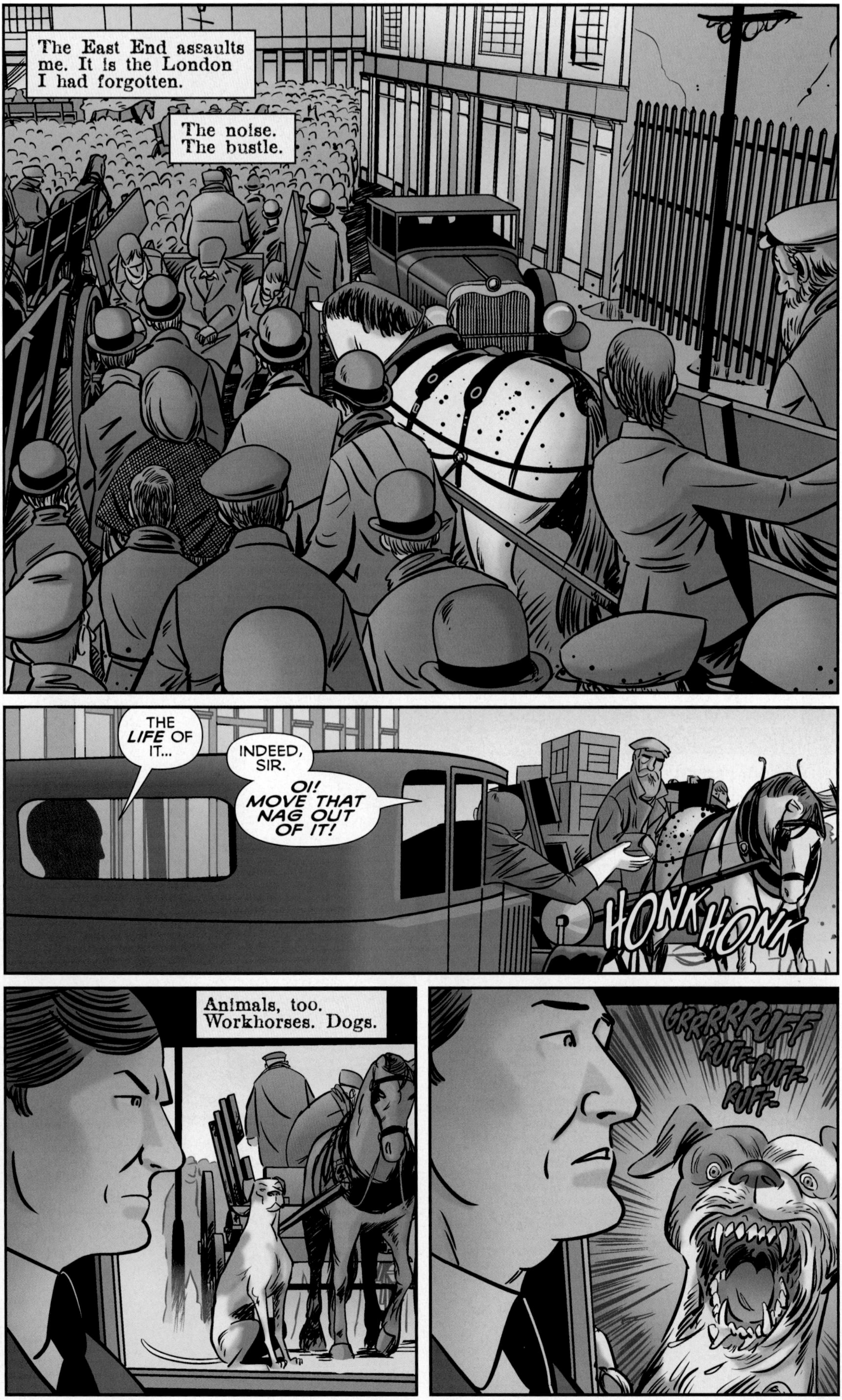
The East End assaults me. It is the London I had forgotten.
The noise. The bustle.
THE *LIFE* OF IT...
INDEED, SIR.
OI! MOVE THAT NAG OUT OF IT!
HONK HONK
Animals, too. Workhorses. Dogs.
GRRRRRUFF RUFF-RUFF-RUFF-

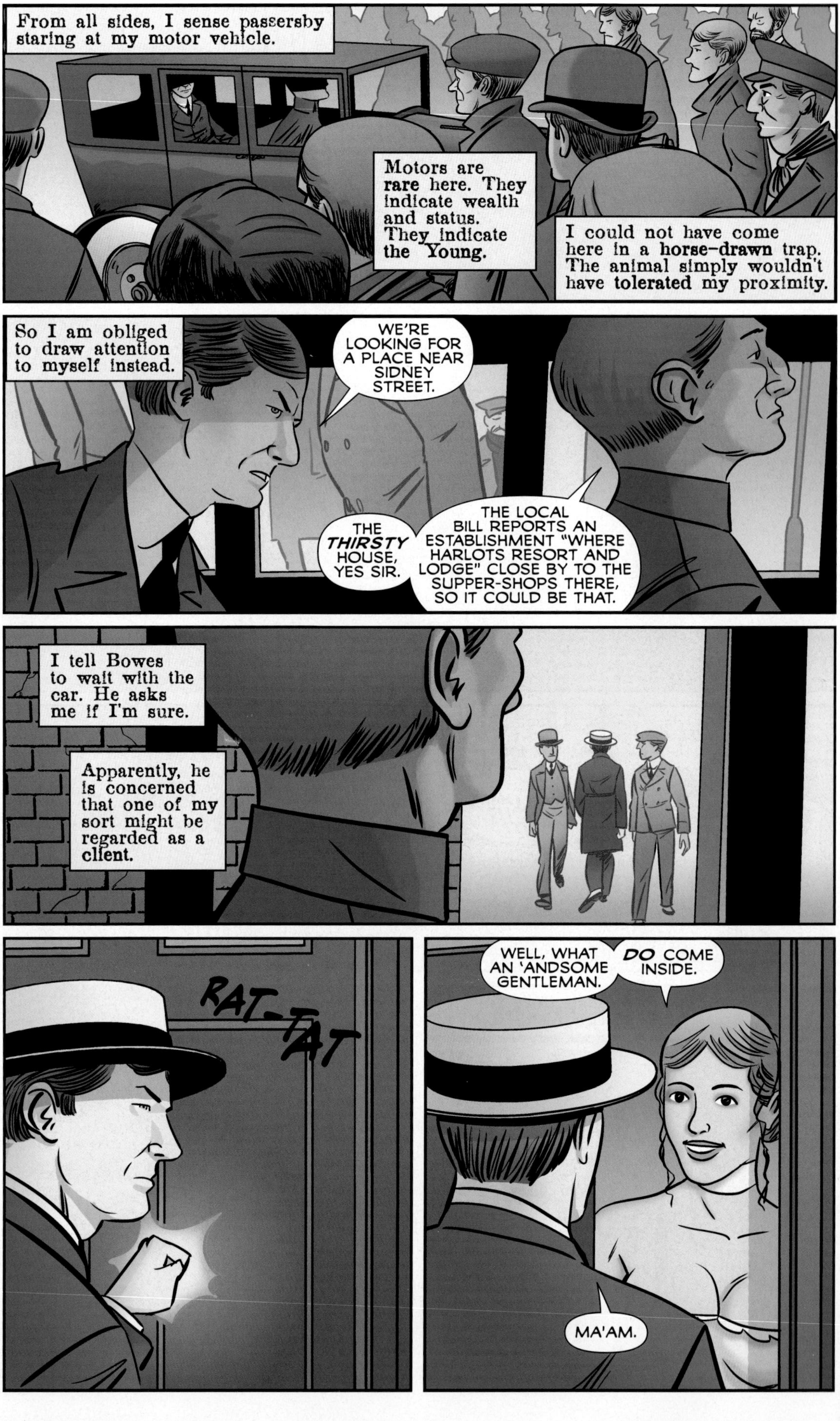
From all sides, I sense passersby staring at my motor vehicle.
Motors are rare here. They indicate wealth and status. They indicate the Young.
I could not have come here in a horse-drawn trap. The animal simply wouldn't have tolerated my proximity.
So I am obliged to draw attention to myself instead.
WE'RE LOOKING FOR A PLACE NEAR SIDNEY STREET.
THE LOCAL BILL REPORTS AN ESTABLISHMENT "WHERE HARLOTS RESORT AND LODGE" CLOSE BY TO THE SUPPER-SHOPS THERE, SO IT COULD BE THAT.
THE THIRSTY HOUSE, YES SIR.
I tell Bowes to wait with the car. He asks me if I'm sure.
Apparently, he is concerned that one of my sort might be regarded as a client.
RAT-TAT
WELL, WHAT AN 'ANDSOME GENTLEMAN.
DO COME INSIDE.
MA'AM.

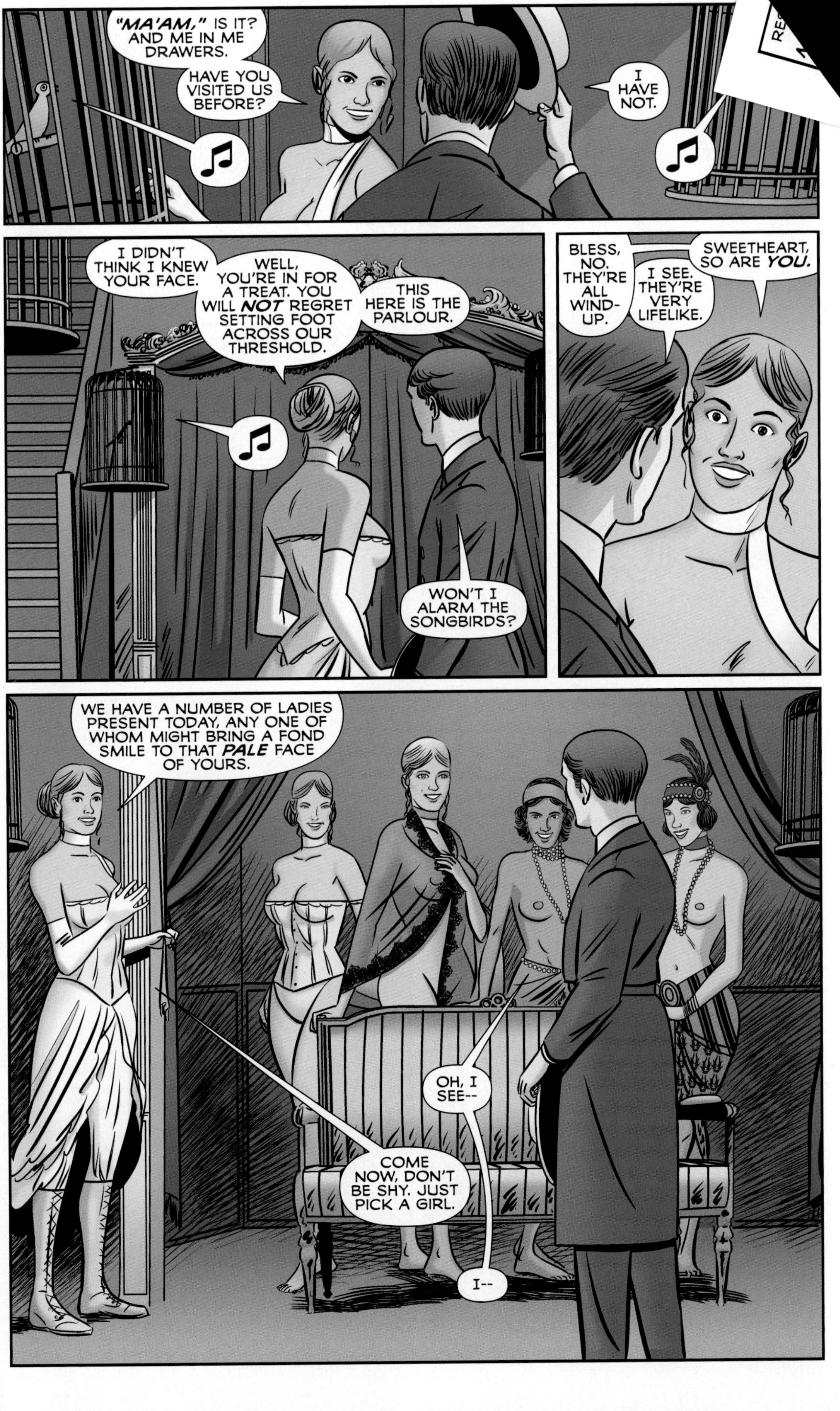
"MA'AM," IS IT? AND ME IN ME DRAWERS.
HAVE YOU VISITED US BEFORE?
♫
I HAVE NOT.
♫
I DIDN'T THINK I KNEW YOUR FACE.
WELL, YOU'RE IN FOR A TREAT. YOU WILL NOT REGRET SETTING FOOT ACROSS OUR THRESHOLD.
THIS HERE IS THE PARLOUR.
♫
WON'T I ALARM THE SONGBIRDS?
BLESS, NO. THEY'RE ALL WIND-UP.
I SEE. THEY'RE VERY LIFELIKE.
SWEETHEART, SO ARE YOU.
WE HAVE A NUMBER OF LADIES PRESENT TODAY, ANY ONE OF WHOM MIGHT BRING A FOND SMILE TO THAT PALE FACE OF YOURS.
OH, I SEE--
COME NOW, DON'T BE SHY. JUST PICK A GIRL.
I--

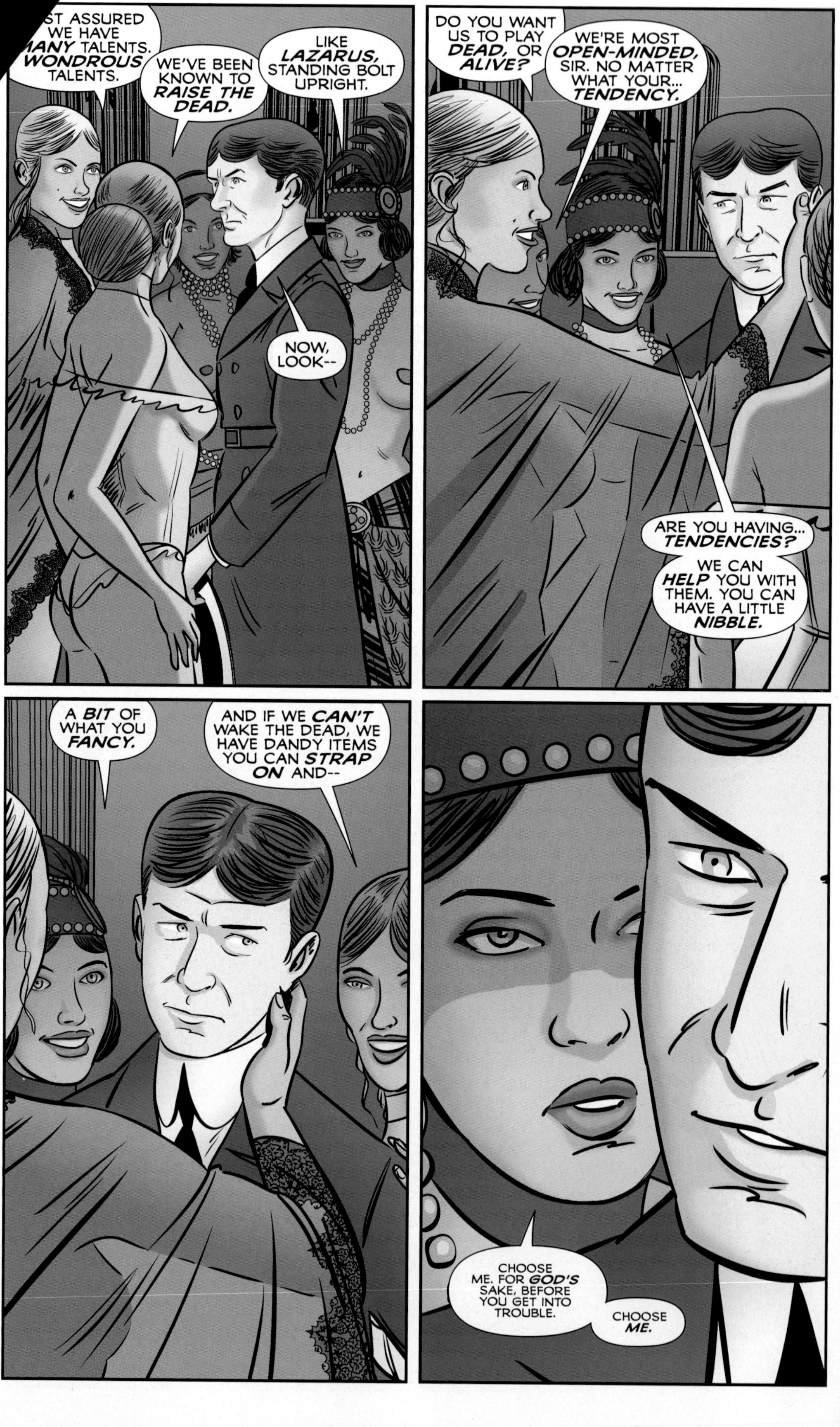
ST ASSURED WE HAVE ANY TALENTS. WONDROUS TALENTS.
WE'VE BEEN KNOWN TO RAISE THE DEAD.
LIKE LAZARUS, STANDING BOLT UPRIGHT.
NOW, LOOK--
DO YOU WANT US TO PLAY DEAD, OR ALIVE?
WE'RE MOST OPEN-MINDED, SIR. NO MATTER WHAT YOUR... TENDENCY.
ARE YOU HAVING... TENDENCIES?
WE CAN HELP YOU WITH THEM. YOU CAN HAVE A LITTLE NIBBLE.
A BIT OF WHAT YOU FANCY.
AND IF WE CAN'T WAKE THE DEAD, WE HAVE DANDY ITEMS YOU CAN STRAP ON AND--
CHOOSE ME. FOR GOD'S SAKE, BEFORE YOU GET INTO TROUBLE.
CHOOSE ME.

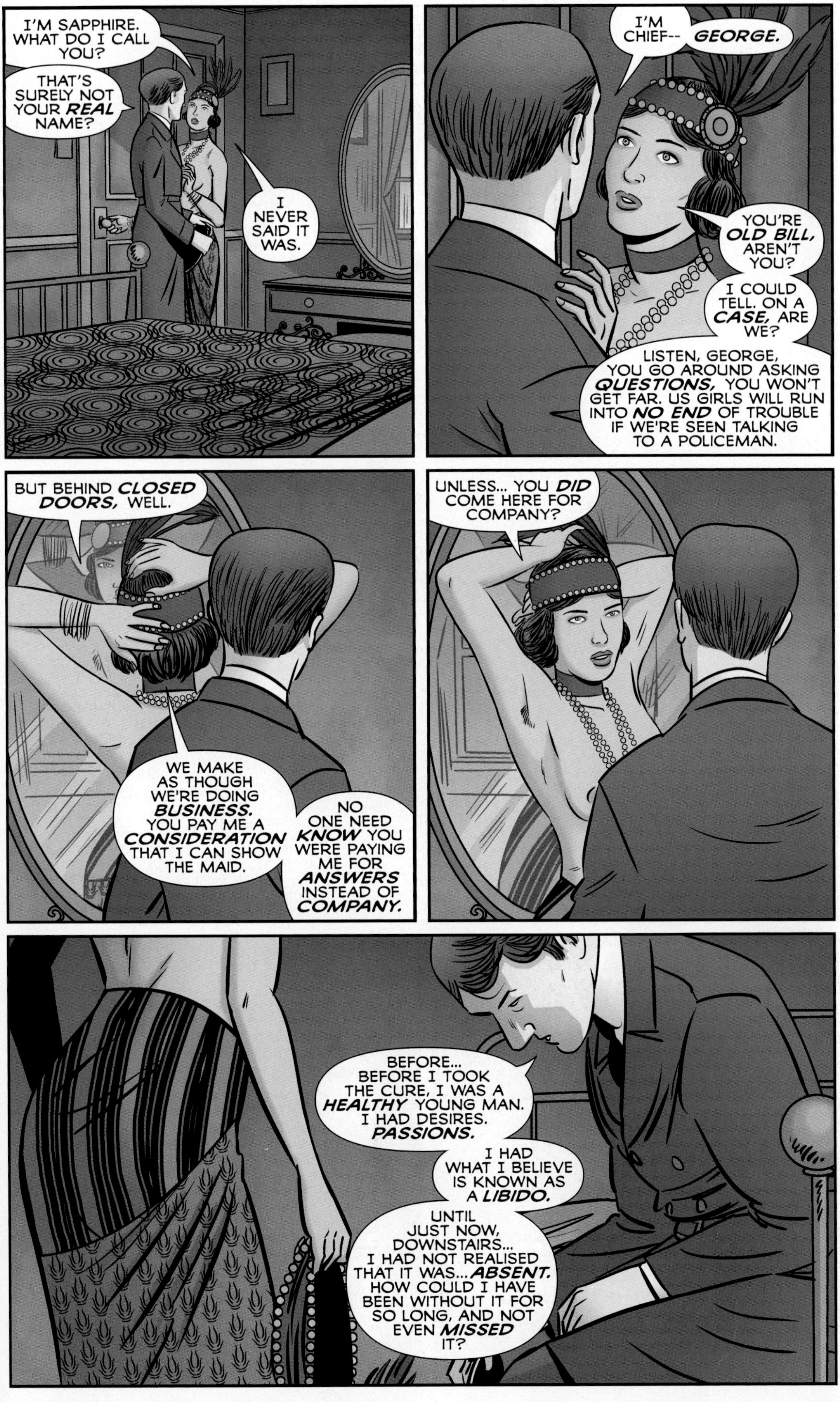

I'M SAPPHIRE. WHAT DO I CALL YOU?
THAT'S SURELY NOT YOUR REAL NAME?
I NEVER SAID IT WAS.
I'M CHIEF-- GEORGE.
YOU'RE OLD BILL, AREN'T YOU?
I COULD TELL. ON A CASE, ARE WE?
LISTEN, GEORGE, YOU GO AROUND ASKING QUESTIONS, YOU WON'T GET FAR. US GIRLS WILL RUN INTO NO END OF TROUBLE IF WE'RE SEEN TALKING TO A POLICEMAN.
BUT BEHIND CLOSED DOORS, WELL.
WE MAKE AS THOUGH WE'RE DOING BUSINESS. YOU PAY ME A CONSIDERATION THAT I CAN SHOW THE MAID.
NO ONE NEED KNOW YOU WERE PAYING ME FOR ANSWERS INSTEAD OF COMPANY.
UNLESS... YOU DID COME HERE FOR COMPANY?
BEFORE... BEFORE I TOOK THE CURE, I WAS A HEALTHY YOUNG MAN. I HAD DESIRES. PASSIONS.
I HAD WHAT I BELIEVE IS KNOWN AS A LIBIDO.
UNTIL JUST NOW, DOWNSTAIRS... I HAD NOT REALISED THAT IT WAS...ABSENT. HOW COULD I HAVE BEEN WITHOUT IT FOR SO LONG, AND NOT EVEN MISSED IT?

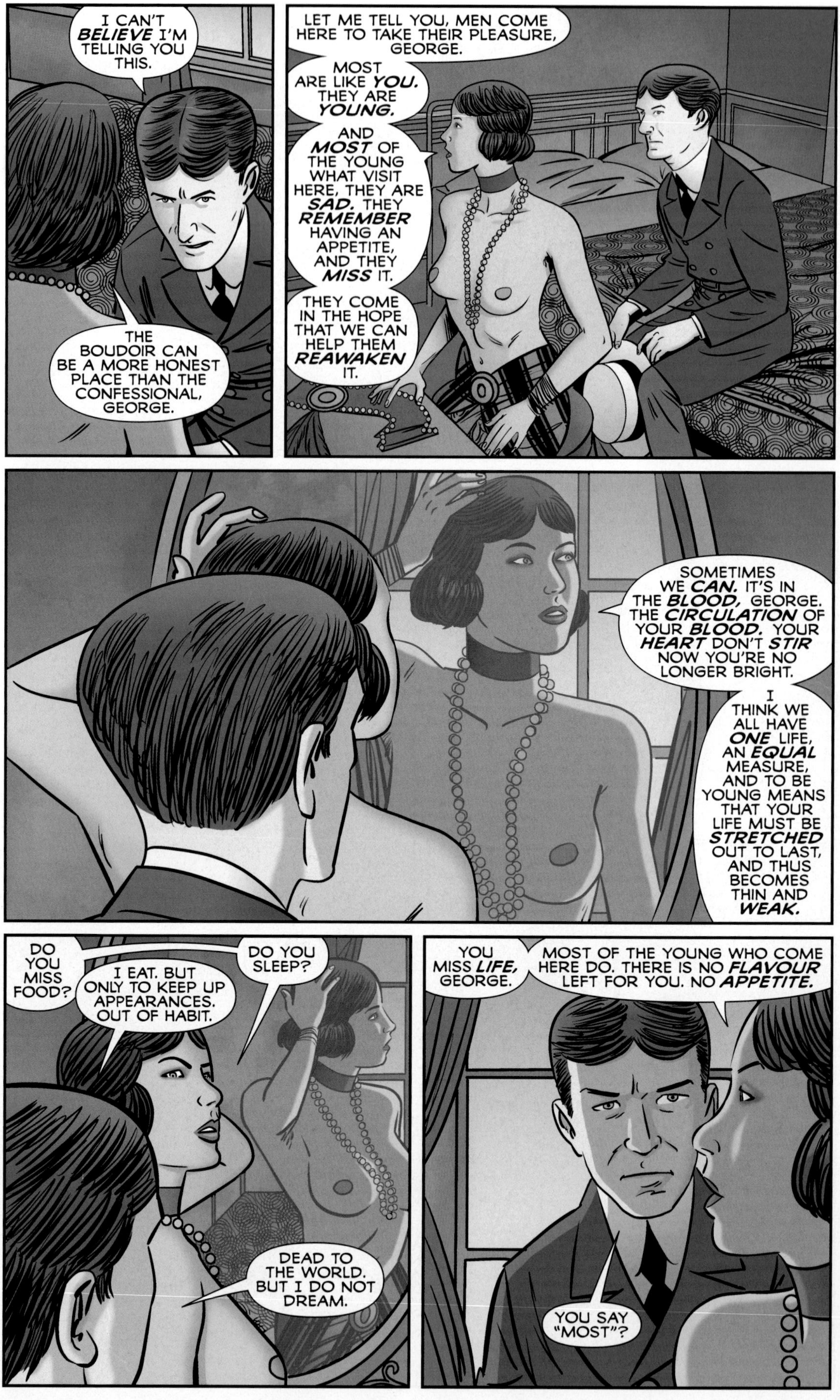
I CAN'T *BELIEVE* I'M TELLING YOU THIS.
THE BOUDOIR CAN BE A MORE HONEST PLACE THAN THE CONFESSIONAL, GEORGE.
LET ME TELL YOU, MEN COME HERE TO TAKE THEIR PLEASURE, GEORGE.
MOST ARE LIKE *YOU.* THEY ARE *YOUNG.*
AND *MOST* OF THE YOUNG WHAT VISIT HERE, THEY ARE *SAD.* THEY *REMEMBER* HAVING AN APPETITE, AND THEY *MISS* IT.
THEY COME IN THE HOPE THAT WE CAN HELP THEM *REAWAKEN* IT.
SOMETIMES WE *CAN.* IT'S IN THE *BLOOD,* GEORGE. THE *CIRCULATION* OF YOUR *BLOOD.* YOUR *HEART* DON'T *STIR* NOW YOU'RE NO LONGER BRIGHT.
I THINK WE ALL HAVE *ONE* LIFE, AN *EQUAL* MEASURE, AND TO BE YOUNG MEANS THAT YOUR LIFE MUST BE *STRETCHED* OUT TO LAST, AND THUS BECOMES THIN AND *WEAK.*
DO YOU MISS FOOD?
I EAT. BUT ONLY TO KEEP UP APPEARANCES. OUT OF HABIT.
DO YOU SLEEP?
DEAD TO THE WORLD. BUT I DO NOT DREAM.
YOU MISS *LIFE,* GEORGE.
MOST OF THE YOUNG WHO COME HERE DO. THERE IS NO *FLAVOUR* LEFT FOR YOU. NO *APPETITE.*
YOU SAY "MOST"?

OH, THERE ARE ALWAYS THE *OTHERS,* GEORGE, *YOU* KNOW THAT.

THE CURE TAKES SOME *RIGHT FUNNY.* GIVES THEM *TENDENCIES.* URGES THEY *CANNOT* CONTROL. URGES TO *BITE* AND *DRINK.*

MOST FOLKS THINK THAT'S *ALL* THAT GOES ON IN A THIRSTY HOUSE LIKE OURS, BUT IN TRUTH, IT'S ONLY ONCE IN A *LONG* WHILE WE GET A *HUNGRY ONE.*

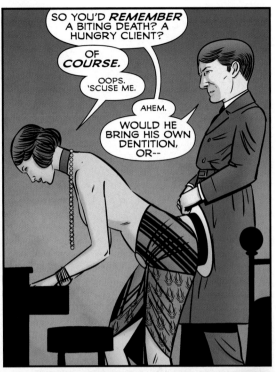

SO YOU'D *REMEMBER* A BITING DEATH? A HUNGRY CLIENT?

OF *COURSE.*

OOPS. 'SCUSE ME.

AHEM.

WOULD HE BRING HIS OWN DENTITION, OR--

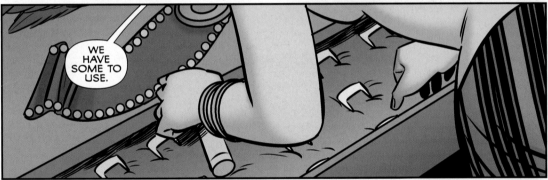

WE HAVE SOME TO USE.

WOULD YOU LIKE A BITE OF ME, GEORGE?

YES.

THAT'S A GOOD SIGN. NOT DEAD YET. NOT *ENTIRELY.*

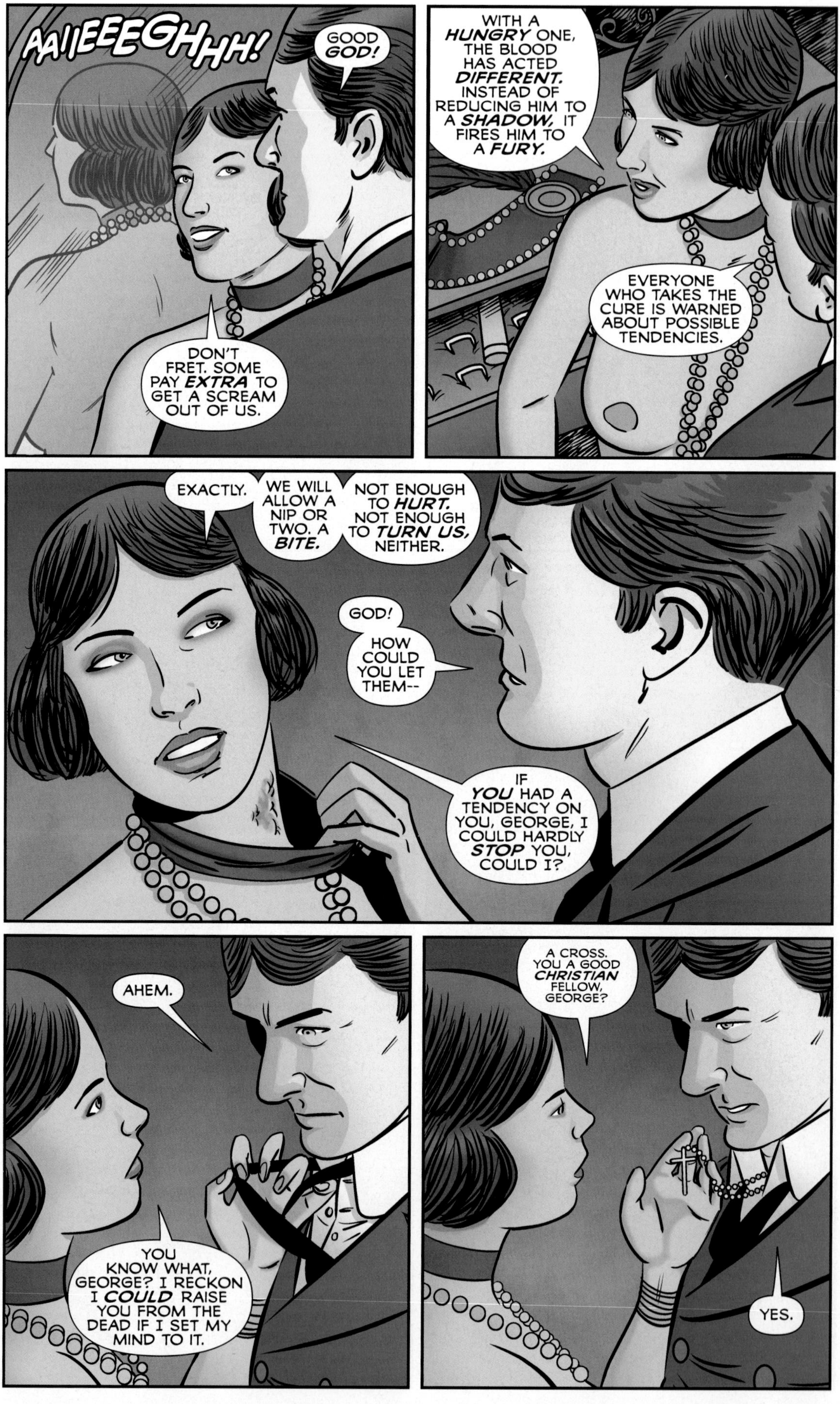
AAIIEEEEGHHH!
GOOD GOD!
DON'T FRET. SOME PAY EXTRA TO GET A SCREAM OUT OF US.
WITH A HUNGRY ONE, THE BLOOD HAS ACTED DIFFERENT. INSTEAD OF REDUCING HIM TO A SHADOW, IT FIRES HIM TO A FURY.
EVERYONE WHO TAKES THE CURE IS WARNED ABOUT POSSIBLE TENDENCIES.
EXACTLY.
WE WILL ALLOW A NIP OR TWO. A BITE.
NOT ENOUGH TO HURT. NOT ENOUGH TO TURN US, NEITHER.
GOD!
HOW COULD YOU LET THEM--
IF YOU HAD A TENDENCY ON YOU, GEORGE, I COULD HARDLY STOP YOU, COULD I?
AHEM.
YOU KNOW WHAT, GEORGE? I RECKON I COULD RAISE YOU FROM THE DEAD IF I SET MY MIND TO IT.
A CROSS. YOU A GOOD CHRISTIAN FELLOW, GEORGE?
YES.

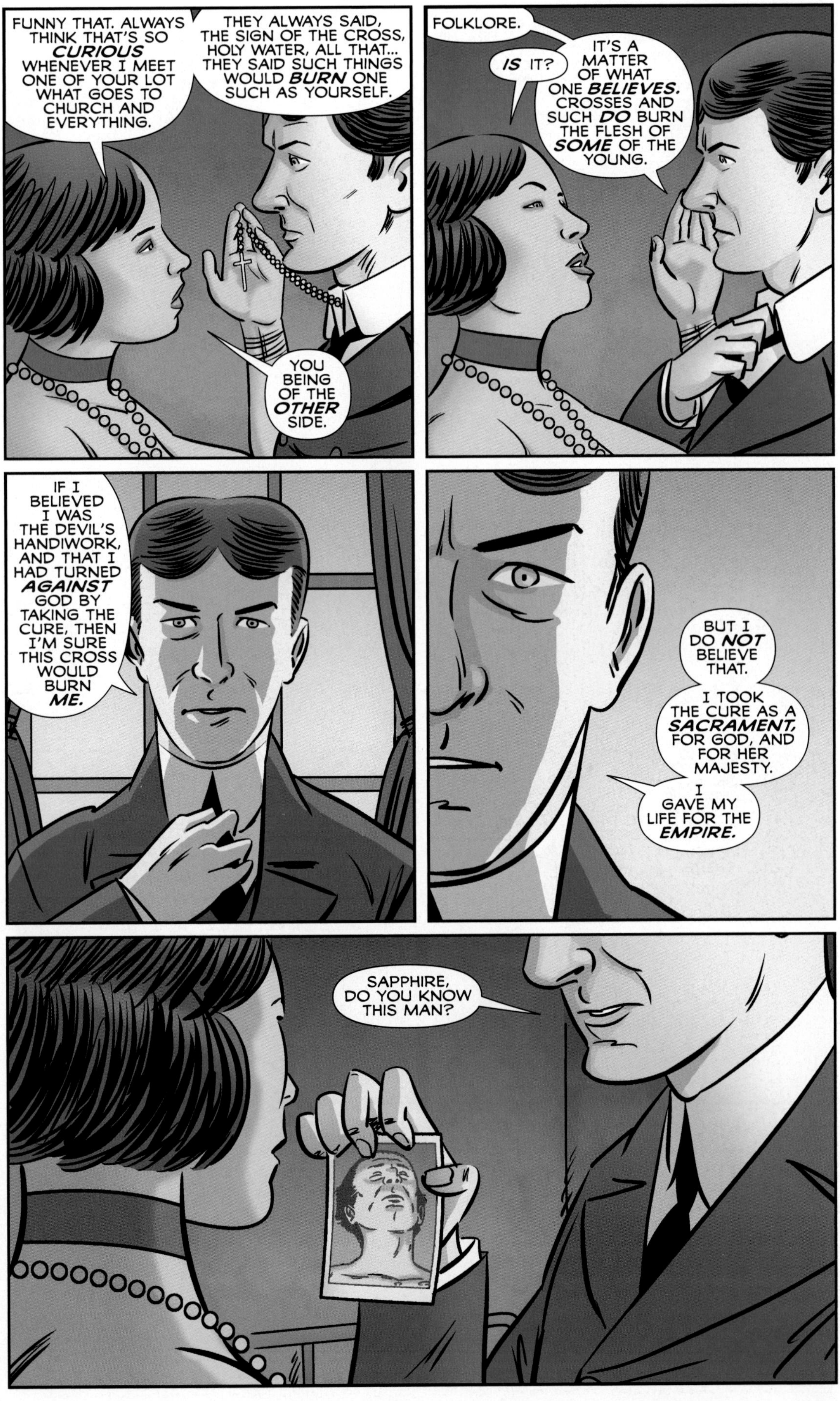
FUNNY THAT. ALWAYS THINK THAT'S SO CURIOUS WHENEVER I MEET ONE OF YOUR LOT WHAT GOES TO CHURCH AND EVERYTHING.
THEY ALWAYS SAID, THE SIGN OF THE CROSS, HOLY WATER, ALL THAT... THEY SAID SUCH THINGS WOULD BURN ONE SUCH AS YOURSELF.
YOU BEING OF THE OTHER SIDE.
FOLKLORE.
IS IT?
IT'S A MATTER OF WHAT ONE BELIEVES. CROSSES AND SUCH DO BURN THE FLESH OF SOME OF THE YOUNG.
IF I BELIEVED I WAS THE DEVIL'S HANDIWORK, AND THAT I HAD TURNED AGAINST GOD BY TAKING THE CURE, THEN I'M SURE THIS CROSS WOULD BURN ME.
BUT I DO NOT BELIEVE THAT.
I TOOK THE CURE AS A SACRAMENT, FOR GOD, AND FOR HER MAJESTY.
I GAVE MY LIFE FOR THE EMPIRE.
SAPPHIRE, DO YOU KNOW THIS MAN?

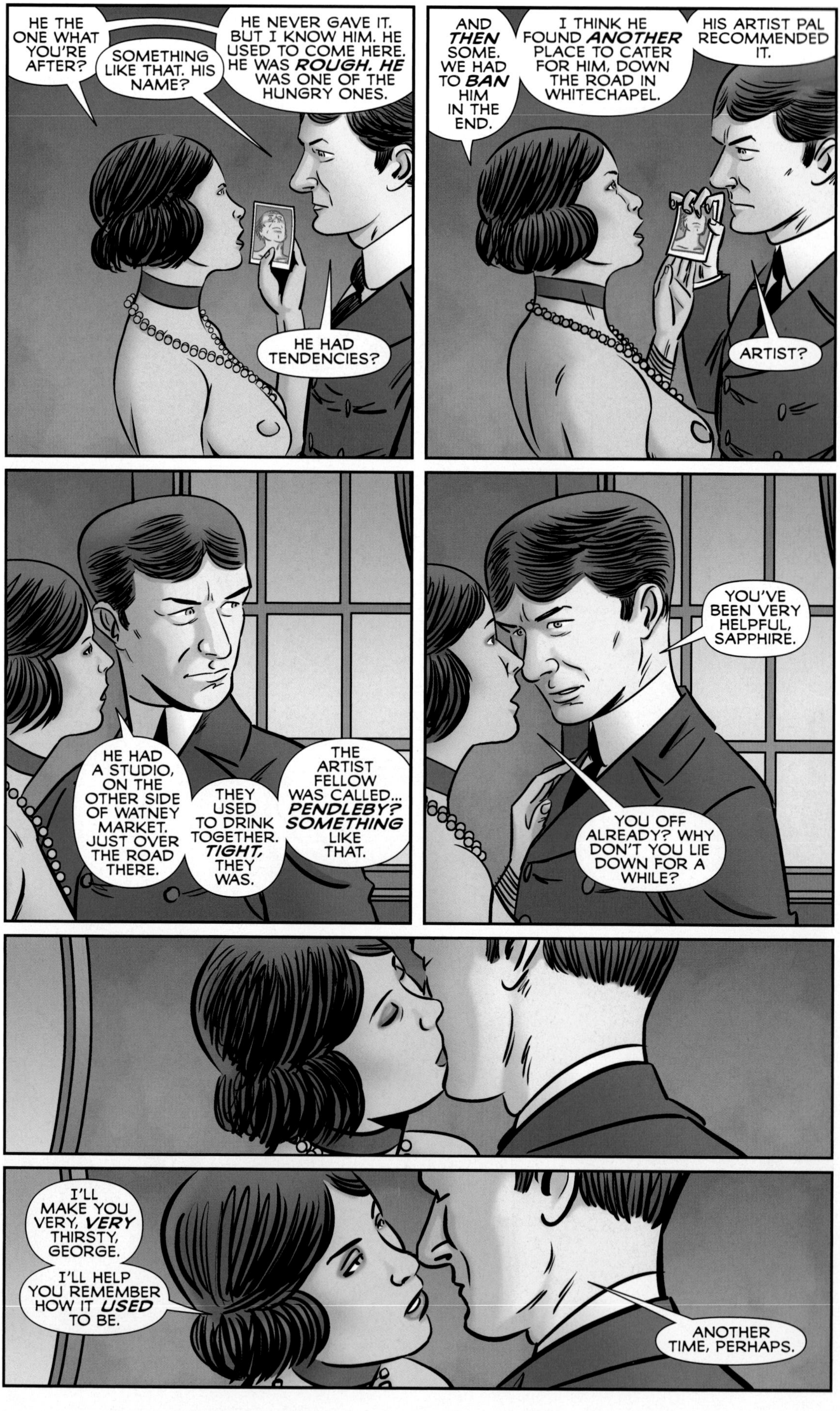
HE THE ONE WHAT YOU'RE AFTER?
SOMETHING LIKE THAT. HIS NAME?
HE NEVER GAVE IT. BUT I KNOW HIM. HE USED TO COME HERE. HE WAS ROUGH. HE WAS ONE OF THE HUNGRY ONES.
HE HAD TENDENCIES?
AND THEN SOME. WE HAD TO BAN HIM IN THE END.
I THINK HE FOUND ANOTHER PLACE TO CATER FOR HIM, DOWN THE ROAD IN WHITECHAPEL.
HIS ARTIST PAL RECOMMENDED IT.
ARTIST?
HE HAD A STUDIO, ON THE OTHER SIDE OF WATNEY MARKET. JUST OVER THE ROAD THERE.
THEY USED TO DRINK TOGETHER. TIGHT, THEY WAS.
THE ARTIST FELLOW WAS CALLED... PENDLEBY? SOMETHING LIKE THAT.
YOU'VE BEEN VERY HELPFUL, SAPPHIRE.
YOU OFF ALREADY? WHY DON'T YOU LIE DOWN FOR A WHILE?
I'LL MAKE YOU VERY, VERY THIRSTY, GEORGE.
I'LL HELP YOU REMEMBER HOW IT USED TO BE.
ANOTHER TIME, PERHAPS.

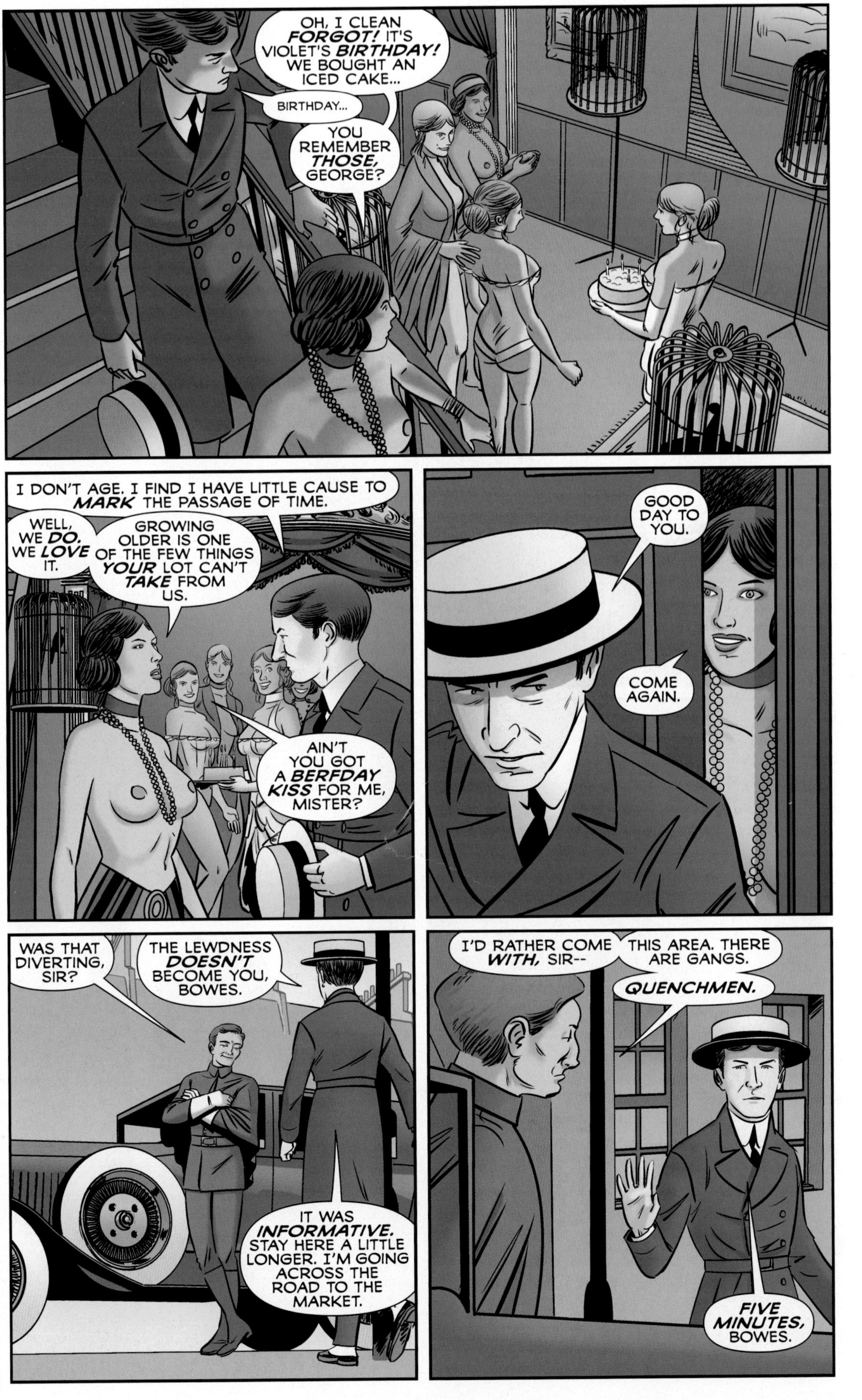
OH, I CLEAN FORGOT! IT'S VIOLET'S BIRTHDAY! WE BOUGHT AN ICED CAKE...
BIRTHDAY...
YOU REMEMBER THOSE, GEORGE?
I DON'T AGE. I FIND I HAVE LITTLE CAUSE TO MARK THE PASSAGE OF TIME.
WELL, WE DO. WE LOVE IT.
GROWING OLDER IS ONE OF THE FEW THINGS YOUR LOT CAN'T TAKE FROM US.
AIN'T YOU GOT A BERFDAY KISS FOR ME, MISTER?
GOOD DAY TO YOU.
COME AGAIN.
WAS THAT DIVERTING, SIR?
THE LEWDNESS DOESN'T BECOME YOU, BOWES.
IT WAS INFORMATIVE. STAY HERE A LITTLE LONGER. I'M GOING ACROSS THE ROAD TO THE MARKET.
I'D RATHER COME WITH, SIR--
THIS AREA. THERE ARE GANGS.
QUENCHMEN.
FIVE MINUTES, BOWES.

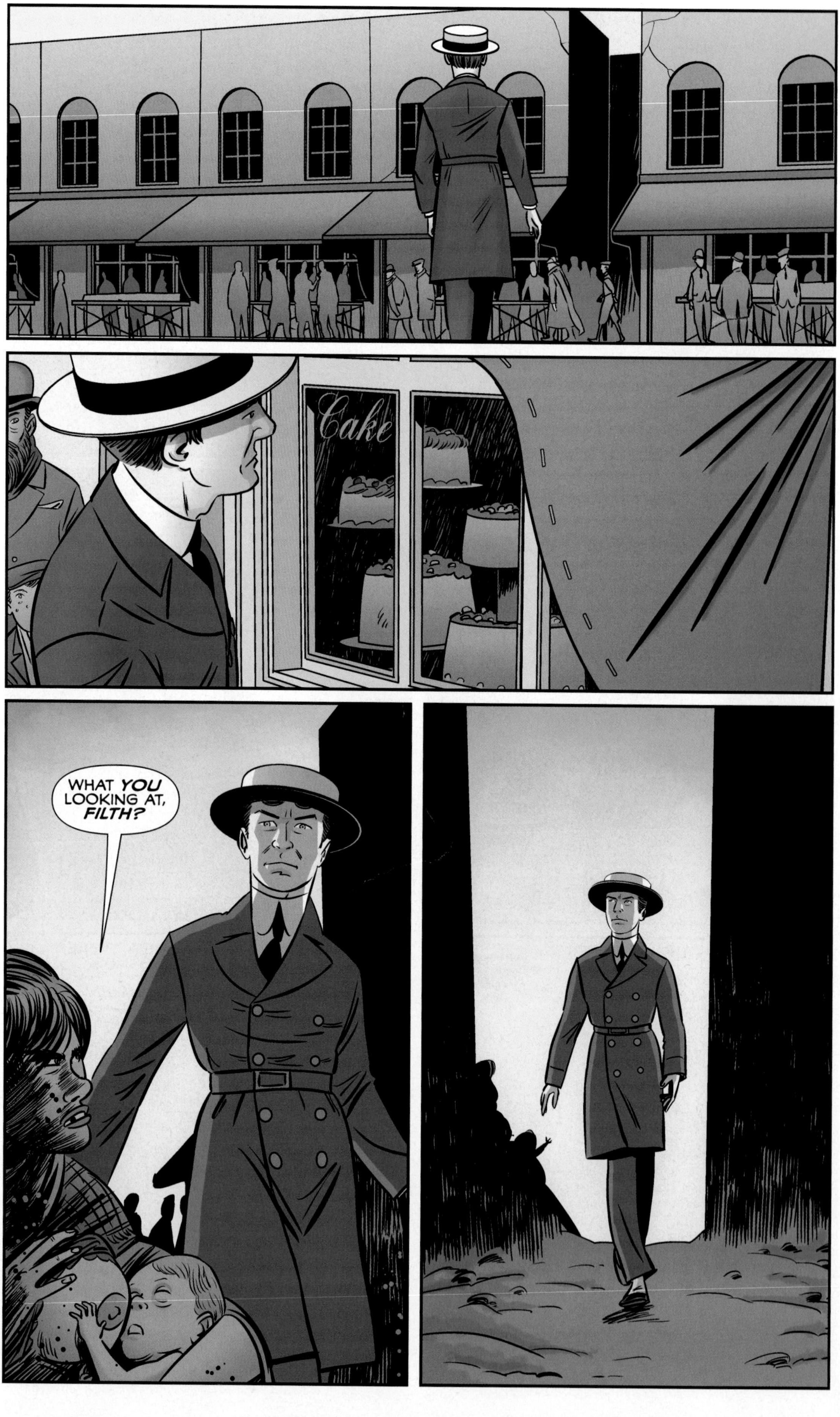
Cake
WHAT YOU LOOKING AT, FILTH?

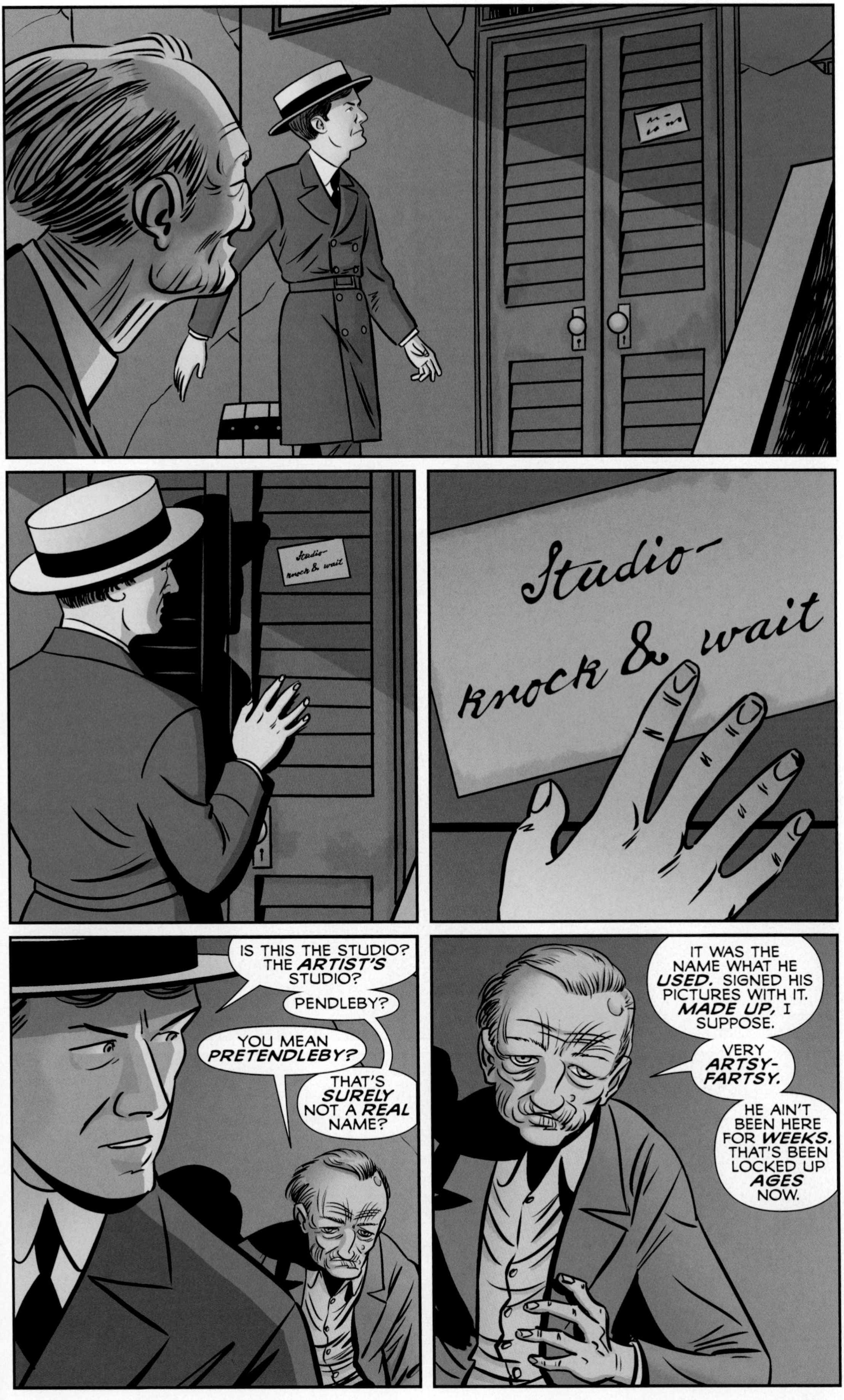
Studio-
knock & wait
Studio-
knock & wait
IS THIS THE STUDIO? THE ARTIST'S STUDIO?
PENDLEBY?
YOU MEAN PRETENDLEBY?
THAT'S SURELY NOT A REAL NAME?
IT WAS THE NAME WHAT HE USED. SIGNED HIS PICTURES WITH IT. MADE UP, I SUPPOSE.
VERY ARTSY-FARTSY.
HE AIN'T BEEN HERE FOR WEEKS. THAT'S BEEN LOCKED UP AGES NOW.

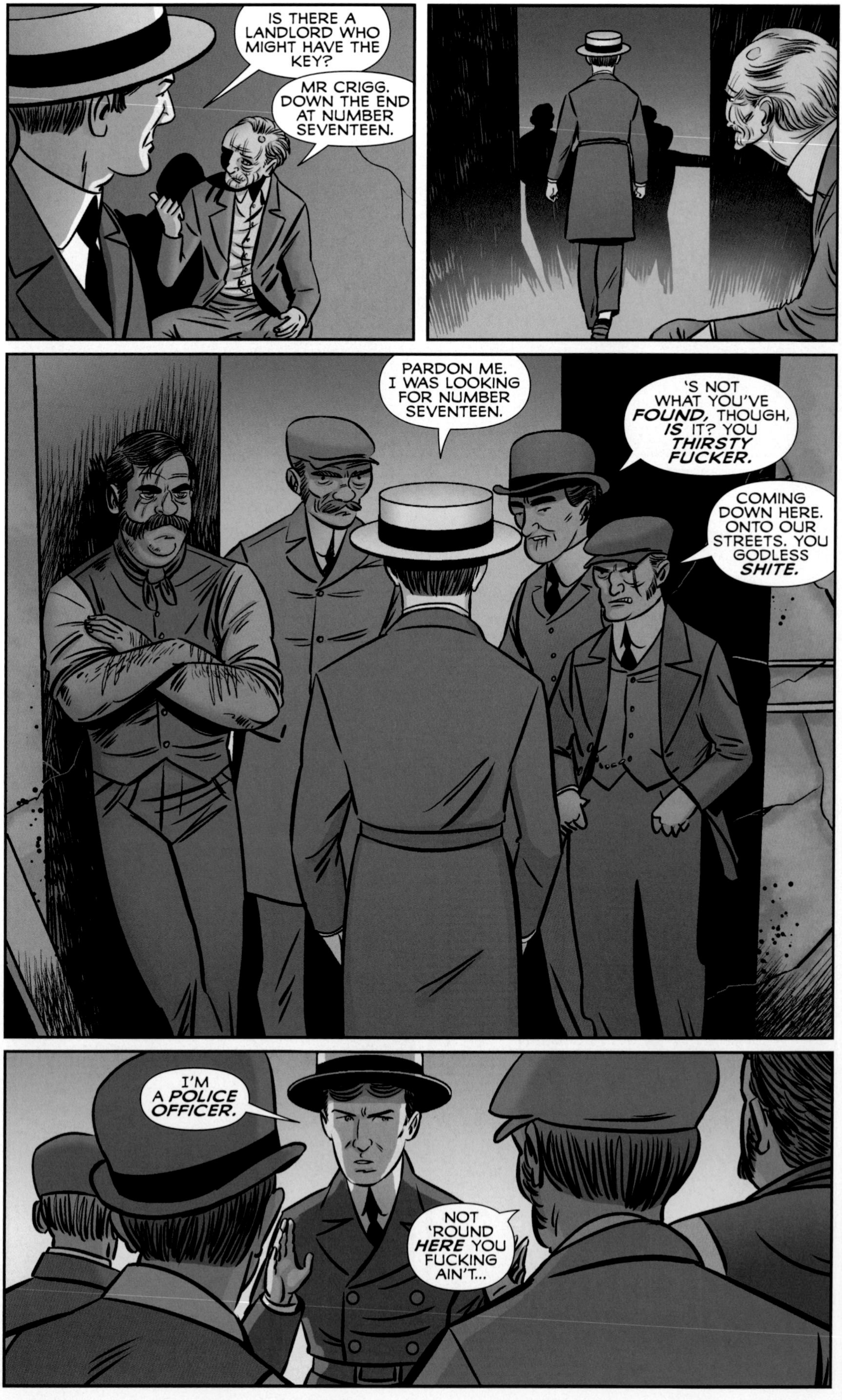
IS THERE A LANDLORD WHO MIGHT HAVE THE KEY?
MR CRIGG. DOWN THE END AT NUMBER SEVENTEEN.
PARDON ME. I WAS LOOKING FOR NUMBER SEVENTEEN.
'S NOT WHAT YOU'VE FOUND, THOUGH, IS IT? YOU THIRSTY FUCKER.
COMING DOWN HERE. ONTO OUR STREETS. YOU GODLESS SHITE.
I'M A POLICE OFFICER.
NOT 'ROUND HERE YOU FUCKING AIN'T...

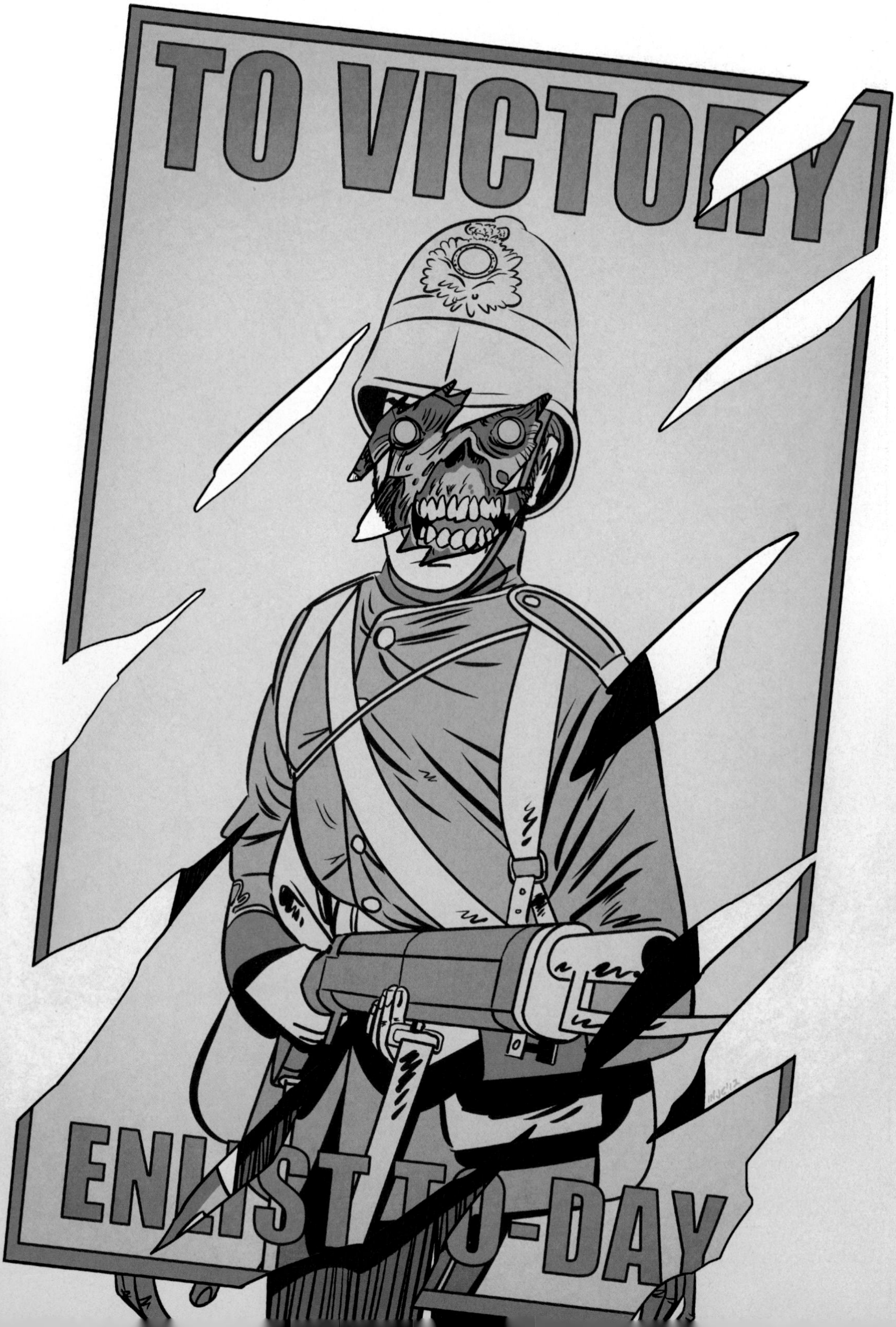
TO VICTORY
ENLIST TO-DAY

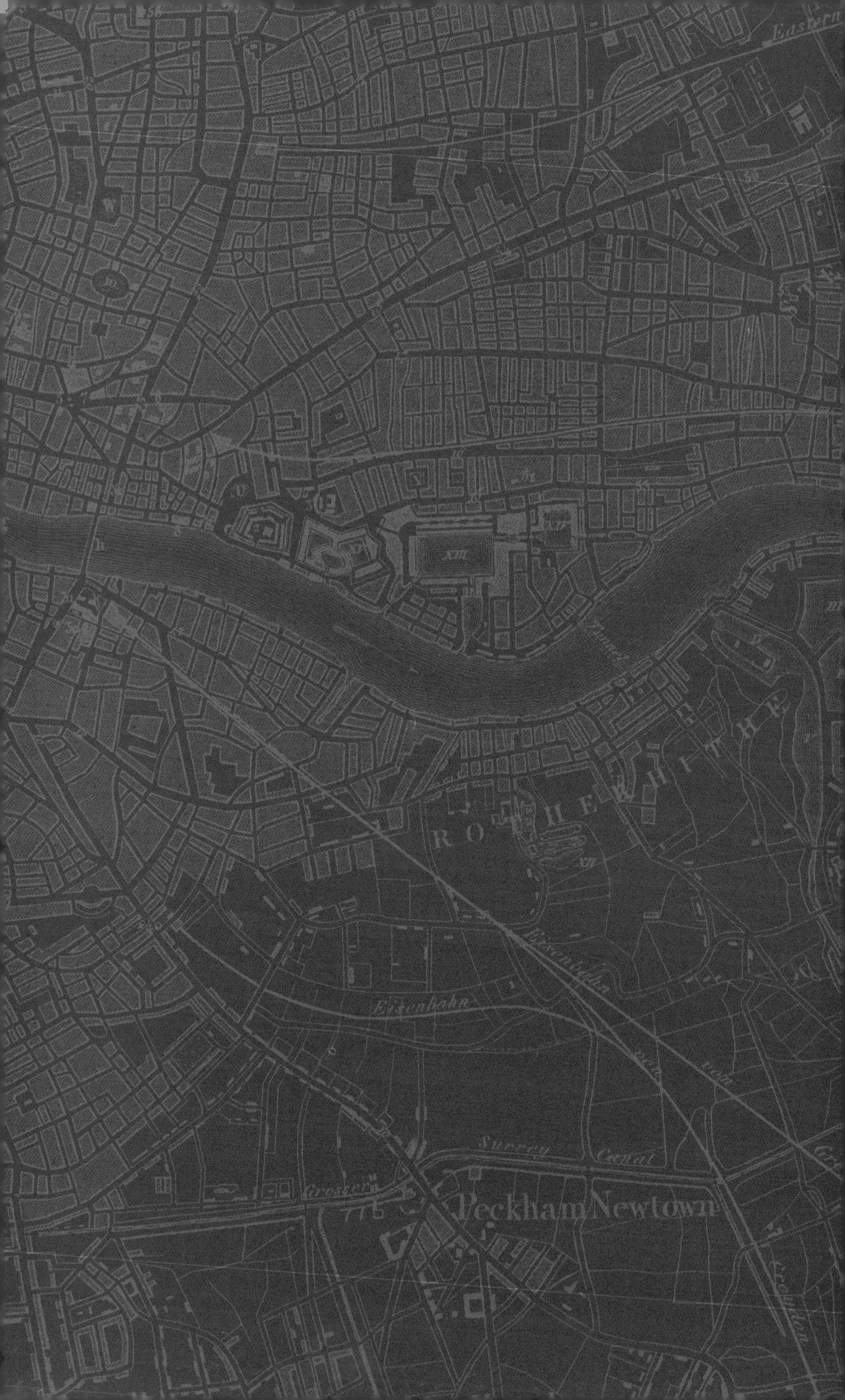
Eastern
R O T H E R H I T H E
Eisenbahn
Surrey Canal
Peckham Newtown

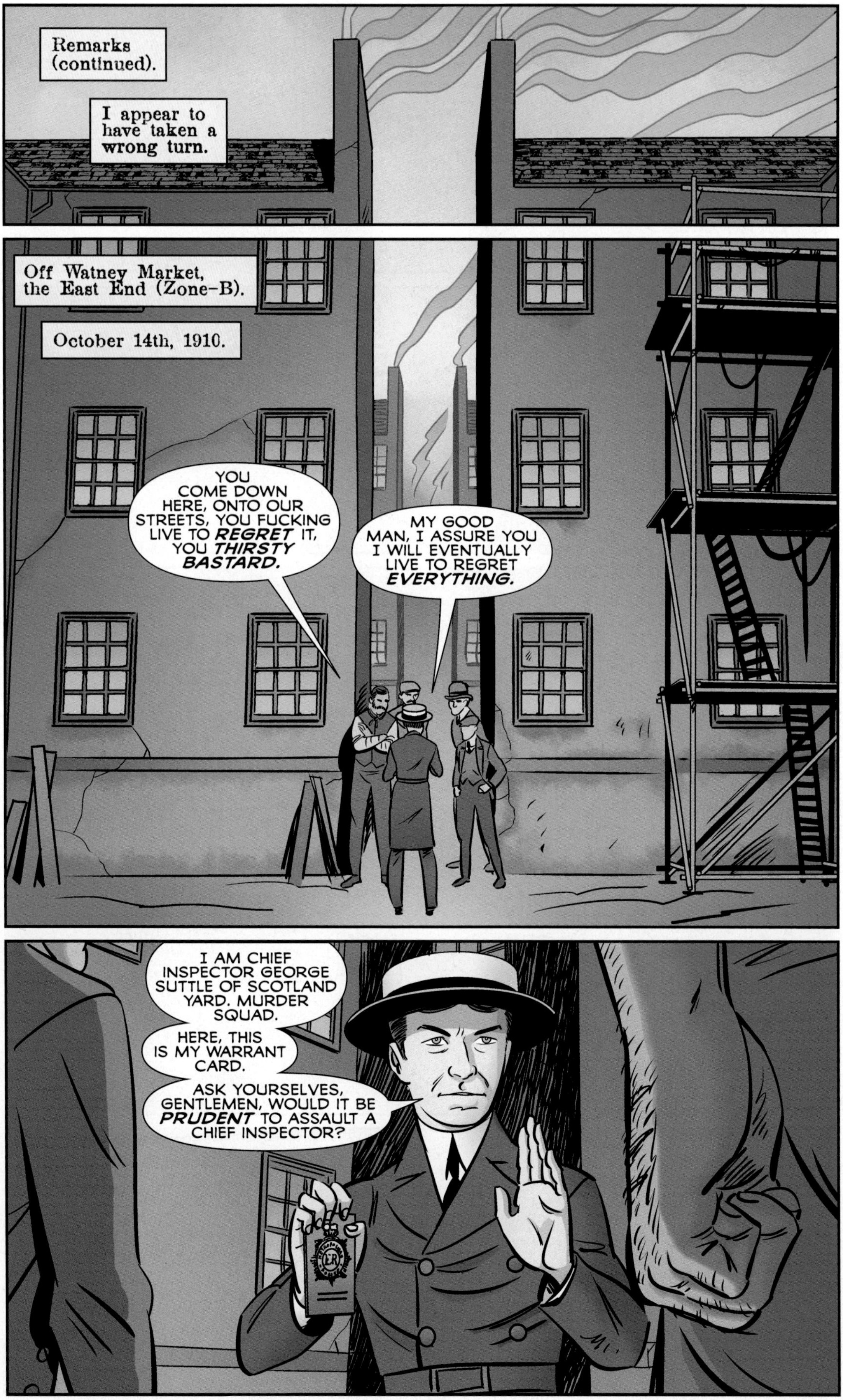
Remarks (continued).
I appear to have taken a wrong turn.
Off Watney Market, the East End (Zone-B).
October 14th, 1910.
YOU COME DOWN HERE, ONTO OUR STREETS, YOU FUCKING LIVE TO REGRET IT, YOU THIRSTY BASTARD.
MY GOOD MAN, I ASSURE YOU I WILL EVENTUALLY LIVE TO REGRET EVERYTHING.
I AM CHIEF INSPECTOR GEORGE SUTTLE OF SCOTLAND YARD. MURDER SQUAD.
HERE, THIS IS MY WARRANT CARD.
ASK YOURSELVES, GENTLEMEN, WOULD IT BE PRUDENT TO ASSAULT A CHIEF INSPECTOR?

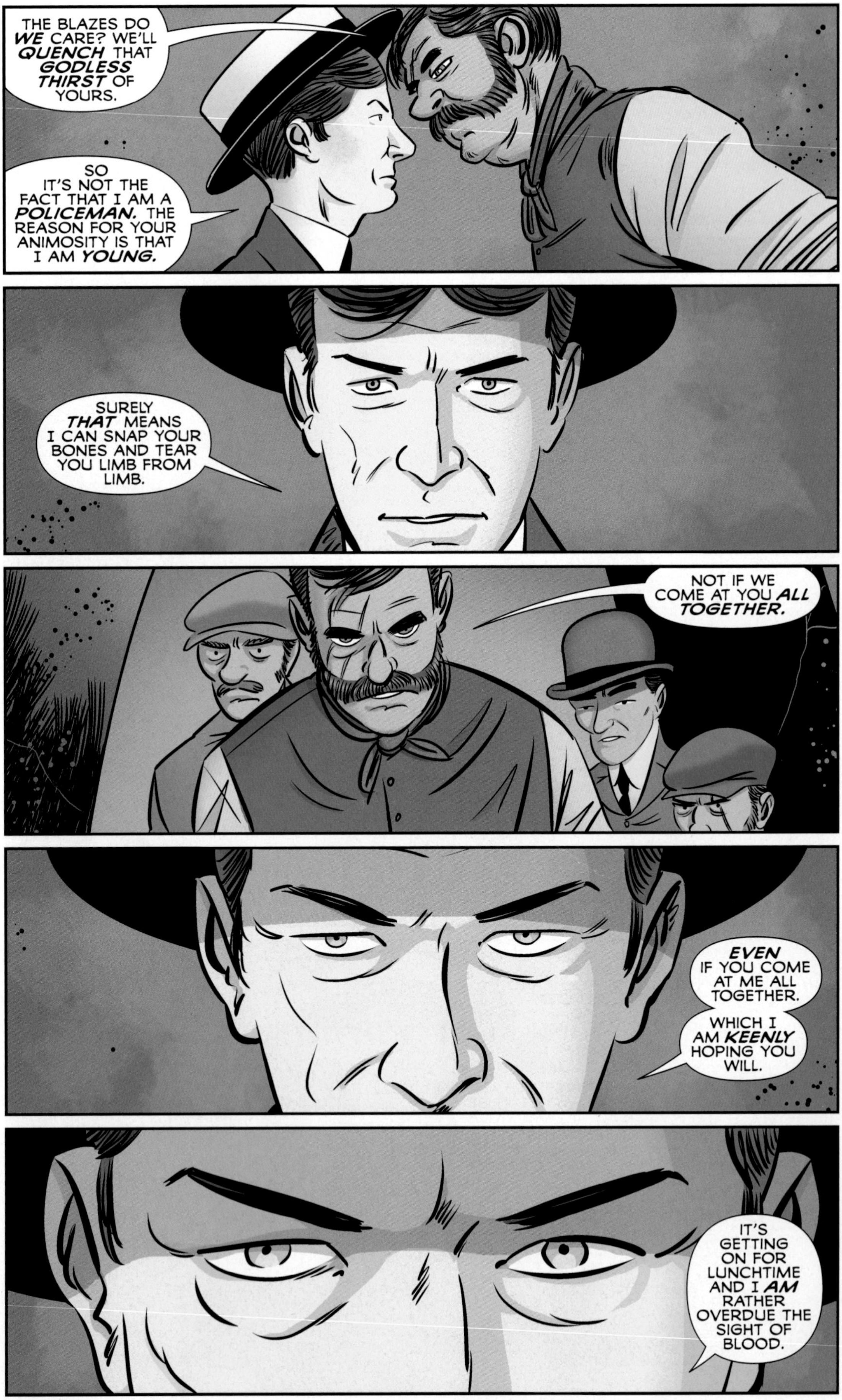
THE BLAZES DO WE CARE? WE'LL QUENCH THAT GODLESS THIRST OF YOURS.
SO IT'S NOT THE FACT THAT I AM A POLICEMAN. THE REASON FOR YOUR ANIMOSITY IS THAT I AM YOUNG.
SURELY THAT MEANS I CAN SNAP YOUR BONES AND TEAR YOU LIMB FROM LIMB.
NOT IF WE COME AT YOU ALL TOGETHER.
EVEN IF YOU COME AT ME ALL TOGETHER.
WHICH I AM KEENLY HOPING YOU WILL.
IT'S GETTING ON FOR LUNCHTIME AND I AM RATHER OVERDUE THE SIGHT OF BLOOD.

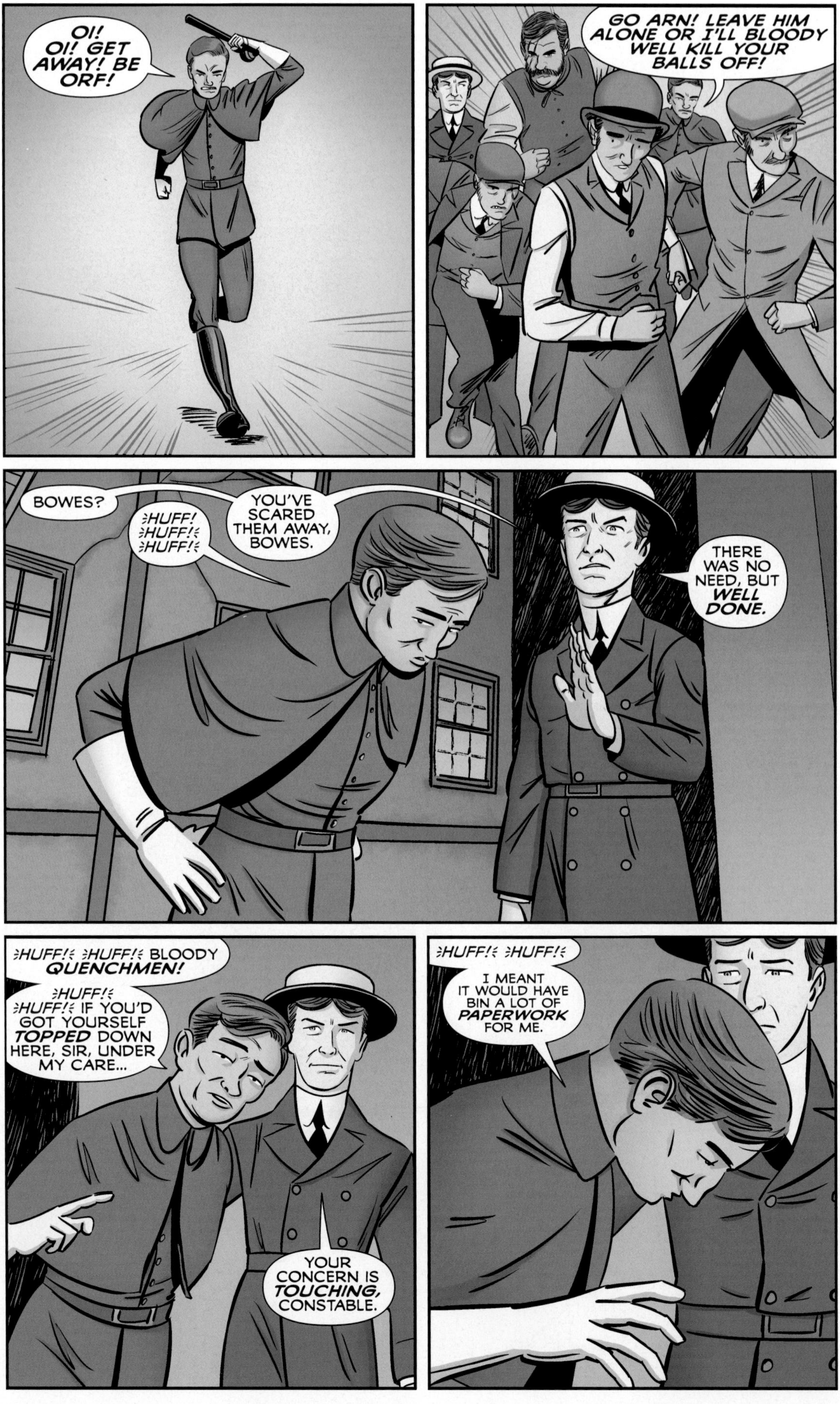
OI!
OI! GET AWAY! BE ORF!
GO ARN! LEAVE HIM ALONE OR I'LL BLOODY WELL KILL YOUR BALLS OFF!
BOWES?
ƷHUFF!Ƹ ƷHUFF!Ƹ ƷHUFF!Ƹ
YOU'VE SCARED THEM AWAY, BOWES.
THERE WAS NO NEED, BUT WELL DONE.
ƷHUFF!Ƹ ƷHUFF!Ƹ BLOODY QUENCHMEN!
ƷHUFF!Ƹ ƷHUFF!Ƹ IF YOU'D GOT YOURSELF TOPPED DOWN HERE, SIR, UNDER MY CARE...
YOUR CONCERN IS TOUCHING, CONSTABLE.
ƷHUFF!Ƹ ƷHUFF!Ƹ
I MEANT IT WOULD HAVE BIN A LOT OF PAPERWORK FOR ME.

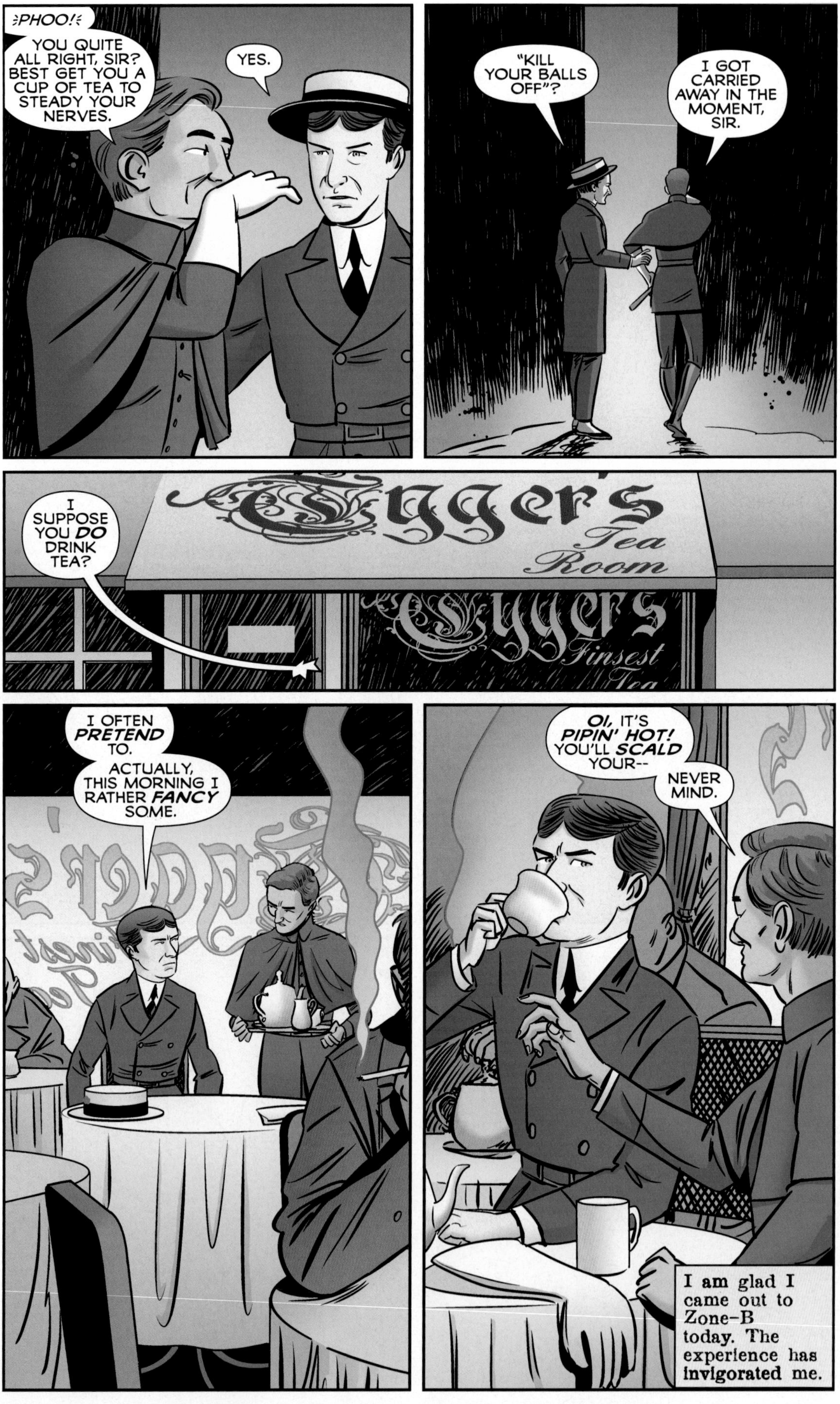
PHOO!
YOU QUITE ALL RIGHT, SIR? BEST GET YOU A CUP OF TEA TO STEADY YOUR NERVES.
YES.
"KILL YOUR BALLS OFF"?
I GOT CARRIED AWAY IN THE MOMENT, SIR.
Tygger's Tea Room
I SUPPOSE YOU DO DRINK TEA?
Tygger's Finsest Tea
I OFTEN PRETEND TO.
ACTUALLY, THIS MORNING I RATHER FANCY SOME.
OI, IT'S PIPIN' HOT! YOU'LL SCALD YOUR--
NEVER MIND.
I am glad I came out to Zone-B today. The experience has invigorated me.

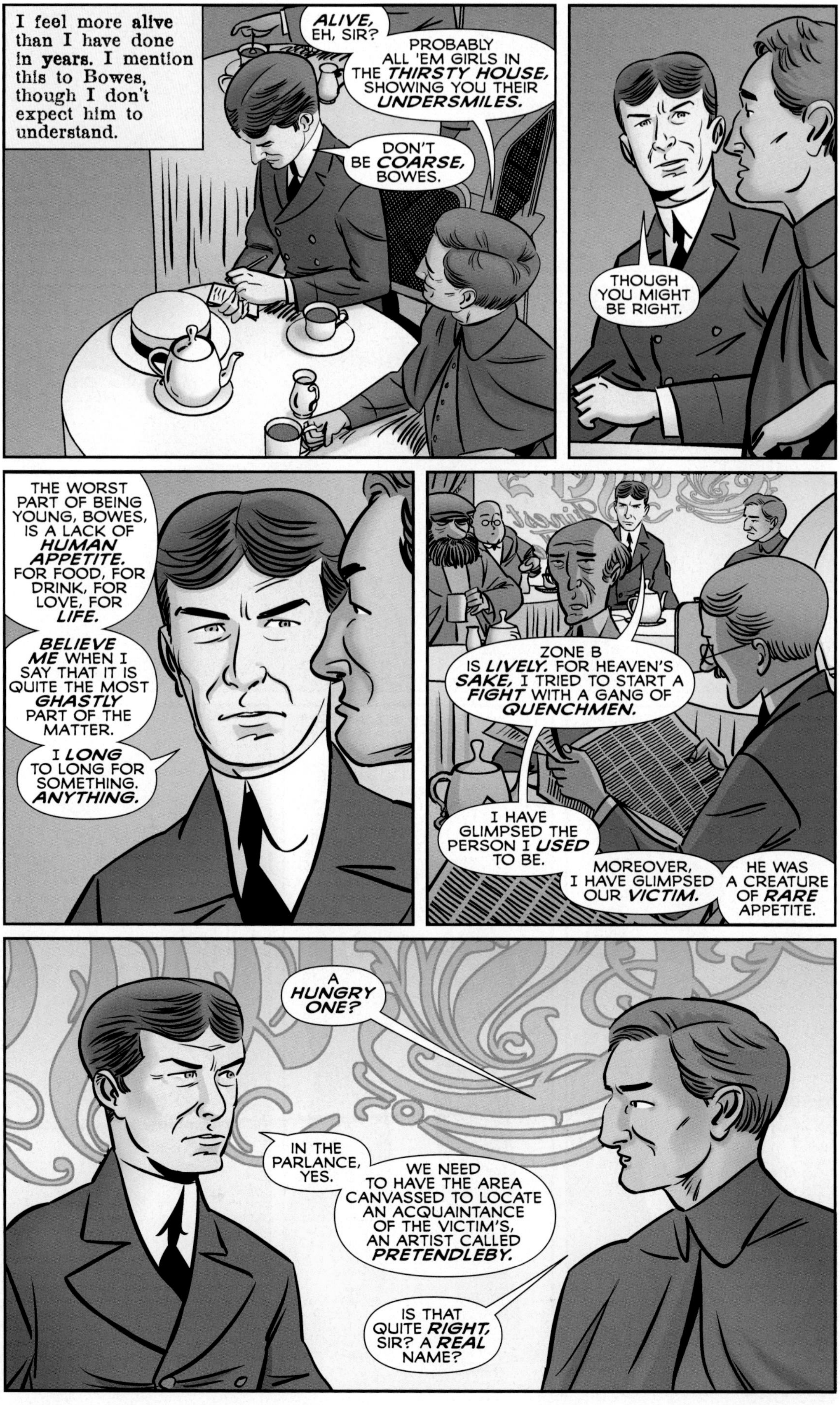
I feel more alive than I have done in years. I mention this to Bowes, though I don't expect him to understand.
ALIVE, EH, SIR?
PROBABLY ALL 'EM GIRLS IN THE THIRSTY HOUSE, SHOWING YOU THEIR UNDERSMILES.
DON'T BE COARSE, BOWES.
THOUGH YOU MIGHT BE RIGHT.
THE WORST PART OF BEING YOUNG, BOWES, IS A LACK OF HUMAN APPETITE. FOR FOOD, FOR DRINK, FOR LOVE, FOR LIFE.
BELIEVE ME WHEN I SAY THAT IT IS QUITE THE MOST GHASTLY PART OF THE MATTER.
I LONG TO LONG FOR SOMETHING. ANYTHING.
ZONE B IS LIVELY. FOR HEAVEN'S SAKE, I TRIED TO START A FIGHT WITH A GANG OF QUENCHMEN.
I HAVE GLIMPSED THE PERSON I USED TO BE.
MOREOVER, I HAVE GLIMPSED OUR VICTIM.
HE WAS A CREATURE OF RARE APPETITE.
A HUNGRY ONE?
IN THE PARLANCE, YES.
WE NEED TO HAVE THE AREA CANVASSED TO LOCATE AN ACQUAINTANCE OF THE VICTIM'S, AN ARTIST CALLED PRETENDLEBY.
IS THAT QUITE RIGHT, SIR? A REAL NAME?

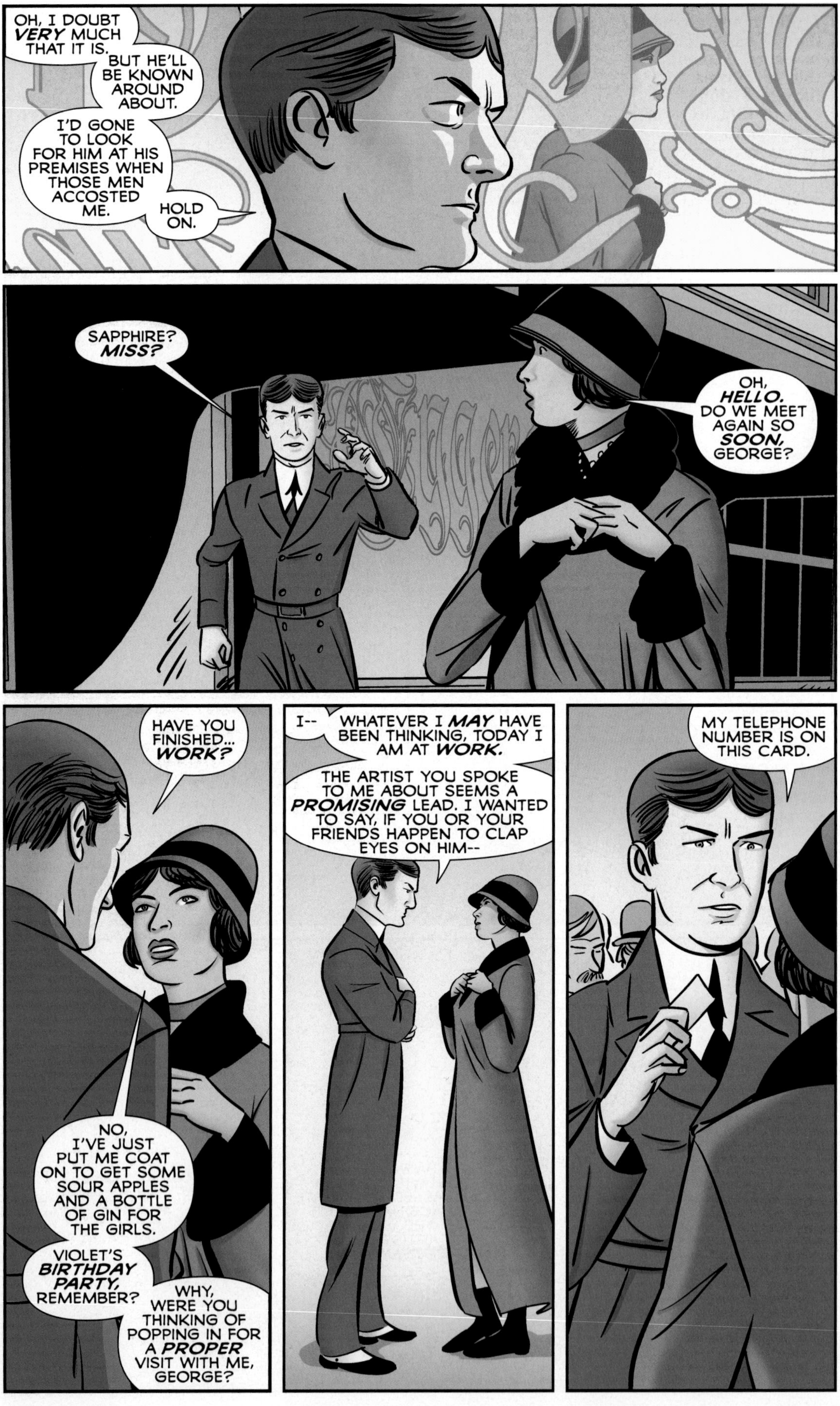
OH, I DOUBT VERY MUCH THAT IT IS.
BUT HE'LL BE KNOWN AROUND ABOUT.
I'D GONE TO LOOK FOR HIM AT HIS PREMISES WHEN THOSE MEN ACCOSTED ME.
HOLD ON.
SAPPHIRE? MISS?
OH, HELLO. DO WE MEET AGAIN SO SOON, GEORGE?
HAVE YOU FINISHED... WORK?
NO, I'VE JUST PUT ME COAT ON TO GET SOME SOUR APPLES AND A BOTTLE OF GIN FOR THE GIRLS.
VIOLET'S BIRTHDAY PARTY, REMEMBER?
WHY, WERE YOU THINKING OF POPPING IN FOR A PROPER VISIT WITH ME, GEORGE?
I--
WHATEVER I MAY HAVE BEEN THINKING, TODAY I AM AT WORK.
THE ARTIST YOU SPOKE TO ME ABOUT SEEMS A PROMISING LEAD. I WANTED TO SAY, IF YOU OR YOUR FRIENDS HAPPEN TO CLAP EYES ON HIM--
MY TELEPHONE NUMBER IS ON THIS CARD.

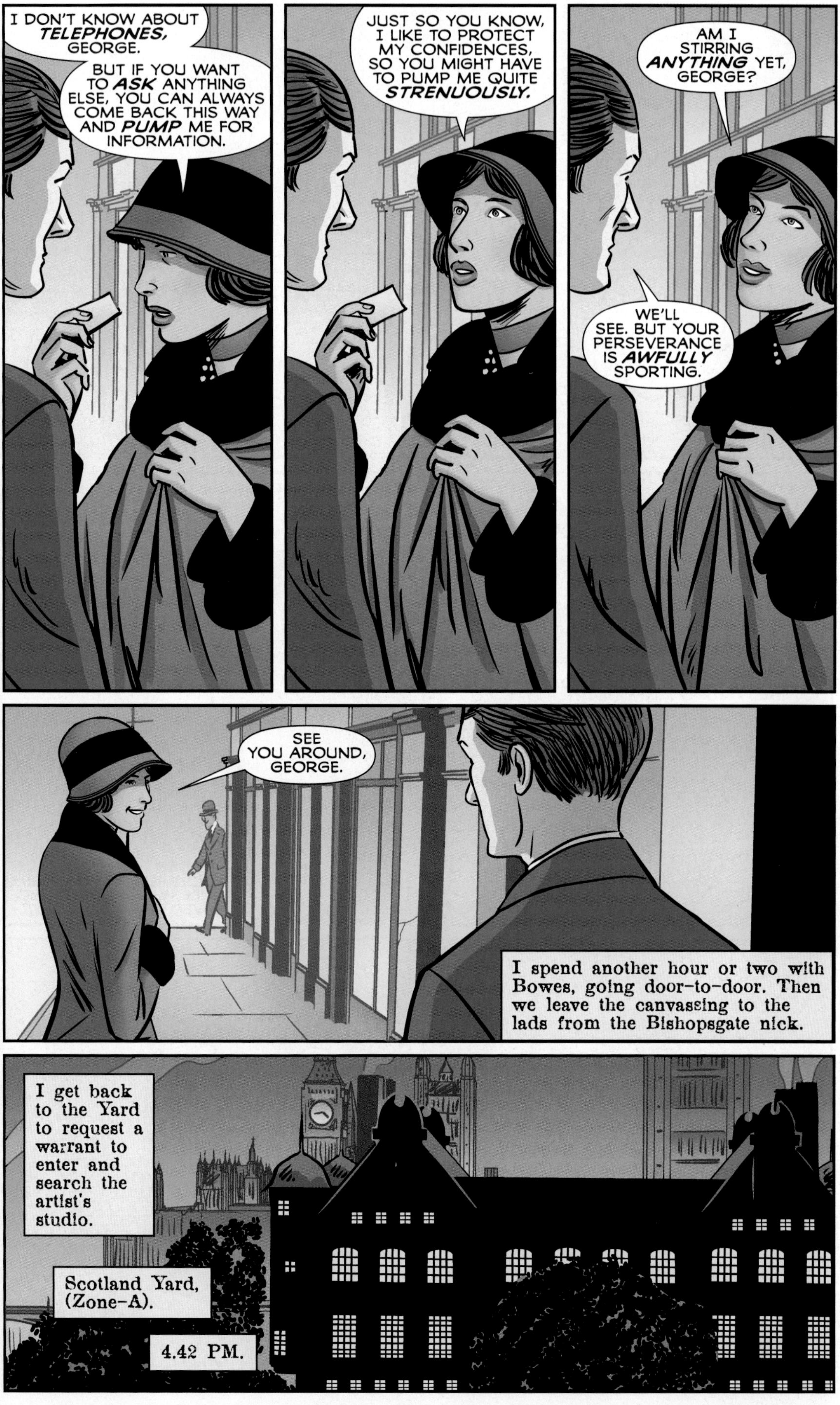
I DON'T KNOW ABOUT TELEPHONES, GEORGE.
BUT IF YOU WANT TO ASK ANYTHING ELSE, YOU CAN ALWAYS COME BACK THIS WAY AND PUMP ME FOR INFORMATION.
JUST SO YOU KNOW, I LIKE TO PROTECT MY CONFIDENCES, SO YOU MIGHT HAVE TO PUMP ME QUITE STRENUOUSLY.
AM I STIRRING ANYTHING YET, GEORGE?
WE'LL SEE. BUT YOUR PERSEVERANCE IS AWFULLY SPORTING.
SEE YOU AROUND, GEORGE.
I spend another hour or two with Bowes, going door-to-door. Then we leave the canvassing to the lads from the Bishopsgate nick.
I get back to the Yard to request a warrant to enter and search the artist's studio.
Scotland Yard, (Zone-A).
4.42 PM.

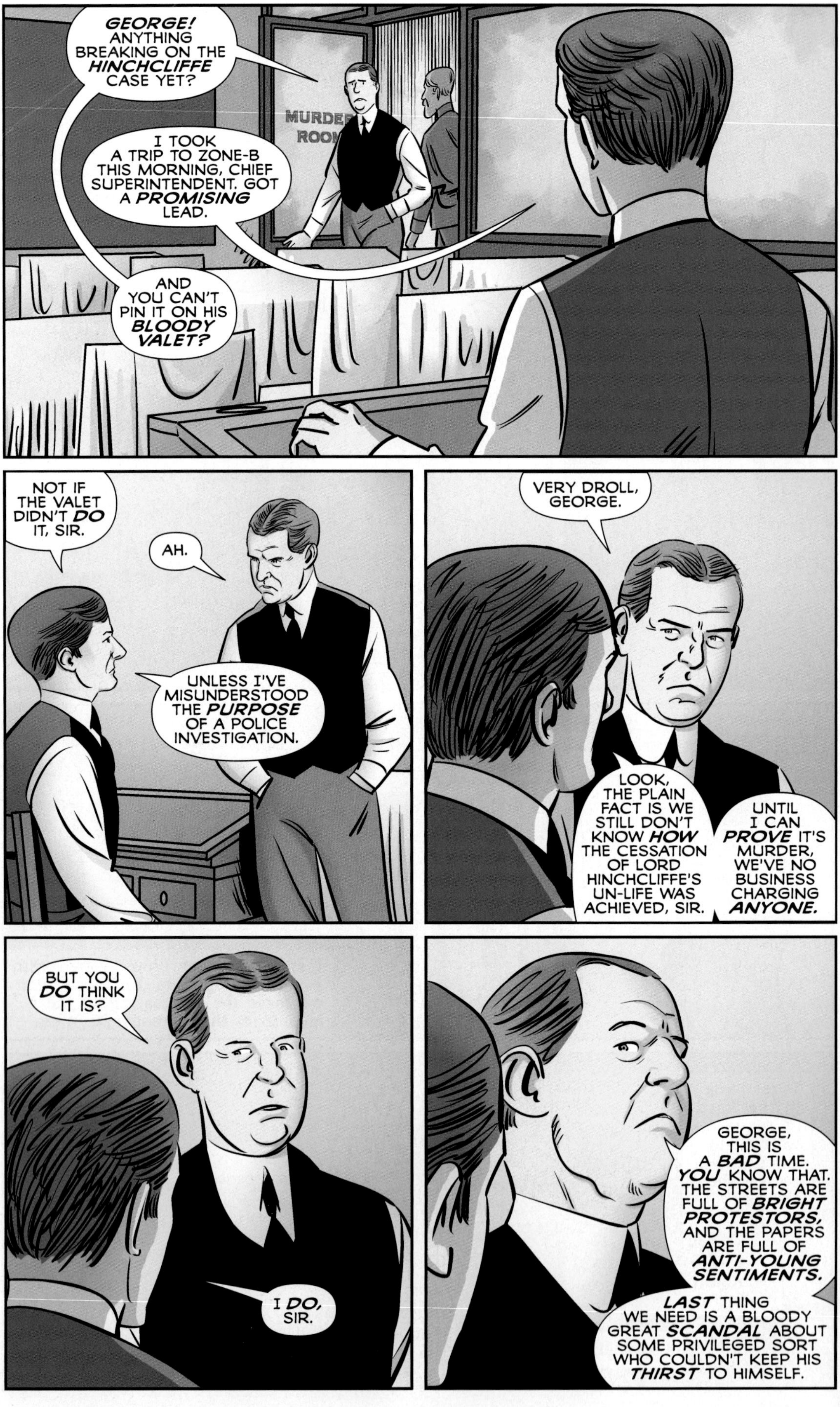

GEORGE! ANYTHING BREAKING ON THE HINCHCLIFFE CASE YET?
MURDER ROOM
I TOOK A TRIP TO ZONE-B THIS MORNING, CHIEF SUPERINTENDENT. GOT A PROMISING LEAD.
AND YOU CAN'T PIN IT ON HIS BLOODY VALET?
NOT IF THE VALET DIDN'T DO IT, SIR.
AH.
UNLESS I'VE MISUNDERSTOOD THE PURPOSE OF A POLICE INVESTIGATION.
VERY DROLL, GEORGE.
LOOK, THE PLAIN FACT IS WE STILL DON'T KNOW HOW THE CESSATION OF LORD HINCHCLIFFE'S UN-LIFE WAS ACHIEVED, SIR.
UNTIL I CAN PROVE IT'S MURDER, WE'VE NO BUSINESS CHARGING ANYONE.
BUT YOU DO THINK IT IS?
I DO, SIR.
GEORGE, THIS IS A BAD TIME. YOU KNOW THAT. THE STREETS ARE FULL OF BRIGHT PROTESTORS, AND THE PAPERS ARE FULL OF ANTI-YOUNG SENTIMENTS.
LAST THING WE NEED IS A BLOODY GREAT SCANDAL ABOUT SOME PRIVILEGED SORT WHO COULDN'T KEEP HIS THIRST TO HIMSELF.

I *WILL* CLOSE THIS CASE, SIR. *DISCREETLY.*

THE PROBLEM IS, THE *FAMILY'S* NOW GOT WIND OF IT ALL. LADY HINCHCLIFFE WANTS HER HUSBAND'S BODY FOR BURIAL.

SHE CAN'T *HAVE* IT. NOT YET.

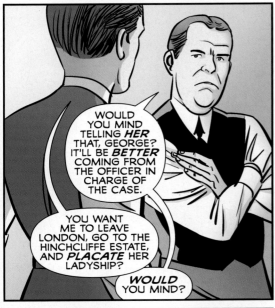

WOULD YOU MIND TELLING *HER* THAT, GEORGE? IT'LL BE *BETTER* COMING FROM THE OFFICER IN CHARGE OF THE CASE.

YOU WANT ME TO LEAVE LONDON, GO TO THE HINCHCLIFFE ESTATE, AND *PLACATE* HER LADYSHIP?

WOULD YOU MIND?

NO. IT MIGHT BE USEFUL TO TALK TO THE FAMILY.

I'LL GO TOMORROW. I'LL NEED A DRIVER.

THE MAN WHO DROVE ME TODAY WILL BE FINE.

NONSENSE, I'LL GET ONE OF THE C.I.D. BOYS TO--

CONSTABLE BOWES WILL BE *FINE.*

I *LIKE* HIM. HE SHOWS *PROMISE.*

"HAVE IT YOUR WAY, GEORGE."

47 Chaney Row, Marylebone (Zone-A).

6.11 PM.

HOW DO YOU *MEAN* YOU'RE *GOING AWAY,* GEORGE?

I *MEAN*, MOTHER, THAT I'M GOING TO BE *GONE* FOR A DAY OR TWO. A CASE IS TAKING ME *OUT OF TOWN*.

BUT YOU *NEVER* GO OUT OF TOWN, GEORGE.

YES, WON'T *THAT* BE FUN?

I WILL *UNDOUBTEDLY* EXPIRE IN YOUR ABSENCE. *NO ONE* WILL LOOK AFTER ME.

ROPER IS HERE. *AND* THE NEW HOUSEKEEPER STARTS TOMORROW. *AND* LOUISA--

I DO NOT *PRETEND* TO KNOW WHAT IS *WRONG* WITH THAT GIRL. I *SUSPECT* SHE'S TAKEN UP WITH THE *WRONG* SORT.

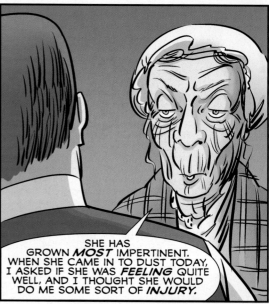

SHE HAS GROWN *MOST* IMPERTINENT. WHEN SHE CAME IN TO DUST TODAY, I ASKED IF SHE WAS *FEELING* QUITE WELL, AND I THOUGHT SHE WOULD DO ME SOME SORT OF *INJURY*.

WITH HER *MOP*.

"I'LL HAVE WORDS WITH HER, MOTHER."

HOW IS IT, LOUISA?

EARLY DAYS, I RECKON, MR SUTTLE. I CAN'T QUITE GET *USED* TO IT, I CAN'T.

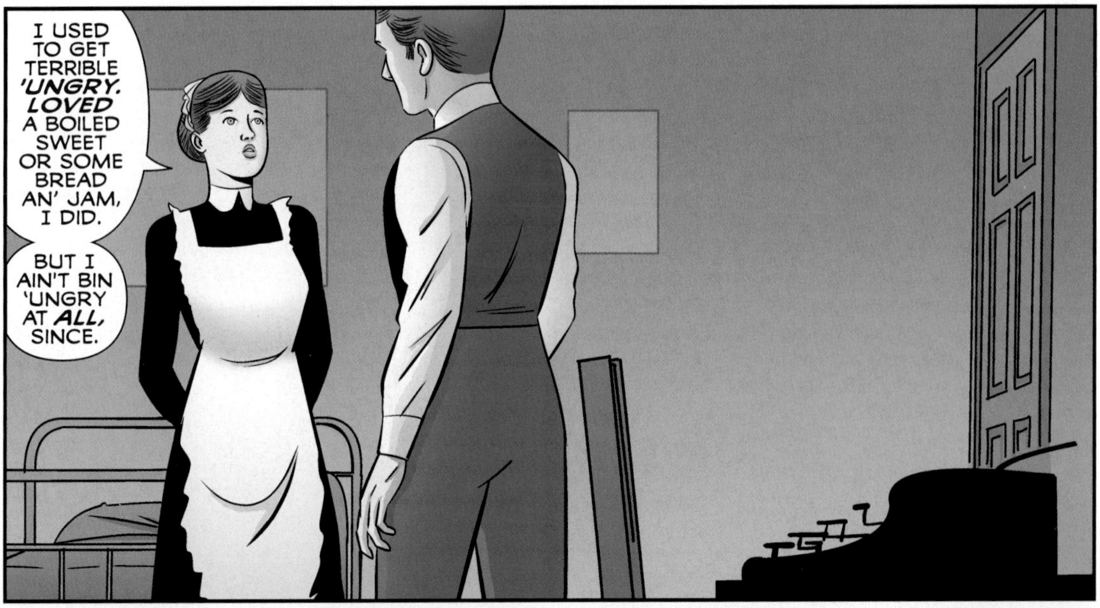
I USED TO GET TERRIBLE *'UNGRY.* *LOVED* A BOILED SWEET OR SOME BREAD AN' JAM, I DID.
BUT I AIN'T BIN 'UNGRY AT *ALL,* SINCE.

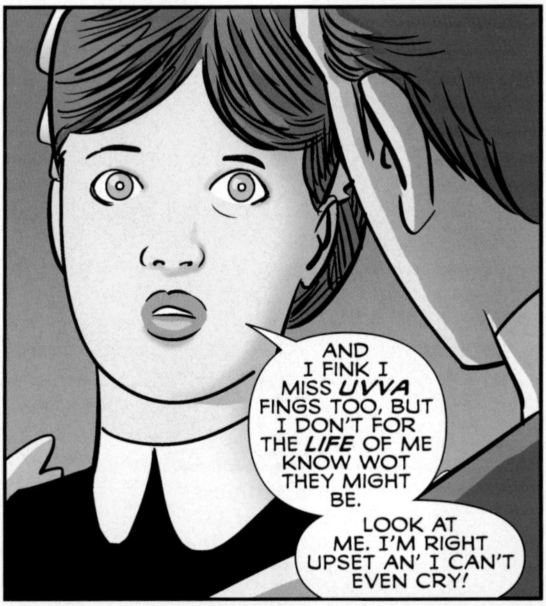
AND I FINK I MISS *UVVA* FINGS TOO, BUT I DON'T FOR THE *LIFE* OF ME KNOW WOT THEY MIGHT BE.
LOOK AT ME. I'M RIGHT UPSET AN' I CAN'T EVEN CRY!

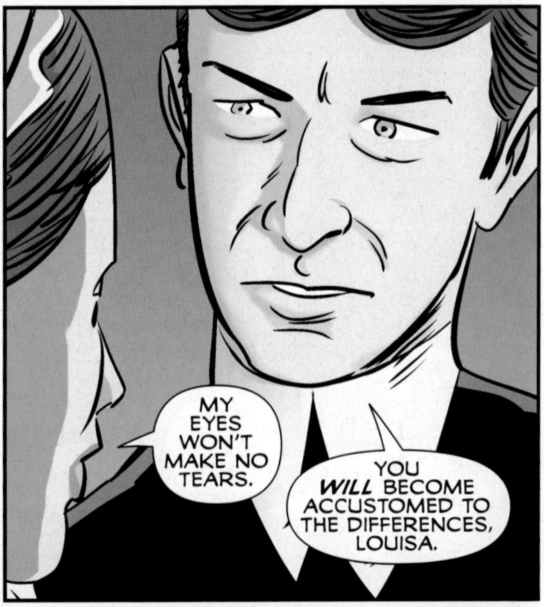
MY EYES WON'T MAKE NO TEARS.
YOU *WILL* BECOME ACCUSTOMED TO THE DIFFERENCES, LOUISA.

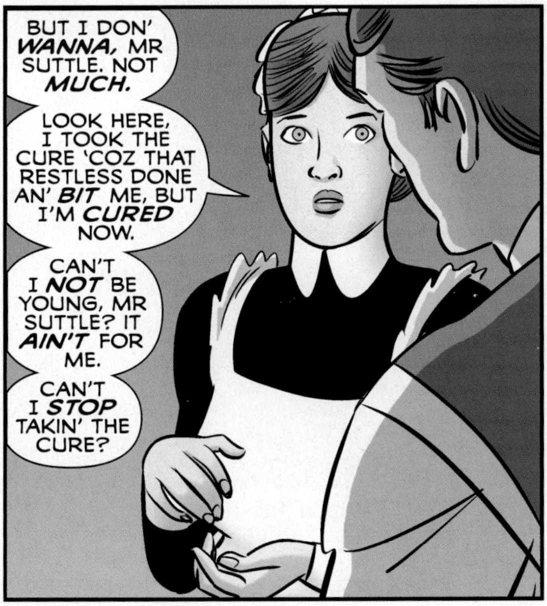
BUT I DON' *WANNA,* MR SUTTLE. NOT *MUCH.*
LOOK HERE, I TOOK THE CURE 'COZ THAT RESTLESS DONE AN' *BIT* ME, BUT I'M *CURED* NOW.
CAN'T I *NOT* BE YOUNG, MR SUTTLE? IT *AIN'T* FOR ME.
CAN'T I *STOP* TAKIN' THE CURE?

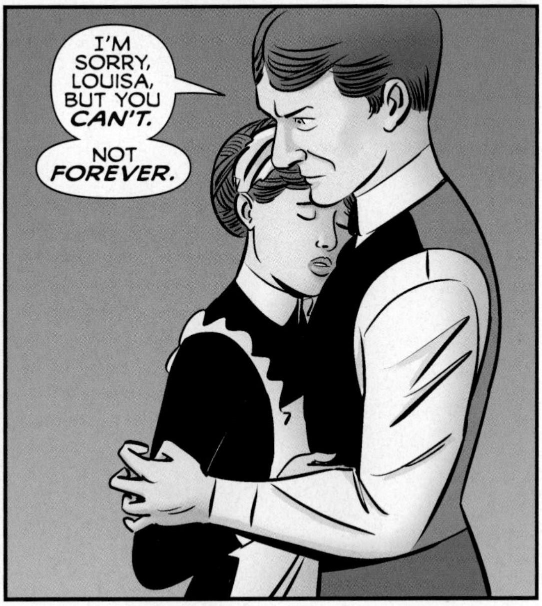
I'M SORRY, LOUISA, BUT YOU *CAN'T.*
NOT *FOREVER.*

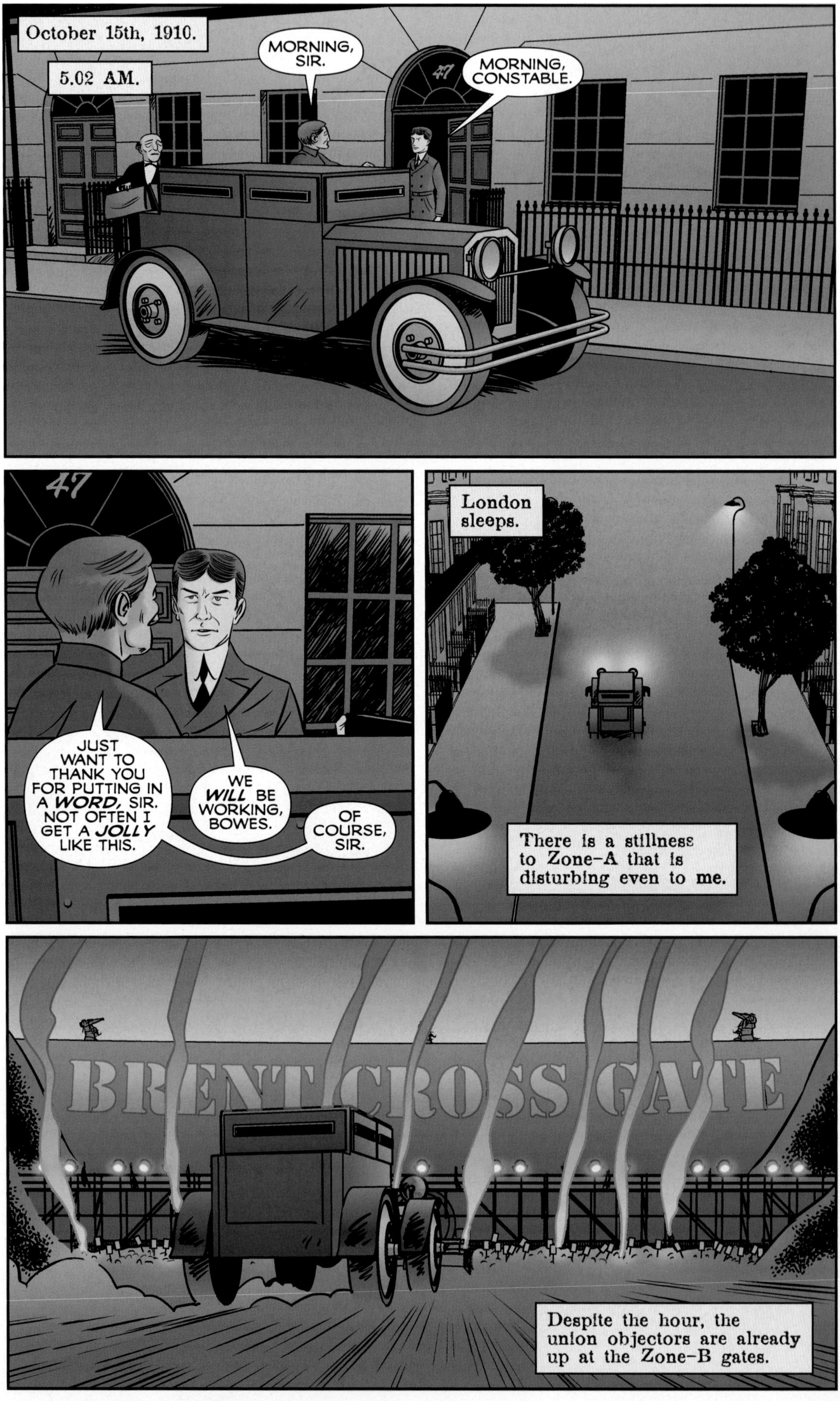
October 15th, 1910.
5.02 AM.
MORNING, SIR.
MORNING, CONSTABLE.
47
JUST WANT TO THANK YOU FOR PUTTING IN A WORD, SIR. NOT OFTEN I GET A JOLLY LIKE THIS.
WE WILL BE WORKING, BOWES.
OF COURSE, SIR.
London sleeps.
There is a stillness to Zone-A that is disturbing even to me.
BRENT CROSS GATE
Despite the hour, the union objectors are already up at the Zone-B gates.

I do not know what to think about the protests. Living conditions should be better for the brights.

But after my visit to the East End yesterday, I believe their circumstance is far, far preferable to ours.

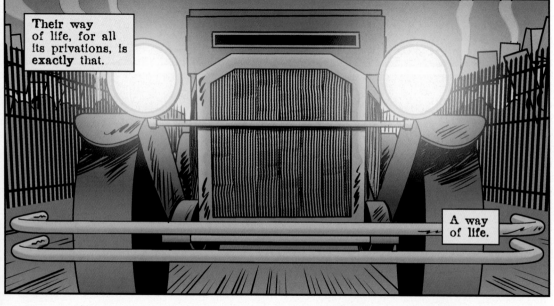

Their way of life, for all its privations, is exactly that.

A way of life.

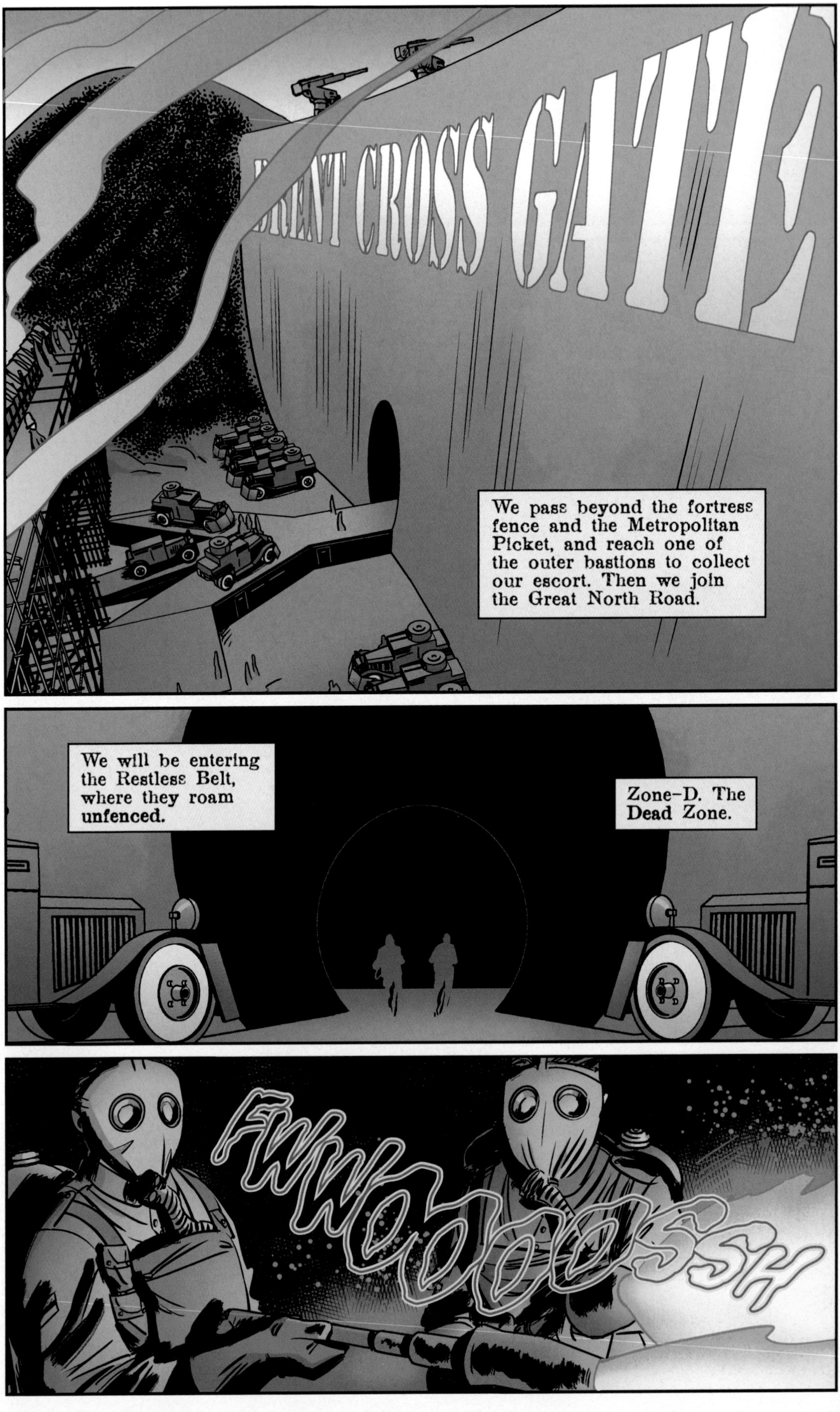
BRENT CROSS GATE
We pass beyond the fortress fence and the Metropolitan Picket, and reach one of the outer bastions to collect our escort. Then we join the Great North Road.
We will be entering the Restless Belt, where they roam unfenced.
Zone-D. The Dead Zone.
FWWOOOOOSSH

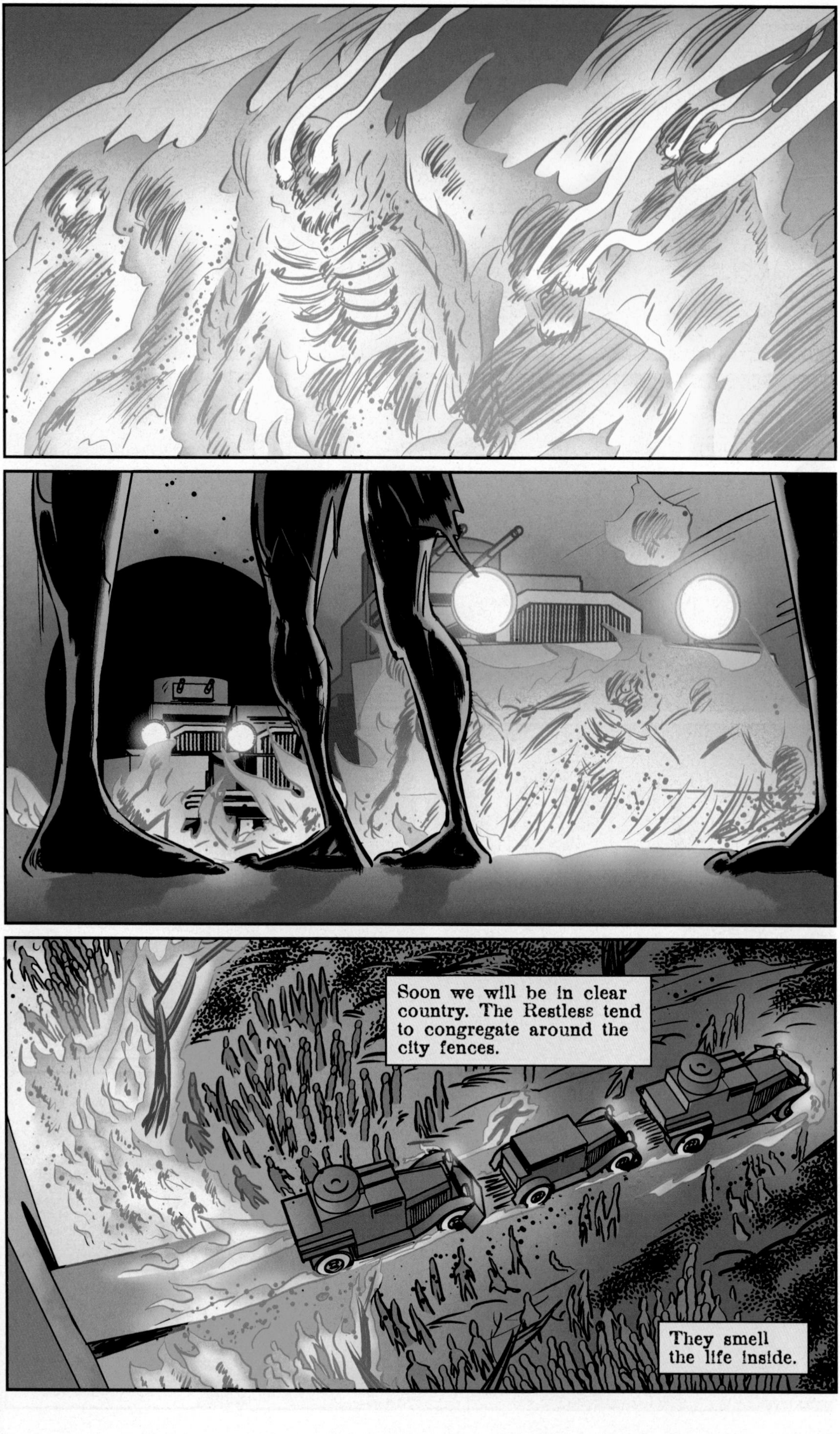
Soon we will be in clear country. The Restless tend to congregate around the city fences.
They smell the life inside.

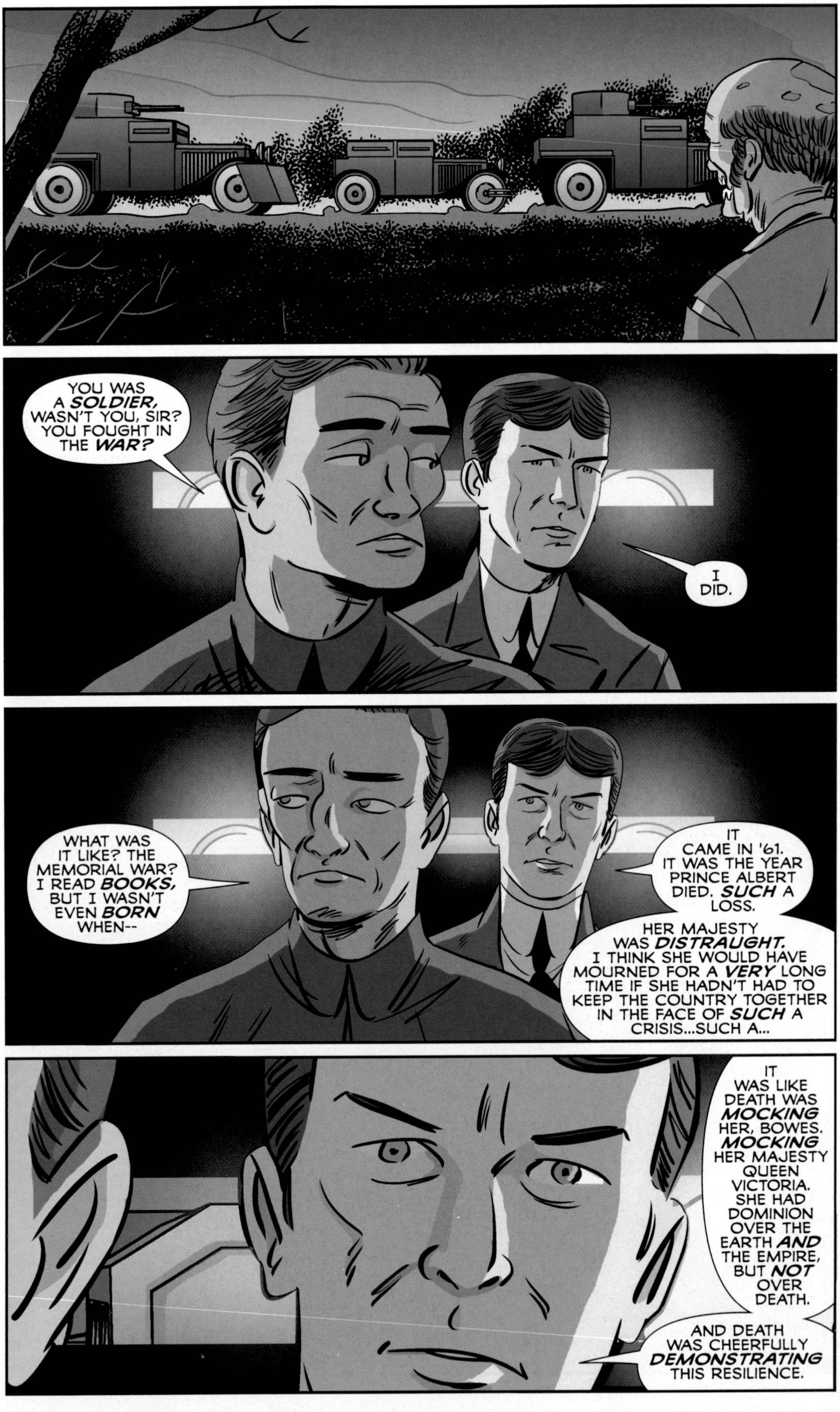
YOU WAS A SOLDIER, WASN'T YOU, SIR? YOU FOUGHT IN THE WAR?
I DID.
WHAT WAS IT LIKE? THE MEMORIAL WAR? I READ BOOKS, BUT I WASN'T EVEN BORN WHEN--
IT CAME IN '61. IT WAS THE YEAR PRINCE ALBERT DIED. SUCH A LOSS.
HER MAJESTY WAS DISTRAUGHT. I THINK SHE WOULD HAVE MOURNED FOR A VERY LONG TIME IF SHE HADN'T HAD TO KEEP THE COUNTRY TOGETHER IN THE FACE OF SUCH A CRISIS...SUCH A...
IT WAS LIKE DEATH WAS MOCKING HER, BOWES. MOCKING HER MAJESTY QUEEN VICTORIA. SHE HAD DOMINION OVER THE EARTH AND THE EMPIRE, BUT NOT OVER DEATH.
AND DEATH WAS CHEERFULLY DEMONSTRATING THIS RESILIENCE.

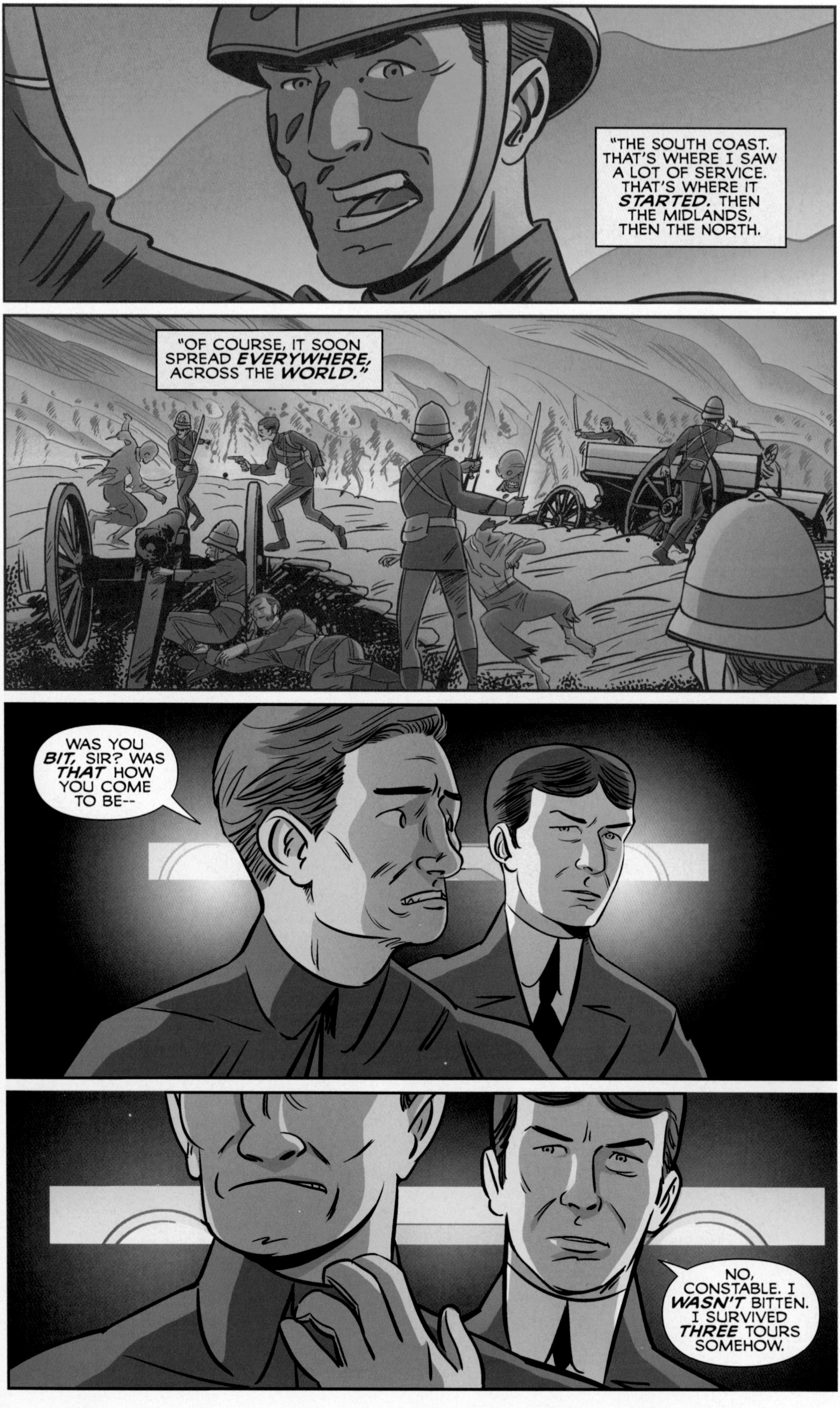
"THE SOUTH COAST. THAT'S WHERE I SAW A LOT OF SERVICE. THAT'S WHERE IT **STARTED.** THEN THE MIDLANDS, THEN THE NORTH.
"OF COURSE, IT SOON SPREAD **EVERYWHERE,** ACROSS THE **WORLD.**"
WAS YOU **BIT,** SIR? WAS **THAT** HOW YOU COME TO BE--
NO, CONSTABLE. I **WASN'T** BITTEN. I SURVIVED **THREE** TOURS SOMEHOW.

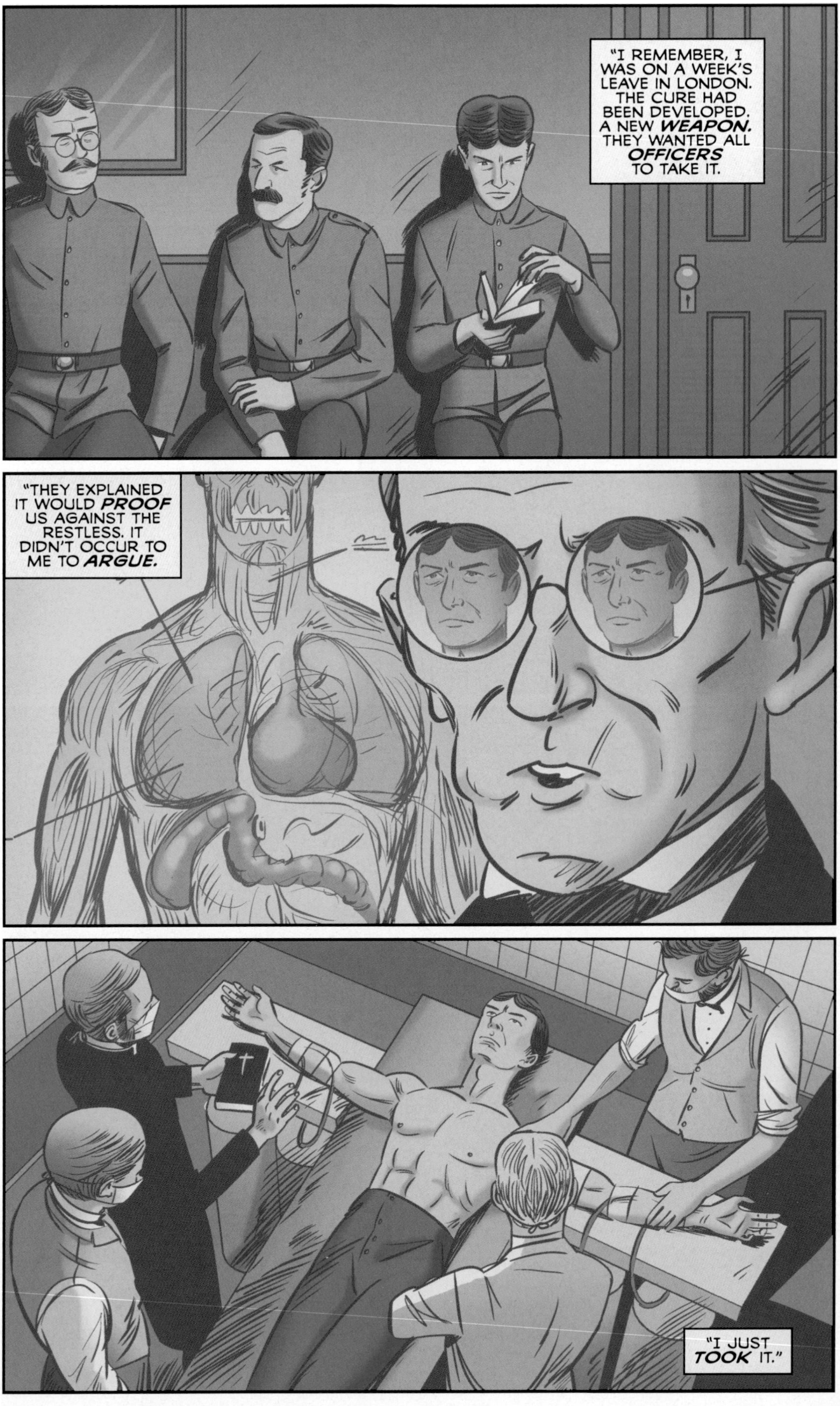
"I REMEMBER, I WAS ON A WEEK'S LEAVE IN LONDON. THE CURE HAD BEEN DEVELOPED. A NEW WEAPON. THEY WANTED ALL OFFICERS TO TAKE IT.
"THEY EXPLAINED IT WOULD PROOF US AGAINST THE RESTLESS. IT DIDN'T OCCUR TO ME TO ARGUE.
"I JUST TOOK IT."

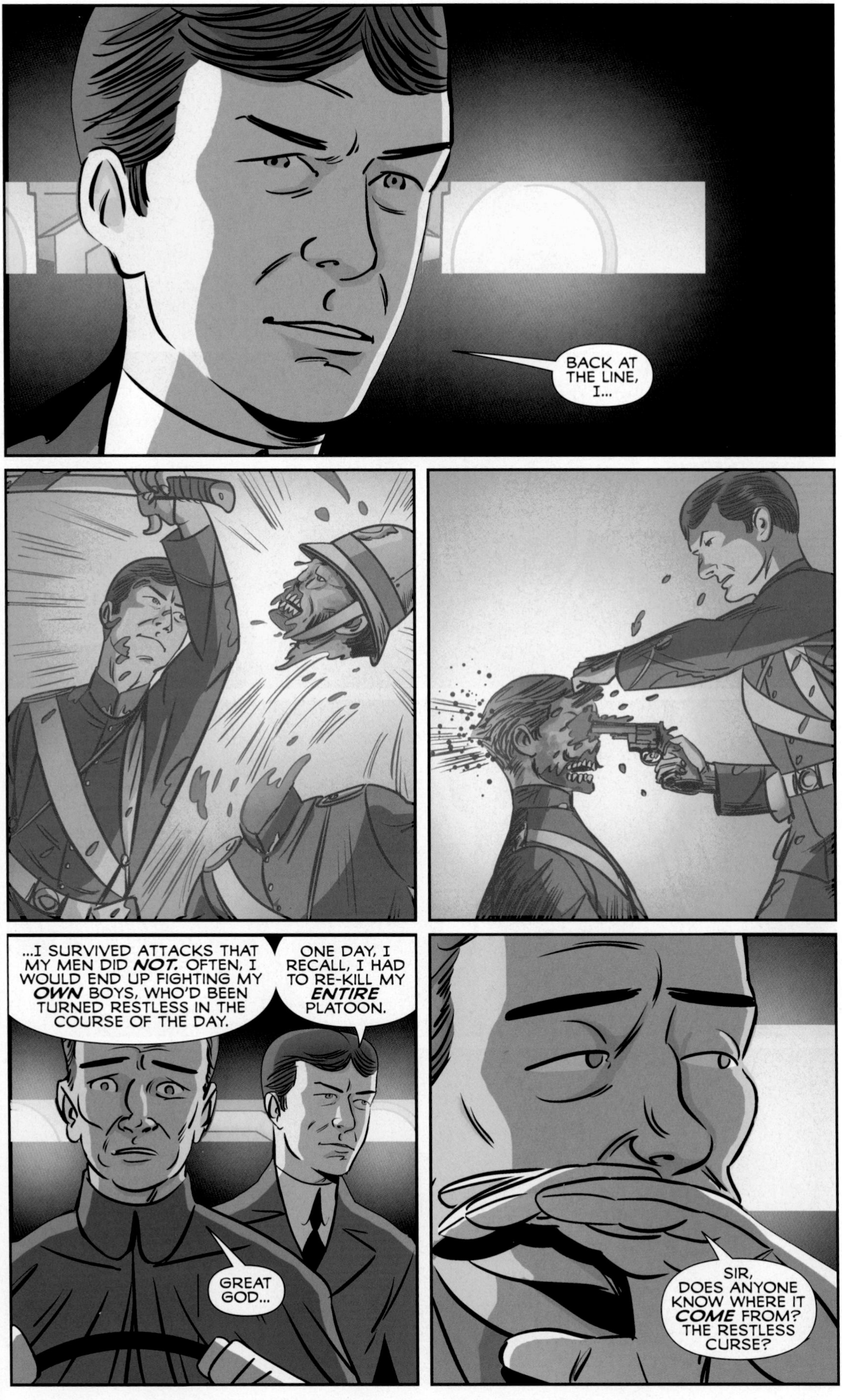
BACK AT THE LINE, I...
...I SURVIVED ATTACKS THAT MY MEN DID NOT. OFTEN, I WOULD END UP FIGHTING MY OWN BOYS, WHO'D BEEN TURNED RESTLESS IN THE COURSE OF THE DAY.
ONE DAY, I RECALL, I HAD TO RE-KILL MY ENTIRE PLATOON.
GREAT GOD...
SIR, DOES ANYONE KNOW WHERE IT COME FROM? THE RESTLESS CURSE?

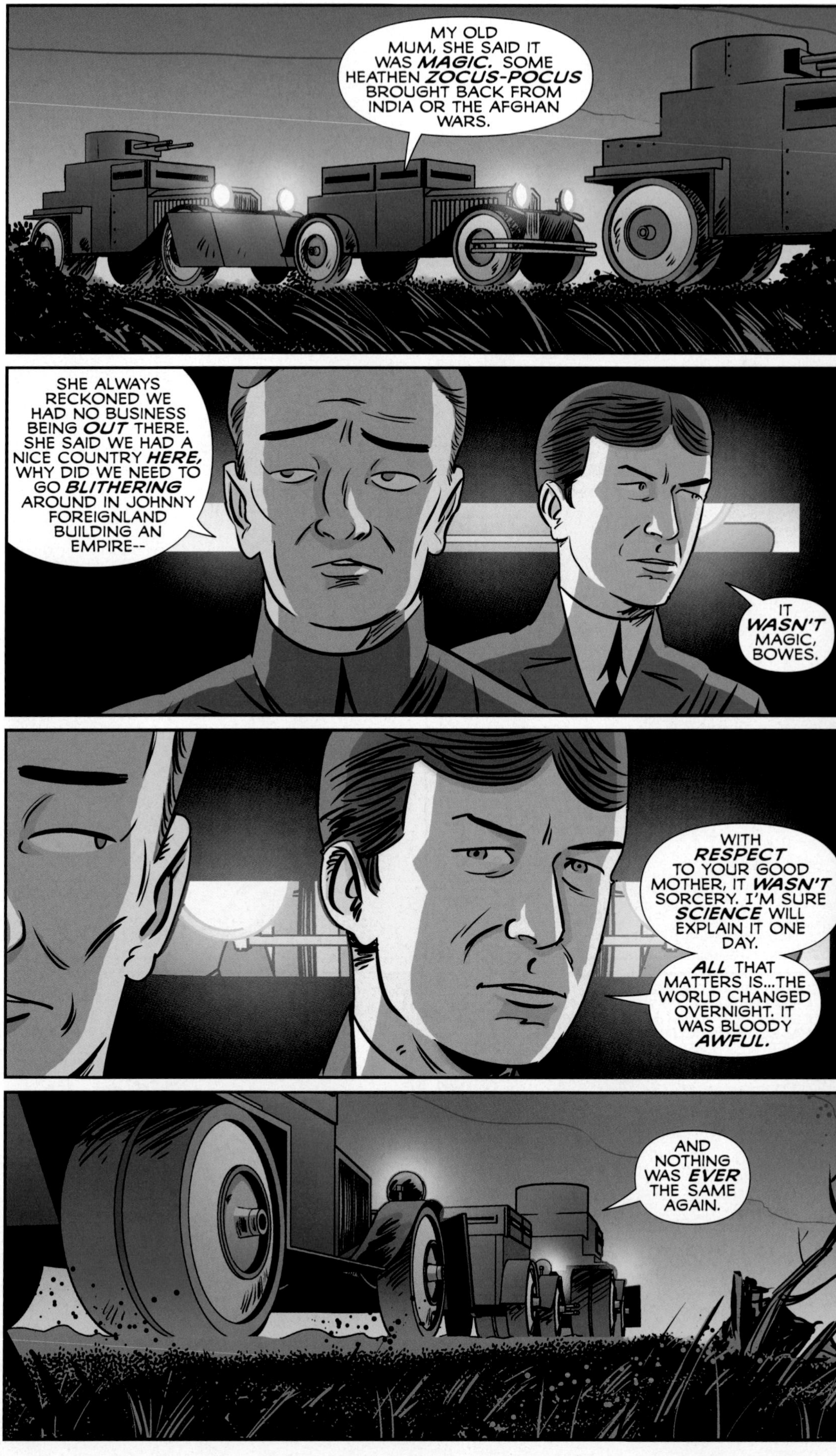
MY OLD MUM, SHE SAID IT WAS MAGIC. SOME HEATHEN ZOCUS-POCUS BROUGHT BACK FROM INDIA OR THE AFGHAN WARS.
SHE ALWAYS RECKONED WE HAD NO BUSINESS BEING OUT THERE. SHE SAID WE HAD A NICE COUNTRY HERE, WHY DID WE NEED TO GO BLITHERING AROUND IN JOHNNY FOREIGNLAND BUILDING AN EMPIRE--
IT WASN'T MAGIC, BOWES.
WITH RESPECT TO YOUR GOOD MOTHER, IT WASN'T SORCERY. I'M SURE SCIENCE WILL EXPLAIN IT ONE DAY.
ALL THAT MATTERS IS...THE WORLD CHANGED OVERNIGHT. IT WAS BLOODY AWFUL.
AND NOTHING WAS EVER THE SAME AGAIN.

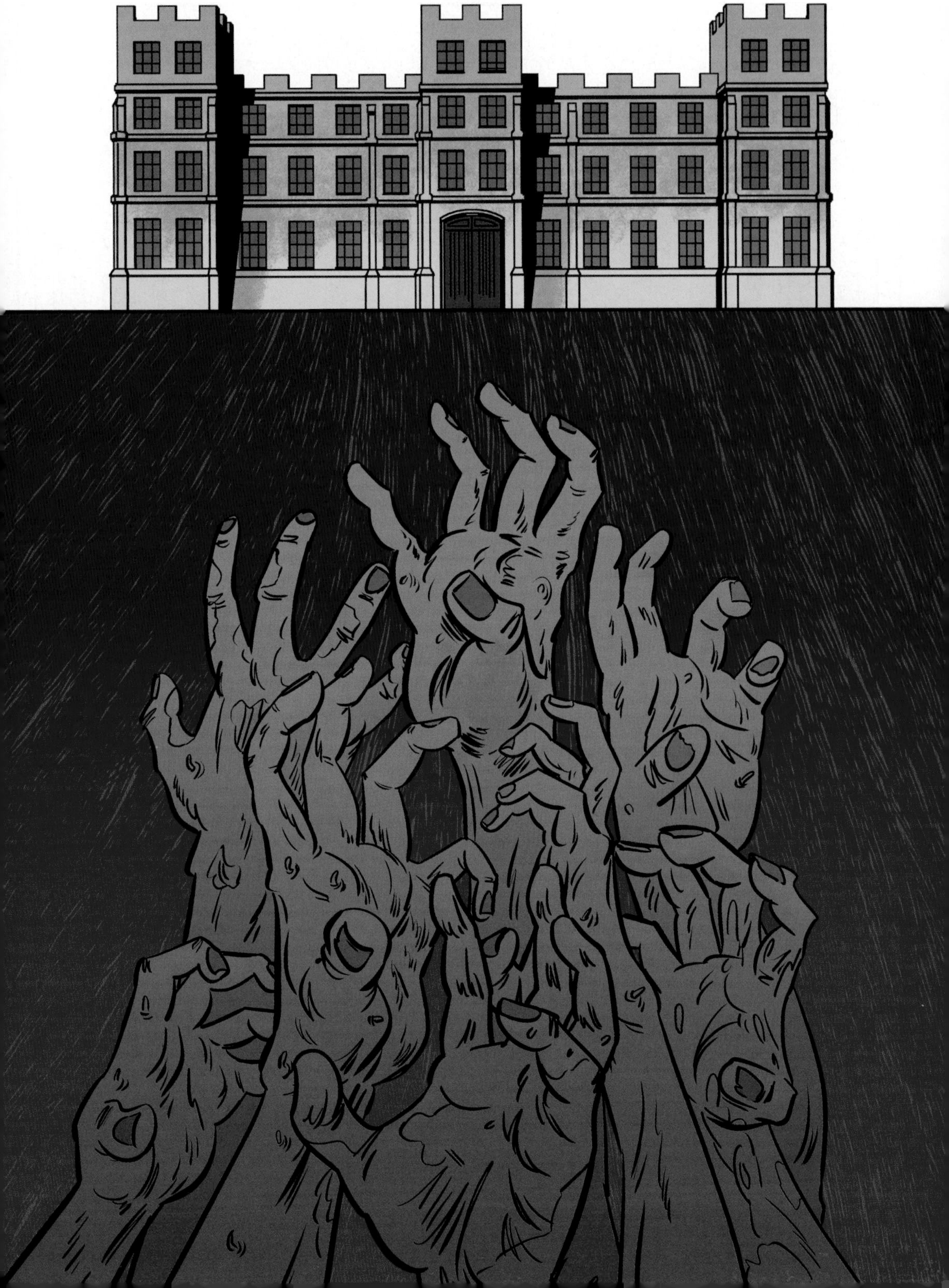

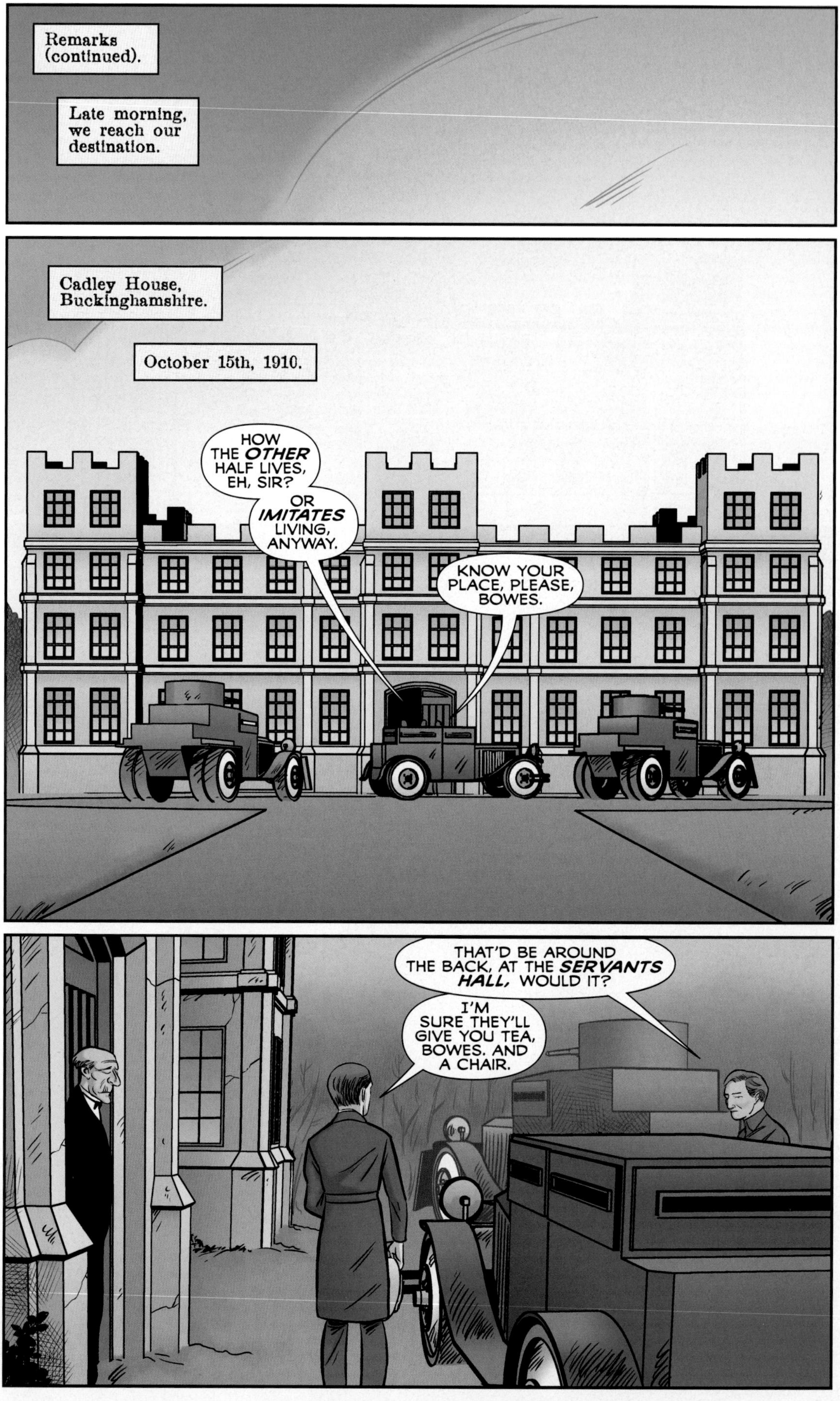
Remarks (continued).
Late morning, we reach our destination.
Cadley House, Buckinghamshire.
October 15th, 1910.
HOW THE OTHER HALF LIVES, EH, SIR?
OR IMITATES LIVING, ANYWAY.
KNOW YOUR PLACE, PLEASE, BOWES.
THAT'D BE AROUND THE BACK, AT THE SERVANTS HALL, WOULD IT?
I'M SURE THEY'LL GIVE YOU TEA, BOWES. AND A CHAIR.

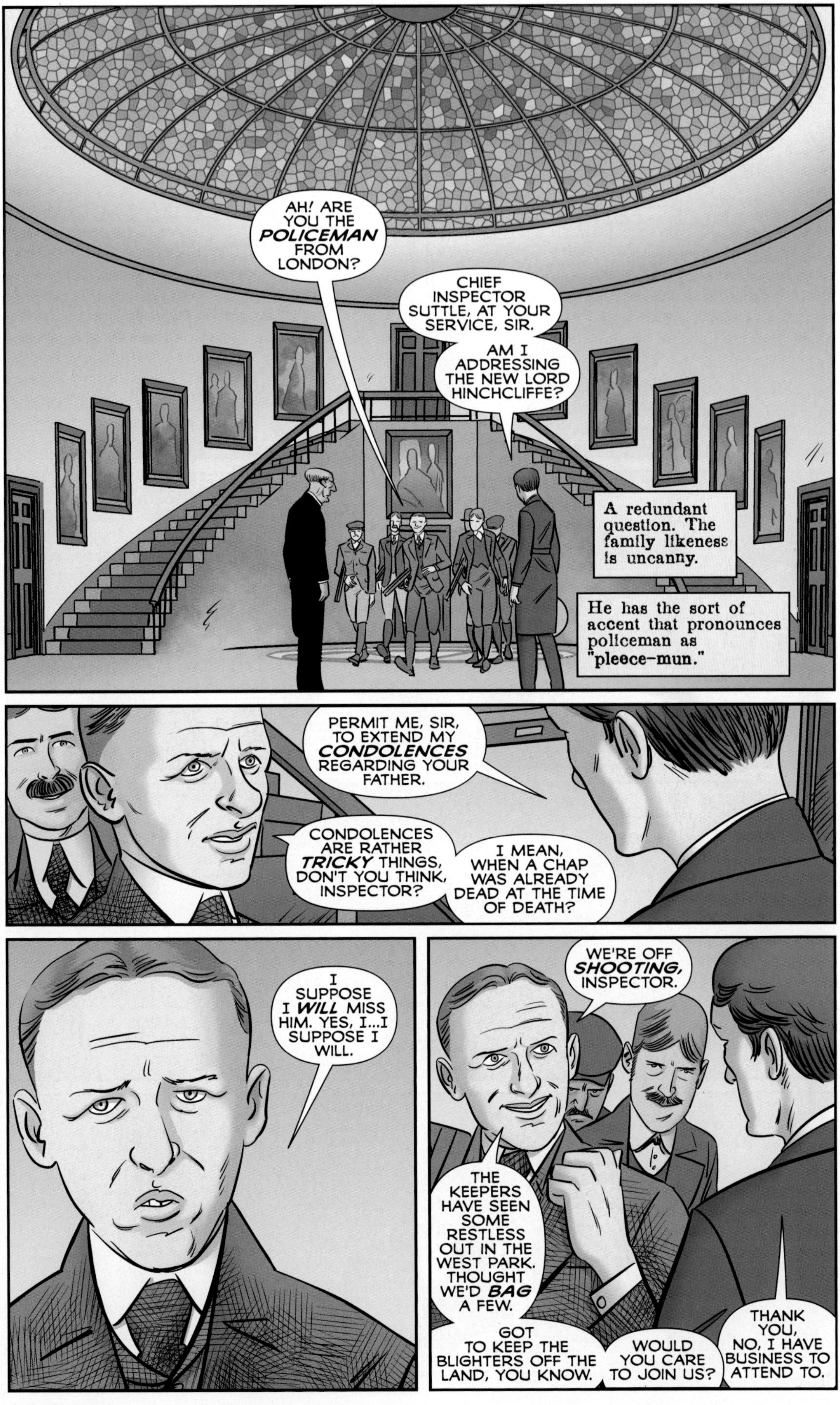
AH! ARE YOU THE *POLICEMAN* FROM LONDON?
CHIEF INSPECTOR SUTTLE, AT YOUR SERVICE, SIR.
AM I ADDRESSING THE NEW LORD HINCHCLIFFE?
A redundant question. The family likeness is uncanny.
He has the sort of accent that pronounces policeman as "pleece-mun."
PERMIT ME, SIR, TO EXTEND MY *CONDOLENCES* REGARDING YOUR FATHER.
CONDOLENCES ARE RATHER *TRICKY* THINGS, DON'T YOU THINK, INSPECTOR?
I MEAN, WHEN A CHAP WAS ALREADY DEAD AT THE TIME OF DEATH?
I SUPPOSE I *WILL* MISS HIM. YES, I...I SUPPOSE I WILL.
WE'RE OFF *SHOOTING,* INSPECTOR.
THE KEEPERS HAVE SEEN SOME RESTLESS OUT IN THE WEST PARK. THOUGHT WE'D *BAG* A FEW.
GOT TO KEEP THE BLIGHTERS OFF THE LAND, YOU KNOW.
WOULD YOU CARE TO JOIN US?
THANK YOU, NO, I HAVE BUSINESS TO ATTEND TO.

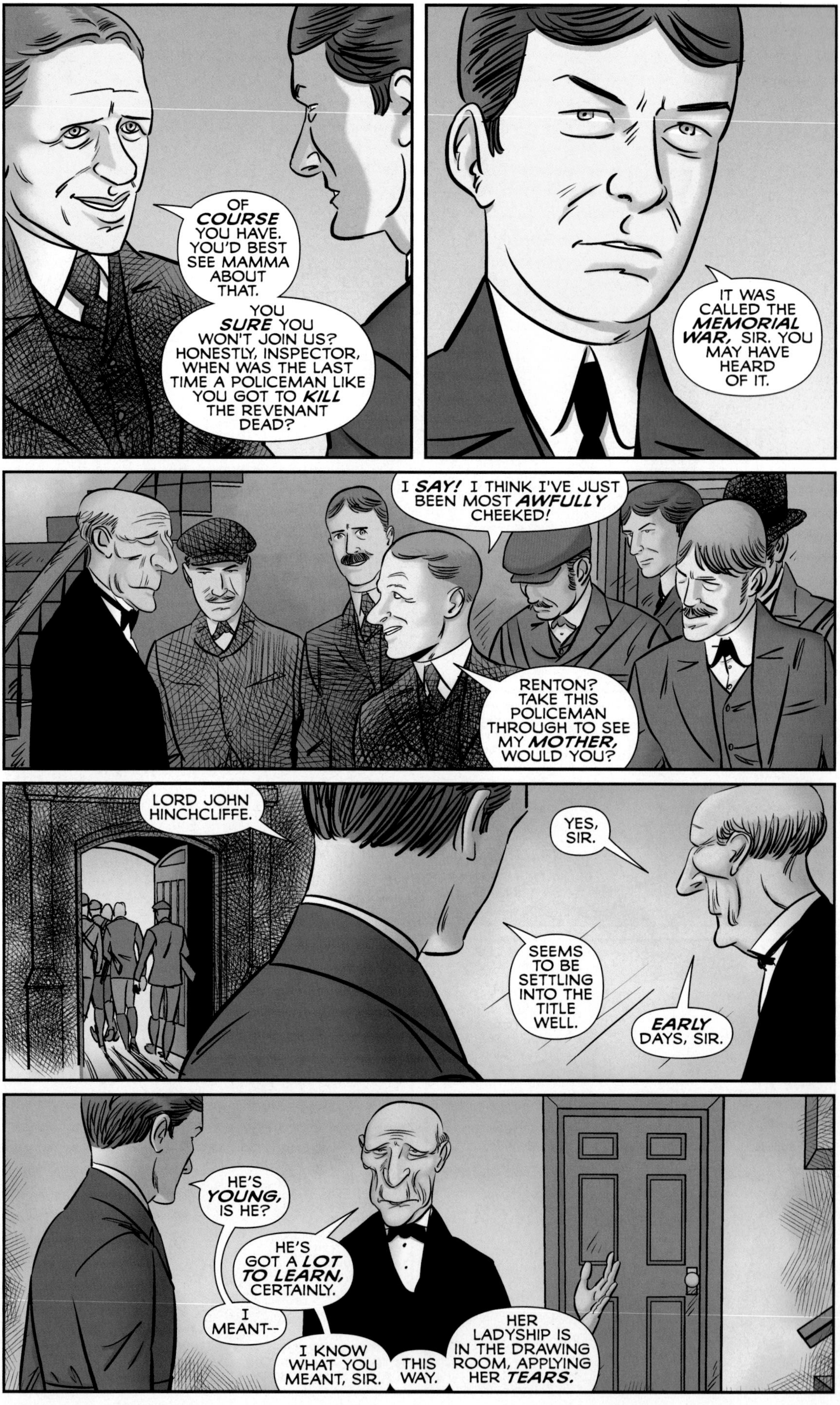
OF COURSE YOU HAVE. YOU'D BEST SEE MAMMA ABOUT THAT.
YOU SURE YOU WON'T JOIN US? HONESTLY, INSPECTOR, WHEN WAS THE LAST TIME A POLICEMAN LIKE YOU GOT TO KILL THE REVENANT DEAD?
IT WAS CALLED THE MEMORIAL WAR, SIR. YOU MAY HAVE HEARD OF IT.
I SAY! I THINK I'VE JUST BEEN MOST AWFULLY CHEEKED!
RENTON? TAKE THIS POLICEMAN THROUGH TO SEE MY MOTHER, WOULD YOU?
LORD JOHN HINCHCLIFFE.
YES, SIR.
SEEMS TO BE SETTLING INTO THE TITLE WELL.
EARLY DAYS, SIR.
HE'S YOUNG, IS HE?
HE'S GOT A LOT TO LEARN, CERTAINLY.
I MEANT--
I KNOW WHAT YOU MEANT, SIR.
THIS WAY.
HER LADYSHIP IS IN THE DRAWING ROOM, APPLYING HER TEARS.

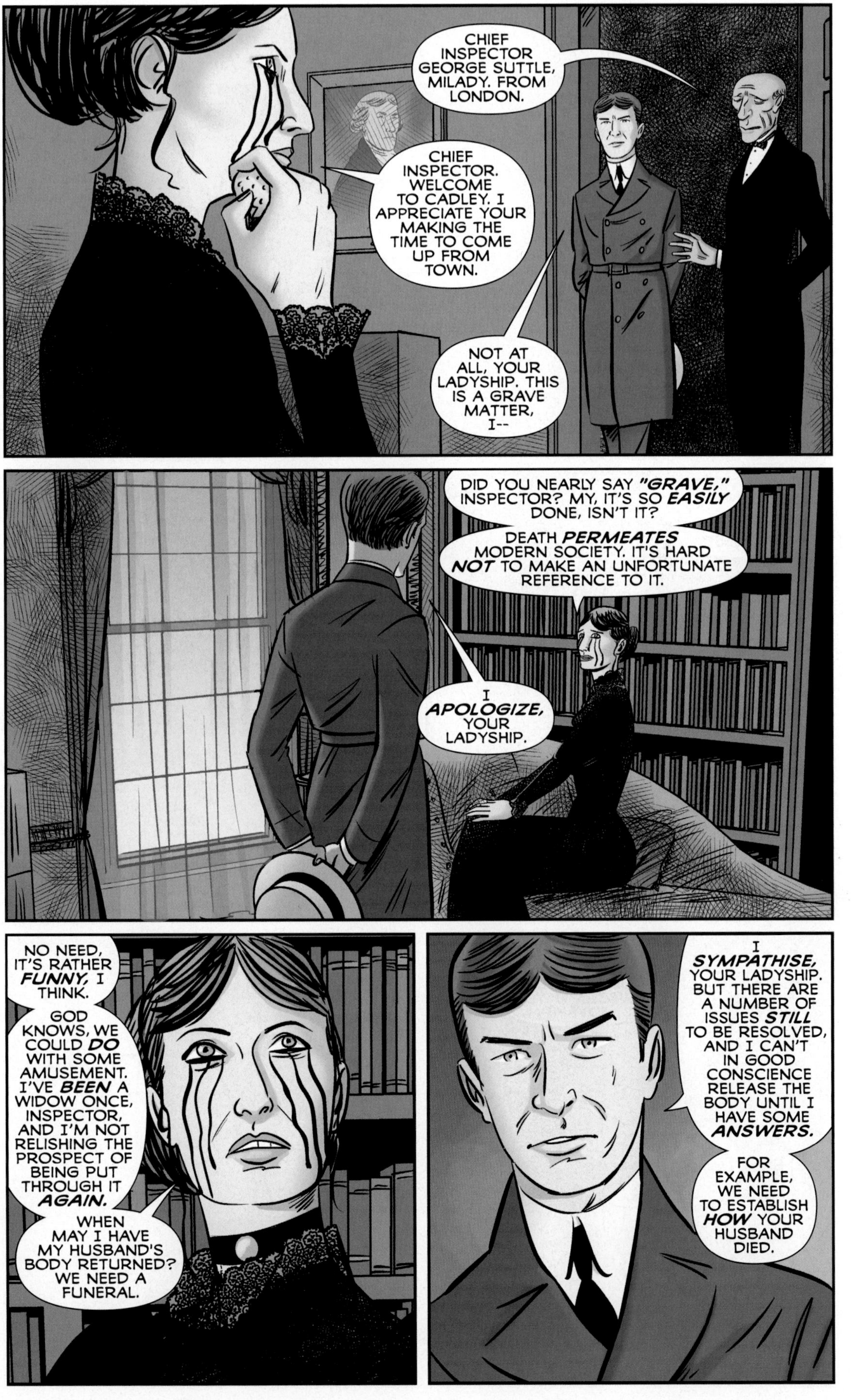
CHIEF INSPECTOR GEORGE SUTTLE, MILADY. FROM LONDON.
CHIEF INSPECTOR. WELCOME TO CADLEY. I APPRECIATE YOUR MAKING THE TIME TO COME UP FROM TOWN.
NOT AT ALL, YOUR LADYSHIP. THIS IS A GRAVE MATTER, I--
DID YOU NEARLY SAY "GRAVE," INSPECTOR? MY, IT'S SO EASILY DONE, ISN'T IT?
DEATH PERMEATES MODERN SOCIETY. IT'S HARD NOT TO MAKE AN UNFORTUNATE REFERENCE TO IT.
I APOLOGIZE, YOUR LADYSHIP.
NO NEED, IT'S RATHER FUNNY, I THINK.
GOD KNOWS, WE COULD DO WITH SOME AMUSEMENT. I'VE BEEN A WIDOW ONCE, INSPECTOR, AND I'M NOT RELISHING THE PROSPECT OF BEING PUT THROUGH IT AGAIN.
WHEN MAY I HAVE MY HUSBAND'S BODY RETURNED? WE NEED A FUNERAL.
I SYMPATHISE, YOUR LADYSHIP. BUT THERE ARE A NUMBER OF ISSUES STILL TO BE RESOLVED, AND I CAN'T IN GOOD CONSCIENCE RELEASE THE BODY UNTIL I HAVE SOME ANSWERS.
FOR EXAMPLE, WE NEED TO ESTABLISH HOW YOUR HUSBAND DIED.

HE DIED IN *1868* WHEN HE TOOK THE *CURE,* INSPECTOR, JUST AS I DIED TWENTY-FOUR YEARS *LATER.*

WHAT YOU *MEAN* IS, HOW HIS *UN-LIFE* WAS *TERMINATED.*

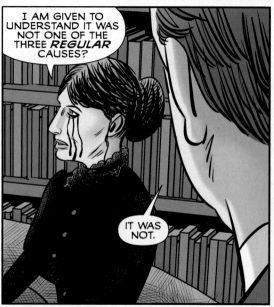

I AM GIVEN TO UNDERSTAND IT WAS NOT ONE OF THE THREE *REGULAR* CAUSES?

IT WAS NOT.

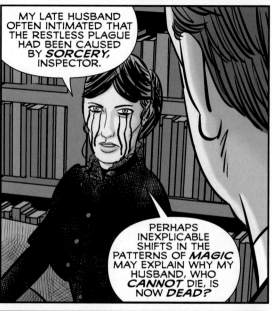

MY LATE HUSBAND OFTEN INTIMATED THAT THE RESTLESS PLAGUE HAD BEEN CAUSED BY *SORCERY,* INSPECTOR.

PERHAPS INEXPLICABLE SHIFTS IN THE PATTERNS OF *MAGIC* MAY EXPLAIN WHY MY HUSBAND, WHO *CANNOT* DIE, IS NOW *DEAD?*

I DON'T SET MUCH STORE BY *SORCERY,* YOUR LADYSHIP.

THEN YOU ARE A WOEFULLY *UNIMAGINATIVE* MAN, MR SUTTLE.

BOOM FBOOM- BOOM

WHAT--

STEADY, INSPECTOR. IT'S JUST THE SHOOTING PARTY.

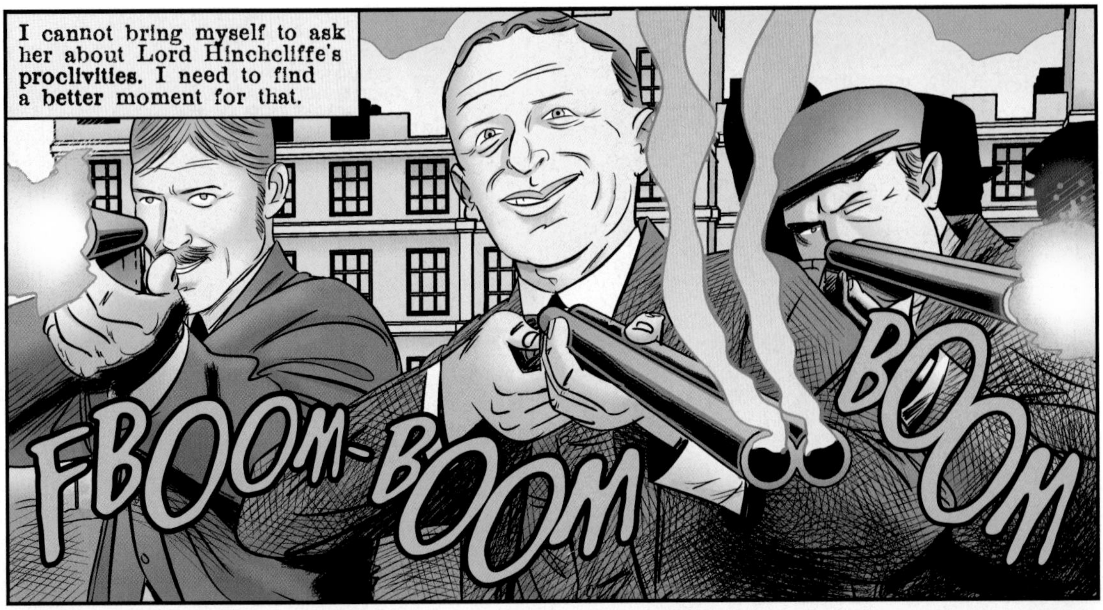
I cannot bring myself to ask her about Lord Hinchcliffe's proclivities. I need to find a better moment for that.
FBOOM-BOOM
BOOOM

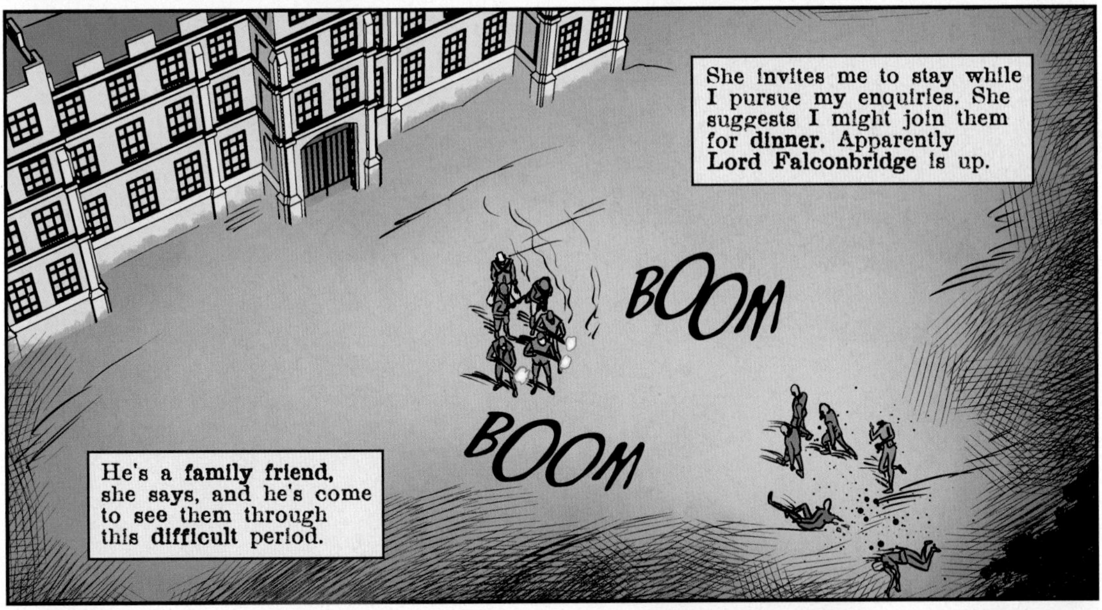
She invites me to stay while I pursue my enquiries. She suggests I might join them for dinner. Apparently Lord Falconbridge is up.
BOOM
BOOM
He's a family friend, she says, and he's come to see them through this difficult period.

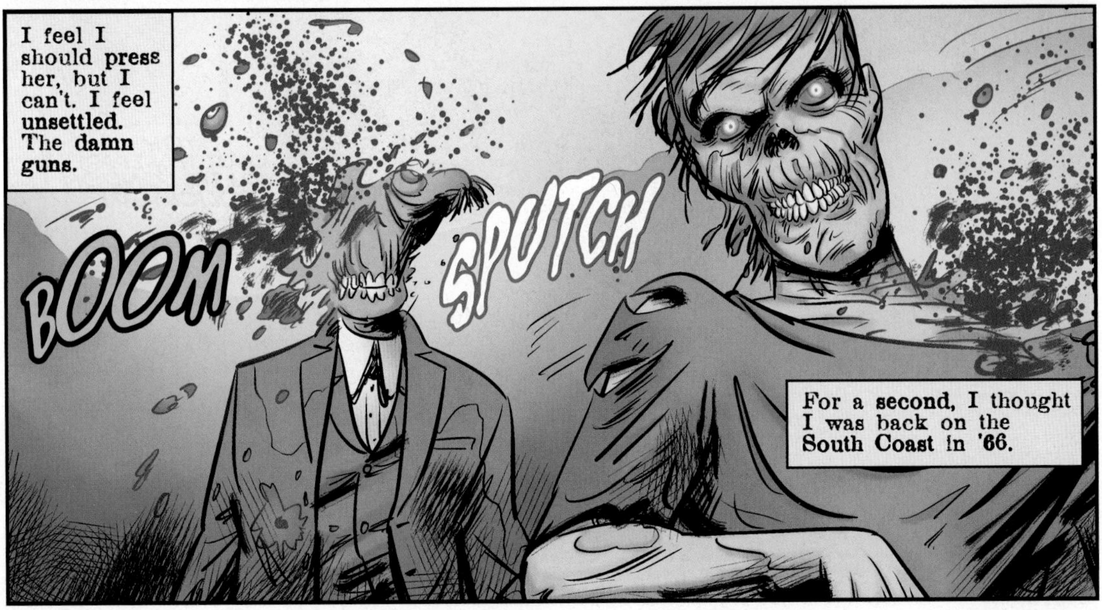
I feel I should press her, but I can't. I feel unsettled. The damn guns.
BOOM
SPUTCH
For a second, I thought I was back on the South Coast in '66.

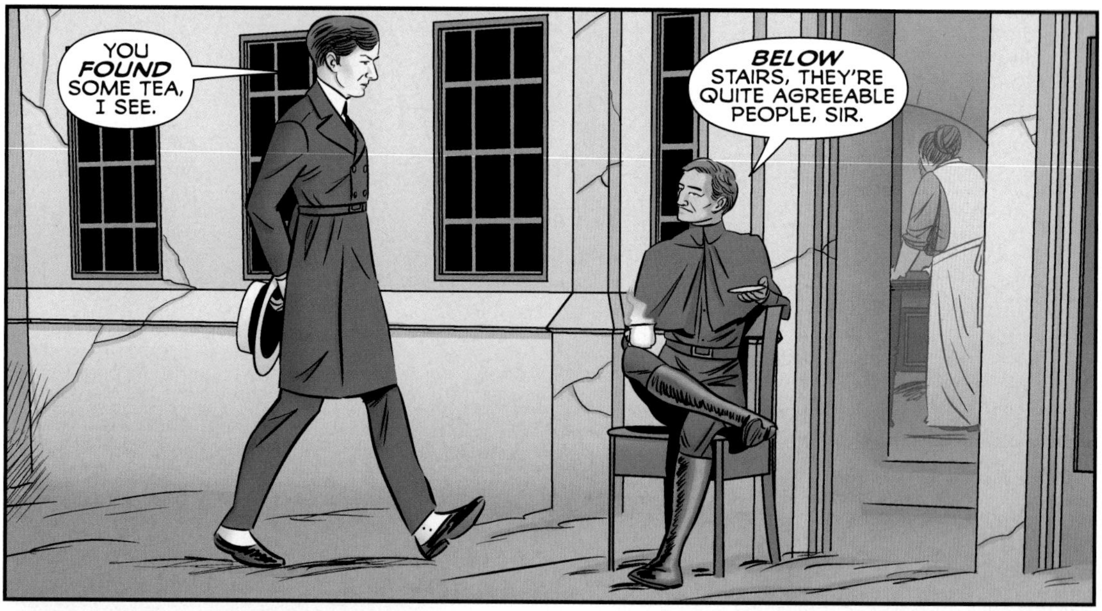
YOU *FOUND* SOME TEA, I SEE.
BELOW STAIRS, THEY'RE QUITE AGREEABLE PEOPLE, SIR.

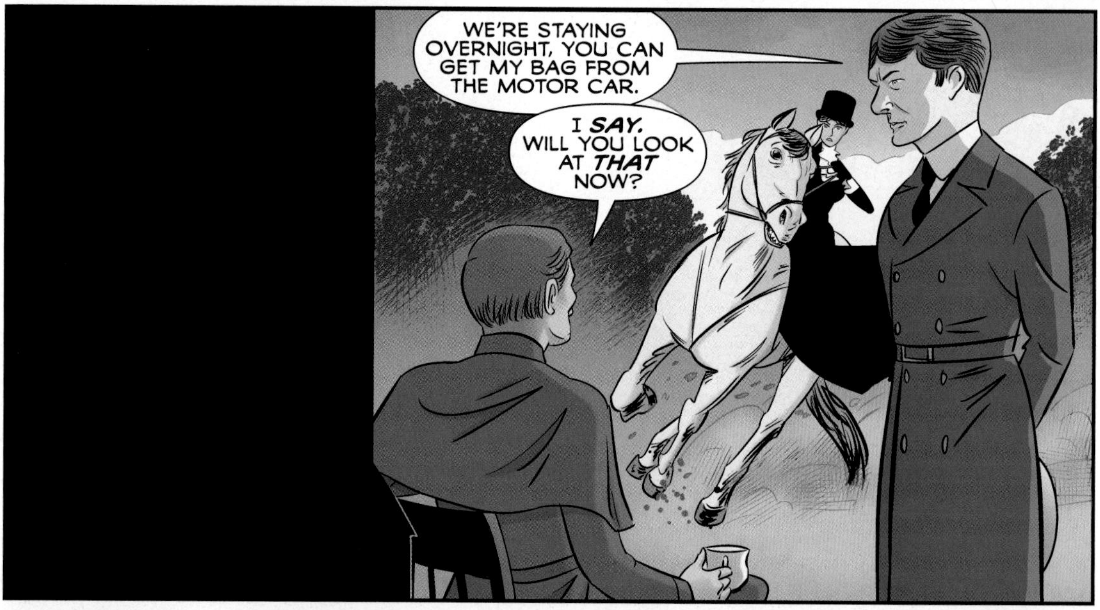
WE'RE STAYING OVERNIGHT, YOU CAN GET MY BAG FROM THE MOTOR CAR.
I *SAY.* WILL YOU LOOK AT *THAT* NOW?

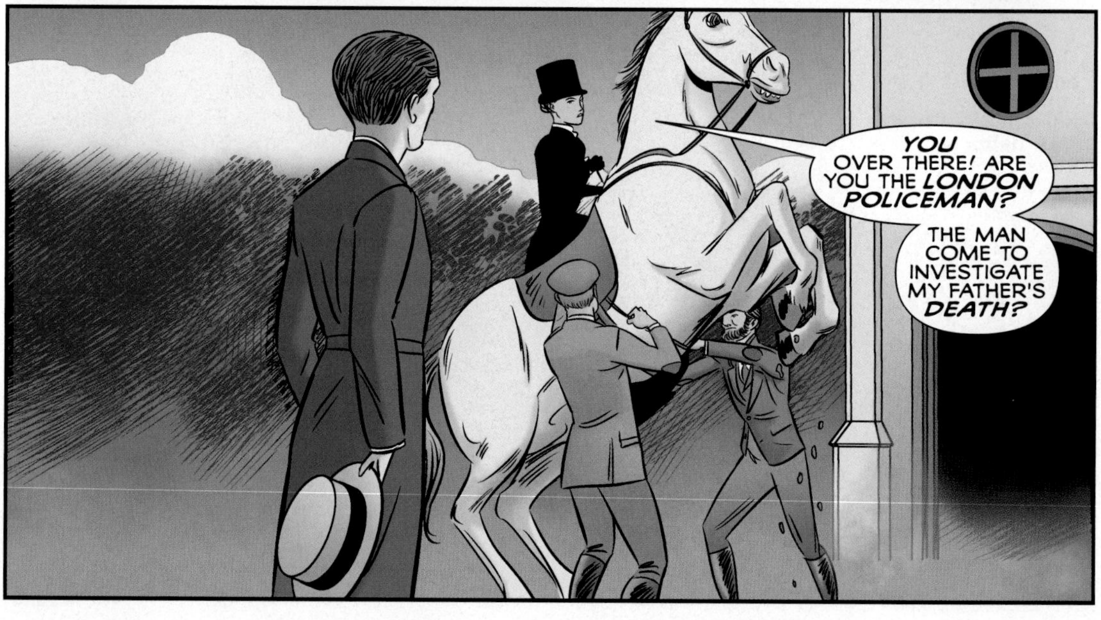
YOU OVER THERE! ARE YOU THE *LONDON POLICEMAN?*
THE MAN COME TO INVESTIGATE MY FATHER'S *DEATH?*

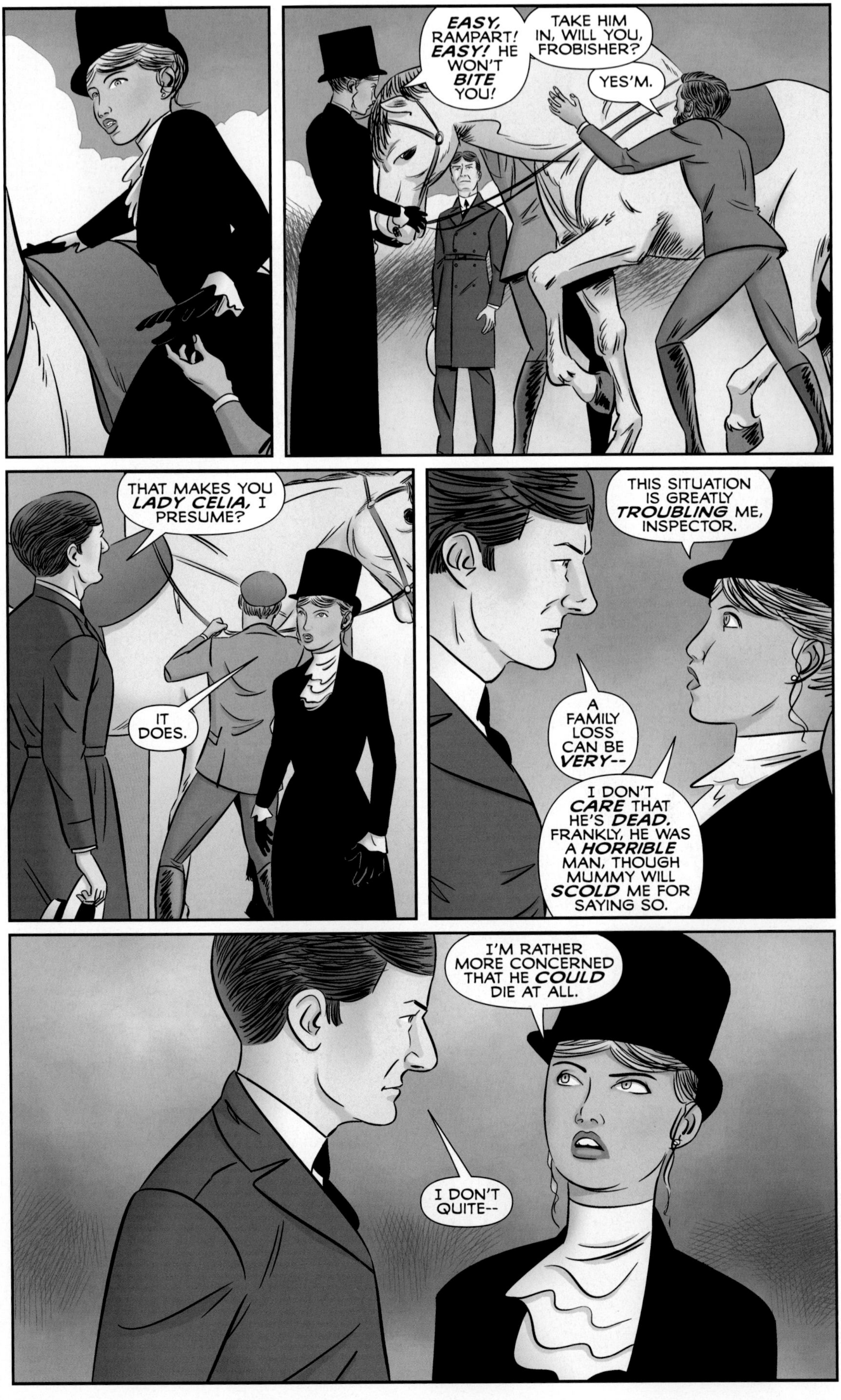
EASY, RAMPART! EASY! HE WON'T BITE YOU!
TAKE HIM IN, WILL YOU, FROBISHER?
YES'M.
THAT MAKES YOU LADY CELIA, I PRESUME?
IT DOES.
THIS SITUATION IS GREATLY TROUBLING ME, INSPECTOR.
A FAMILY LOSS CAN BE VERY--
I DON'T CARE THAT HE'S DEAD. FRANKLY, HE WAS A HORRIBLE MAN, THOUGH MUMMY WILL SCOLD ME FOR SAYING SO.
I'M RATHER MORE CONCERNED THAT HE COULD DIE AT ALL.
I DON'T QUITE--

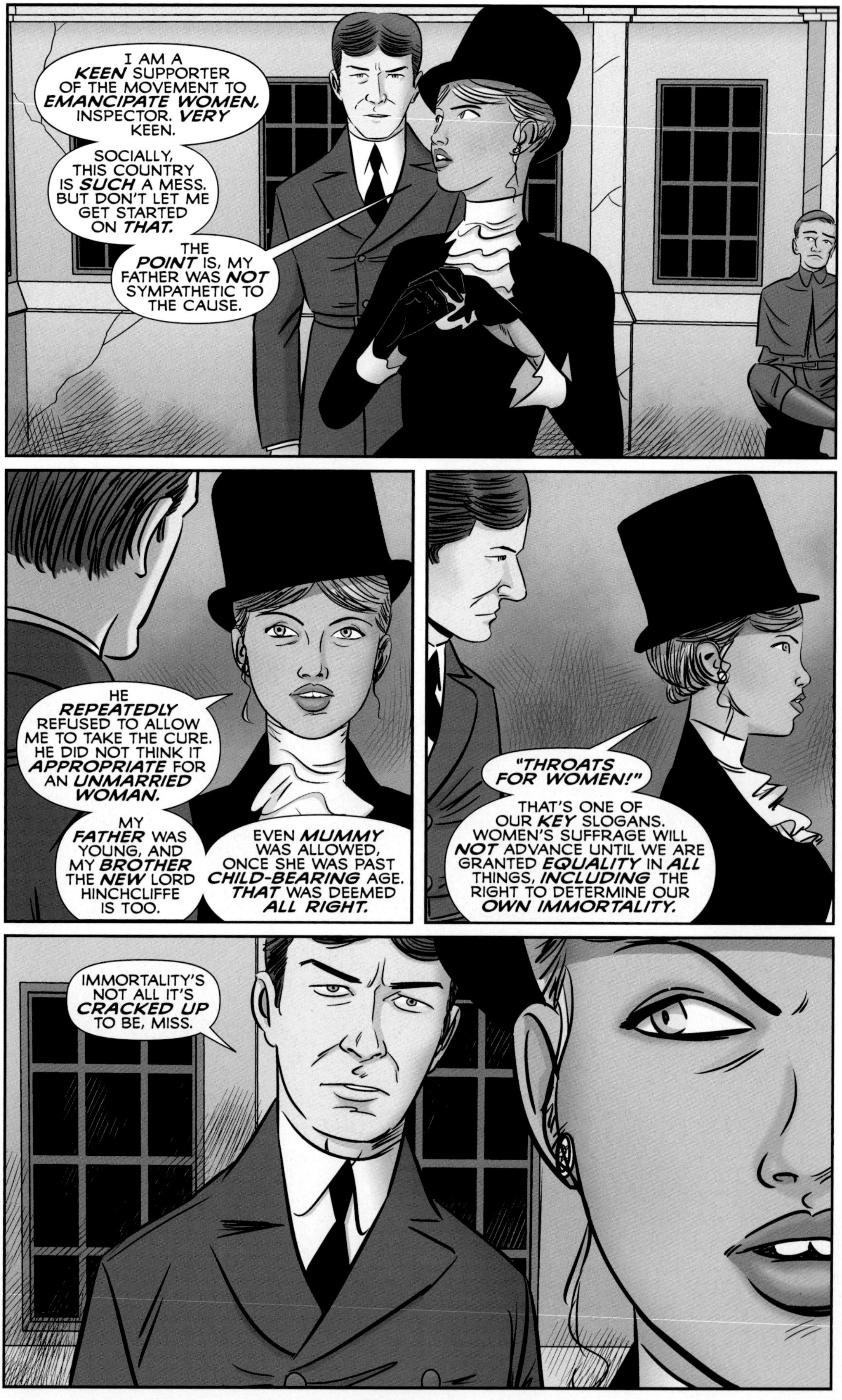
I AM A KEEN SUPPORTER OF THE MOVEMENT TO EMANCIPATE WOMEN, INSPECTOR. VERY KEEN.
SOCIALLY, THIS COUNTRY IS SUCH A MESS. BUT DON'T LET ME GET STARTED ON THAT.
THE POINT IS, MY FATHER WAS NOT SYMPATHETIC TO THE CAUSE.
HE REPEATEDLY REFUSED TO ALLOW ME TO TAKE THE CURE. HE DID NOT THINK IT APPROPRIATE FOR AN UNMARRIED WOMAN.
MY FATHER WAS YOUNG, AND MY BROTHER THE NEW LORD HINCHCLIFFE IS TOO.
EVEN MUMMY WAS ALLOWED, ONCE SHE WAS PAST CHILD-BEARING AGE. THAT WAS DEEMED ALL RIGHT.
"THROATS FOR WOMEN!"
THAT'S ONE OF OUR KEY SLOGANS. WOMEN'S SUFFRAGE WILL NOT ADVANCE UNTIL WE ARE GRANTED EQUALITY IN ALL THINGS, INCLUDING THE RIGHT TO DETERMINE OUR OWN IMMORTALITY.
IMMORTALITY'S NOT ALL IT'S CRACKED UP TO BE, MISS.

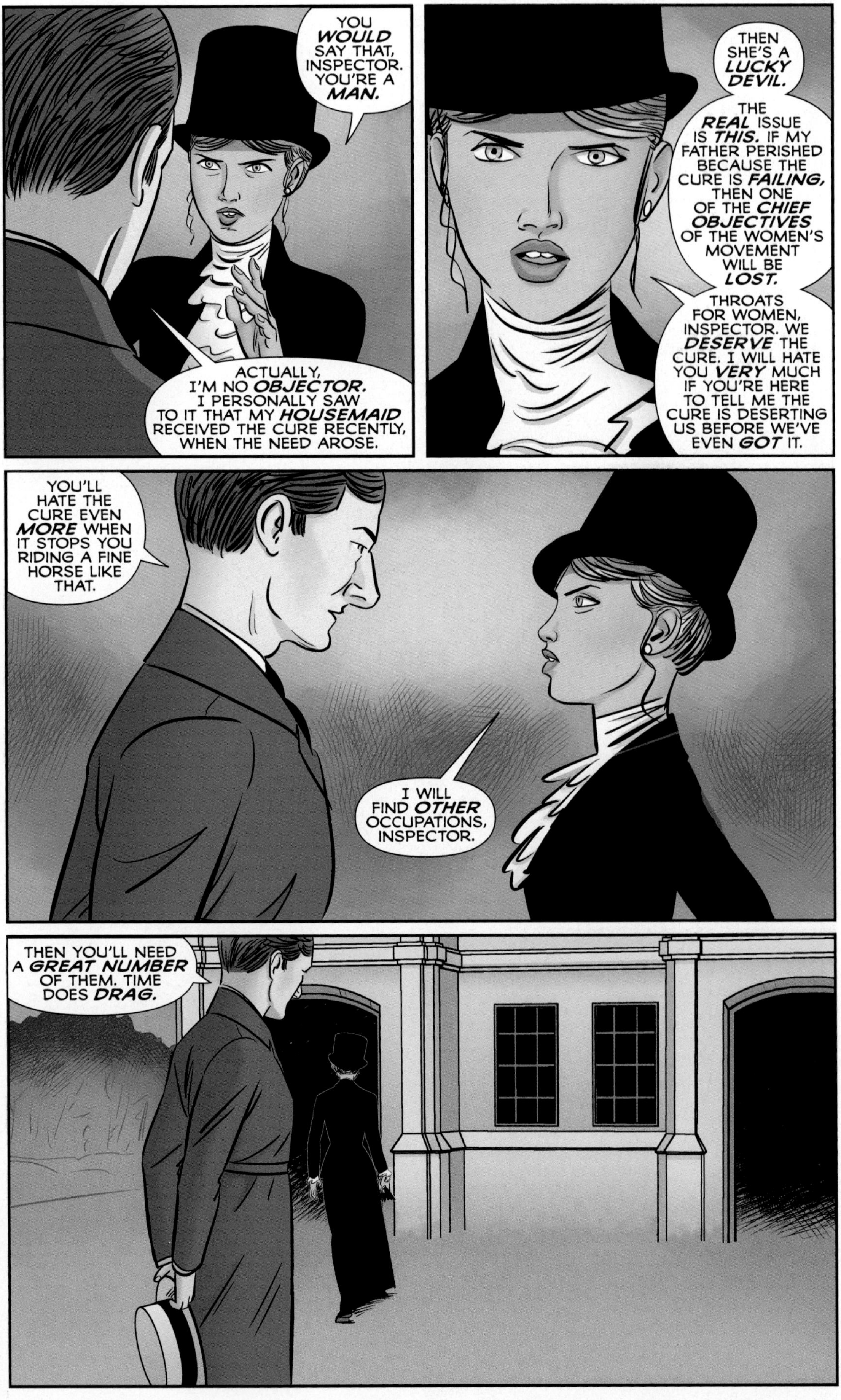
YOU WOULD SAY THAT, INSPECTOR. YOU'RE A MAN.
ACTUALLY, I'M NO OBJECTOR. I PERSONALLY SAW TO IT THAT MY HOUSEMAID RECEIVED THE CURE RECENTLY, WHEN THE NEED AROSE.
THEN SHE'S A LUCKY DEVIL.
THE REAL ISSUE IS THIS. IF MY FATHER PERISHED BECAUSE THE CURE IS FAILING, THEN ONE OF THE CHIEF OBJECTIVES OF THE WOMEN'S MOVEMENT WILL BE LOST.
THROATS FOR WOMEN, INSPECTOR. WE DESERVE THE CURE. I WILL HATE YOU VERY MUCH IF YOU'RE HERE TO TELL ME THE CURE IS DESERTING US BEFORE WE'VE EVEN GOT IT.
YOU'LL HATE THE CURE EVEN MORE WHEN IT STOPS YOU RIDING A FINE HORSE LIKE THAT.
I WILL FIND OTHER OCCUPATIONS, INSPECTOR.
THEN YOU'LL NEED A GREAT NUMBER OF THEM. TIME DOES DRAG.

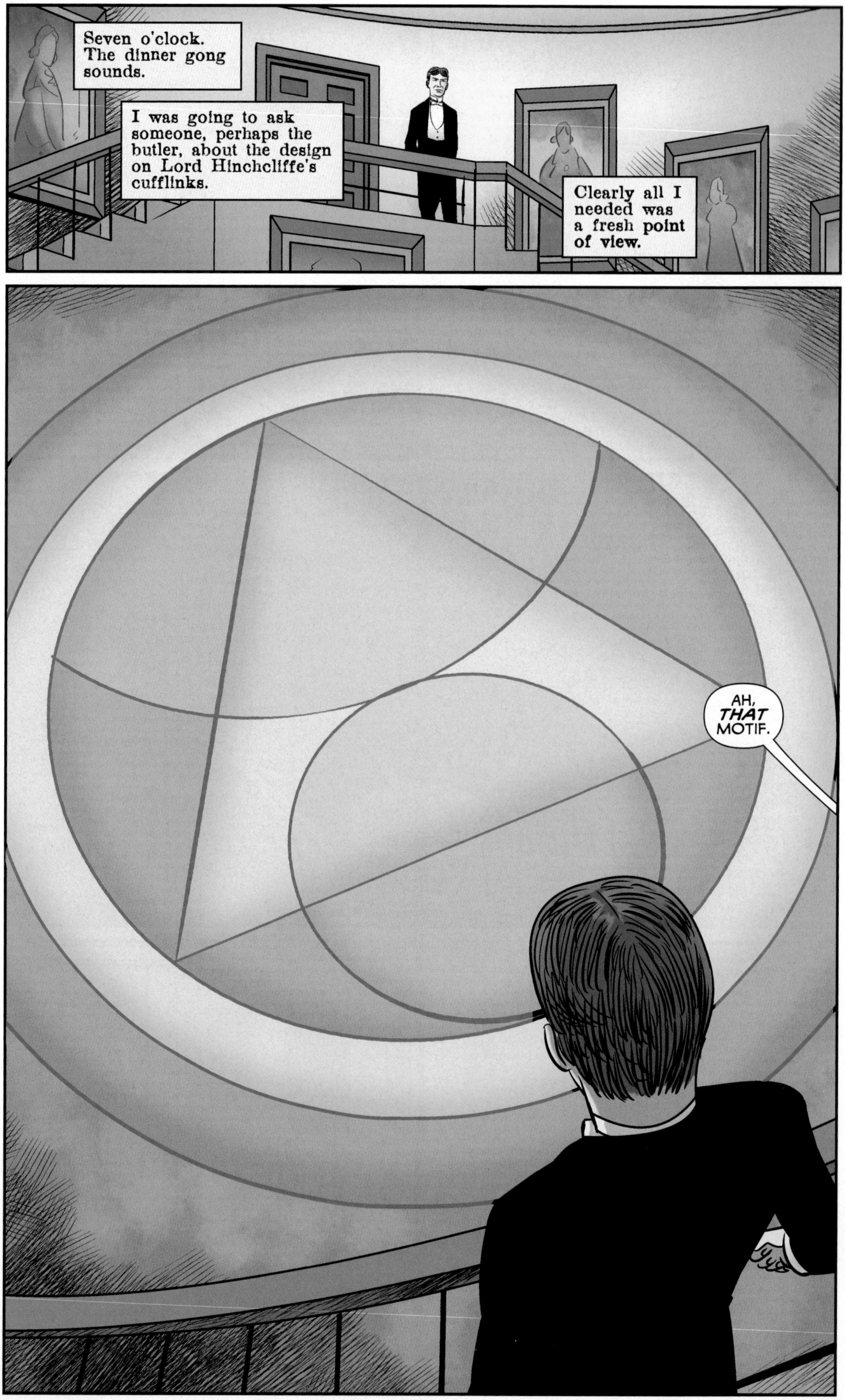
Seven o'clock. The dinner gong sounds.
I was going to ask someone, perhaps the butler, about the design on Lord Hinchcliffe's cufflinks.
Clearly all I needed was a fresh point of view.
AH, THAT MOTIF.

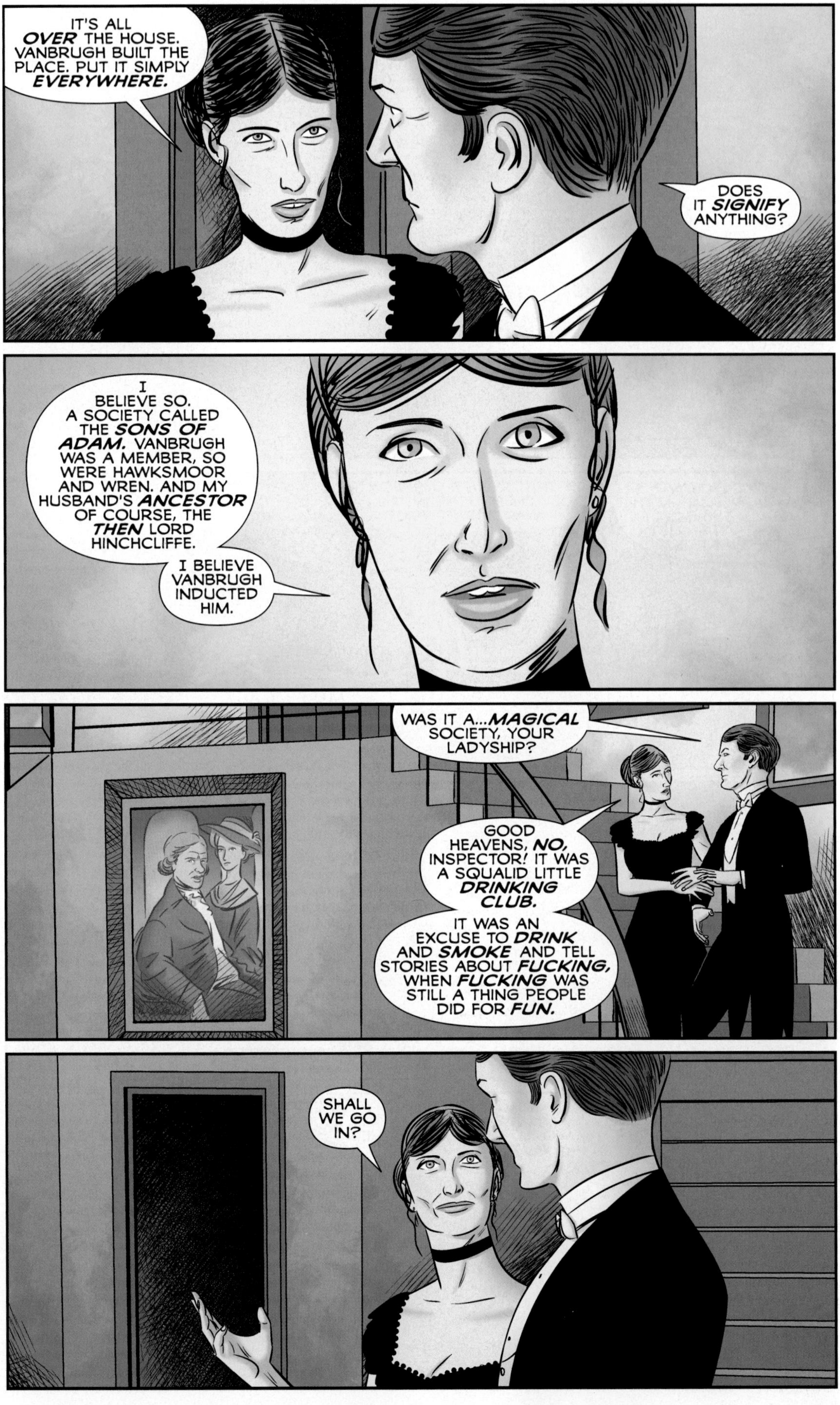
IT'S ALL OVER THE HOUSE. VANBRUGH BUILT THE PLACE. PUT IT SIMPLY EVERYWHERE.
DOES IT SIGNIFY ANYTHING?
I BELIEVE SO. A SOCIETY CALLED THE SONS OF ADAM. VANBRUGH WAS A MEMBER, SO WERE HAWKSMOOR AND WREN. AND MY HUSBAND'S ANCESTOR OF COURSE, THE THEN LORD HINCHCLIFFE.
I BELIEVE VANBRUGH INDUCTED HIM.
WAS IT A...MAGICAL SOCIETY, YOUR LADYSHIP?
GOOD HEAVENS, NO, INSPECTOR! IT WAS A SQUALID LITTLE DRINKING CLUB.
IT WAS AN EXCUSE TO DRINK AND SMOKE AND TELL STORIES ABOUT FUCKING, WHEN FUCKING WAS STILL A THING PEOPLE DID FOR FUN.
SHALL WE GO IN?

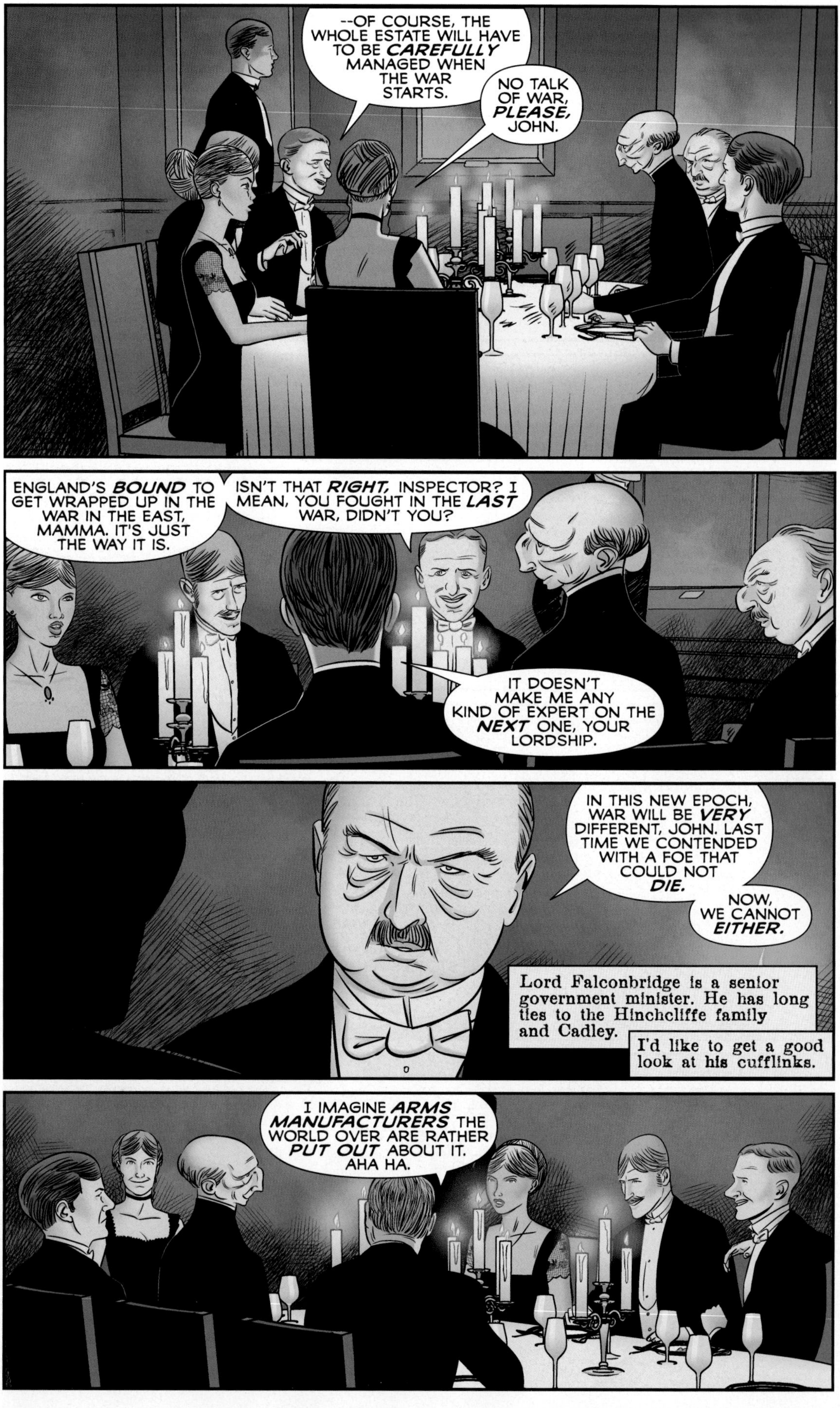
--OF COURSE, THE WHOLE ESTATE WILL HAVE TO BE CAREFULLY MANAGED WHEN THE WAR STARTS.
NO TALK OF WAR, PLEASE, JOHN.
ENGLAND'S BOUND TO GET WRAPPED UP IN THE WAR IN THE EAST, MAMMA. IT'S JUST THE WAY IT IS.
ISN'T THAT RIGHT, INSPECTOR? I MEAN, YOU FOUGHT IN THE LAST WAR, DIDN'T YOU?
IT DOESN'T MAKE ME ANY KIND OF EXPERT ON THE NEXT ONE, YOUR LORDSHIP.
IN THIS NEW EPOCH, WAR WILL BE VERY DIFFERENT, JOHN. LAST TIME WE CONTENDED WITH A FOE THAT COULD NOT DIE.
NOW, WE CANNOT EITHER.
Lord Falconbridge is a senior government minister. He has long ties to the Hinchcliffe family and Cadley.
I'd like to get a good look at his cufflinks.
I IMAGINE ARMS MANUFACTURERS THE WORLD OVER ARE RATHER PUT OUT ABOUT IT. AHA HA.

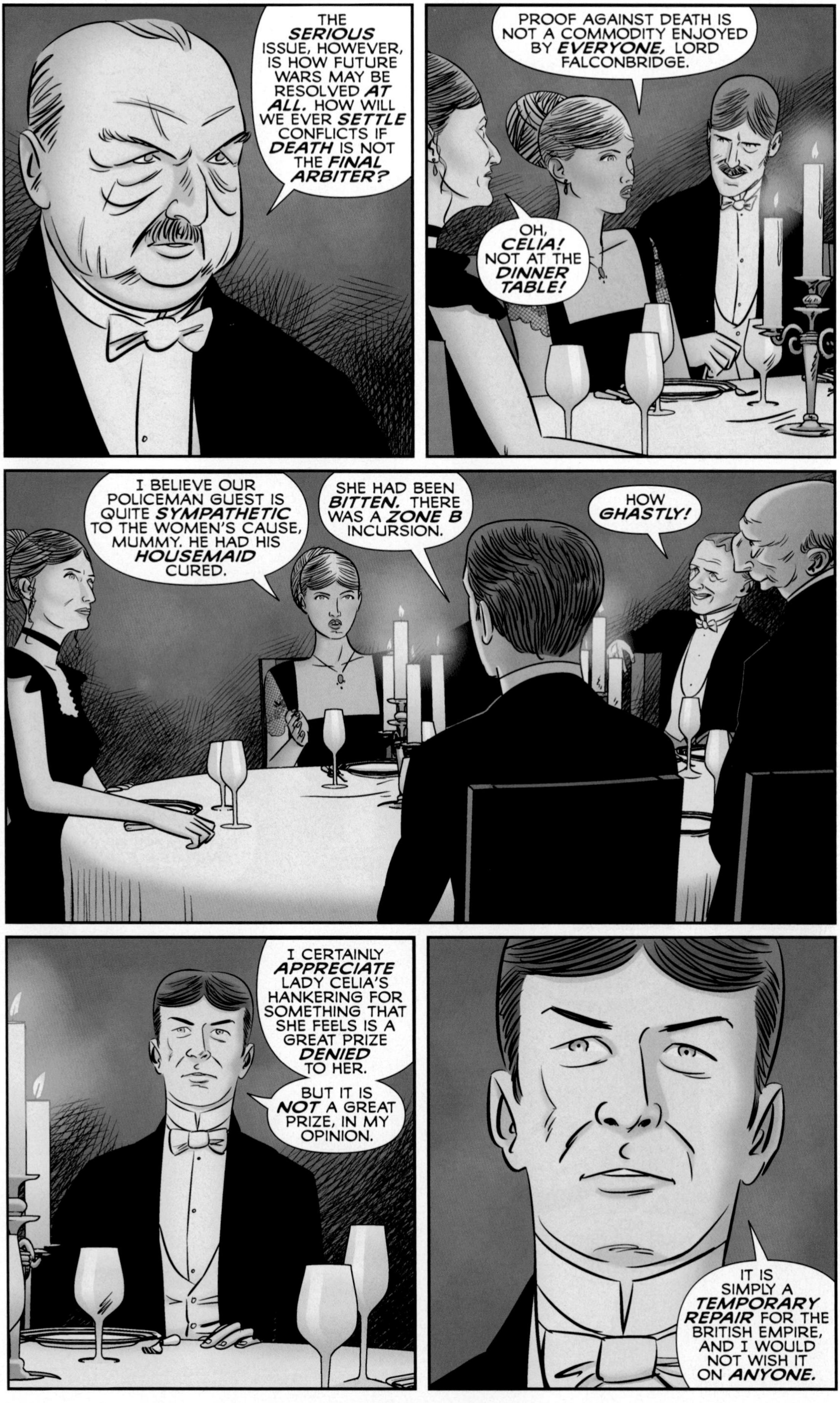
THE SERIOUS ISSUE, HOWEVER, IS HOW FUTURE WARS MAY BE RESOLVED AT ALL. HOW WILL WE EVER SETTLE CONFLICTS IF DEATH IS NOT THE FINAL ARBITER?
PROOF AGAINST DEATH IS NOT A COMMODITY ENJOYED BY EVERYONE, LORD FALCONBRIDGE.
OH, CELIA! NOT AT THE DINNER TABLE!
I BELIEVE OUR POLICEMAN GUEST IS QUITE SYMPATHETIC TO THE WOMEN'S CAUSE, MUMMY. HE HAD HIS HOUSEMAID CURED.
SHE HAD BEEN BITTEN. THERE WAS A ZONE B INCURSION.
HOW GHASTLY!
I CERTAINLY APPRECIATE LADY CELIA'S HANKERING FOR SOMETHING THAT SHE FEELS IS A GREAT PRIZE DENIED TO HER.
BUT IT IS NOT A GREAT PRIZE, IN MY OPINION.
IT IS SIMPLY A TEMPORARY REPAIR FOR THE BRITISH EMPIRE, AND I WOULD NOT WISH IT ON ANYONE.

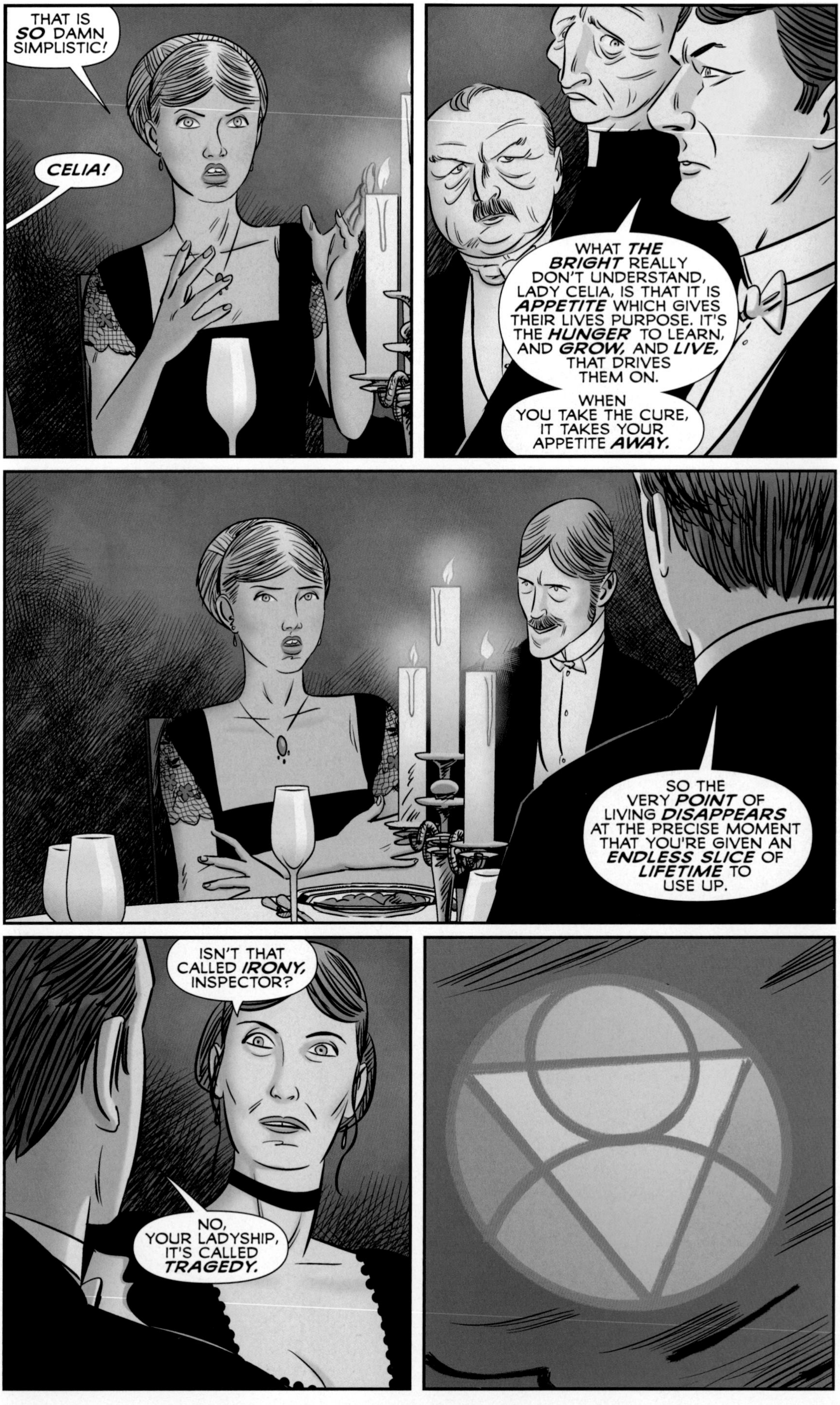
THAT IS SO DAMN SIMPLISTIC!
CELIA!
WHAT THE BRIGHT REALLY DON'T UNDERSTAND, LADY CELIA, IS THAT IT IS APPETITE WHICH GIVES THEIR LIVES PURPOSE. IT'S THE HUNGER TO LEARN, AND GROW, AND LIVE, THAT DRIVES THEM ON.
WHEN YOU TAKE THE CURE, IT TAKES YOUR APPETITE AWAY.
SO THE VERY POINT OF LIVING DISAPPEARS AT THE PRECISE MOMENT THAT YOU'RE GIVEN AN ENDLESS SLICE OF LIFETIME TO USE UP.
ISN'T THAT CALLED IRONY, INSPECTOR?
NO, YOUR LADYSHIP, IT'S CALLED TRAGEDY.

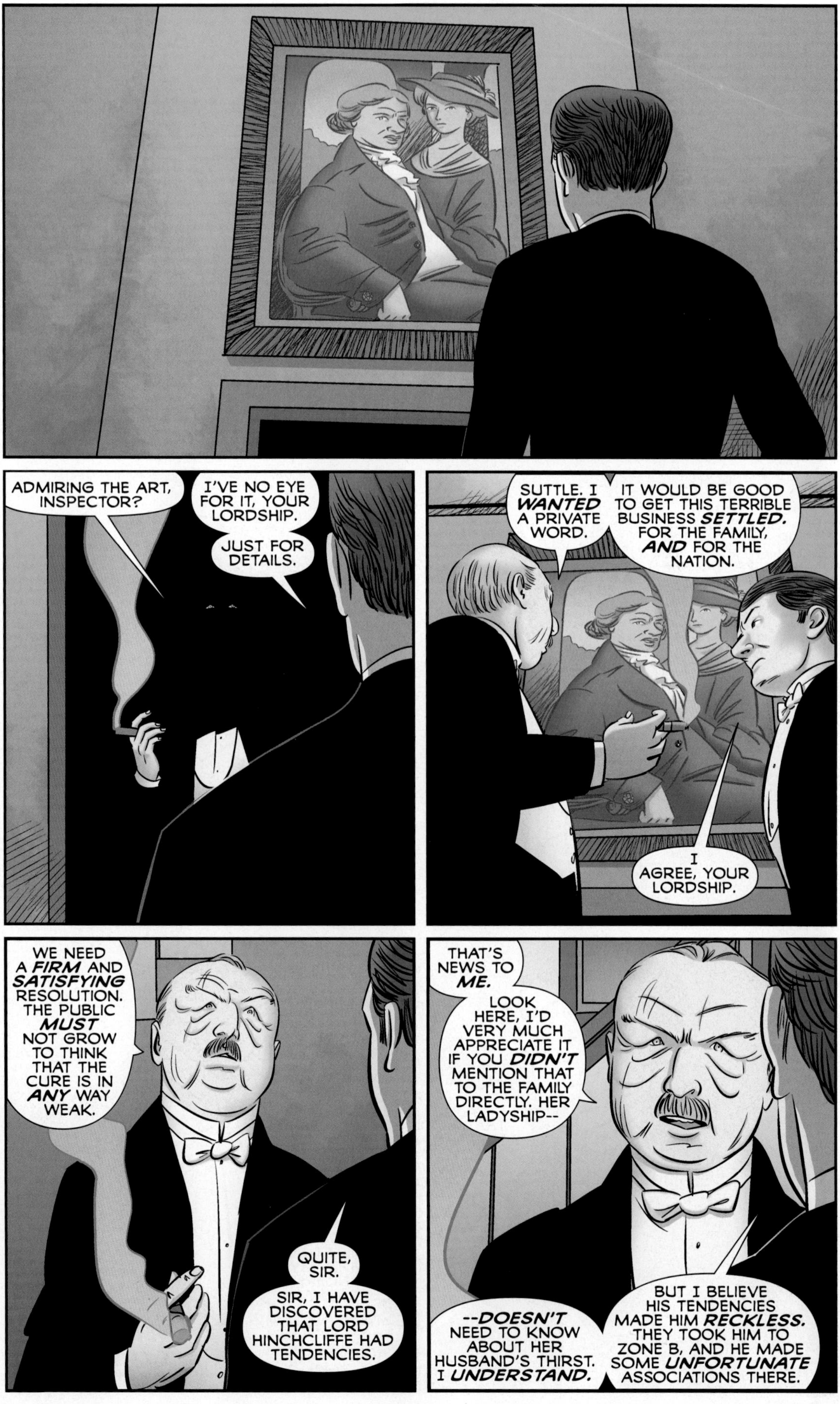
ADMIRING THE ART, INSPECTOR?
I'VE NO EYE FOR IT, YOUR LORDSHIP.
JUST FOR DETAILS.
SUTTLE. I *WANTED* A PRIVATE WORD.
IT WOULD BE GOOD TO GET THIS TERRIBLE BUSINESS *SETTLED.* FOR THE FAMILY, *AND* FOR THE NATION.
I AGREE, YOUR LORDSHIP.
WE NEED A *FIRM* AND *SATISFYING* RESOLUTION. THE PUBLIC *MUST* NOT GROW TO THINK THAT THE CURE IS IN *ANY* WAY WEAK.
QUITE, SIR.
SIR, I HAVE DISCOVERED THAT LORD HINCHCLIFFE HAD TENDENCIES.
THAT'S NEWS TO *ME.*
LOOK HERE, I'D VERY MUCH APPRECIATE IT IF YOU *DIDN'T* MENTION THAT TO THE FAMILY DIRECTLY. HER LADYSHIP--
--*DOESN'T* NEED TO KNOW ABOUT HER HUSBAND'S THIRST. I *UNDERSTAND.*
BUT I BELIEVE HIS TENDENCIES MADE HIM *RECKLESS.* THEY TOOK HIM TO ZONE B, AND HE MADE SOME *UNFORTUNATE* ASSOCIATIONS THERE.

SUCH AS?

THERE'S AN ARTIST WHOSE NAME *KEEPS* RECURRING.

AND YOU *LIKE* THIS FELLOW FOR THE MURDER, DO YOU?

TO BE *HONEST*, SIR, HE'S THE ONLY THING I HAVE THAT EVEN *RESEMBLES* A SUSPECT.

AND I'M NOT EVEN SURE IT *IS* A MURDER.

LISTEN, SUTTLE, YOU SEEM LIKE A GOOD SORT.

ISN'T THERE SOME WAY WE COULD DRAW A *LINE* UNDER THIS? PRODUCE, SHALL WE SAY, AN *ADEQUATE VERDICT?*

I CAN HAVE MY PEOPLE PROVIDE YOU WITH *ANYTHING* YOU NEED. DOCUMENTATION. WITNESSES. *THAT* SORT OF THING.

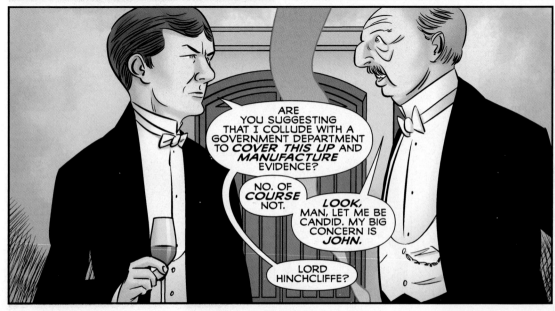

ARE YOU SUGGESTING THAT I COLLUDE WITH A GOVERNMENT DEPARTMENT TO *COVER THIS UP* AND *MANUFACTURE* EVIDENCE?

NO. OF *COURSE* NOT.

LOOK, MAN, LET ME BE CANDID. MY BIG CONCERN IS *JOHN.*

LORD HINCHCLIFFE?

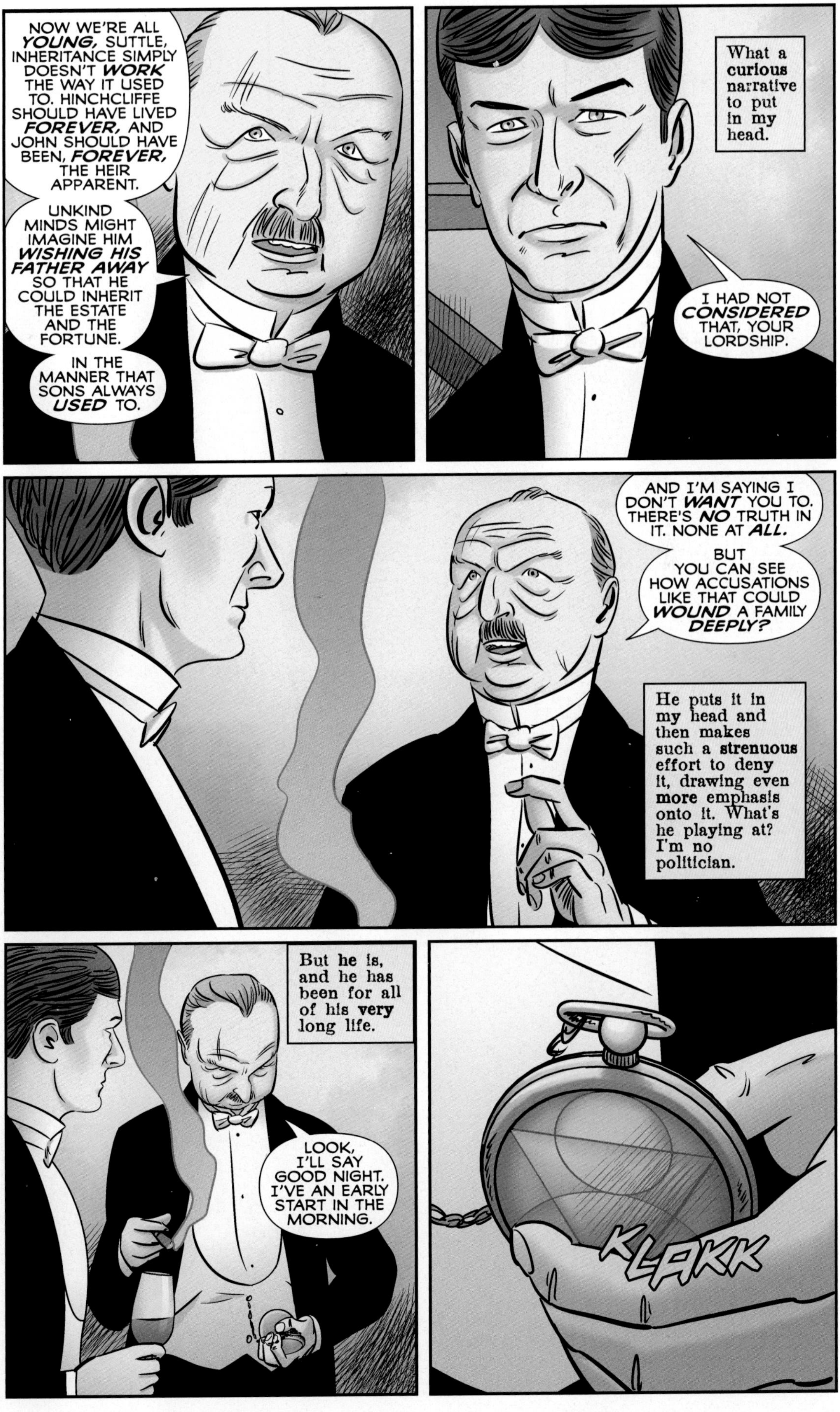
NOW WE'RE ALL YOUNG, SUTTLE, INHERITANCE SIMPLY DOESN'T WORK THE WAY IT USED TO. HINCHCLIFFE SHOULD HAVE LIVED FOREVER, AND JOHN SHOULD HAVE BEEN, FOREVER, THE HEIR APPARENT.
UNKIND MINDS MIGHT IMAGINE HIM WISHING HIS FATHER AWAY SO THAT HE COULD INHERIT THE ESTATE AND THE FORTUNE.
IN THE MANNER THAT SONS ALWAYS USED TO.
What a curious narrative to put in my head.
I HAD NOT CONSIDERED THAT, YOUR LORDSHIP.
AND I'M SAYING I DON'T WANT YOU TO. THERE'S NO TRUTH IN IT. NONE AT ALL.
BUT YOU CAN SEE HOW ACCUSATIONS LIKE THAT COULD WOUND A FAMILY DEEPLY?
He puts it in my head and then makes such a strenuous effort to deny it, drawing even more emphasis onto it. What's he playing at? I'm no politician.
But he is, and he has been for all of his very long life.
LOOK, I'LL SAY GOOD NIGHT. I'VE AN EARLY START IN THE MORNING.
KLAKK

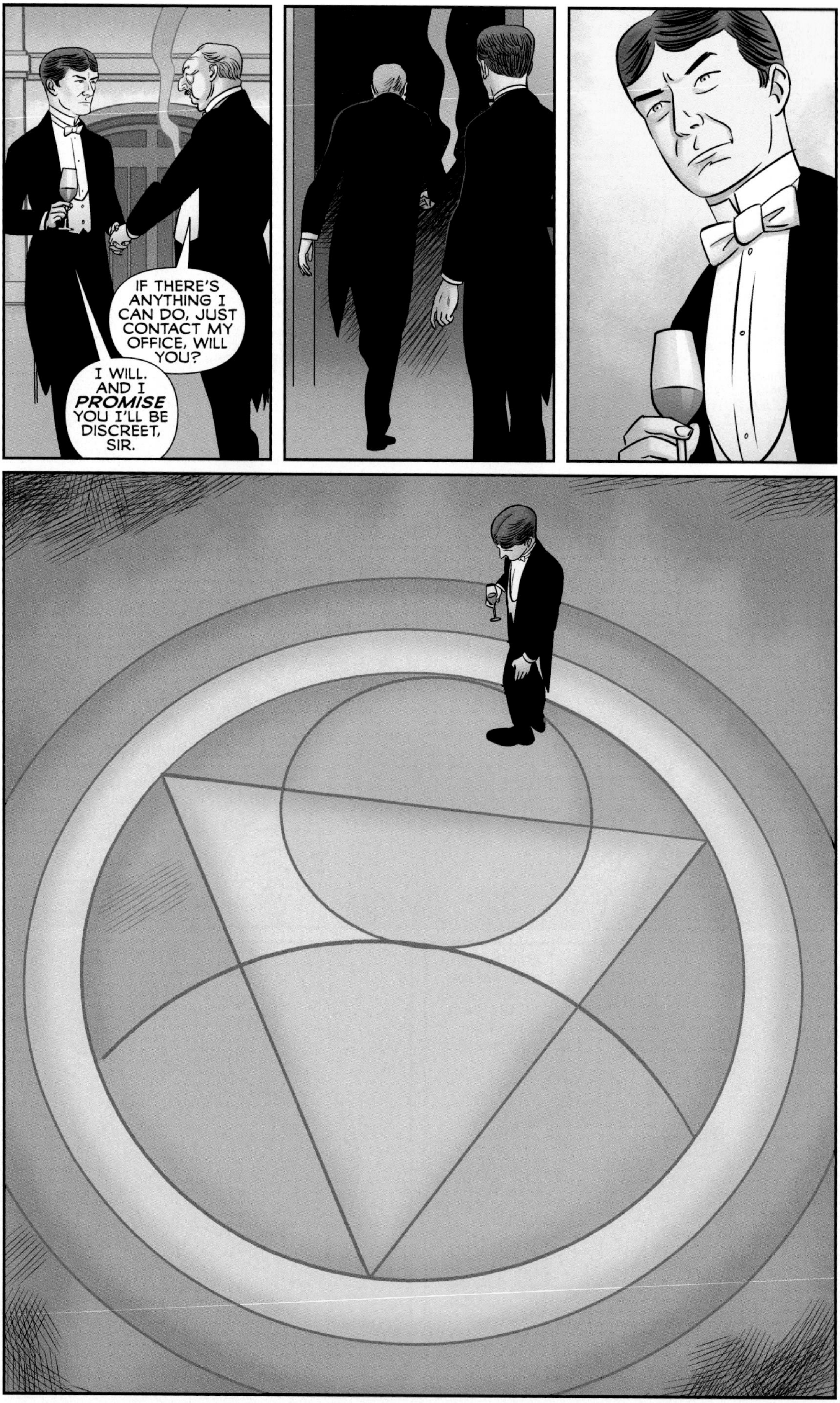
IF THERE'S ANYTHING I CAN DO, JUST CONTACT MY OFFICE, WILL YOU?
I WILL. AND I *PROMISE* YOU I'LL BE DISCREET, SIR.

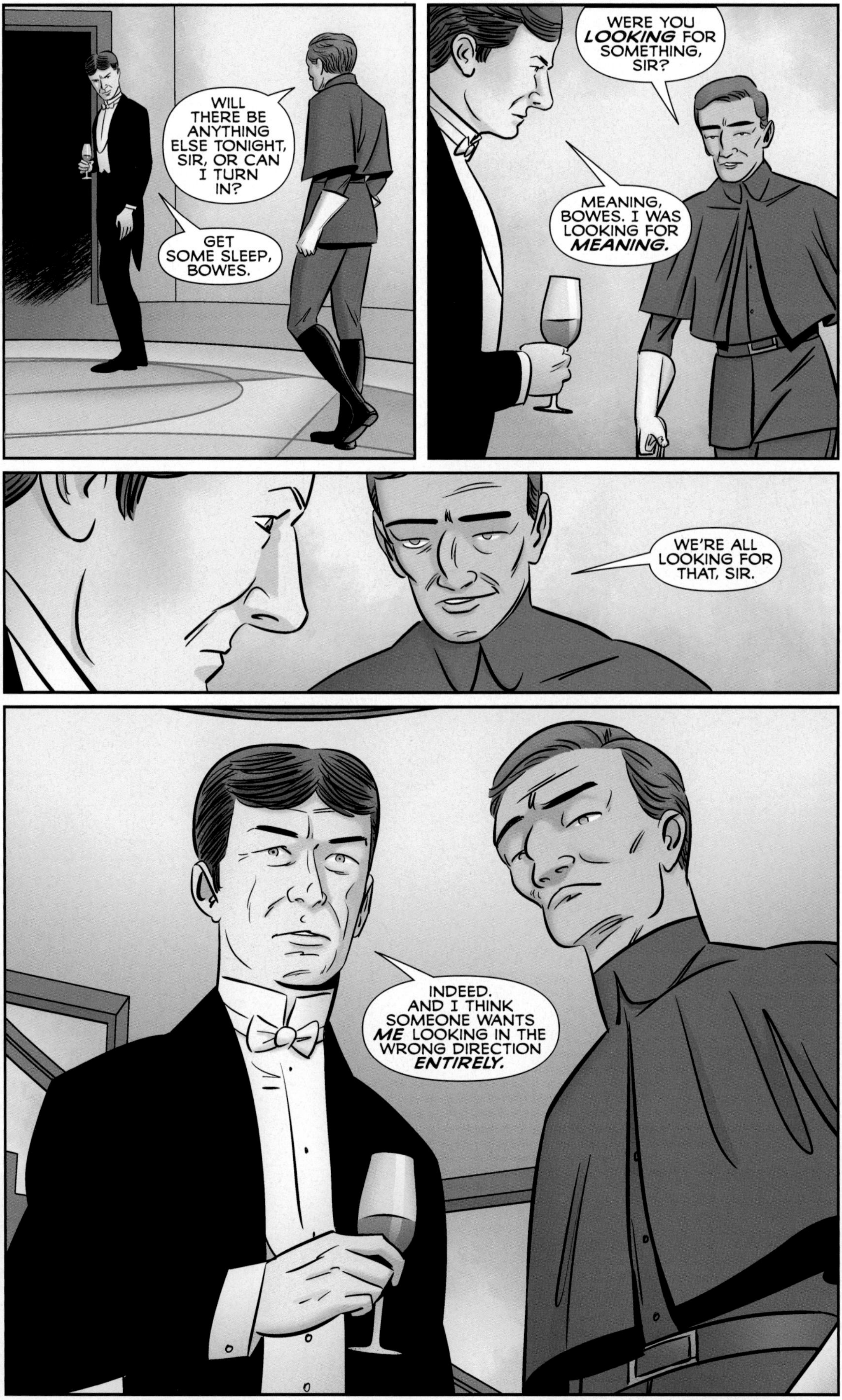
WILL THERE BE ANYTHING ELSE TONIGHT, SIR, OR CAN I TURN IN?
GET SOME SLEEP, BOWES.
WERE YOU LOOKING FOR SOMETHING, SIR?
MEANING, BOWES. I WAS LOOKING FOR MEANING.
WE'RE ALL LOOKING FOR THAT, SIR.
INDEED. AND I THINK SOMEONE WANTS ME LOOKING IN THE WRONG DIRECTION ENTIRELY.

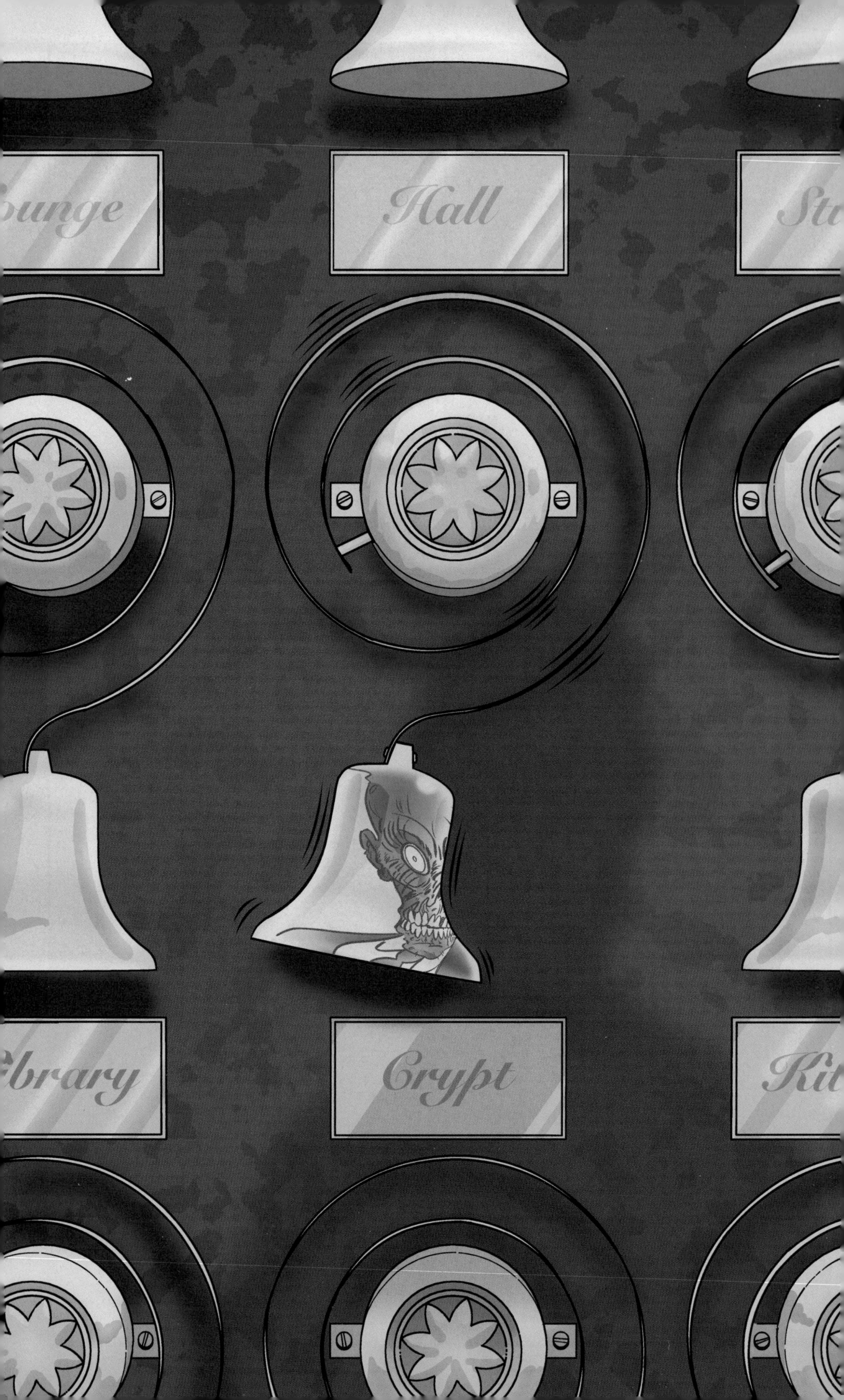

Hall
Crypt

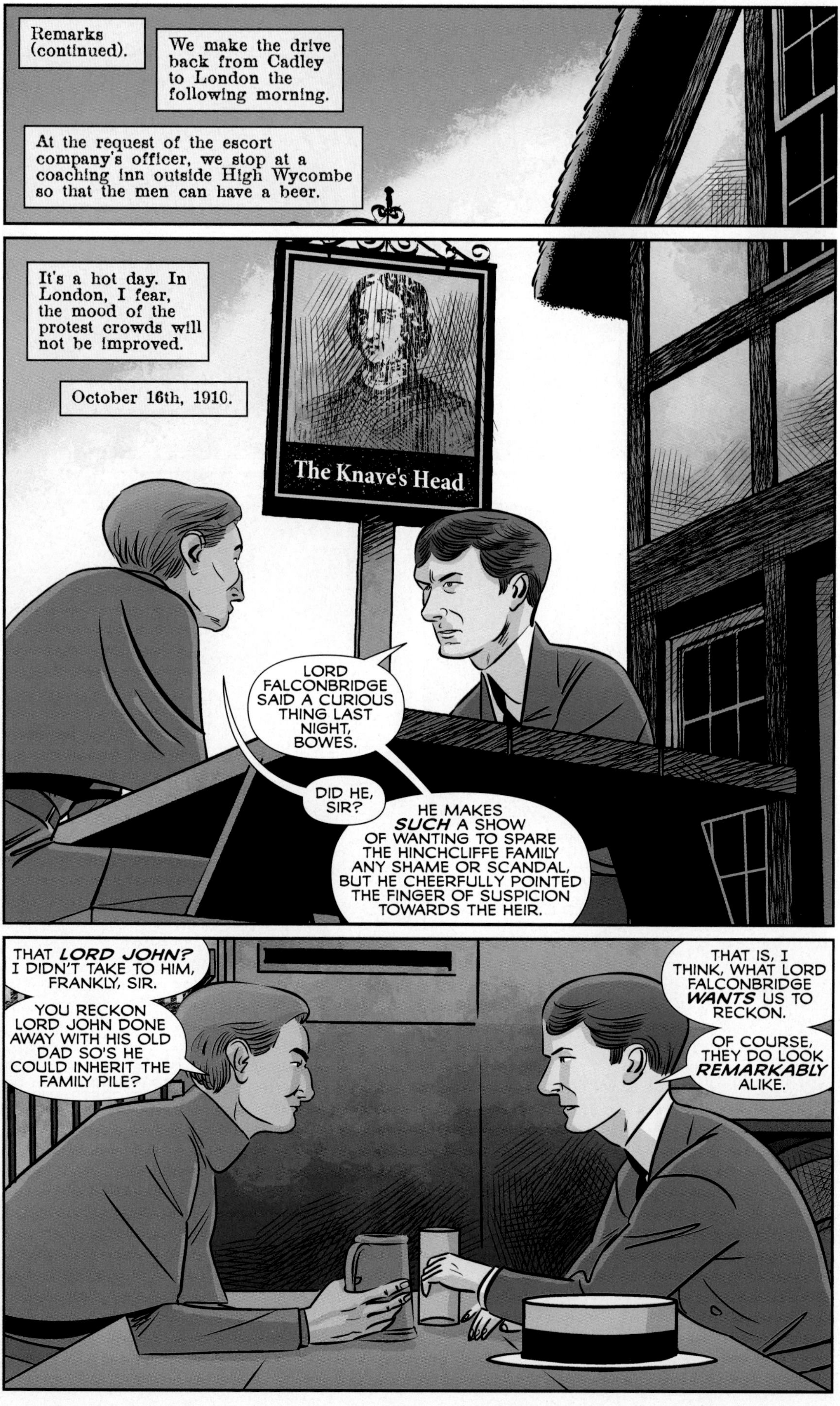
Remarks (continued).
We make the drive back from Cadley to London the following morning.
At the request of the escort company's officer, we stop at a coaching inn outside High Wycombe so that the men can have a beer.
It's a hot day. In London, I fear, the mood of the protest crowds will not be improved.
October 16th, 1910.
The Knave's Head
LORD FALCONBRIDGE SAID A CURIOUS THING LAST NIGHT, BOWES.
DID HE, SIR?
HE MAKES *SUCH* A SHOW OF WANTING TO SPARE THE HINCHCLIFFE FAMILY ANY SHAME OR SCANDAL, BUT HE CHEERFULLY POINTED THE FINGER OF SUSPICION TOWARDS THE HEIR.
THAT *LORD JOHN?* I DIDN'T TAKE TO HIM, FRANKLY, SIR.
YOU RECKON LORD JOHN DONE AWAY WITH HIS OLD DAD SO'S HE COULD INHERIT THE FAMILY PILE?
THAT IS, I THINK, WHAT LORD FALCONBRIDGE *WANTS* US TO RECKON.
OF COURSE, THEY DO LOOK *REMARKABLY* ALIKE.

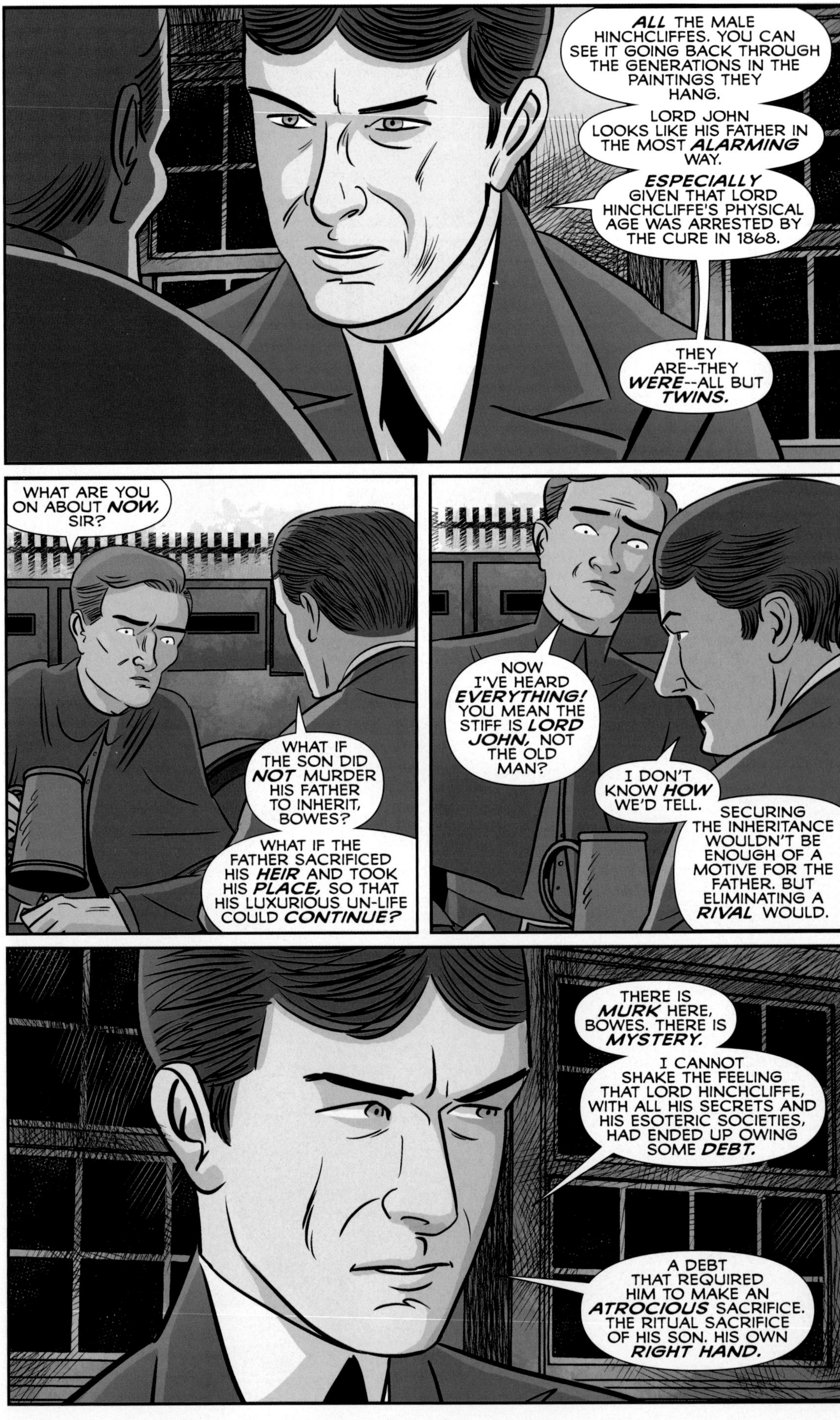
ALL THE MALE HINCHCLIFFES. YOU CAN SEE IT GOING BACK THROUGH THE GENERATIONS IN THE PAINTINGS THEY HANG.
LORD JOHN LOOKS LIKE HIS FATHER IN THE MOST ALARMING WAY.
ESPECIALLY GIVEN THAT LORD HINCHCLIFFE'S PHYSICAL AGE WAS ARRESTED BY THE CURE IN 1868.
THEY ARE--THEY WERE--ALL BUT TWINS.
WHAT ARE YOU ON ABOUT NOW, SIR?
WHAT IF THE SON DID NOT MURDER HIS FATHER TO INHERIT, BOWES?
WHAT IF THE FATHER SACRIFICED HIS HEIR AND TOOK HIS PLACE, SO THAT HIS LUXURIOUS UN-LIFE COULD CONTINUE?
NOW I'VE HEARD EVERYTHING! YOU MEAN THE STIFF IS LORD JOHN, NOT THE OLD MAN?
I DON'T KNOW HOW WE'D TELL.
SECURING THE INHERITANCE WOULDN'T BE ENOUGH OF A MOTIVE FOR THE FATHER. BUT ELIMINATING A RIVAL WOULD.
THERE IS MURK HERE, BOWES. THERE IS MYSTERY.
I CANNOT SHAKE THE FEELING THAT LORD HINCHCLIFFE, WITH ALL HIS SECRETS AND HIS ESOTERIC SOCIETIES, HAD ENDED UP OWING SOME DEBT.
A DEBT THAT REQUIRED HIM TO MAKE AN ATROCIOUS SACRIFICE. THE RITUAL SACRIFICE OF HIS SON. HIS OWN RIGHT HAND.

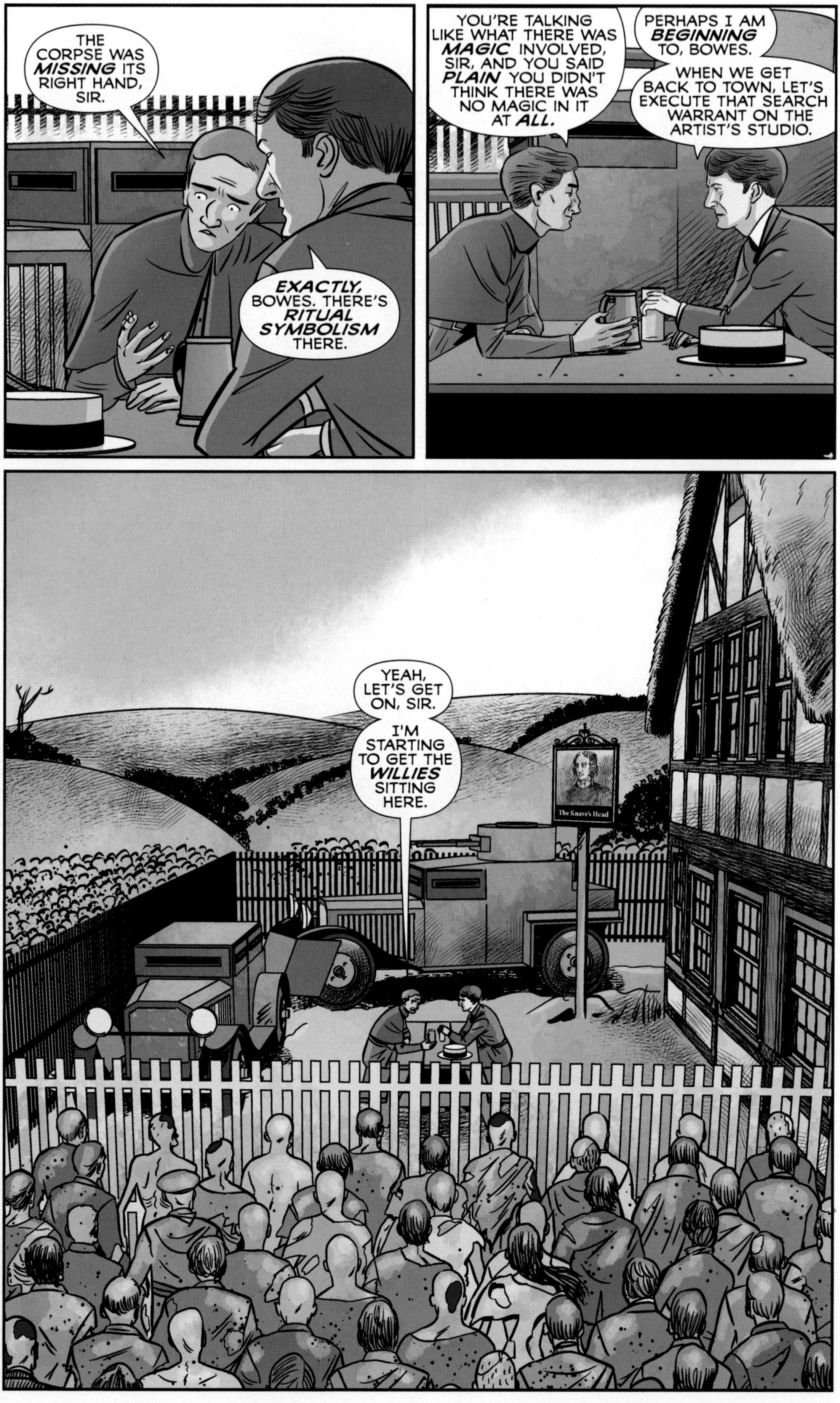
THE CORPSE WAS MISSING ITS RIGHT HAND, SIR.
EXACTLY, BOWES. THERE'S RITUAL SYMBOLISM THERE.
YOU'RE TALKING LIKE WHAT THERE WAS MAGIC INVOLVED, SIR, AND YOU SAID PLAIN YOU DIDN'T THINK THERE WAS NO MAGIC IN IT AT ALL.
PERHAPS I AM BEGINNING TO, BOWES.
WHEN WE GET BACK TO TOWN, LET'S EXECUTE THAT SEARCH WARRANT ON THE ARTIST'S STUDIO.
YEAH, LET'S GET ON, SIR.
I'M STARTING TO GET THE WILLIES SITTING HERE.
The Knave's Head

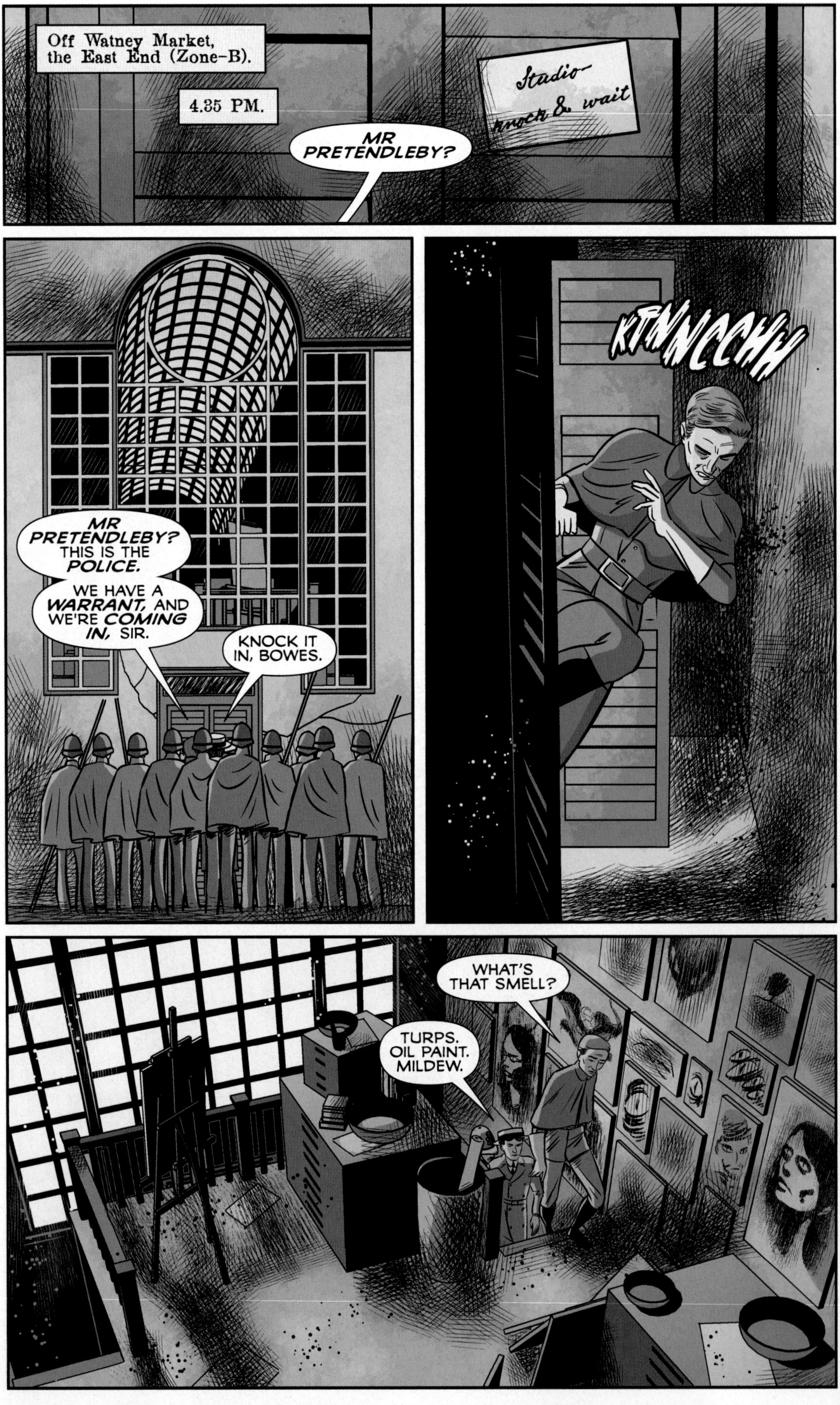
Off Watney Market,
the East End (Zone-B).
4.35 PM.
Studio-
knock & wait
MR PRETENDLEBY?
MR PRETENDLEBY? THIS IS THE POLICE.
WE HAVE A WARRANT, AND WE'RE COMING IN, SIR.
KNOCK IT IN, BOWES.
KTNNCCHH
WHAT'S THAT SMELL?
TURPS. OIL PAINT. MILDEW.

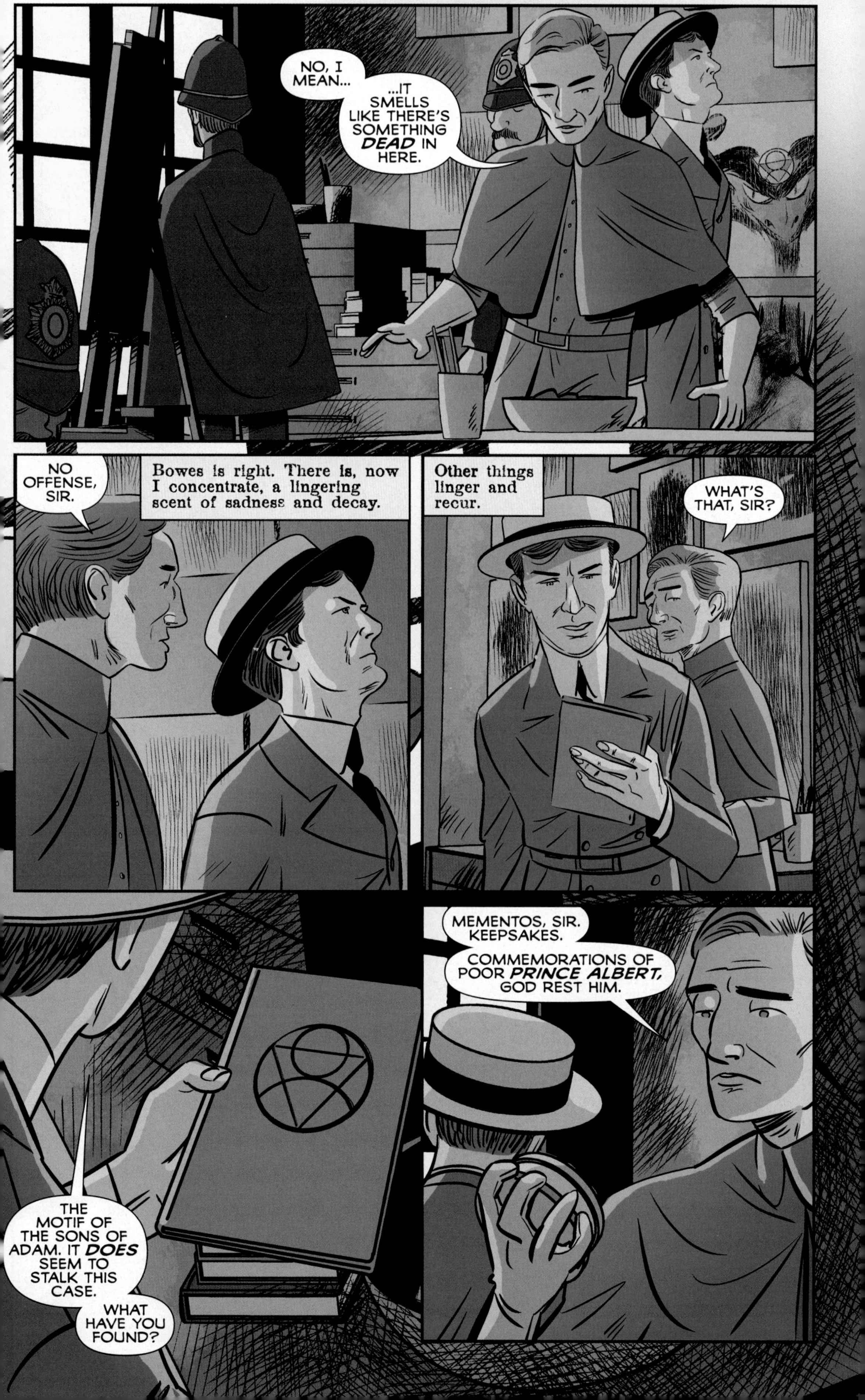
NO, I MEAN...
...IT SMELLS LIKE THERE'S SOMETHING *DEAD* IN HERE.
NO OFFENSE, SIR.
Bowes is right. There is, now I concentrate, a lingering scent of sadness and decay.
Other things linger and recur.
WHAT'S THAT, SIR?
THE MOTIF OF THE SONS OF ADAM. IT *DOES* SEEM TO STALK THIS CASE.
WHAT HAVE YOU FOUND?
MEMENTOS, SIR. KEEPSAKES.
COMMEMORATIONS OF POOR *PRINCE ALBERT,* GOD REST HIM.

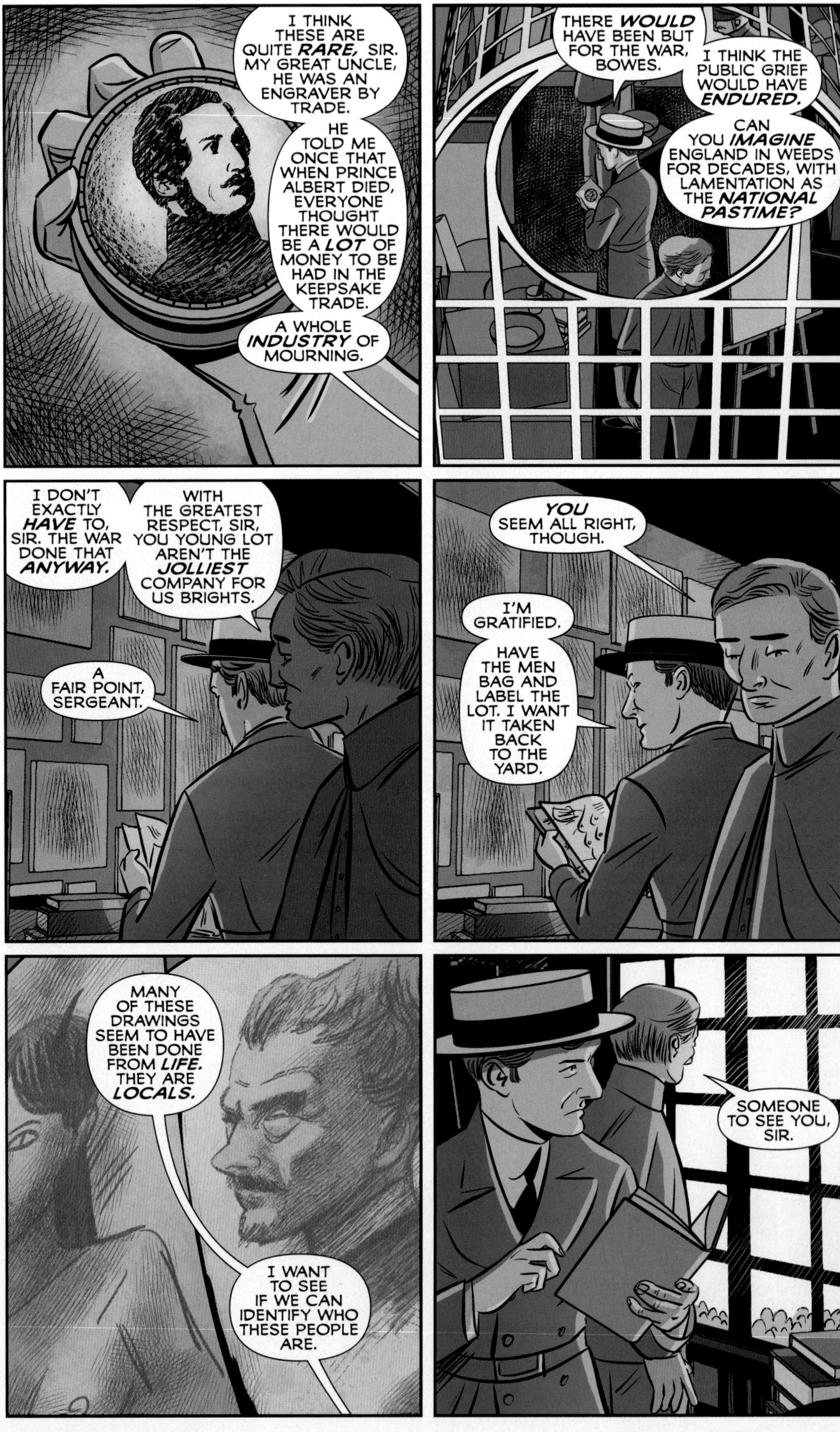
I THINK THESE ARE QUITE RARE, SIR. MY GREAT UNCLE, HE WAS AN ENGRAVER BY TRADE.
HE TOLD ME ONCE THAT WHEN PRINCE ALBERT DIED, EVERYONE THOUGHT THERE WOULD BE A LOT OF MONEY TO BE HAD IN THE KEEPSAKE TRADE.
A WHOLE INDUSTRY OF MOURNING.
THERE WOULD HAVE BEEN BUT FOR THE WAR, BOWES.
I THINK THE PUBLIC GRIEF WOULD HAVE ENDURED.
CAN YOU IMAGINE ENGLAND IN WEEDS FOR DECADES, WITH LAMENTATION AS THE NATIONAL PASTIME?
I DON'T EXACTLY HAVE TO, SIR. THE WAR DONE THAT ANYWAY.
WITH THE GREATEST RESPECT, SIR, YOU YOUNG LOT AREN'T THE JOLLIEST COMPANY FOR US BRIGHTS.
A FAIR POINT, SERGEANT.
YOU SEEM ALL RIGHT, THOUGH.
I'M GRATIFIED.
HAVE THE MEN BAG AND LABEL THE LOT. I WANT IT TAKEN BACK TO THE YARD.
MANY OF THESE DRAWINGS SEEM TO HAVE BEEN DONE FROM LIFE. THEY ARE LOCALS.
I WANT TO SEE IF WE CAN IDENTIFY WHO THESE PEOPLE ARE.
SOMEONE TO SEE YOU, SIR.

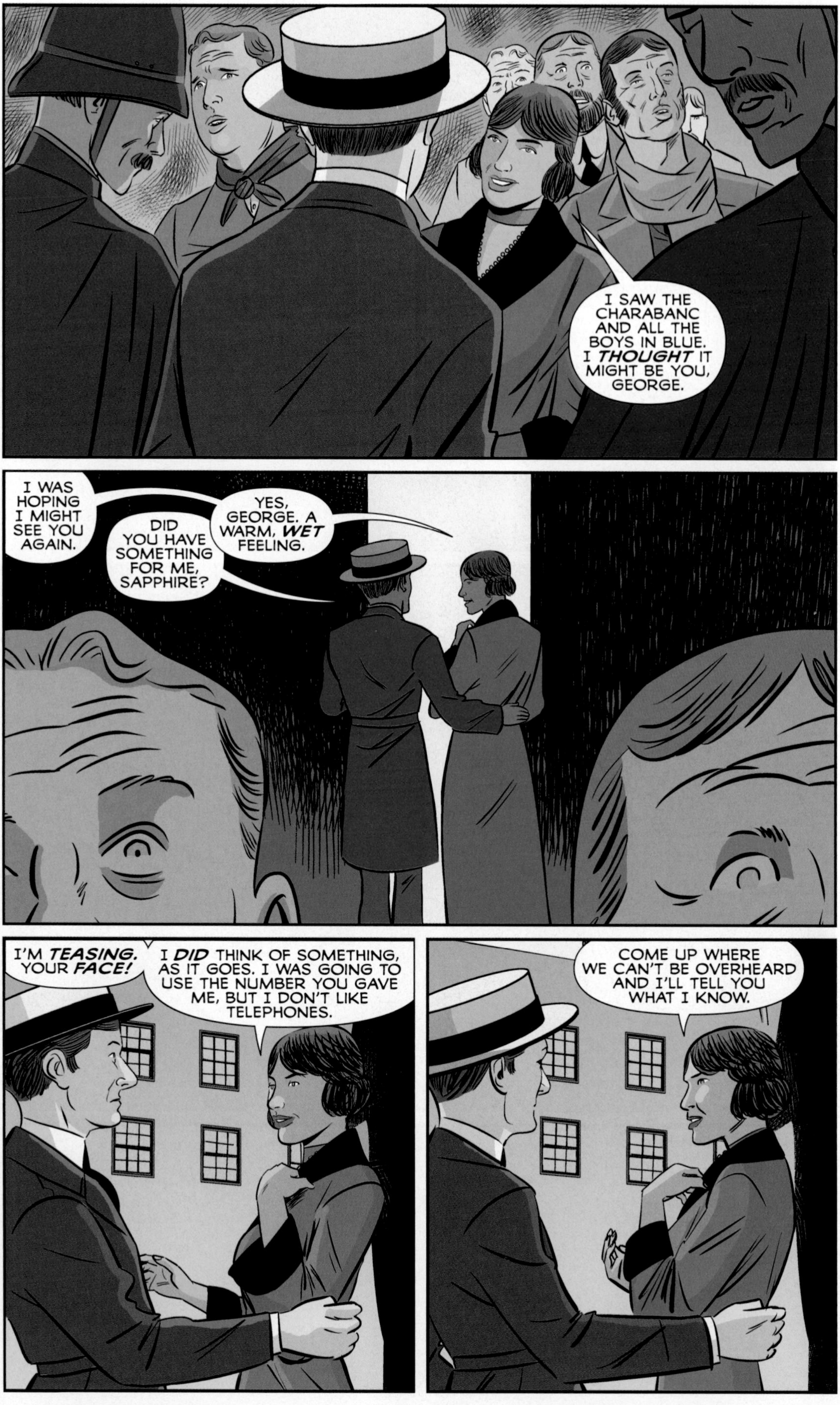
I SAW THE CHARABANC AND ALL THE BOYS IN BLUE. I *THOUGHT* IT MIGHT BE YOU, GEORGE.
I WAS HOPING I MIGHT SEE YOU AGAIN.
DID YOU HAVE SOMETHING FOR ME, SAPPHIRE?
YES, GEORGE. A WARM, *WET* FEELING.
I'M *TEASING.* YOUR *FACE!*
I *DID* THINK OF SOMETHING, AS IT GOES. I WAS GOING TO USE THE NUMBER YOU GAVE ME, BUT I DON'T LIKE TELEPHONES.
COME UP WHERE WE CAN'T BE OVERHEARD AND I'LL TELL YOU WHAT I KNOW.

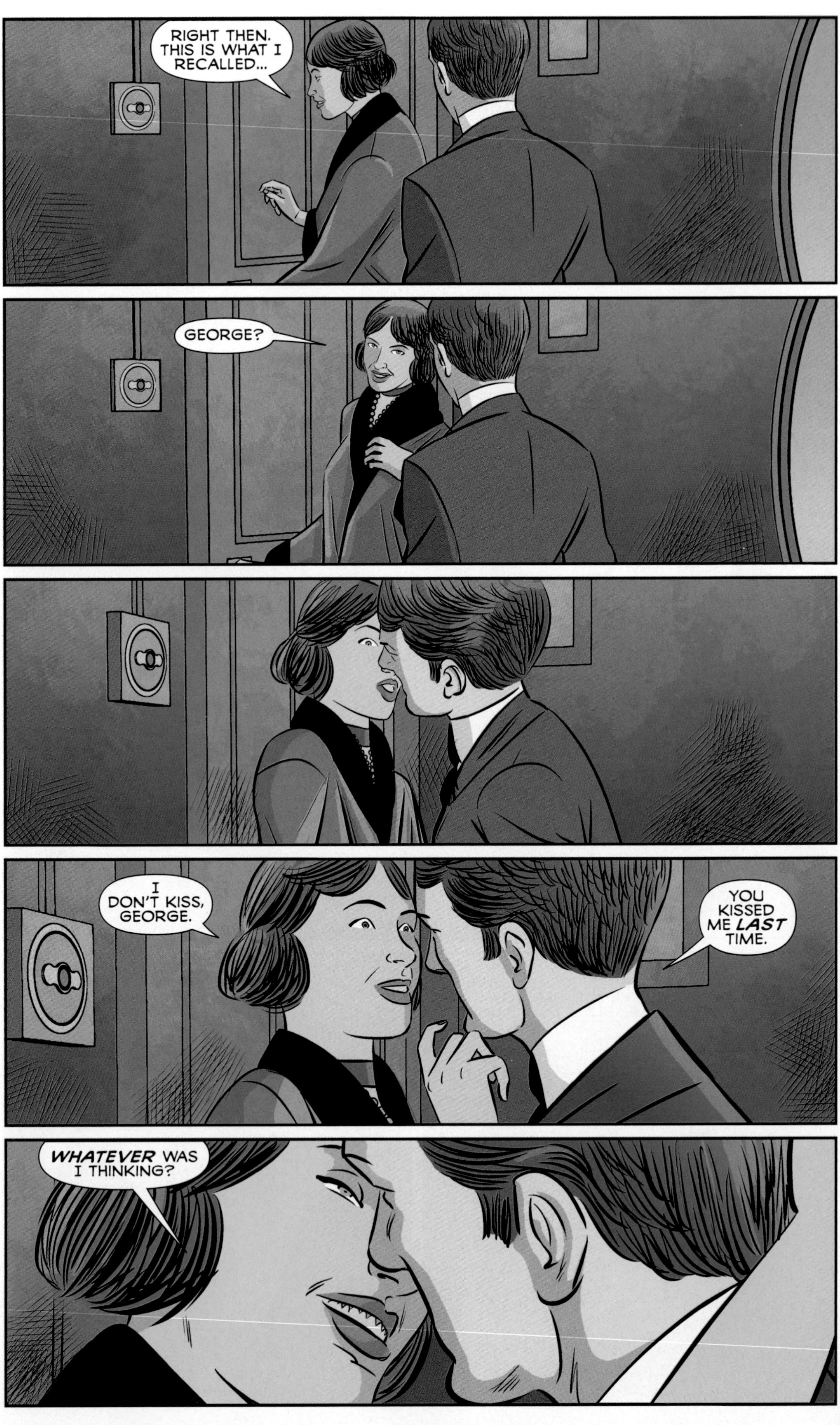
RIGHT THEN. THIS IS WHAT I RECALLED...
GEORGE?
I DON'T KISS, GEORGE.
YOU KISSED ME *LAST* TIME.
WHATEVER WAS I THINKING?

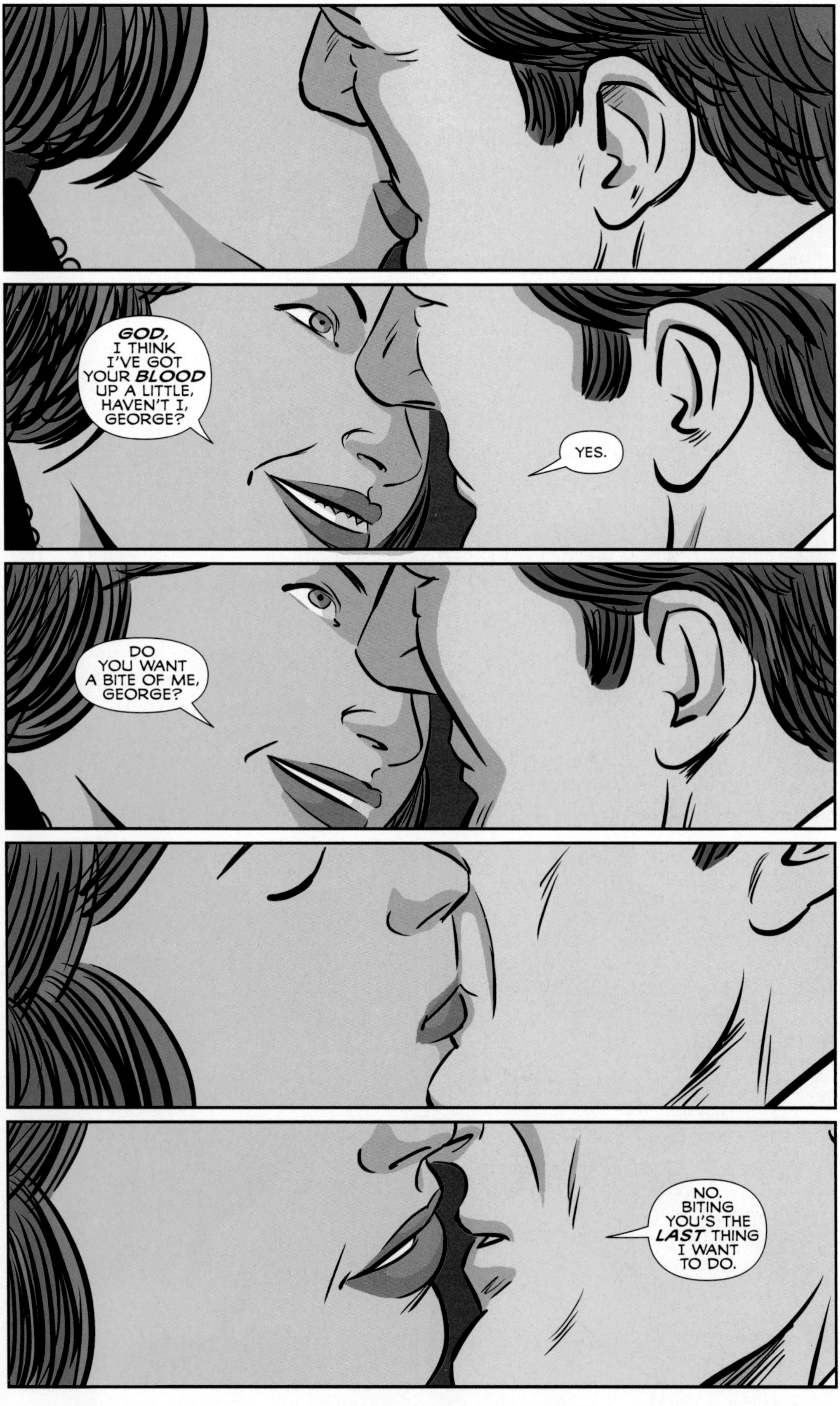
GOD, I THINK I'VE GOT YOUR BLOOD UP A LITTLE, HAVEN'T I, GEORGE?
YES.
DO YOU WANT A BITE OF ME, GEORGE?
NO. BITING YOU'S THE LAST THING I WANT TO DO.

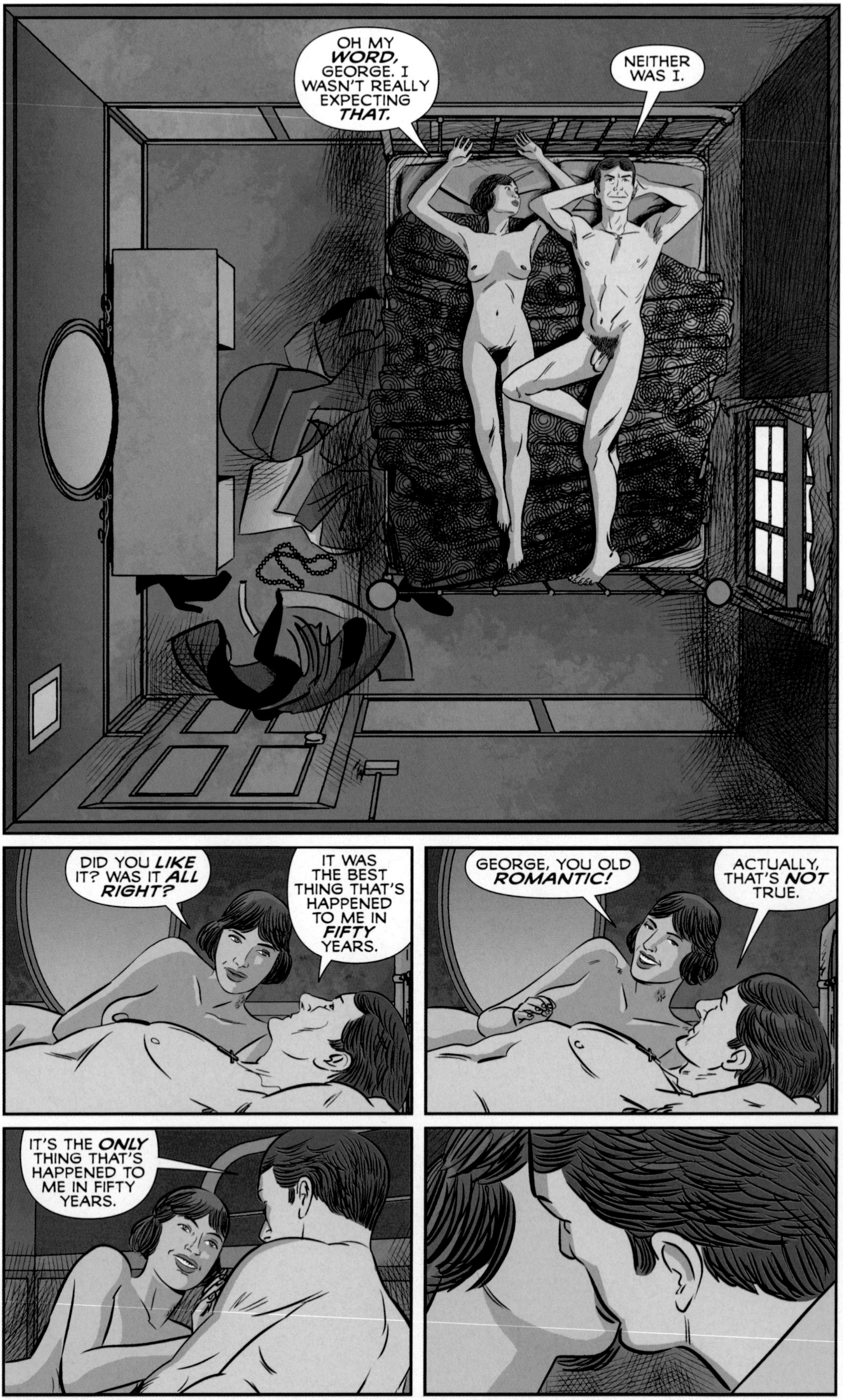
OH MY WORD, GEORGE. I WASN'T REALLY EXPECTING THAT.
NEITHER WAS I.
DID YOU LIKE IT? WAS IT ALL RIGHT?
IT WAS THE BEST THING THAT'S HAPPENED TO ME IN FIFTY YEARS.
GEORGE, YOU OLD ROMANTIC!
ACTUALLY, THAT'S NOT TRUE.
IT'S THE ONLY THING THAT'S HAPPENED TO ME IN FIFTY YEARS.

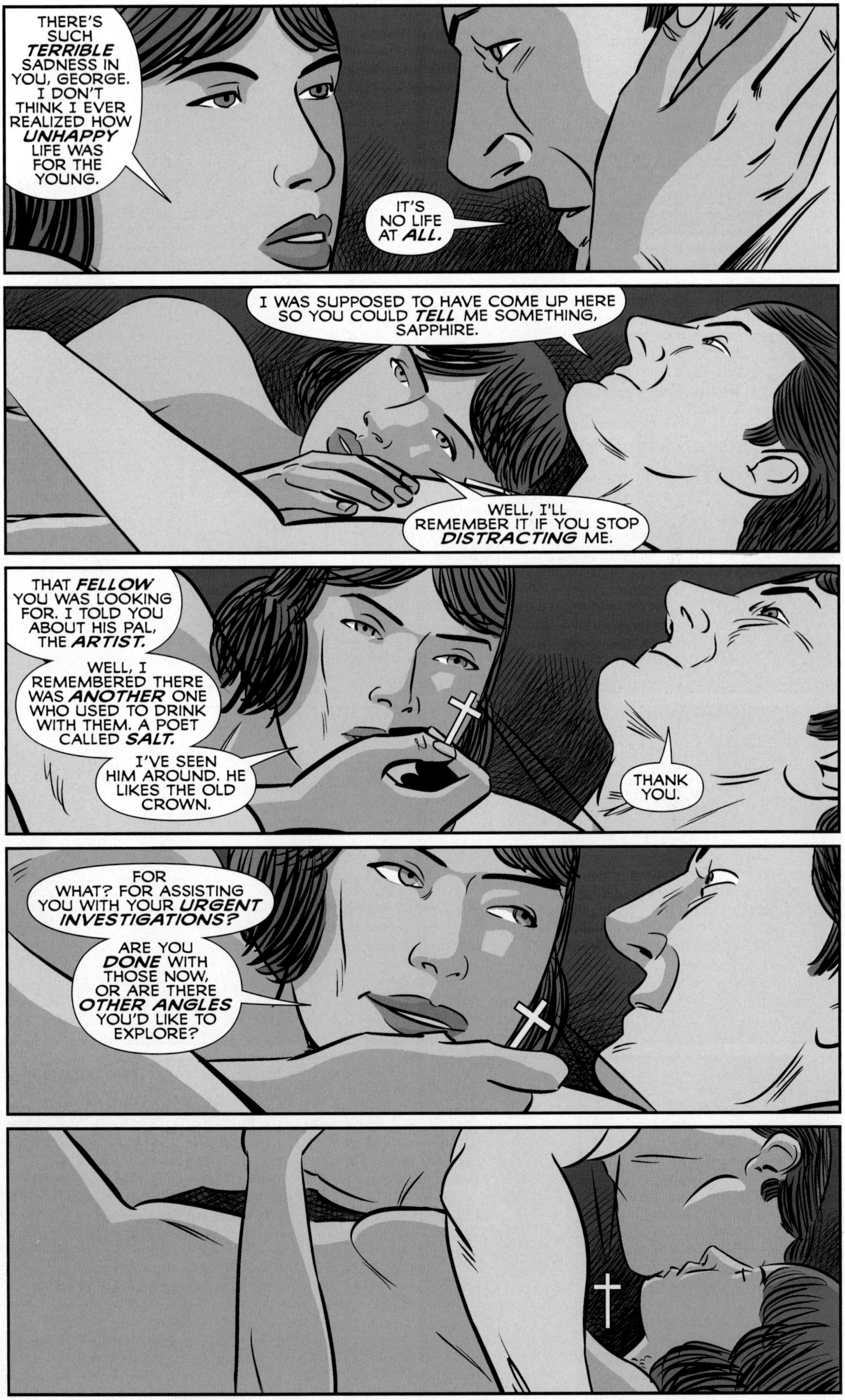
THERE'S SUCH TERRIBLE SADNESS IN YOU, GEORGE. I DON'T THINK I EVER REALIZED HOW UNHAPPY LIFE WAS FOR THE YOUNG.
IT'S NO LIFE AT ALL.
I WAS SUPPOSED TO HAVE COME UP HERE SO YOU COULD TELL ME SOMETHING, SAPPHIRE.
WELL, I'LL REMEMBER IT IF YOU STOP DISTRACTING ME.
THAT FELLOW YOU WAS LOOKING FOR. I TOLD YOU ABOUT HIS PAL, THE ARTIST.
WELL, I REMEMBERED THERE WAS ANOTHER ONE WHO USED TO DRINK WITH THEM. A POET CALLED SALT.
I'VE SEEN HIM AROUND. HE LIKES THE OLD CROWN.
THANK YOU.
FOR WHAT? FOR ASSISTING YOU WITH YOUR URGENT INVESTIGATIONS?
ARE YOU DONE WITH THOSE NOW, OR ARE THERE OTHER ANGLES YOU'D LIKE TO EXPLORE?

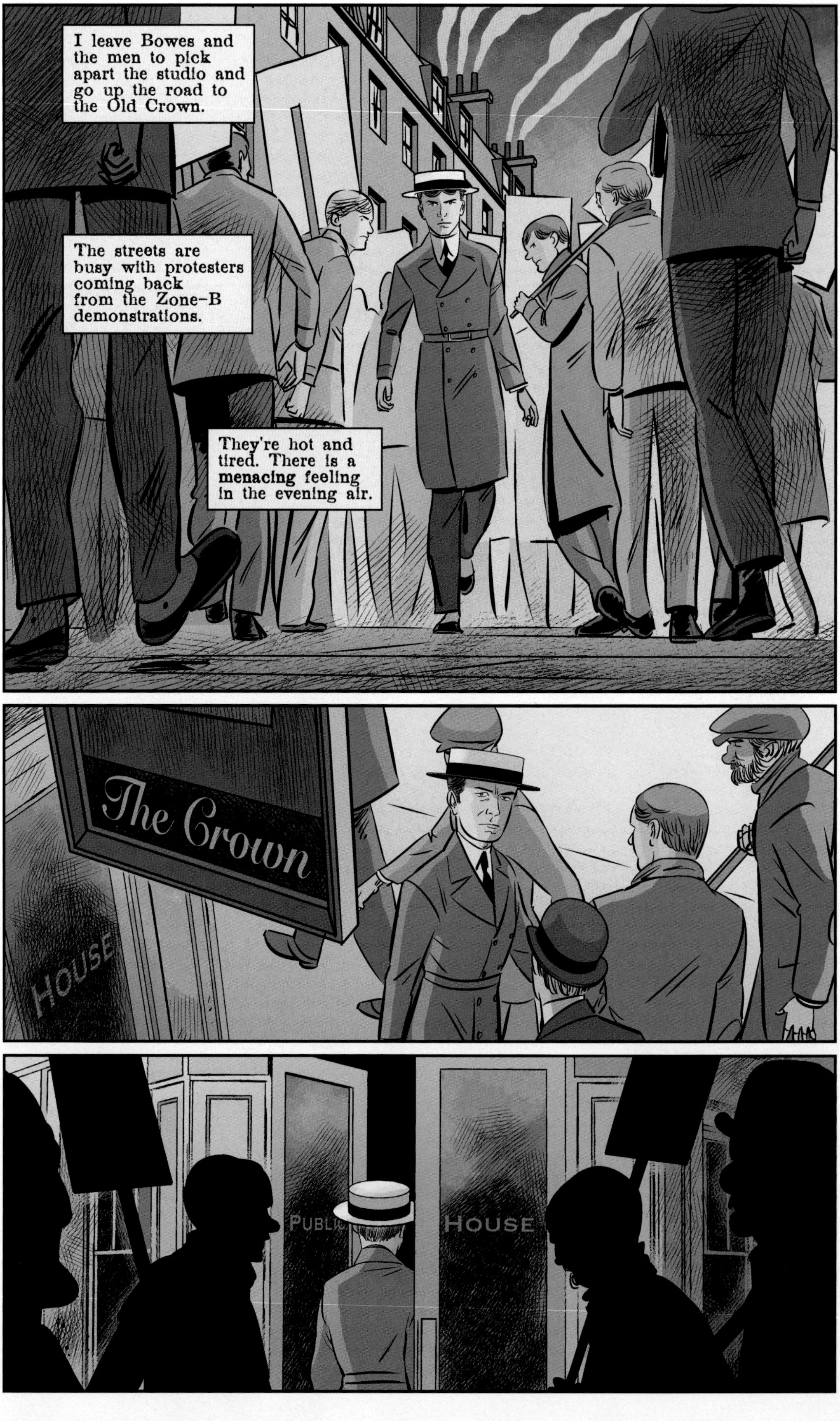
I leave Bowes and the men to pick apart the studio and go up the road to the Old Crown.
The streets are busy with protesters coming back from the Zone-B demonstrations.
They're hot and tired. There is a **menacing** feeling in the evening air.
The Crown
HOUSE
PUBLIC
HOUSE

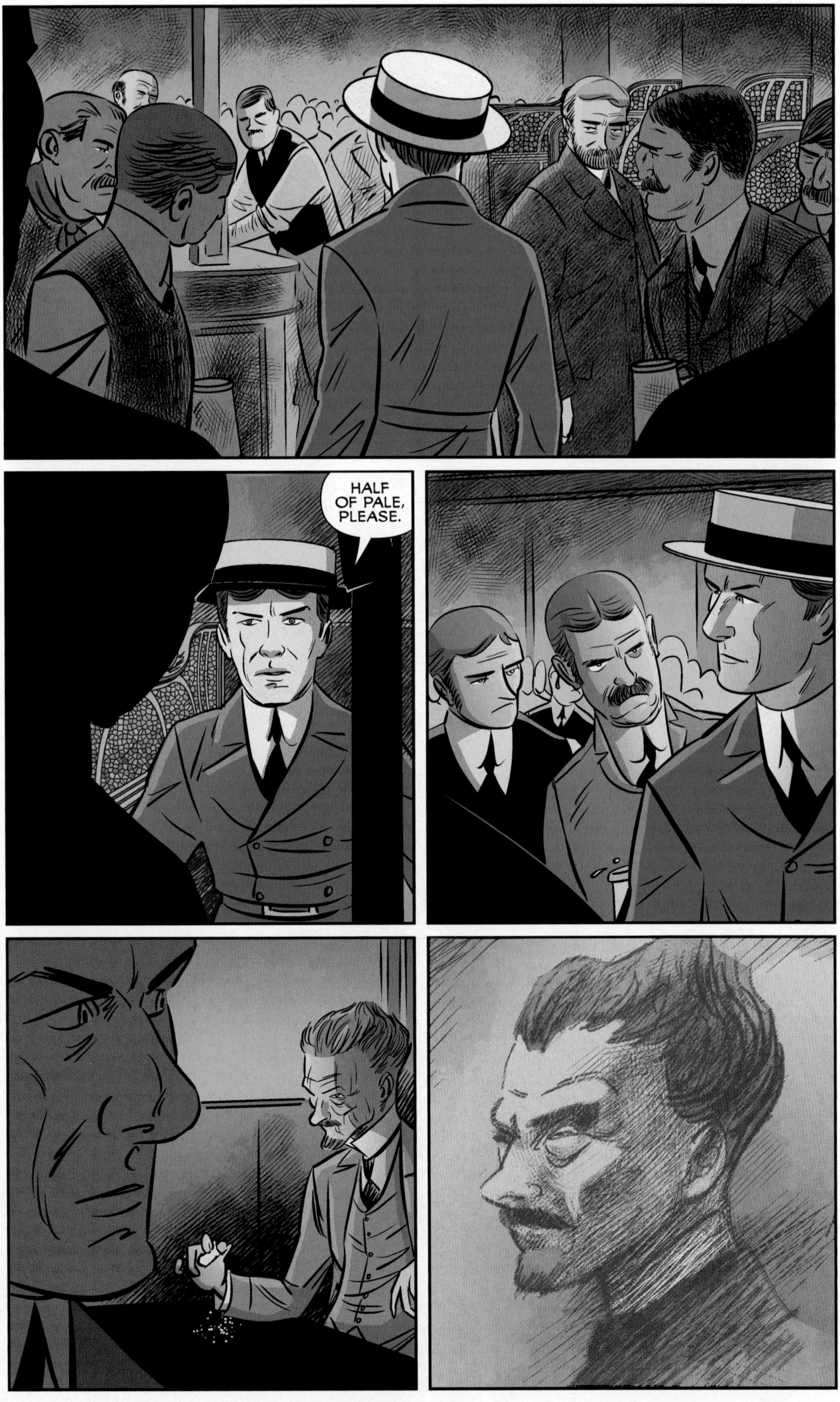
HALF
OF PALE,
PLEASE.

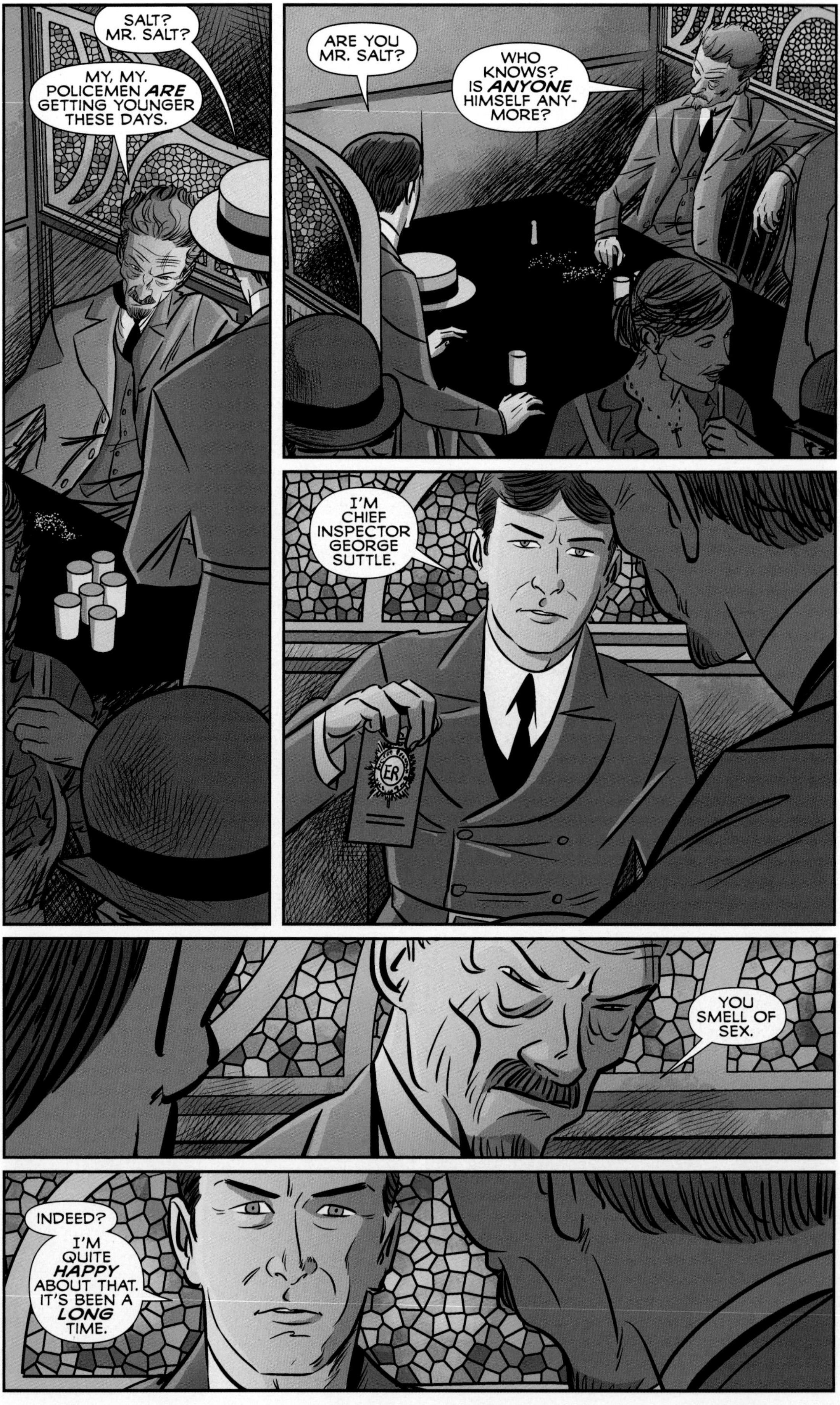
SALT? MR. SALT?
MY, MY. POLICEMEN ARE GETTING YOUNGER THESE DAYS.
ARE YOU MR. SALT?
WHO KNOWS? IS ANYONE HIMSELF ANY-MORE?
I'M CHIEF INSPECTOR GEORGE SUTTLE.
YOU SMELL OF SEX.
INDEED?
I'M QUITE HAPPY ABOUT THAT. IT'S BEEN A LONG TIME.

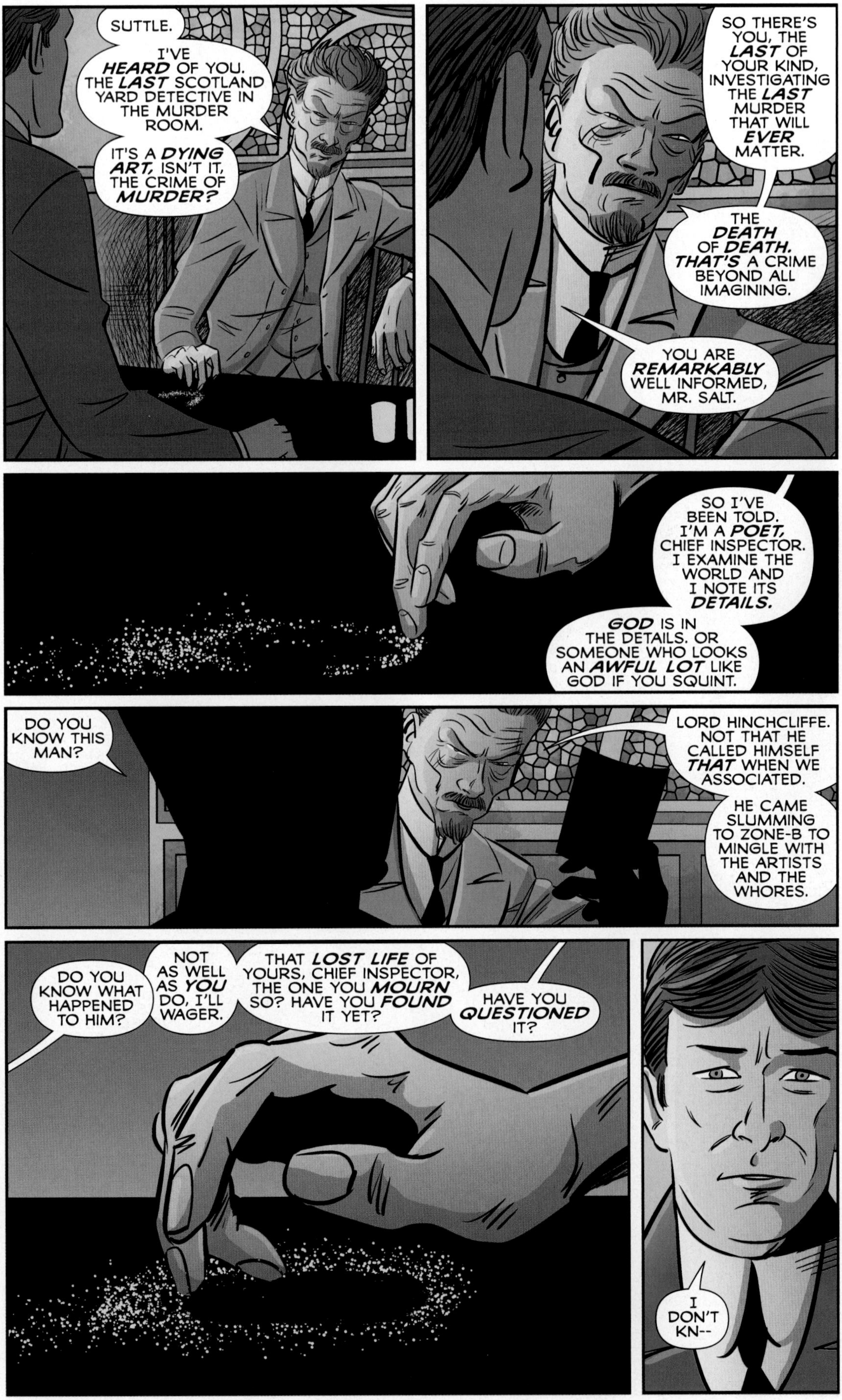
SUTTLE.
I'VE HEARD OF YOU. THE LAST SCOTLAND YARD DETECTIVE IN THE MURDER ROOM.
IT'S A DYING ART, ISN'T IT, THE CRIME OF MURDER?
SO THERE'S YOU, THE LAST OF YOUR KIND, INVESTIGATING THE LAST MURDER THAT WILL EVER MATTER.
THE DEATH OF DEATH. THAT'S A CRIME BEYOND ALL IMAGINING.
YOU ARE REMARKABLY WELL INFORMED, MR. SALT.
SO I'VE BEEN TOLD. I'M A POET, CHIEF INSPECTOR. I EXAMINE THE WORLD AND I NOTE ITS DETAILS.
GOD IS IN THE DETAILS. OR SOMEONE WHO LOOKS AN AWFUL LOT LIKE GOD IF YOU SQUINT.
DO YOU KNOW THIS MAN?
LORD HINCHCLIFFE. NOT THAT HE CALLED HIMSELF THAT WHEN WE ASSOCIATED.
HE CAME SLUMMING TO ZONE-B TO MINGLE WITH THE ARTISTS AND THE WHORES.
DO YOU KNOW WHAT HAPPENED TO HIM?
NOT AS WELL AS YOU DO, I'LL WAGER.
THAT LOST LIFE OF YOURS, CHIEF INSPECTOR, THE ONE YOU MOURN SO? HAVE YOU FOUND IT YET?
HAVE YOU QUESTIONED IT?
I DON'T KN--

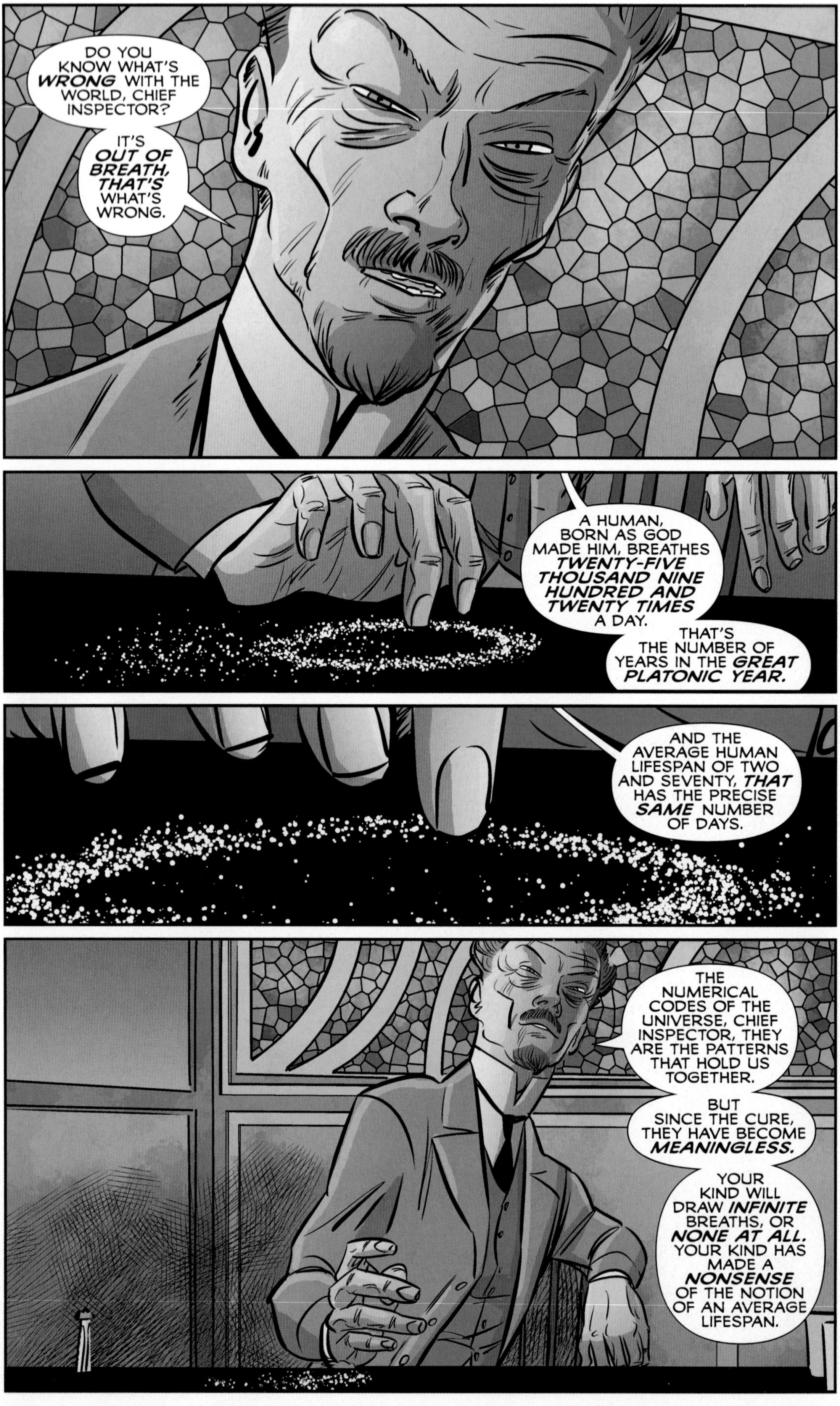
DO YOU KNOW WHAT'S WRONG WITH THE WORLD, CHIEF INSPECTOR?
IT'S OUT OF BREATH, THAT'S WHAT'S WRONG.
A HUMAN, BORN AS GOD MADE HIM, BREATHES TWENTY-FIVE THOUSAND NINE HUNDRED AND TWENTY TIMES A DAY.
THAT'S THE NUMBER OF YEARS IN THE GREAT PLATONIC YEAR.
AND THE AVERAGE HUMAN LIFESPAN OF TWO AND SEVENTY, THAT HAS THE PRECISE SAME NUMBER OF DAYS.
THE NUMERICAL CODES OF THE UNIVERSE, CHIEF INSPECTOR, THEY ARE THE PATTERNS THAT HOLD US TOGETHER.
BUT SINCE THE CURE, THEY HAVE BECOME MEANINGLESS.
YOUR KIND WILL DRAW INFINITE BREATHS, OR NONE AT ALL. YOUR KIND HAS MADE A NONSENSE OF THE NOTION OF AN AVERAGE LIFESPAN.

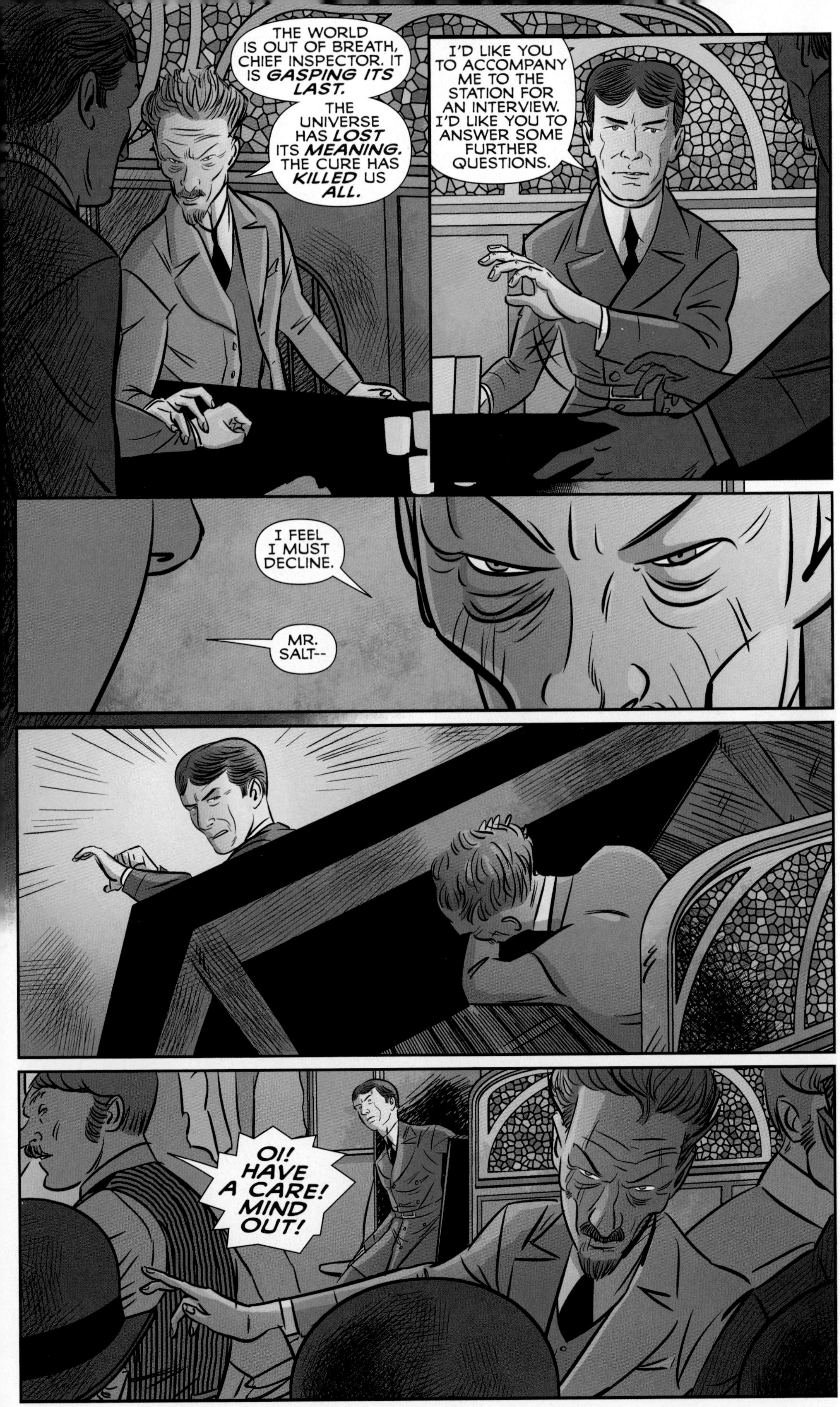
THE WORLD IS OUT OF BREATH, CHIEF INSPECTOR. IT IS GASPING ITS LAST.
THE UNIVERSE HAS LOST ITS MEANING. THE CURE HAS KILLED US ALL.
I'D LIKE YOU TO ACCOMPANY ME TO THE STATION FOR AN INTERVIEW. I'D LIKE YOU TO ANSWER SOME FURTHER QUESTIONS.
I FEEL I MUST DECLINE.
MR. SALT--
OI! HAVE A CARE! MIND OUT!

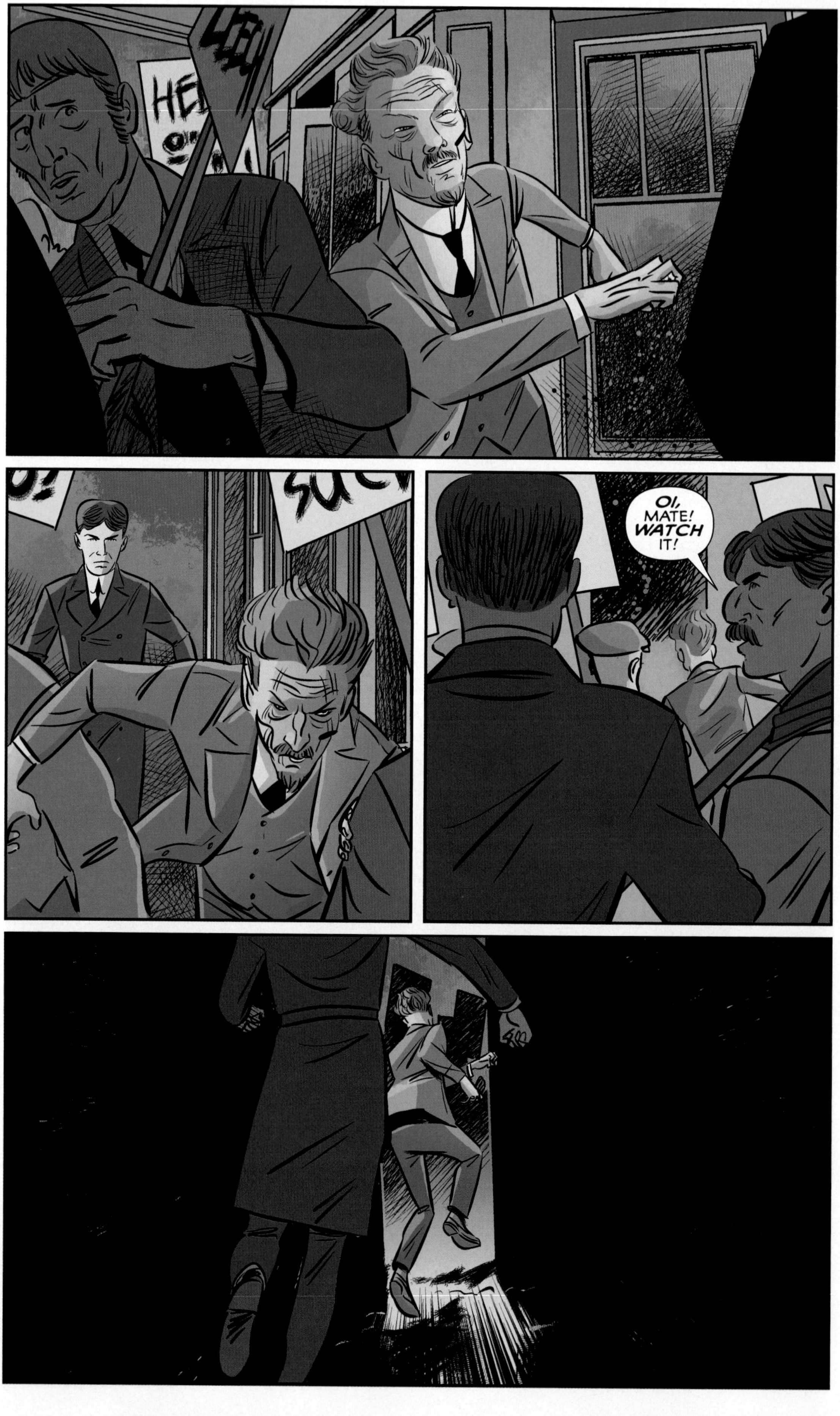
OI, MATE! WATCH IT!

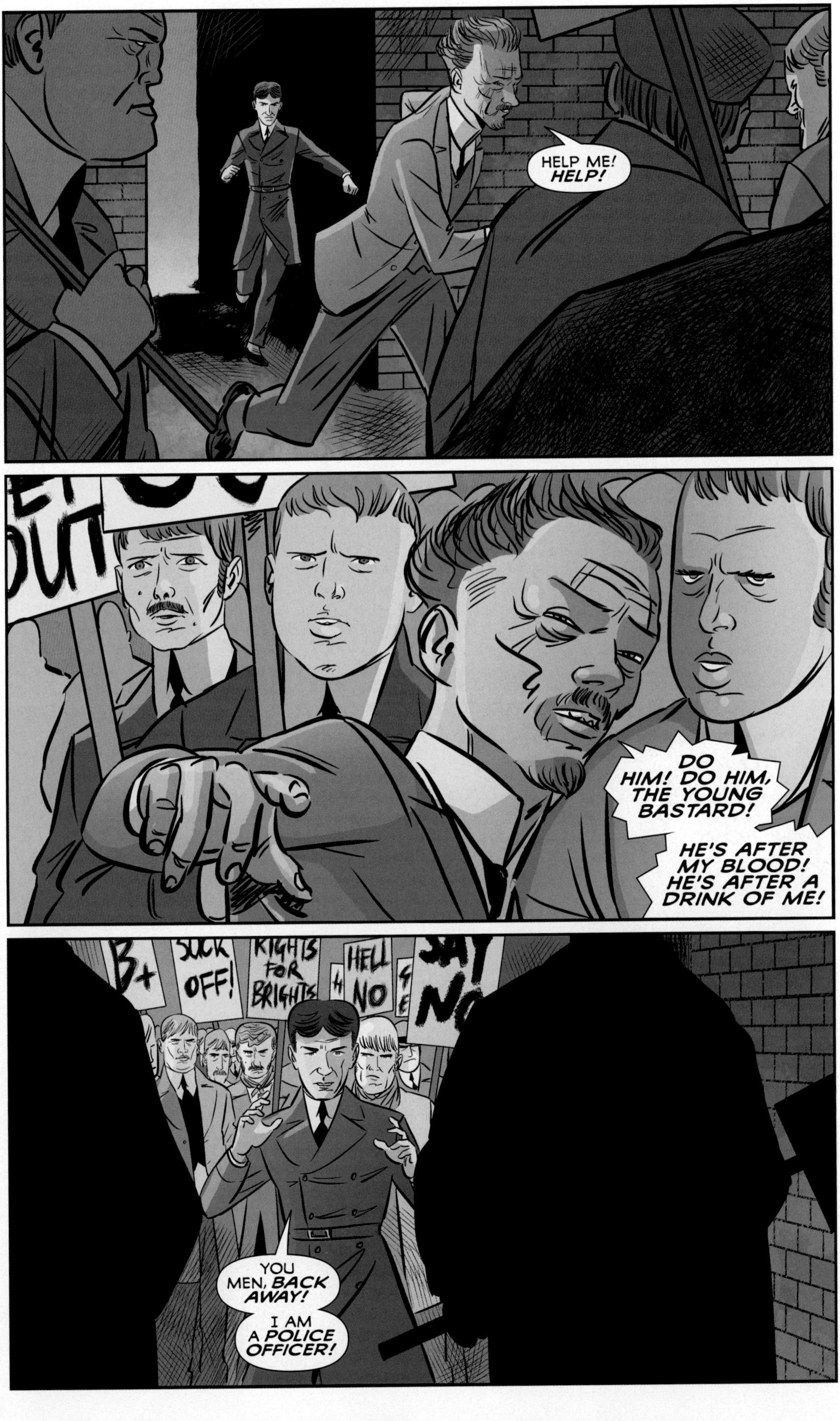
HELP ME! HELP!
DO HIM! DO HIM, THE YOUNG BASTARD!
HE'S AFTER MY BLOOD! HE'S AFTER A DRINK OF ME!
SUCK OFF!
RIGHTS FOR BRIGHTS
HELL NO
YOU MEN, BACK AWAY!
I AM A POLICE OFFICER!

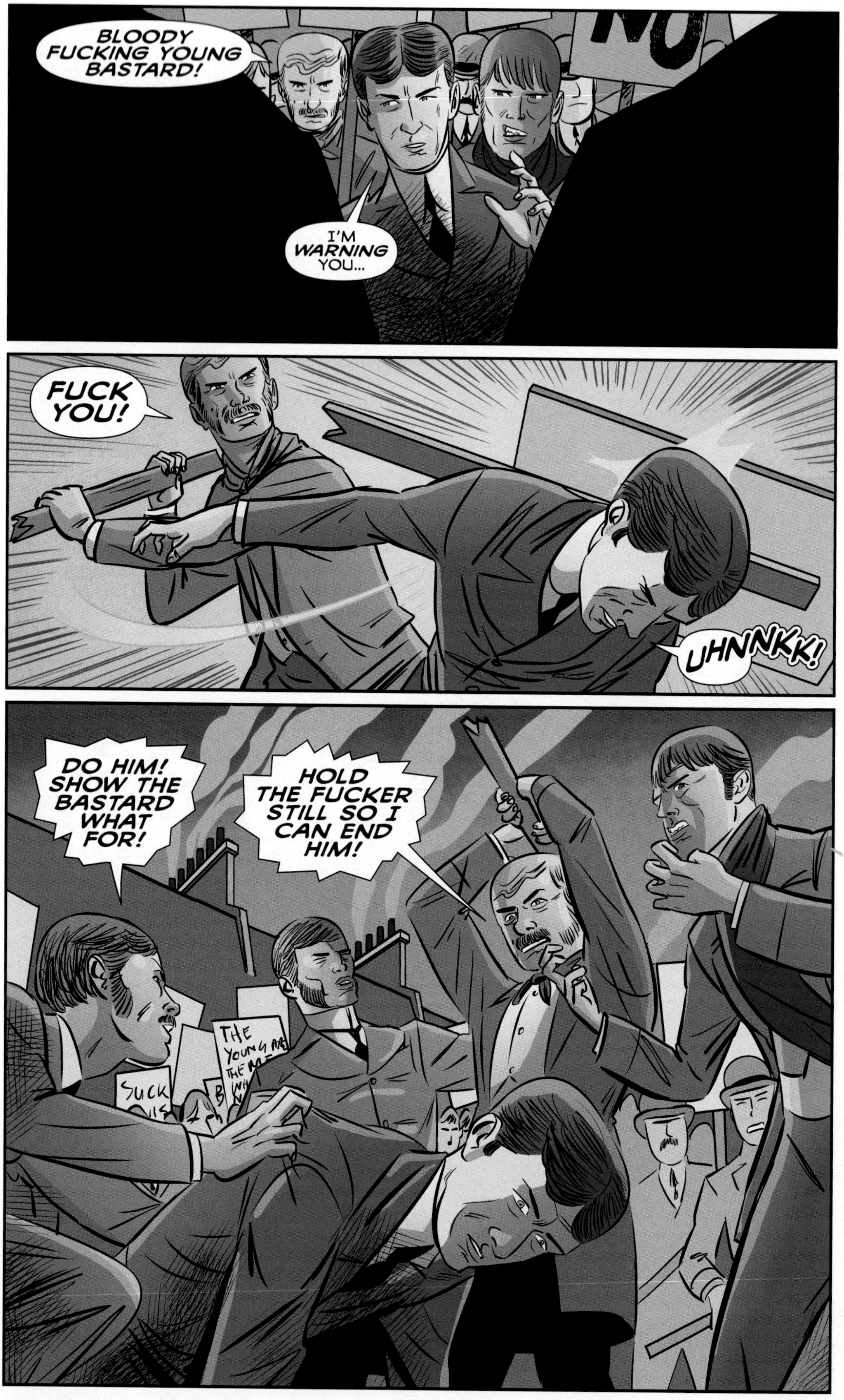
BLOODY FUCKING YOUNG BASTARD!
I'M WARNING YOU...
FUCK YOU!
UHNNKK!
DO HIM! SHOW THE BASTARD WHAT FOR!
HOLD THE FUCKER STILL SO I CAN END HIM!

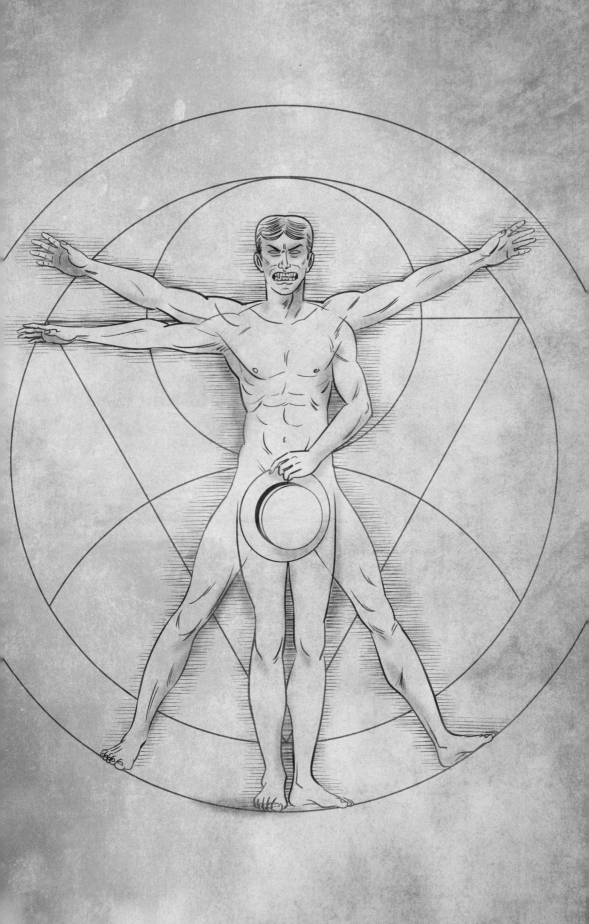

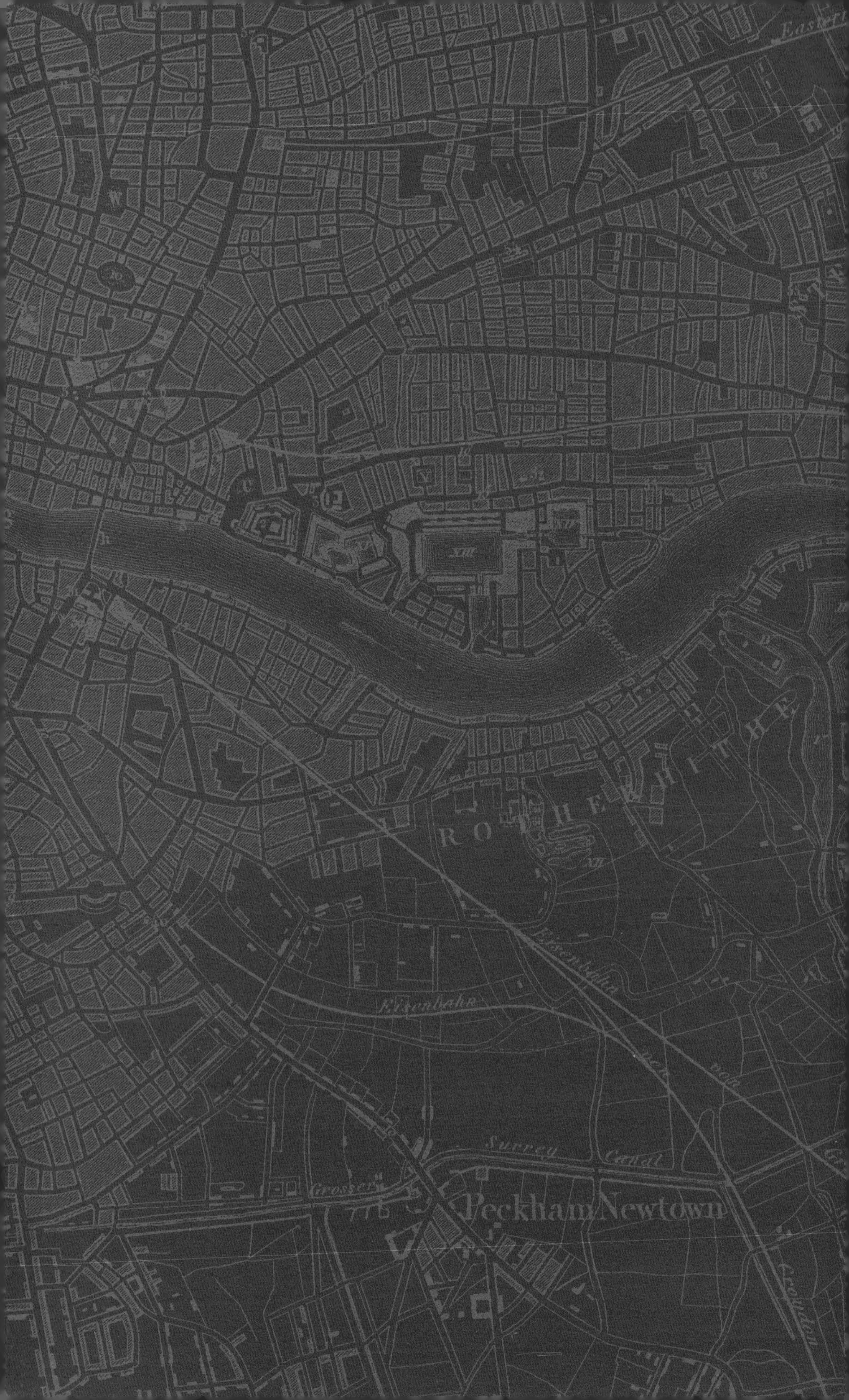

ROTHERHITHE
Eisenbahn
Surrey Canal
Grosser
Peckham Newtown

Remarks (continued).

Mobs are very easily provoked to violence.

Outside the Old Crown public house, Zone-B.

October 16th, 1910.

HOLD THE FUCKING YOUNG BASTARD DOWN!

DO NOT! DO NOT DO THIS!

I AM A POLICE OFFICER!

DESIST--

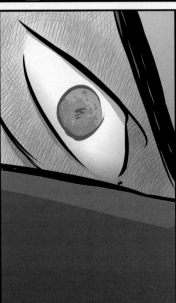

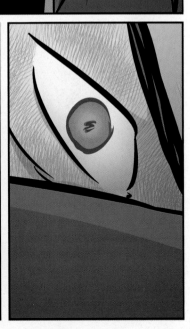

FUCK 'IM UP!

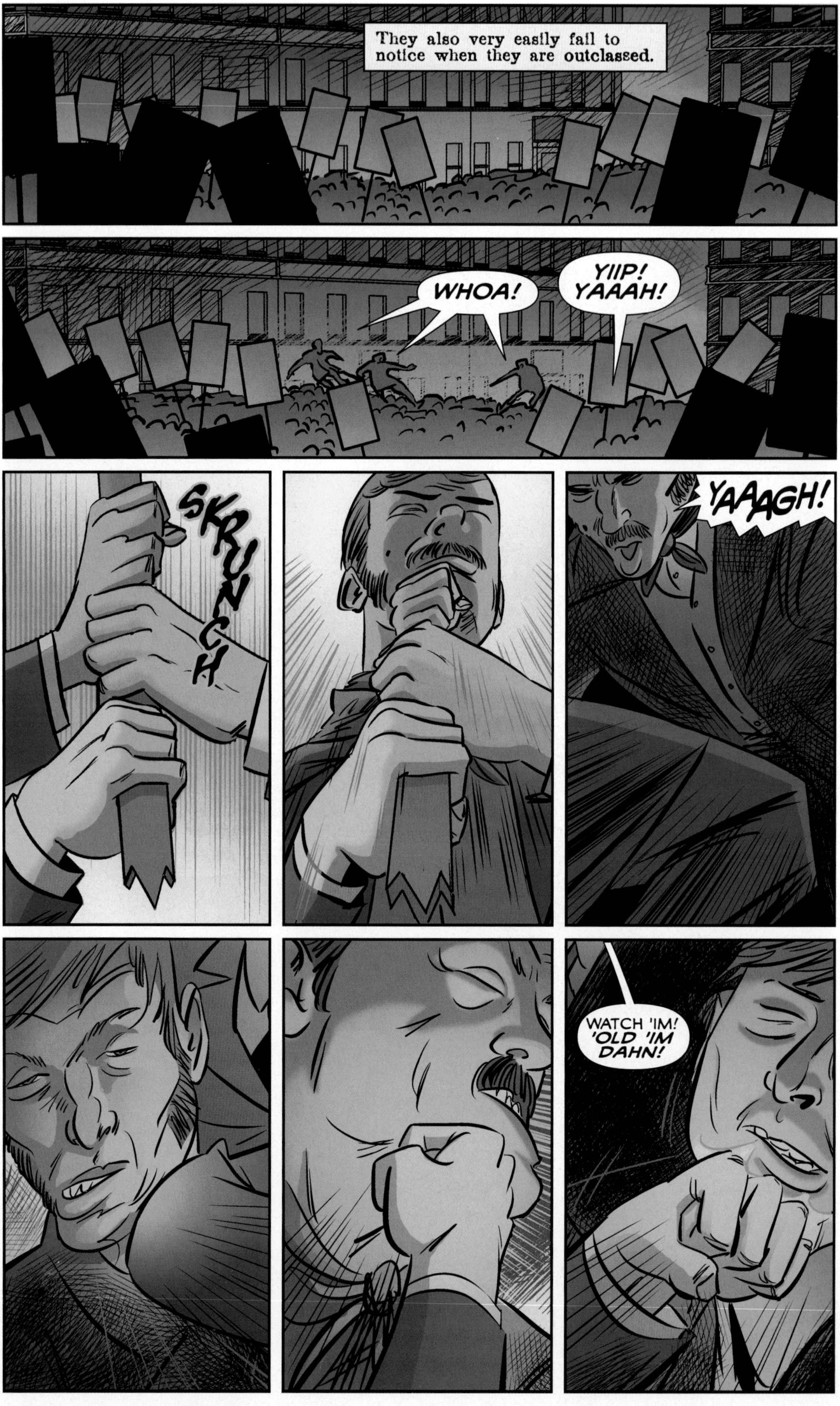
They also very easily fail to notice when they are outclassed.
WHOA!
YIIP! YAAAH!
SKRUNCH
YAAAGH!
WATCH 'IM! 'OLD 'IM DAHN!

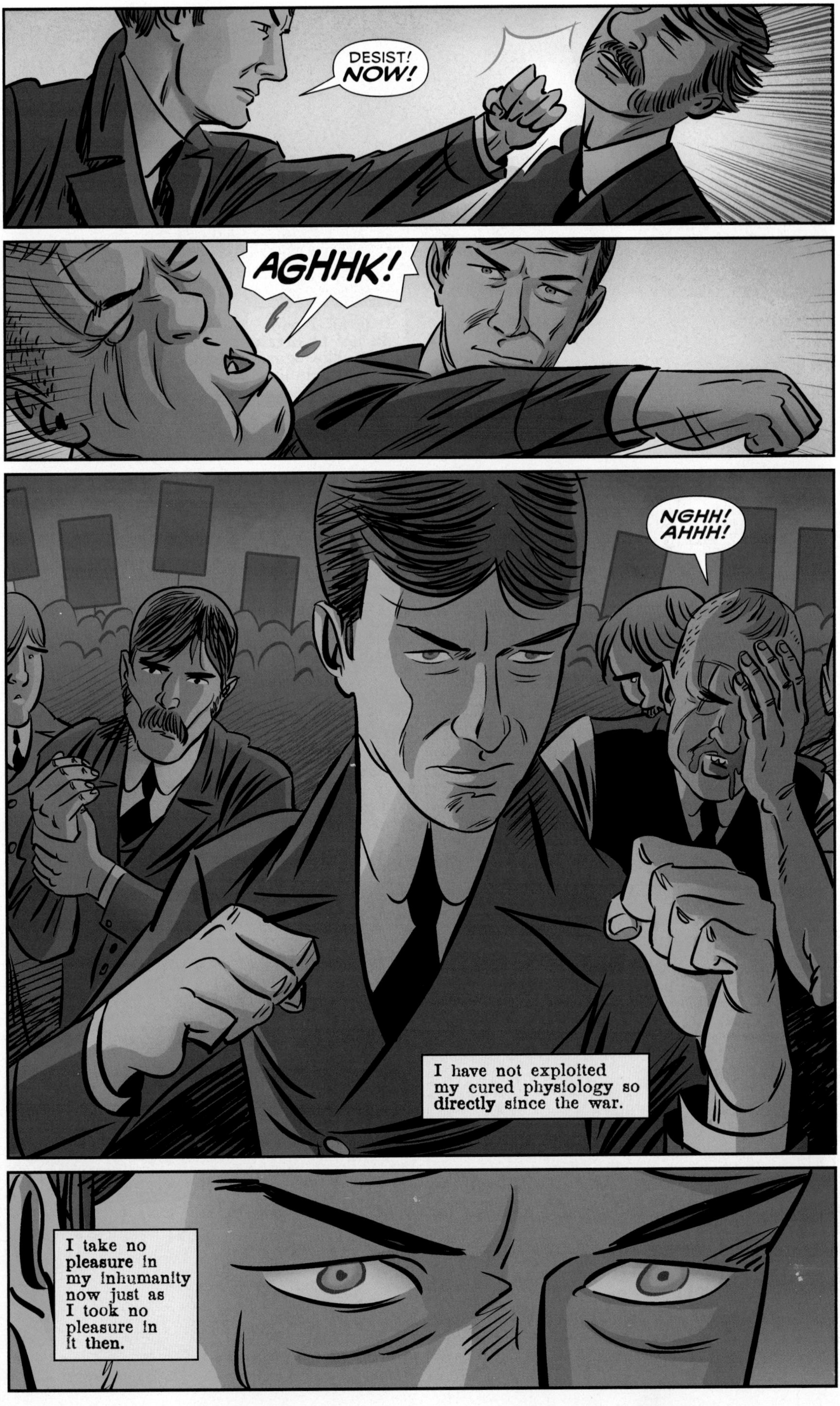

DESIST! NOW!
AGHHK!
NGHH! AHHH!
I have not exploited my cured physiology so directly since the war.
I take no pleasure in my inhumanity now just as I took no pleasure in it then.

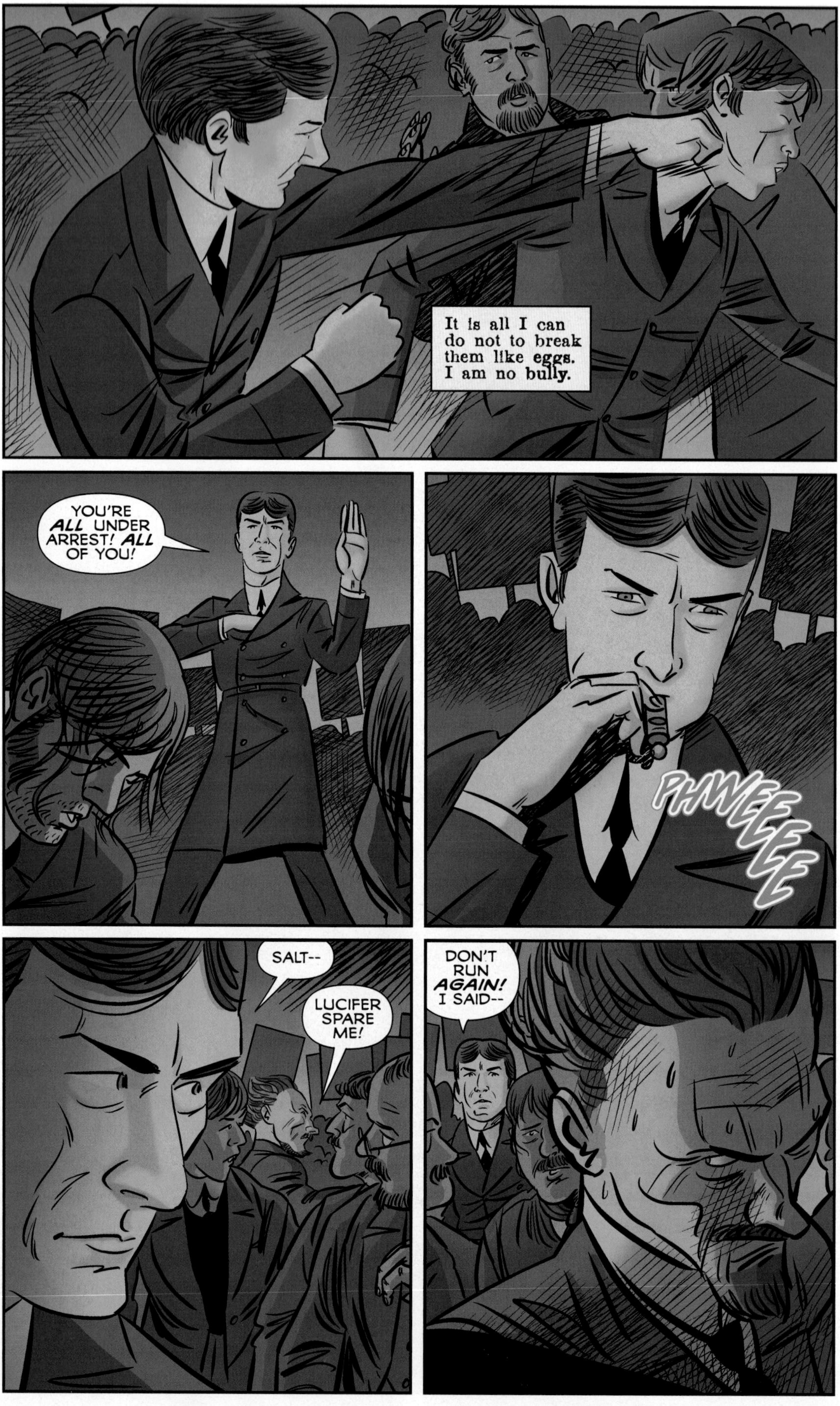
It is all I can do not to break them like eggs. I am no bully.
YOU'RE ALL UNDER ARREST! ALL OF YOU!
PHWEEEEE
SALT--
LUCIFER SPARE ME!
DON'T RUN AGAIN! I SAID--

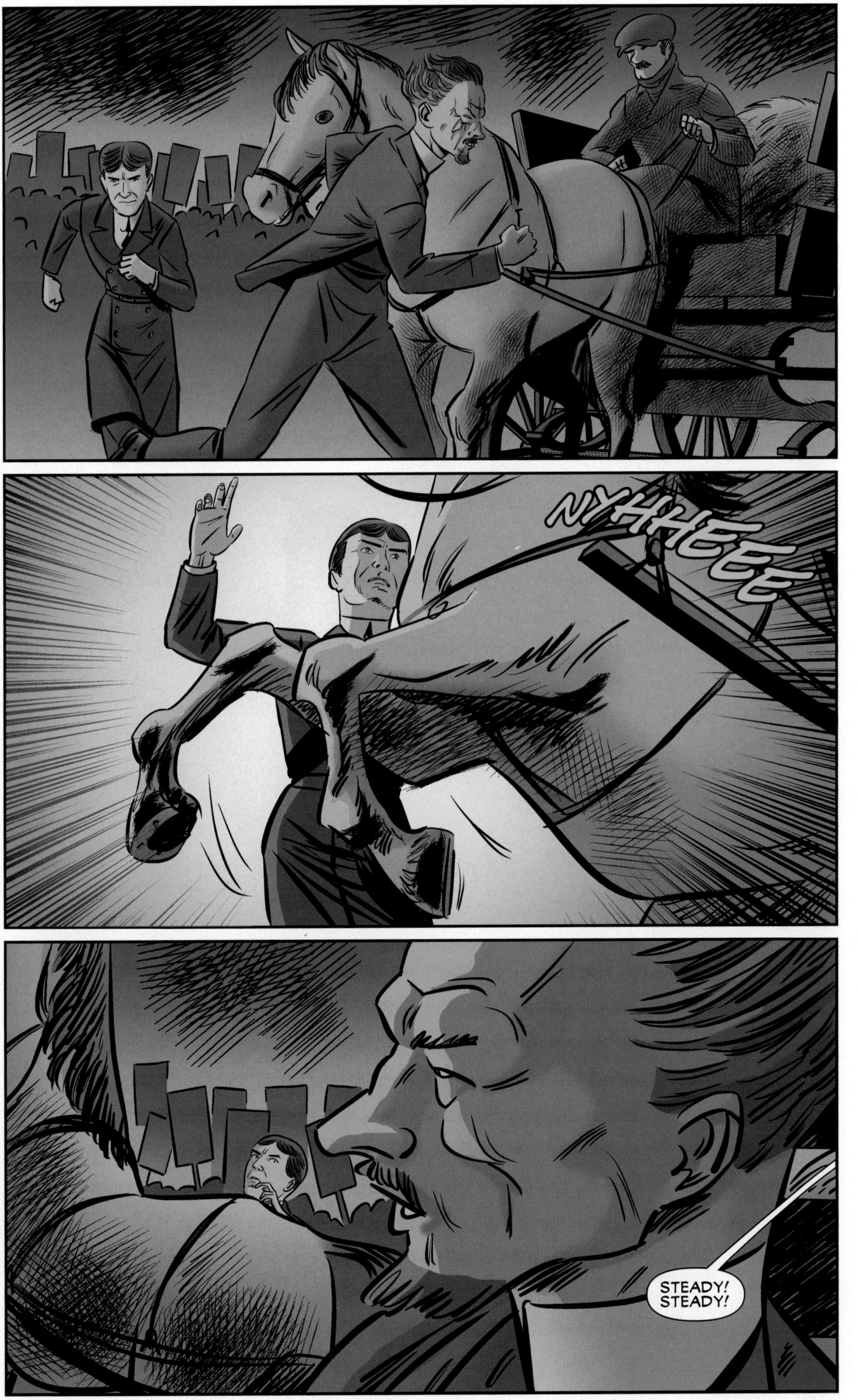
NYHHEEE
STEADY! STEADY!

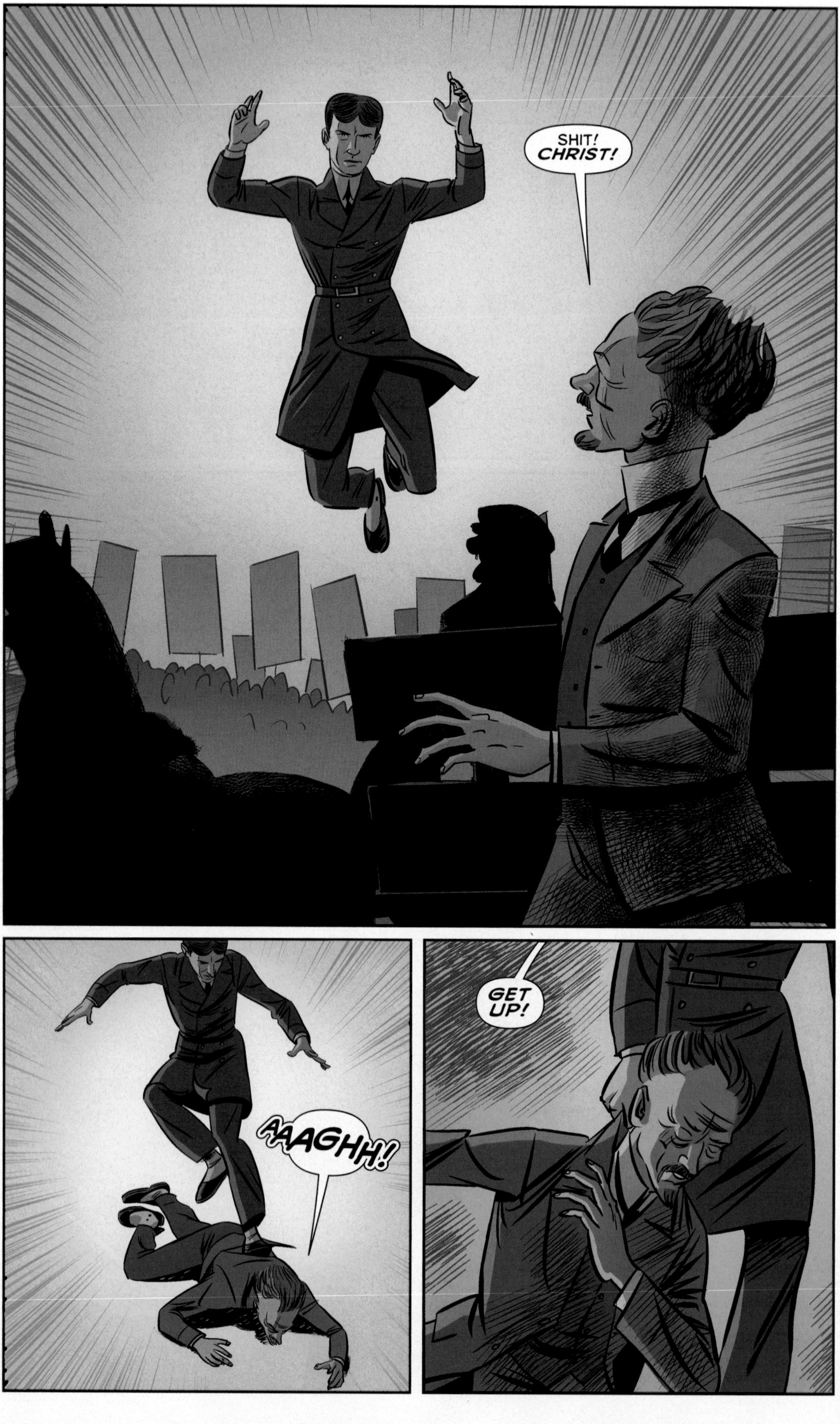

SHIT! CHRIST!
AAAGHH!
GET UP!

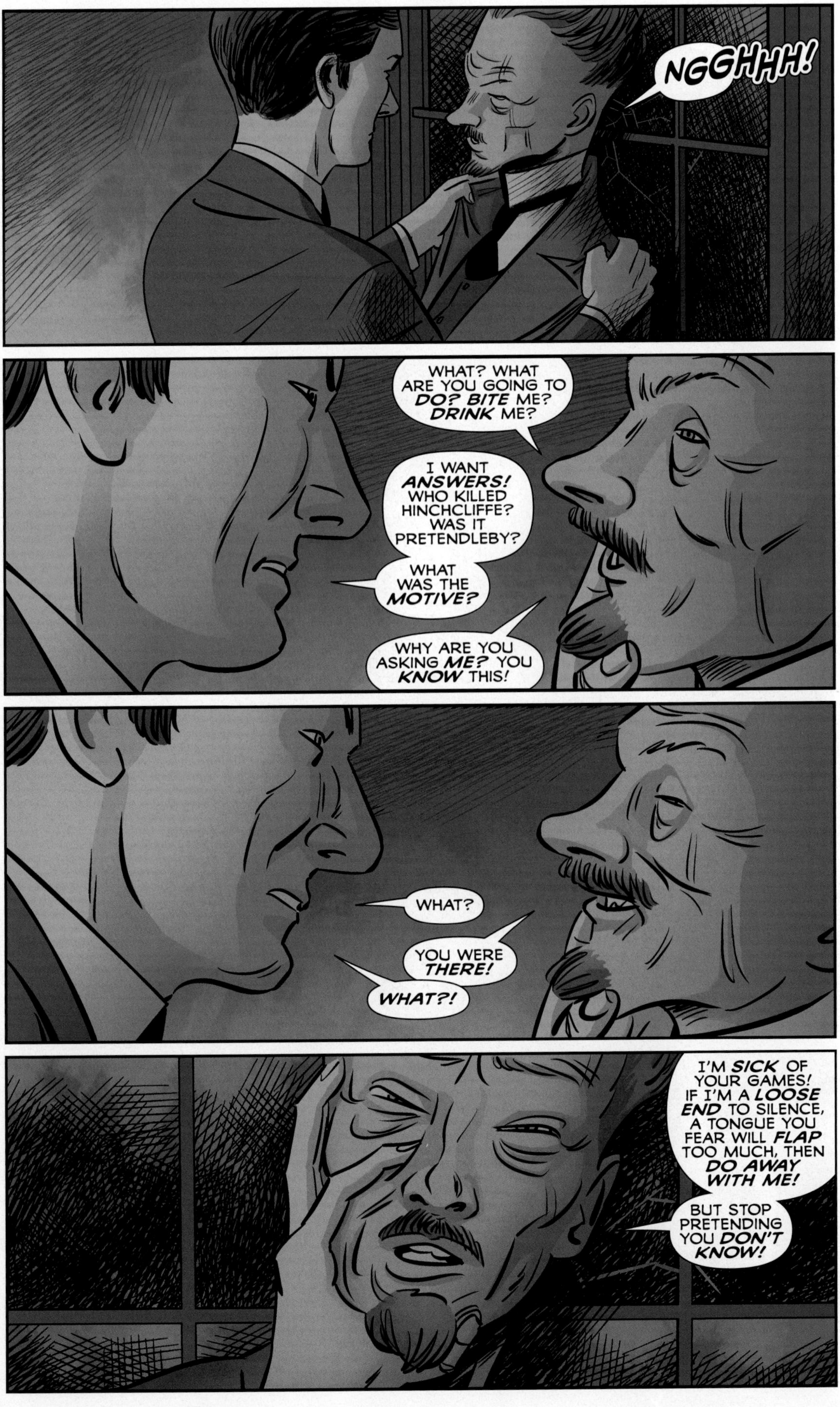
NGGHHH!
WHAT? WHAT ARE YOU GOING TO DO? BITE ME? DRINK ME?
I WANT ANSWERS! WHO KILLED HINCHCLIFFE? WAS IT PRETENDLEBY?
WHAT WAS THE MOTIVE?
WHY ARE YOU ASKING ME? YOU KNOW THIS!
WHAT?
YOU WERE THERE!
WHAT?!
I'M SICK OF YOUR GAMES! IF I'M A LOOSE END TO SILENCE, A TONGUE YOU FEAR WILL FLAP TOO MUCH, THEN DO AWAY WITH ME!
BUT STOP PRETENDING YOU DON'T KNOW!

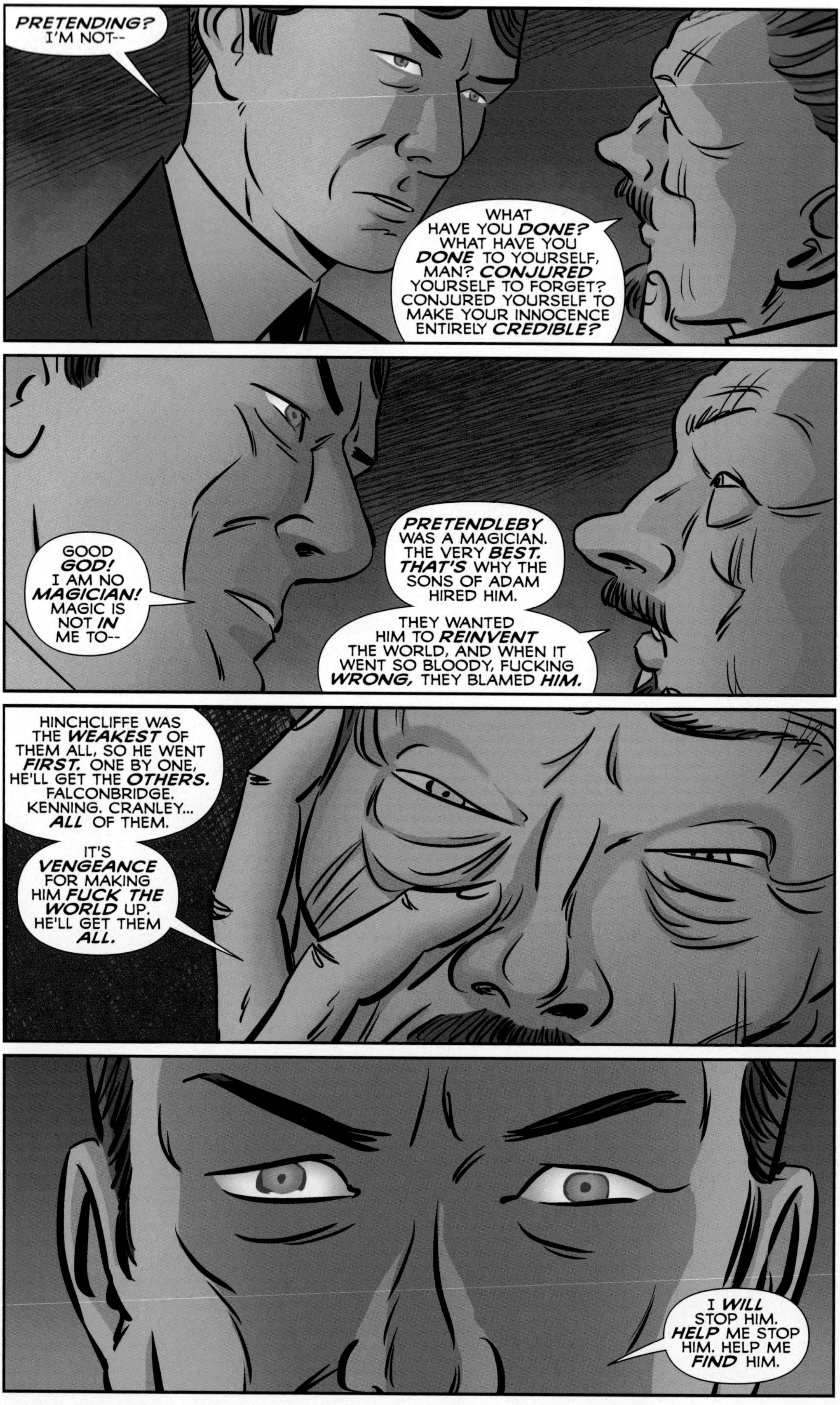
PRETENDING? I'M NOT--
WHAT HAVE YOU DONE? WHAT HAVE YOU DONE TO YOURSELF, MAN? CONJURED YOURSELF TO FORGET? CONJURED YOURSELF TO MAKE YOUR INNOCENCE ENTIRELY CREDIBLE?
GOOD GOD! I AM NO MAGICIAN! MAGIC IS NOT IN ME TO--
PRETENDLEBY WAS A MAGICIAN. THE VERY BEST. THAT'S WHY THE SONS OF ADAM HIRED HIM.
THEY WANTED HIM TO REINVENT THE WORLD, AND WHEN IT WENT SO BLOODY, FUCKING WRONG, THEY BLAMED HIM.
HINCHCLIFFE WAS THE WEAKEST OF THEM ALL, SO HE WENT FIRST. ONE BY ONE, HE'LL GET THE OTHERS. FALCONBRIDGE. KENNING. CRANLEY... ALL OF THEM.
IT'S VENGEANCE FOR MAKING HIM FUCK THE WORLD UP. HE'LL GET THEM ALL.
I WILL STOP HIM. HELP ME STOP HIM. HELP ME FIND HIM.

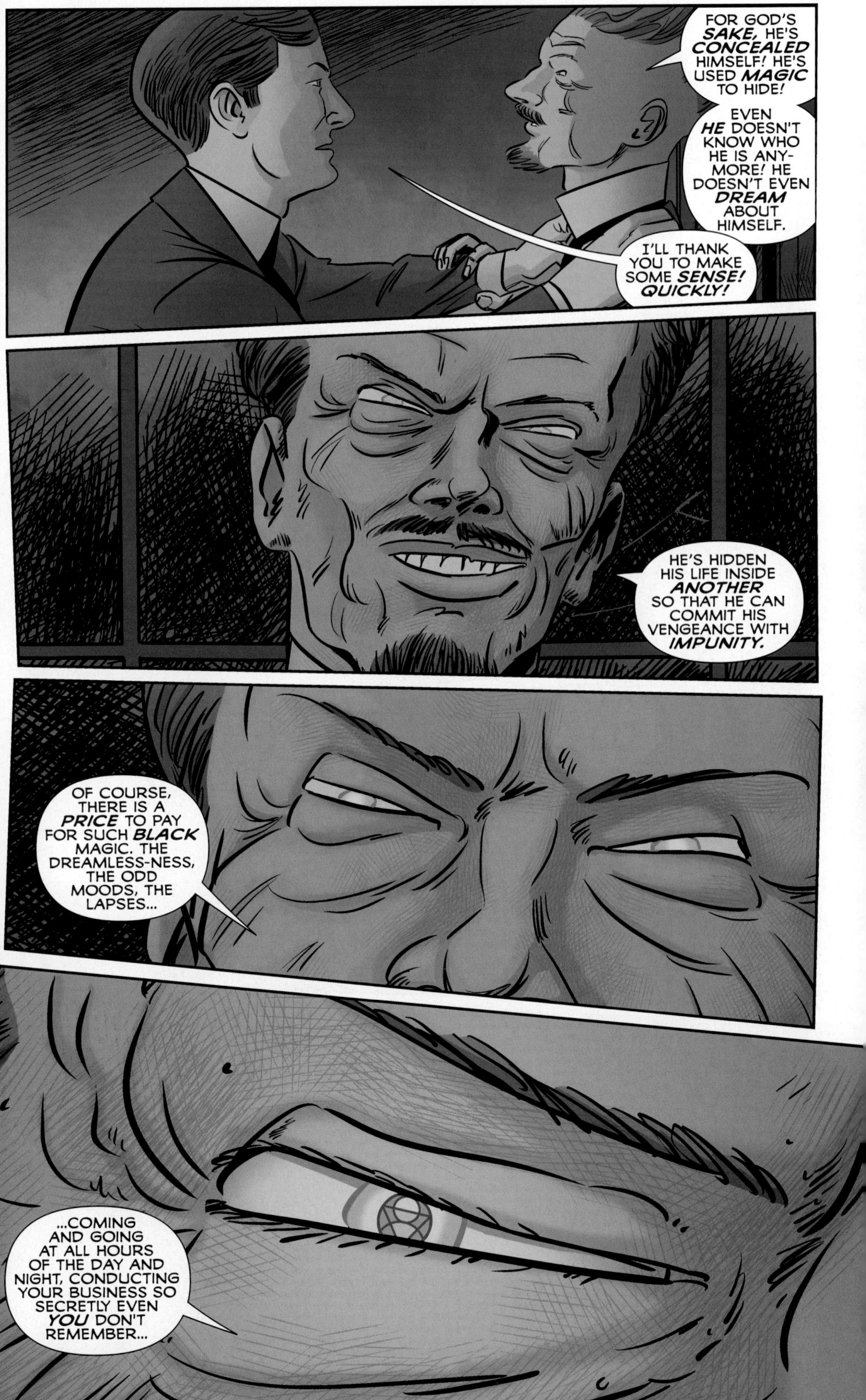
FOR GOD'S SAKE, HE'S CONCEALED HIMSELF! HE'S USED MAGIC TO HIDE!
EVEN HE DOESN'T KNOW WHO HE IS ANY-MORE! HE DOESN'T EVEN DREAM ABOUT HIMSELF.
I'LL THANK YOU TO MAKE SOME SENSE! QUICKLY!
HE'S HIDDEN HIS LIFE INSIDE ANOTHER SO THAT HE CAN COMMIT HIS VENGEANCE WITH IMPUNITY.
OF COURSE, THERE IS A PRICE TO PAY FOR SUCH BLACK MAGIC. THE DREAMLESS-NESS, THE ODD MOODS, THE LAPSES...
...COMING AND GOING AT ALL HOURS OF THE DAY AND NIGHT, CONDUCTING YOUR BUSINESS SO SECRETLY EVEN YOU DON'T REMEMBER...

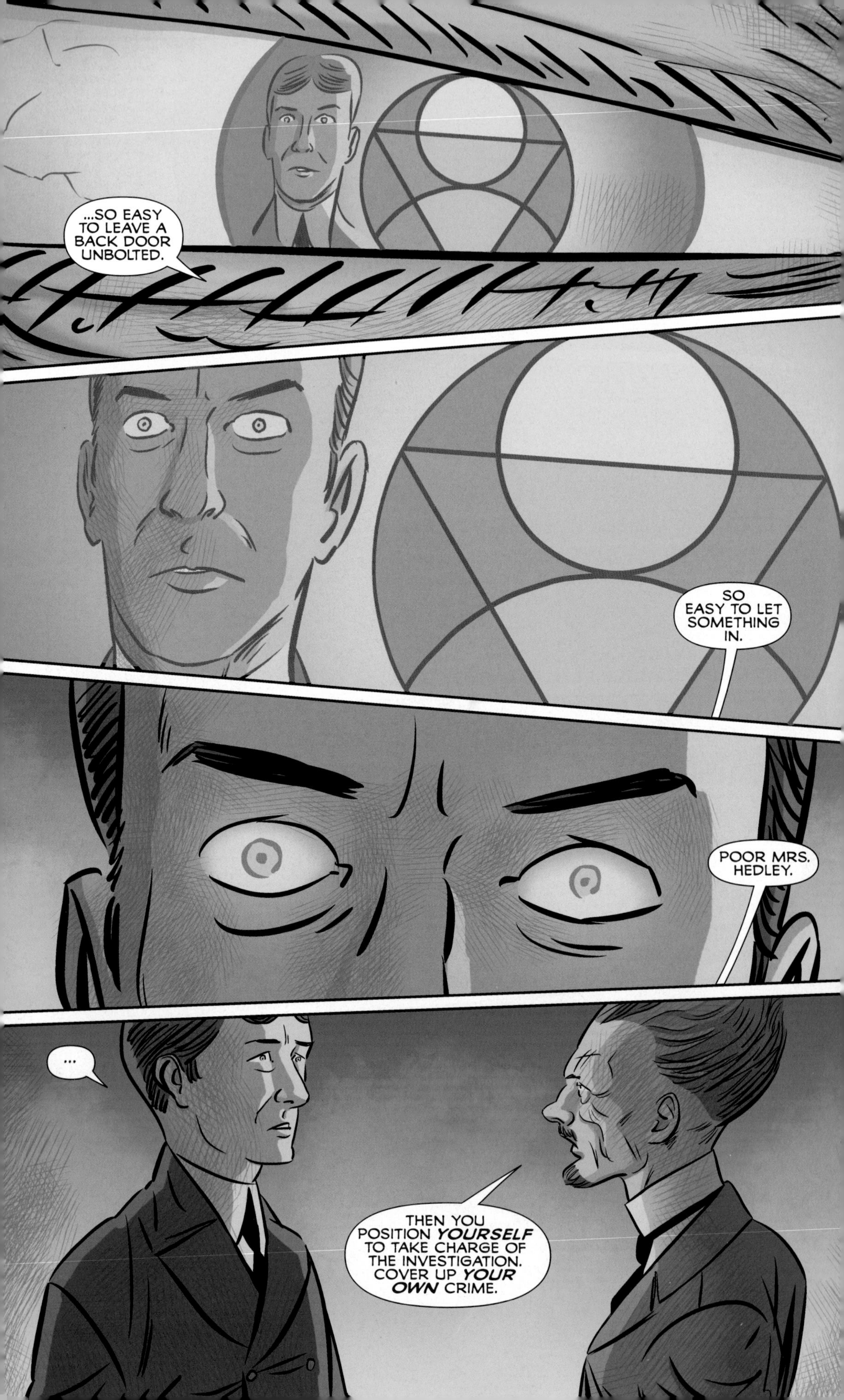
...SO EASY TO LEAVE A BACK DOOR UNBOLTED.
SO EASY TO LET SOMETHING IN.
POOR MRS. HEDLEY.
...
THEN YOU POSITION *YOURSELF* TO TAKE CHARGE OF THE INVESTIGATION. COVER UP *YOUR OWN* CRIME.

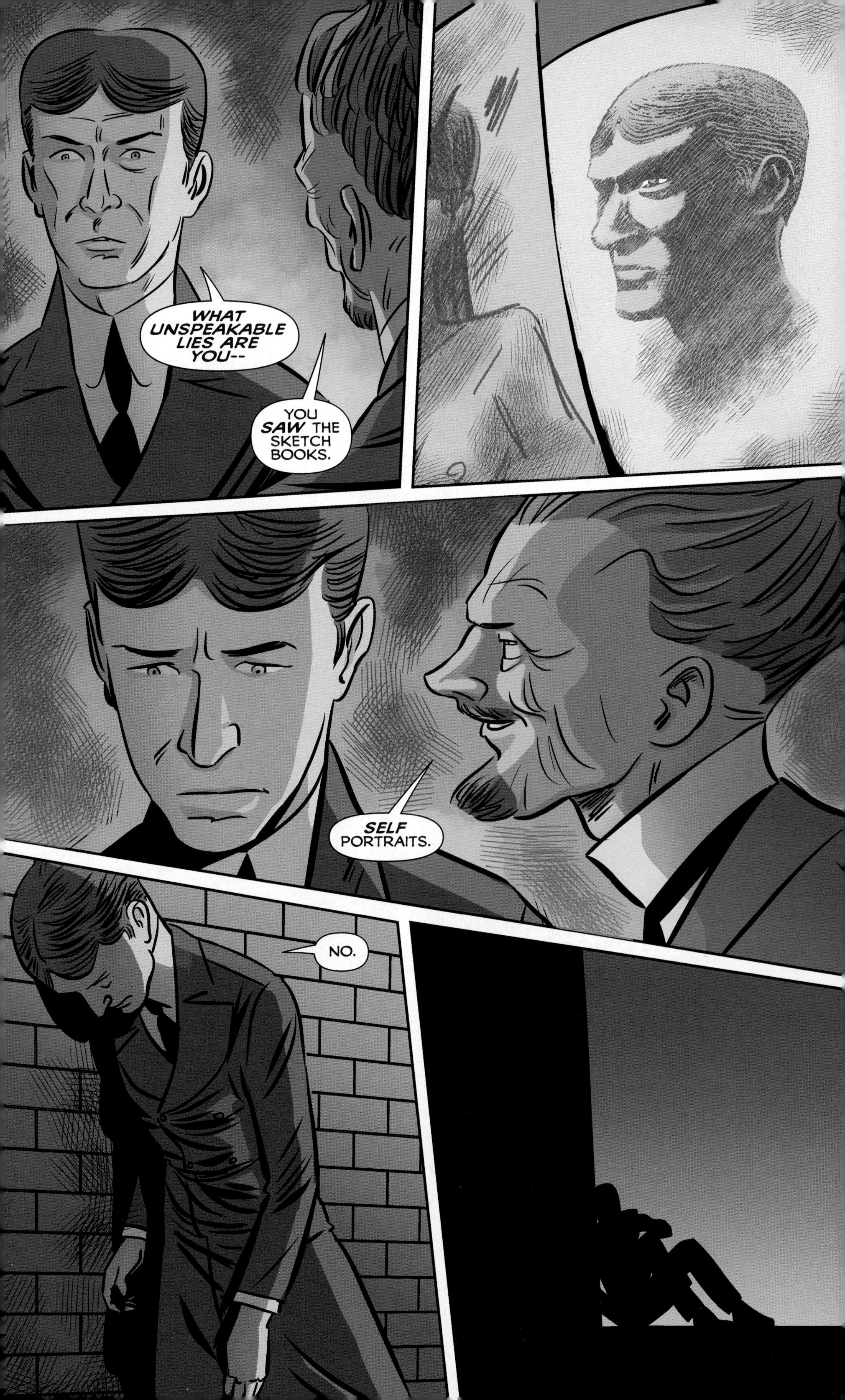
WHAT UNSPEAKABLE LIES ARE YOU--
YOU SAW THE SKETCH BOOKS.
SELF PORTRAITS.
NO.

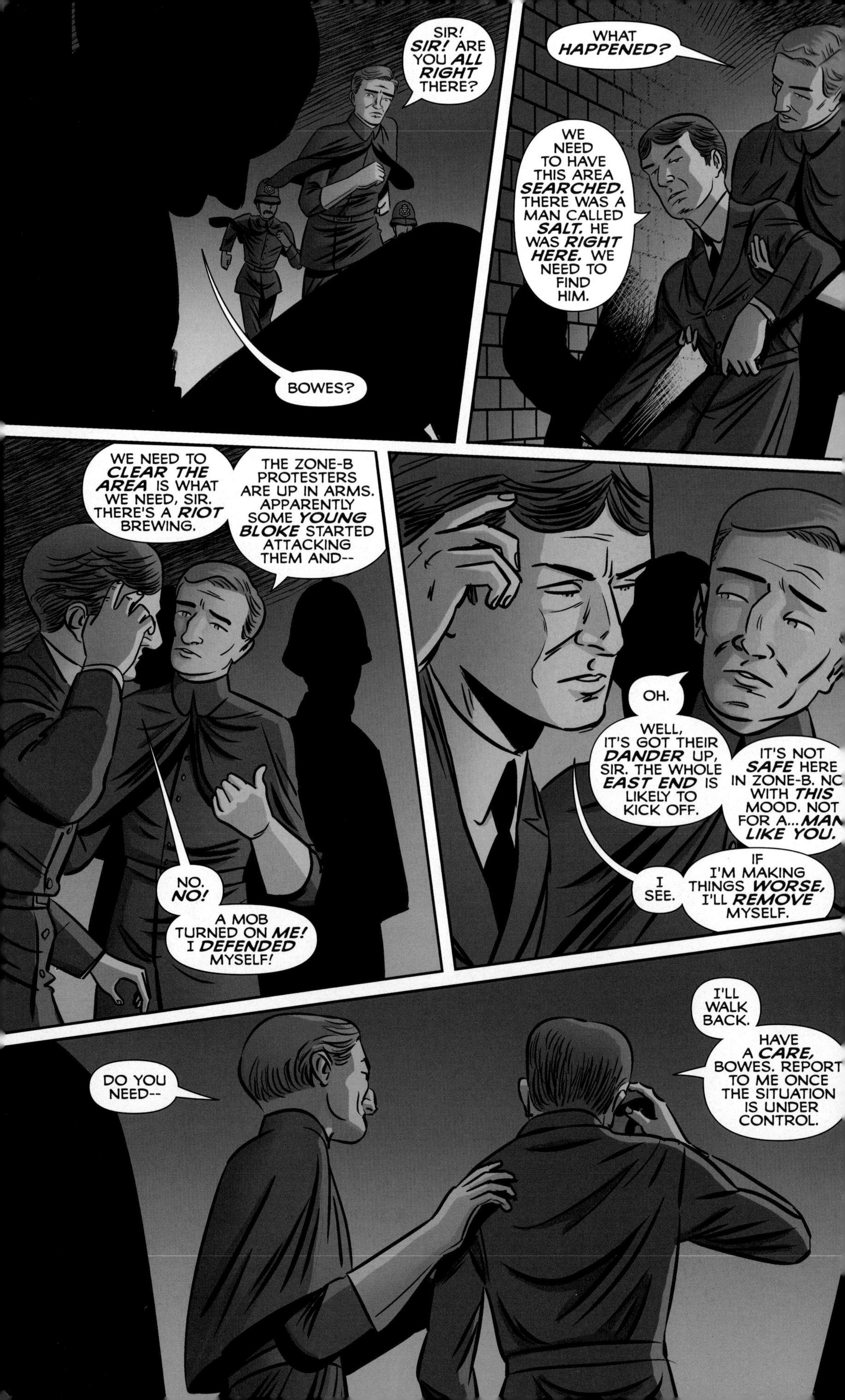
SIR! SIR! ARE YOU ALL RIGHT THERE?
BOWES?
WHAT HAPPENED?
WE NEED TO HAVE THIS AREA SEARCHED. THERE WAS A MAN CALLED SALT. HE WAS RIGHT HERE. WE NEED TO FIND HIM.
WE NEED TO CLEAR THE AREA IS WHAT WE NEED, SIR. THERE'S A RIOT BREWING.
THE ZONE-B PROTESTERS ARE UP IN ARMS. APPARENTLY SOME YOUNG BLOKE STARTED ATTACKING THEM AND--
NO. NO!
A MOB TURNED ON ME! I DEFENDED MYSELF!
OH.
WELL, IT'S GOT THEIR DANDER UP, SIR. THE WHOLE EAST END IS LIKELY TO KICK OFF.
IT'S NOT SAFE HERE IN ZONE-B. NO WITH THIS MOOD. NOT FOR A...MAN LIKE YOU.
I SEE.
IF I'M MAKING THINGS WORSE, I'LL REMOVE MYSELF.
DO YOU NEED--
I'LL WALK BACK.
HAVE A CARE, BOWES. REPORT TO ME ONCE THE SITUATION IS UNDER CONTROL.

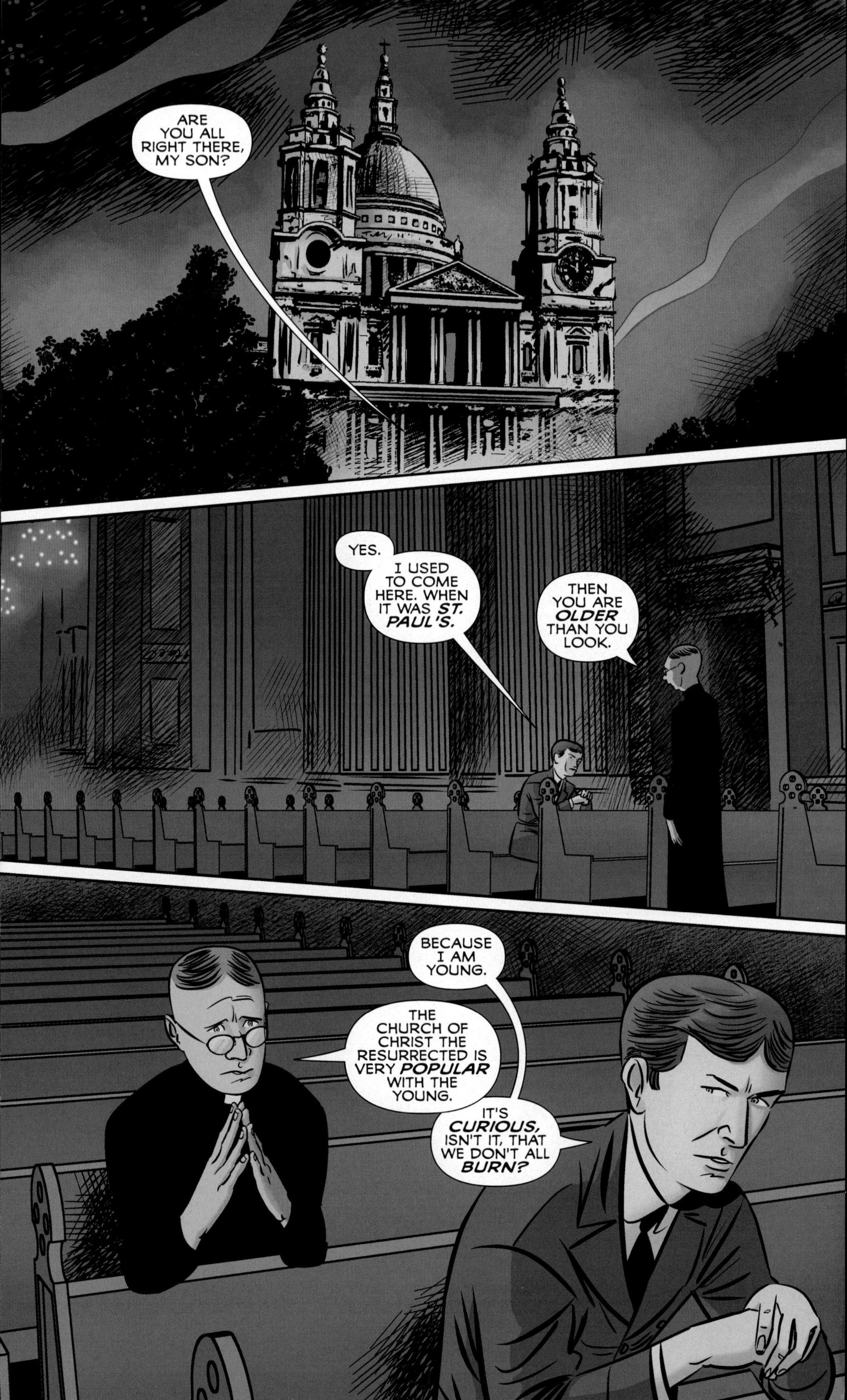
ARE YOU ALL RIGHT THERE, MY SON?
YES.
I USED TO COME HERE. WHEN IT WAS ST. PAUL'S.
THEN YOU ARE OLDER THAN YOU LOOK.
BECAUSE I AM YOUNG.
THE CHURCH OF CHRIST THE RESURRECTED IS VERY POPULAR WITH THE YOUNG.
IT'S CURIOUS, ISN'T IT, THAT WE DON'T ALL BURN?

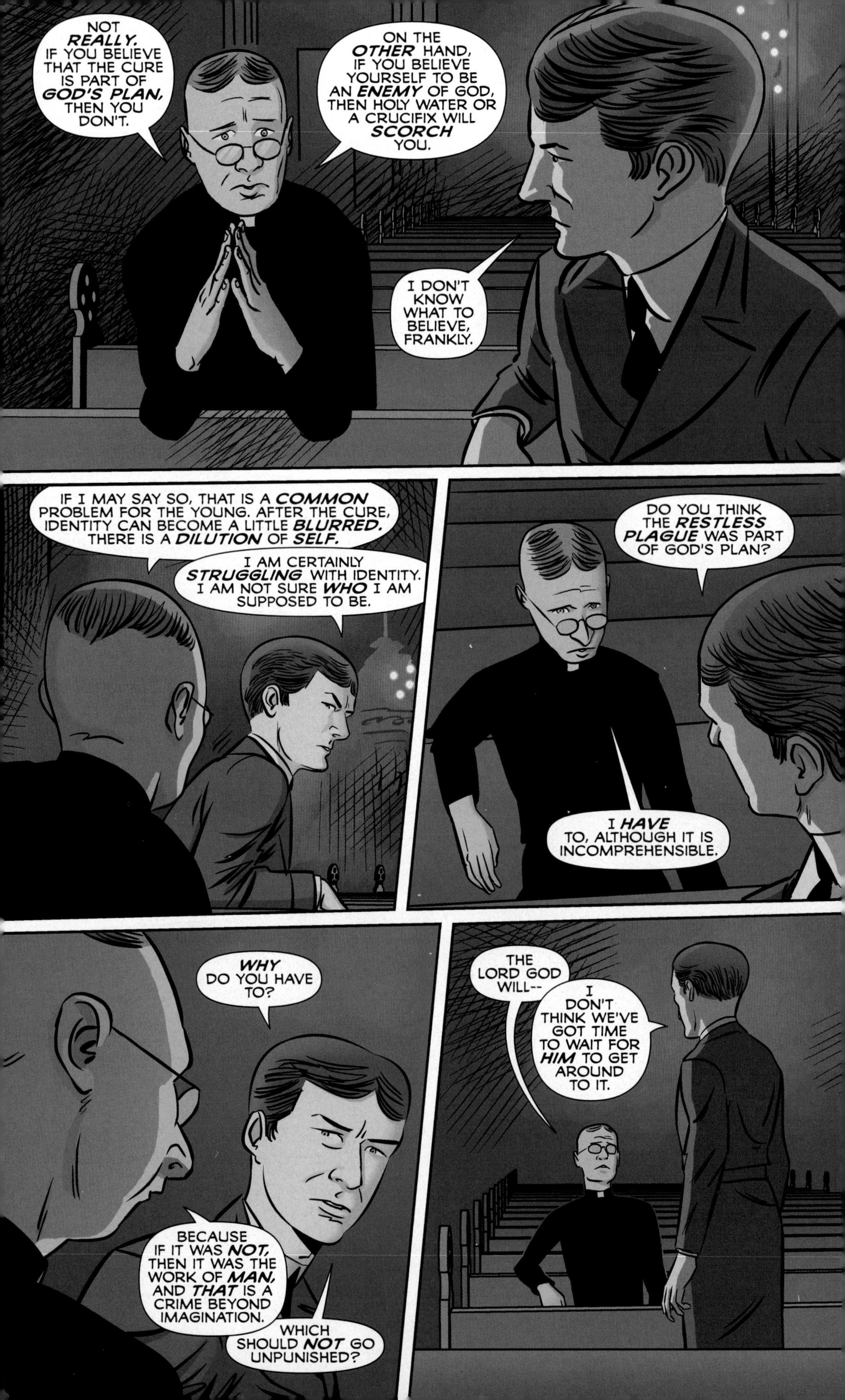
NOT REALLY. IF YOU BELIEVE THAT THE CURE IS PART OF GOD'S PLAN, THEN YOU DON'T.
ON THE OTHER HAND, IF YOU BELIEVE YOURSELF TO BE AN ENEMY OF GOD, THEN HOLY WATER OR A CRUCIFIX WILL SCORCH YOU.
I DON'T KNOW WHAT TO BELIEVE, FRANKLY.
IF I MAY SAY SO, THAT IS A COMMON PROBLEM FOR THE YOUNG. AFTER THE CURE, IDENTITY CAN BECOME A LITTLE BLURRED. THERE IS A DILUTION OF SELF.
I AM CERTAINLY STRUGGLING WITH IDENTITY. I AM NOT SURE WHO I AM SUPPOSED TO BE.
DO YOU THINK THE RESTLESS PLAGUE WAS PART OF GOD'S PLAN?
I HAVE TO, ALTHOUGH IT IS INCOMPREHENSIBLE.
WHY DO YOU HAVE TO?
BECAUSE IF IT WAS NOT, THEN IT WAS THE WORK OF MAN, AND THAT IS A CRIME BEYOND IMAGINATION.
WHICH SHOULD NOT GO UNPUNISHED?
THE LORD GOD WILL--
I DON'T THINK WE'VE GOT TIME TO WAIT FOR HIM TO GET AROUND TO IT.

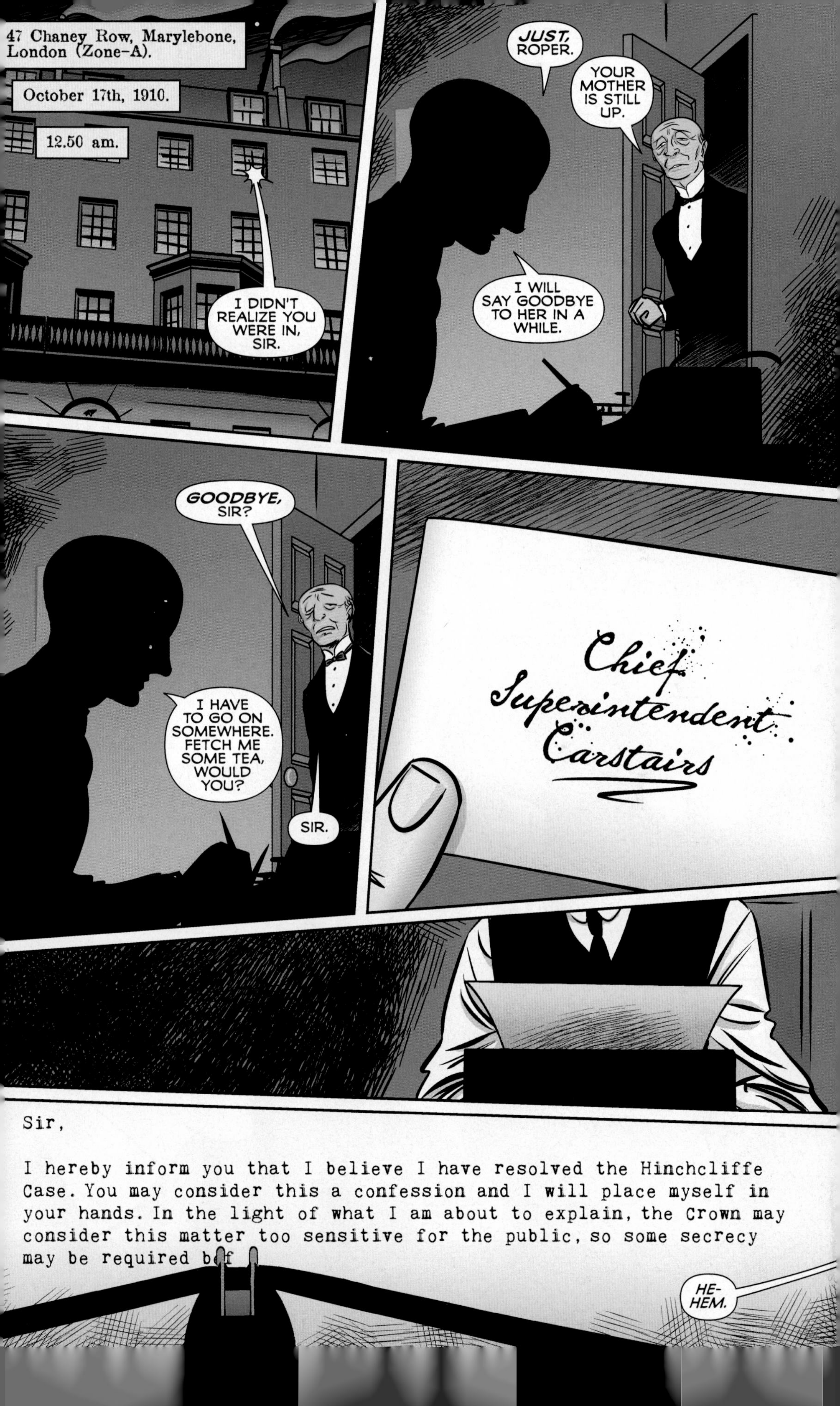
47 Chaney Row, Marylebone, London (Zone-A).
October 17th, 1910.
12.50 am.
I DIDN'T REALIZE YOU WERE IN, SIR.
JUST, ROPER.
YOUR MOTHER IS STILL UP.
I WILL SAY GOODBYE TO HER IN A WHILE.
GOODBYE, SIR?
I HAVE TO GO ON SOMEWHERE. FETCH ME SOME TEA, WOULD YOU?
SIR.
Chief Superintendent Carstairs
Sir,
I hereby inform you that I believe I have resolved the Hinchcliffe Case. You may consider this a confession and I will place myself in your hands. In the light of what I am about to explain, the Crown may consider this matter too sensitive for the public, so some secrecy may be required bef
HE-HEM.

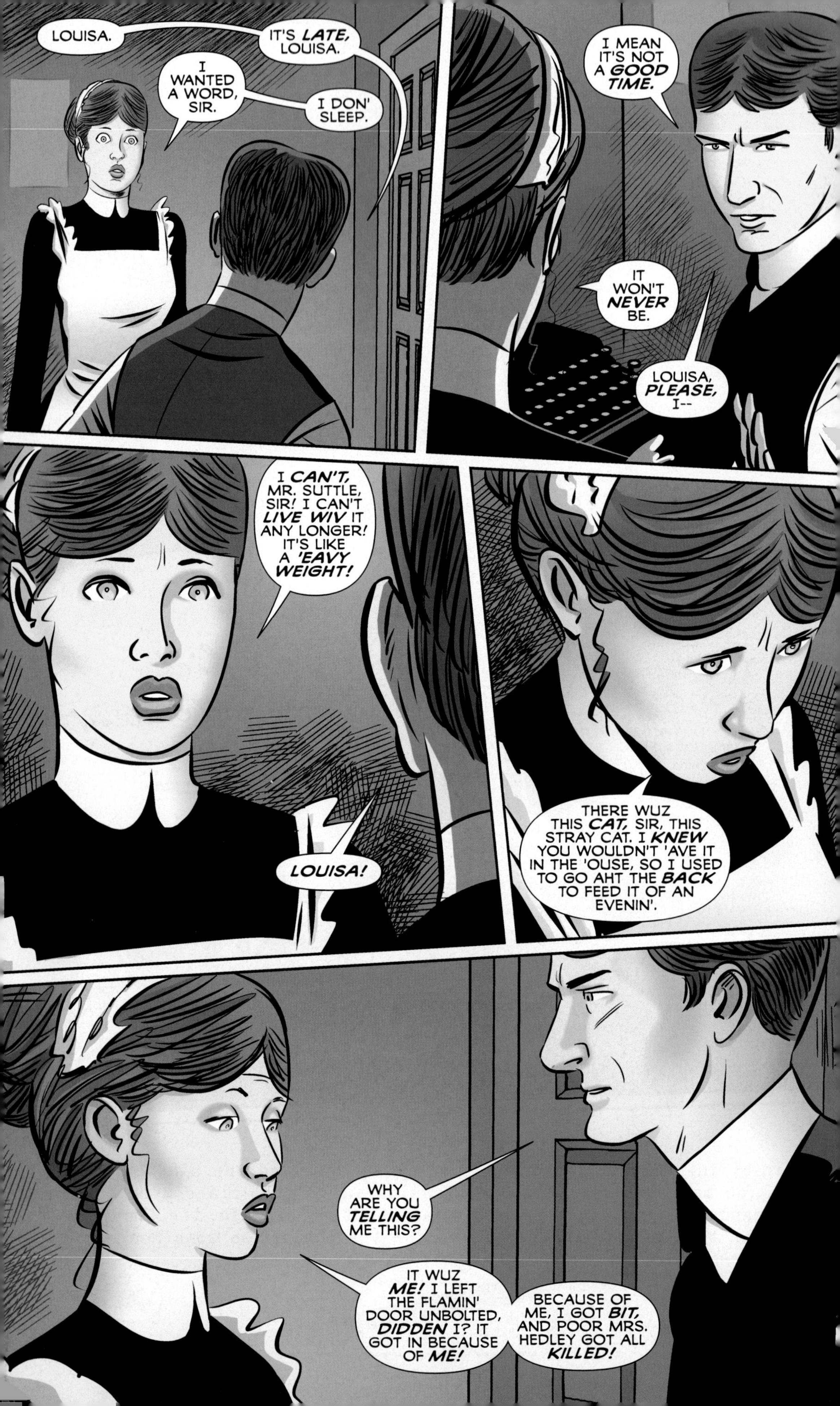

LOUISA.
IT'S *LATE,* LOUISA.
I WANTED A WORD, SIR.
I DON' SLEEP.
I MEAN IT'S NOT A *GOOD TIME.*
IT WON'T *NEVER* BE.
LOUISA, *PLEASE,* I--
I *CAN'T,* MR. SUTTLE, SIR! I CAN'T *LIVE WIV* IT ANY LONGER! IT'S LIKE A *'EAVY WEIGHT!*
LOUISA!
THERE WUZ THIS *CAT,* SIR, THIS STRAY CAT. I *KNEW* YOU WOULDN'T 'AVE IT IN THE 'OUSE, SO I USED TO GO AHT THE *BACK* TO FEED IT OF AN EVENIN'.
WHY ARE YOU *TELLING* ME THIS?
IT WUZ *ME!* I LEFT THE FLAMIN' DOOR UNBOLTED, *DIDDEN* I? IT GOT IN BECAUSE OF *ME!*
BECAUSE OF ME, I GOT *BIT,* AND POOR MRS. HEDLEY GOT ALL *KILLED!*

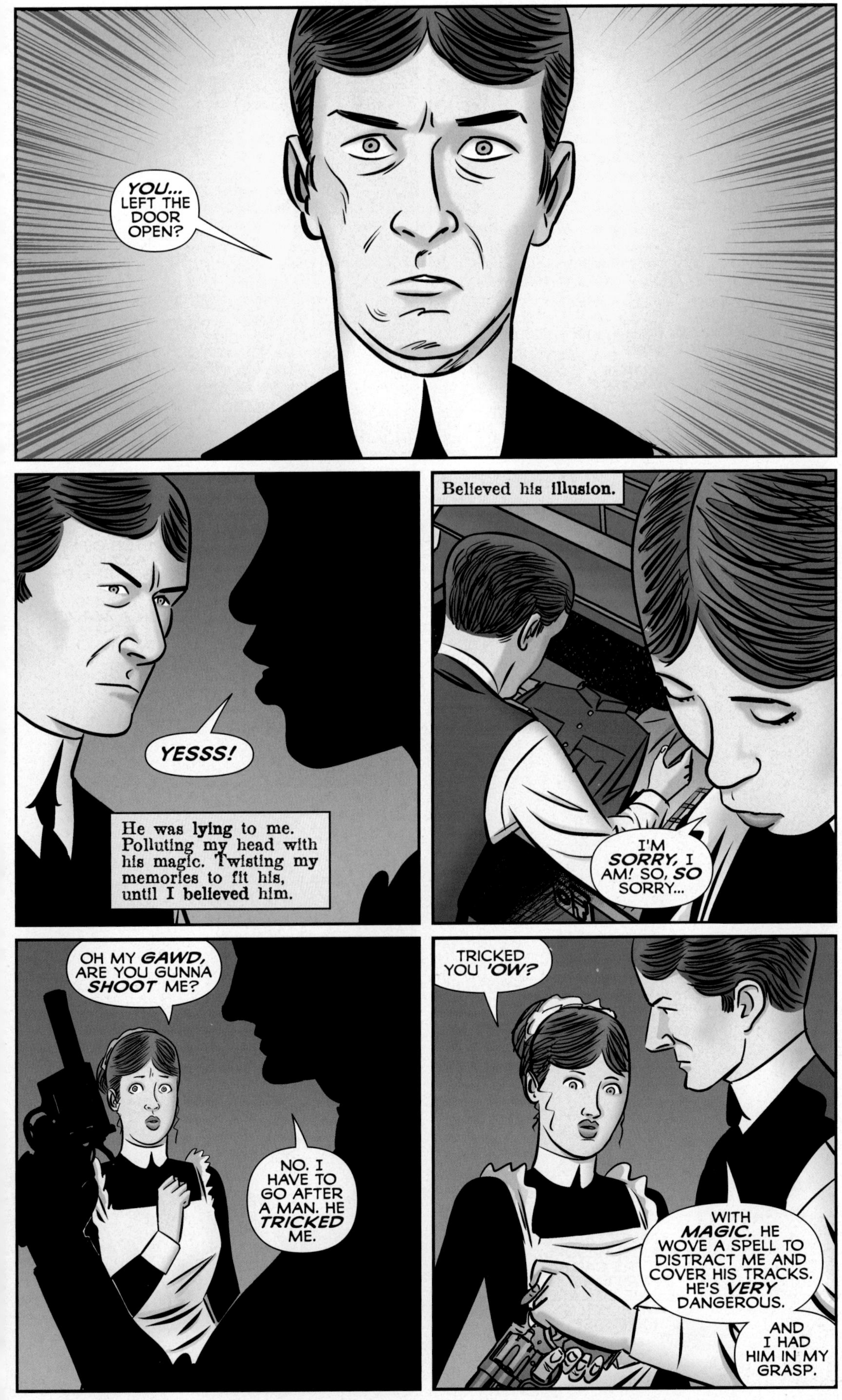
YOU... LEFT THE DOOR OPEN?
YESSS!
He was lying to me. Polluting my head with his magic. Twisting my memories to fit his, until I believed him.
Believed his illusion.
I'M SORRY, I AM! SO, SO SORRY...
OH MY GAWD, ARE YOU GUNNA SHOOT ME?
NO. I HAVE TO GO AFTER A MAN. HE TRICKED ME.
TRICKED YOU 'OW?
WITH MAGIC. HE WOVE A SPELL TO DISTRACT ME AND COVER HIS TRACKS. HE'S VERY DANGEROUS.
AND I HAD HIM IN MY GRASP.

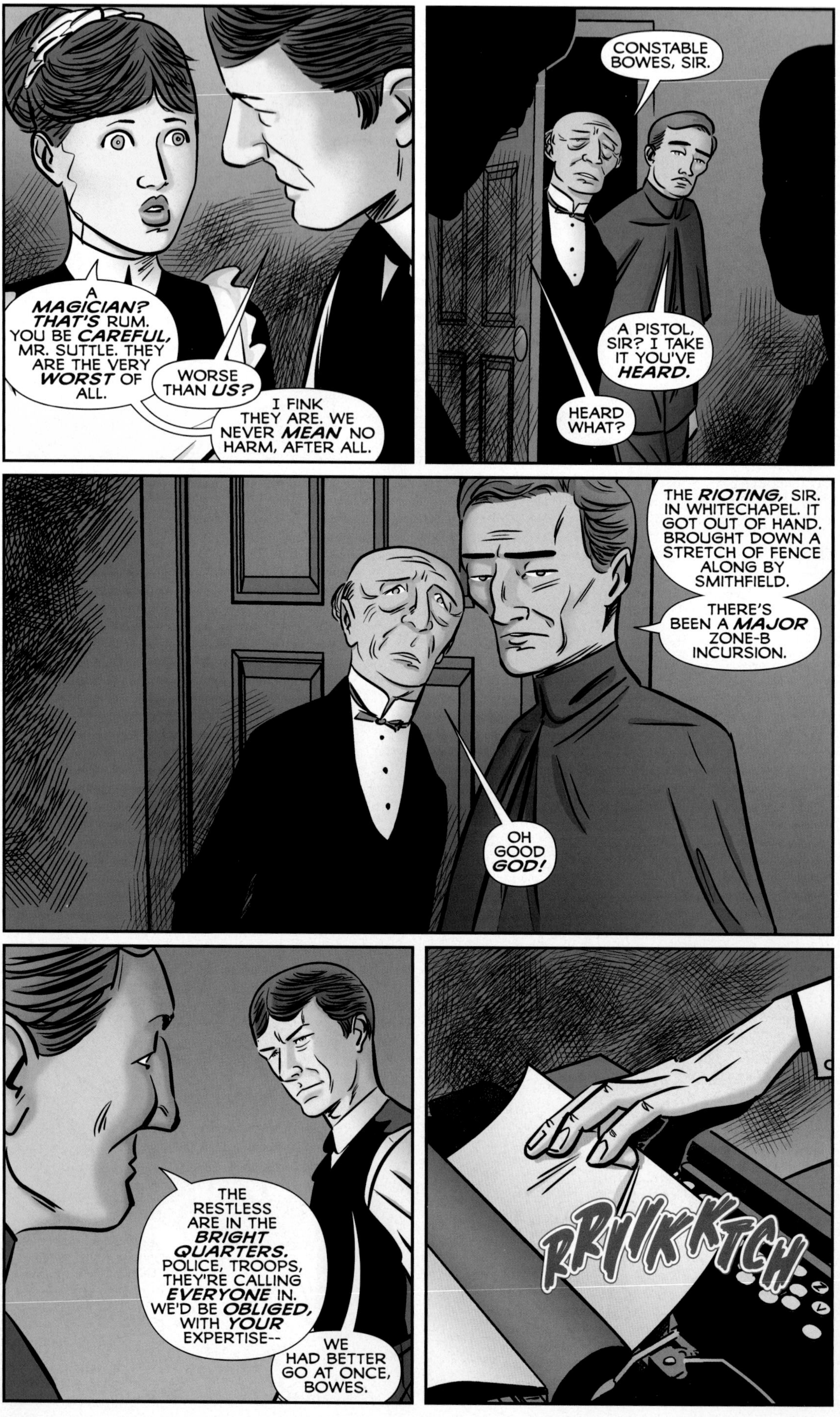
A MAGICIAN? THAT'S RUM. YOU BE CAREFUL, MR. SUTTLE. THEY ARE THE VERY WORST OF ALL.
WORSE THAN US?
I FINK THEY ARE. WE NEVER MEAN NO HARM, AFTER ALL.
CONSTABLE BOWES, SIR.
A PISTOL, SIR? I TAKE IT YOU'VE HEARD.
HEARD WHAT?
THE RIOTING, SIR. IN WHITECHAPEL. IT GOT OUT OF HAND. BROUGHT DOWN A STRETCH OF FENCE ALONG BY SMITHFIELD.
THERE'S BEEN A MAJOR ZONE-B INCURSION.
OH GOOD GOD!
THE RESTLESS ARE IN THE BRIGHT QUARTERS. POLICE, TROOPS, THEY'RE CALLING EVERYONE IN. WE'D BE OBLIGED, WITH YOUR EXPERTISE--
WE HAD BETTER GO AT ONCE, BOWES.
RRYKKTCH

SKRRTCH

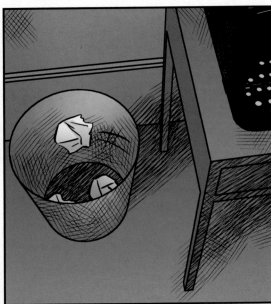

ONE MOMENT.

RIGHT.

ROPER? LOUISA? STAY WITH MOTHER AND KEEP THE DOORS BOLTED. *ALL* OF THEM.

BOWES. LEAD THE WAY.

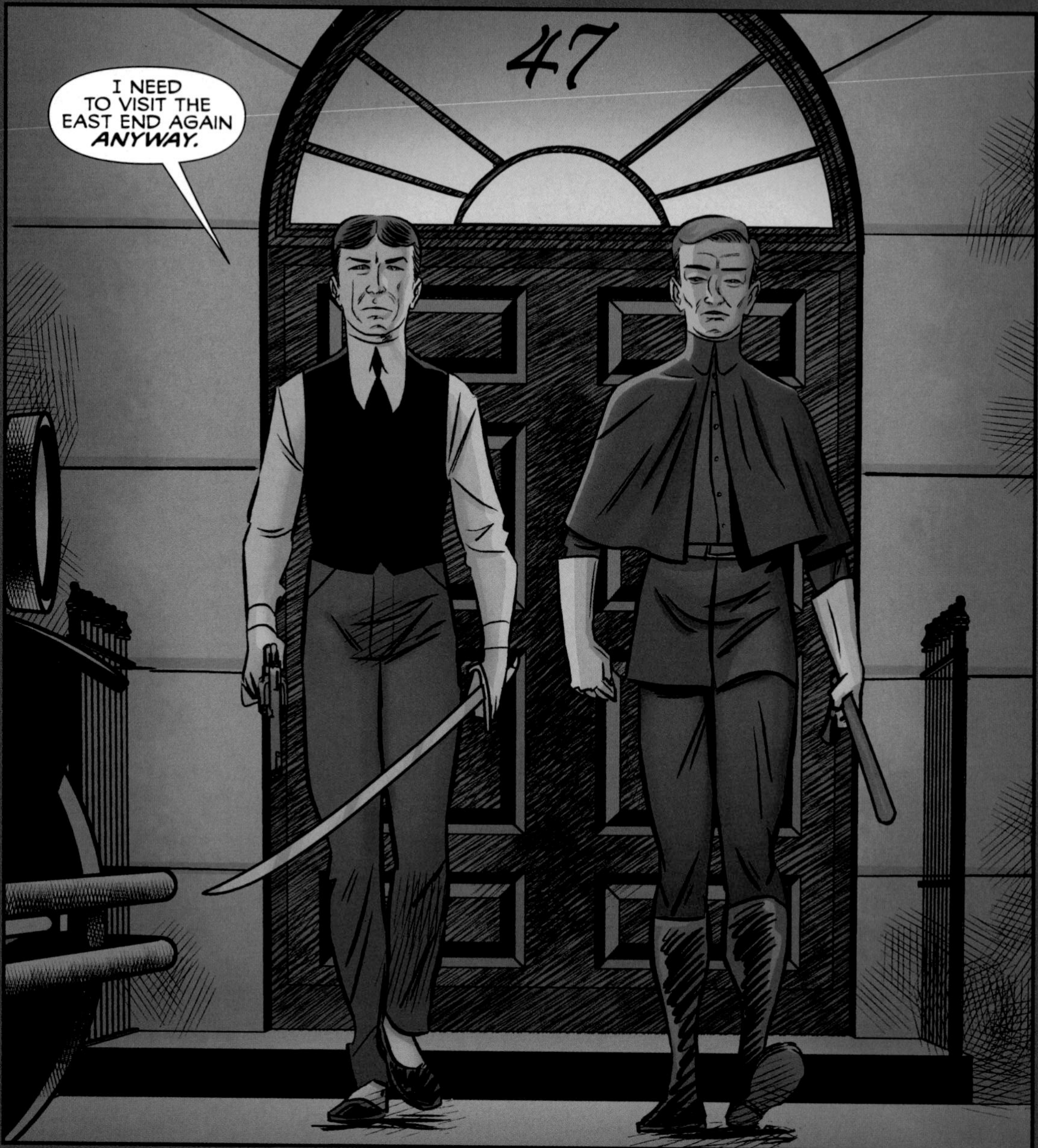
I NEED TO VISIT THE EAST END AGAIN *ANYWAY.*
47

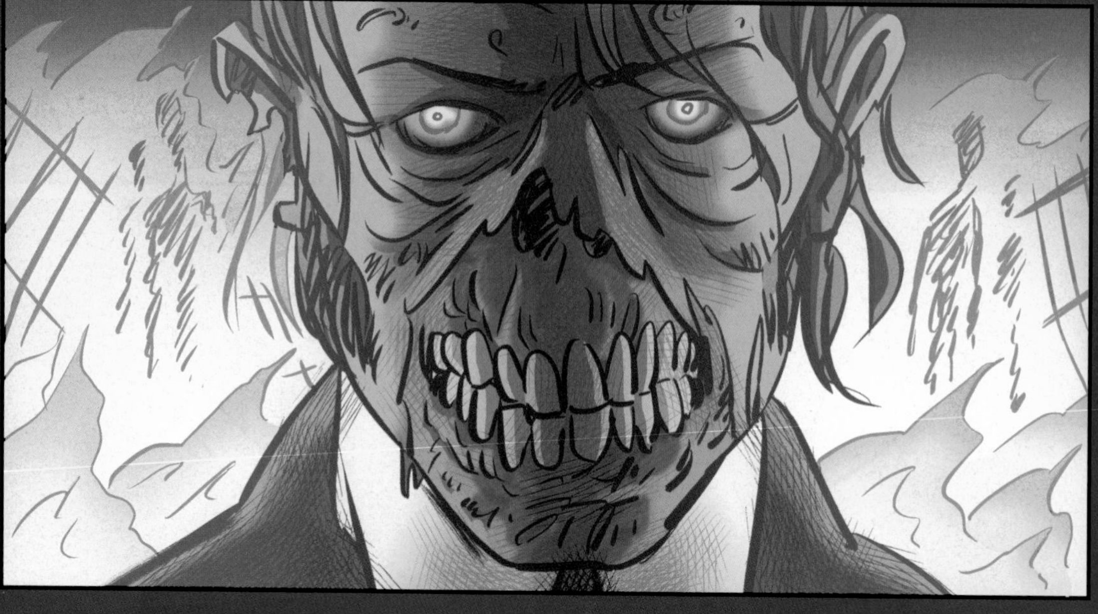

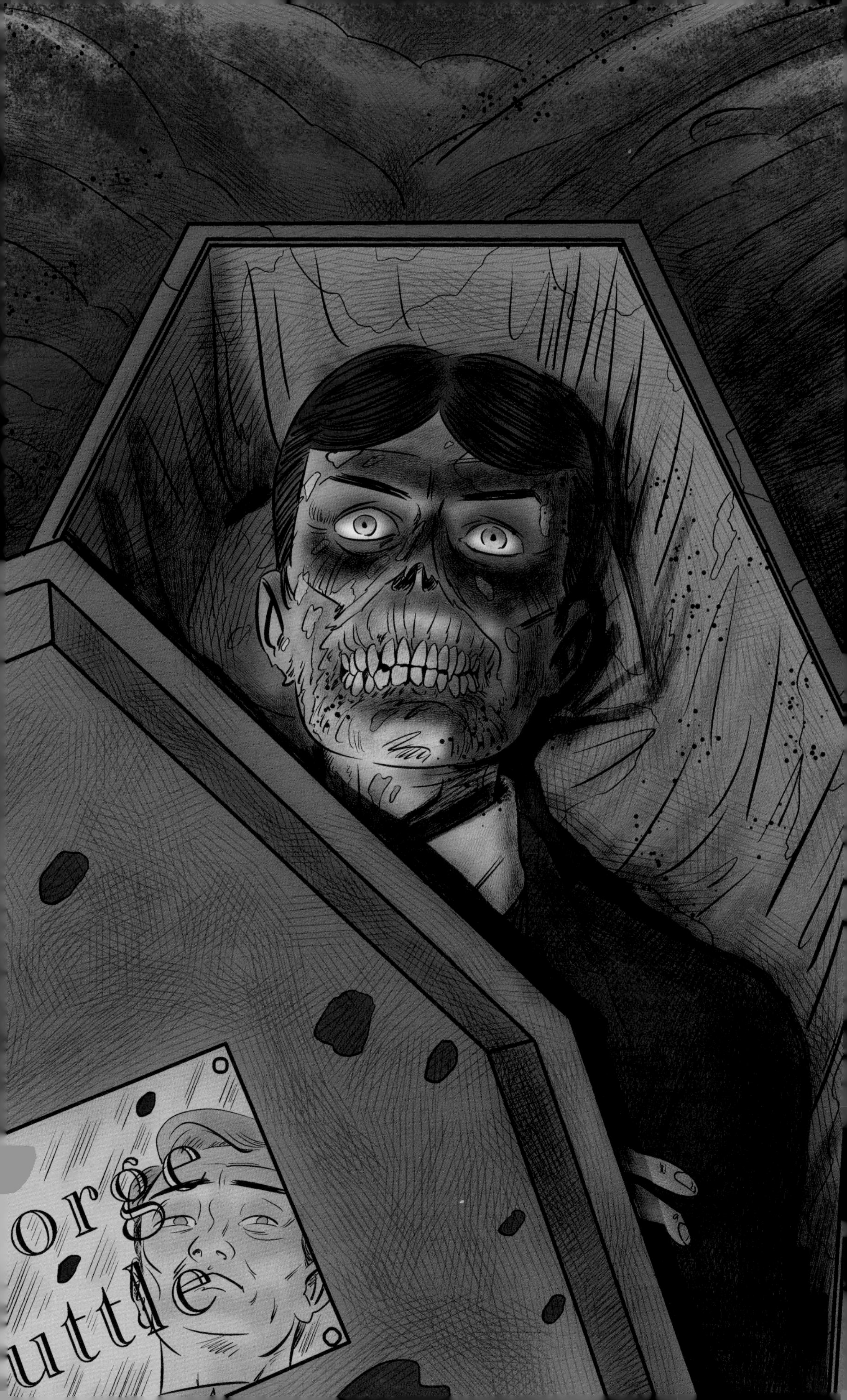
orge
uttle

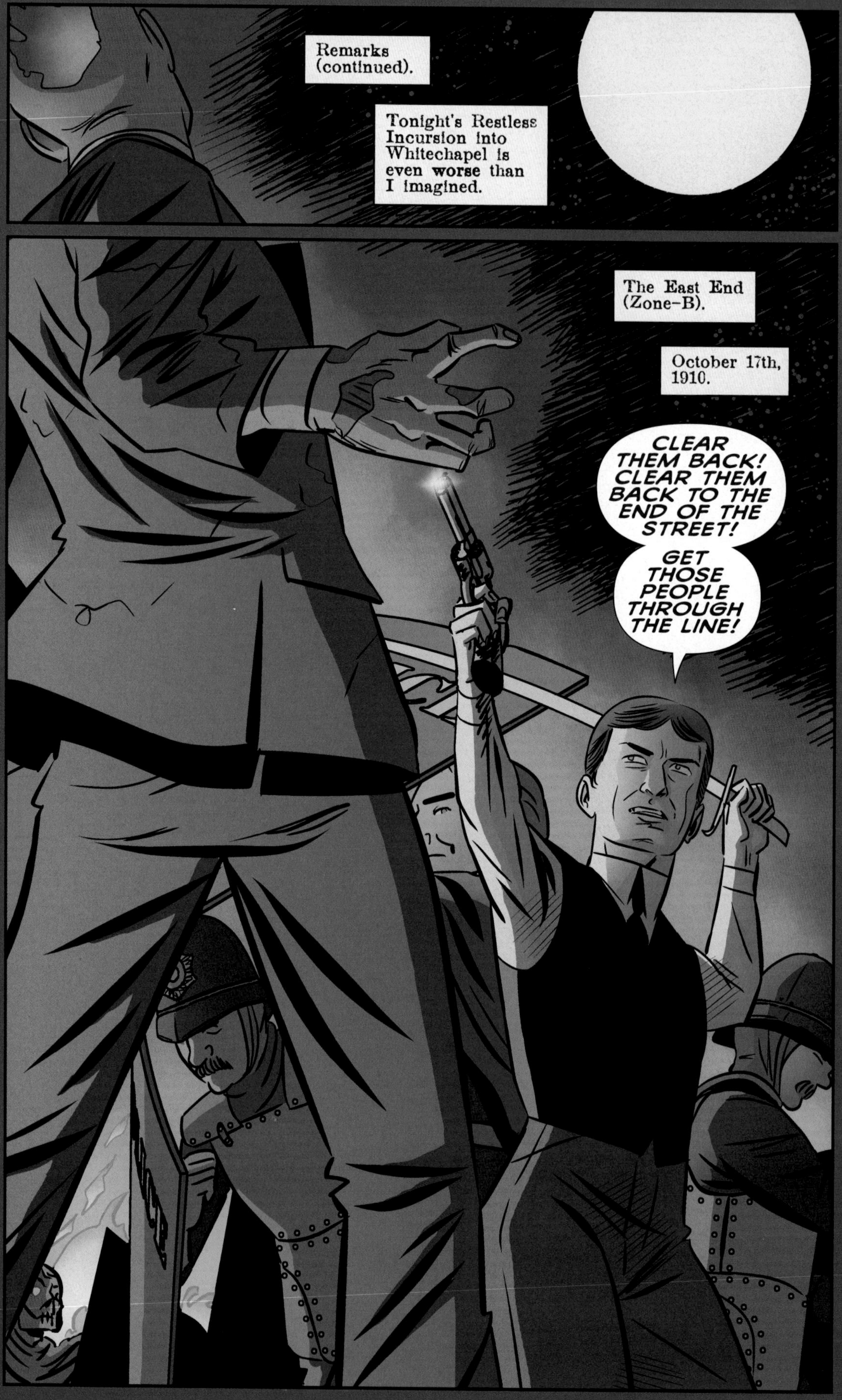
Remarks (continued).
Tonight's Restless Incursion into Whitechapel is even **worse** than I imagined.
The East End (Zone-B).
October 17th, 1910.
CLEAR THEM BACK! CLEAR THEM BACK TO THE END OF THE STREET!
GET THOSE PEOPLE THROUGH THE LINE!

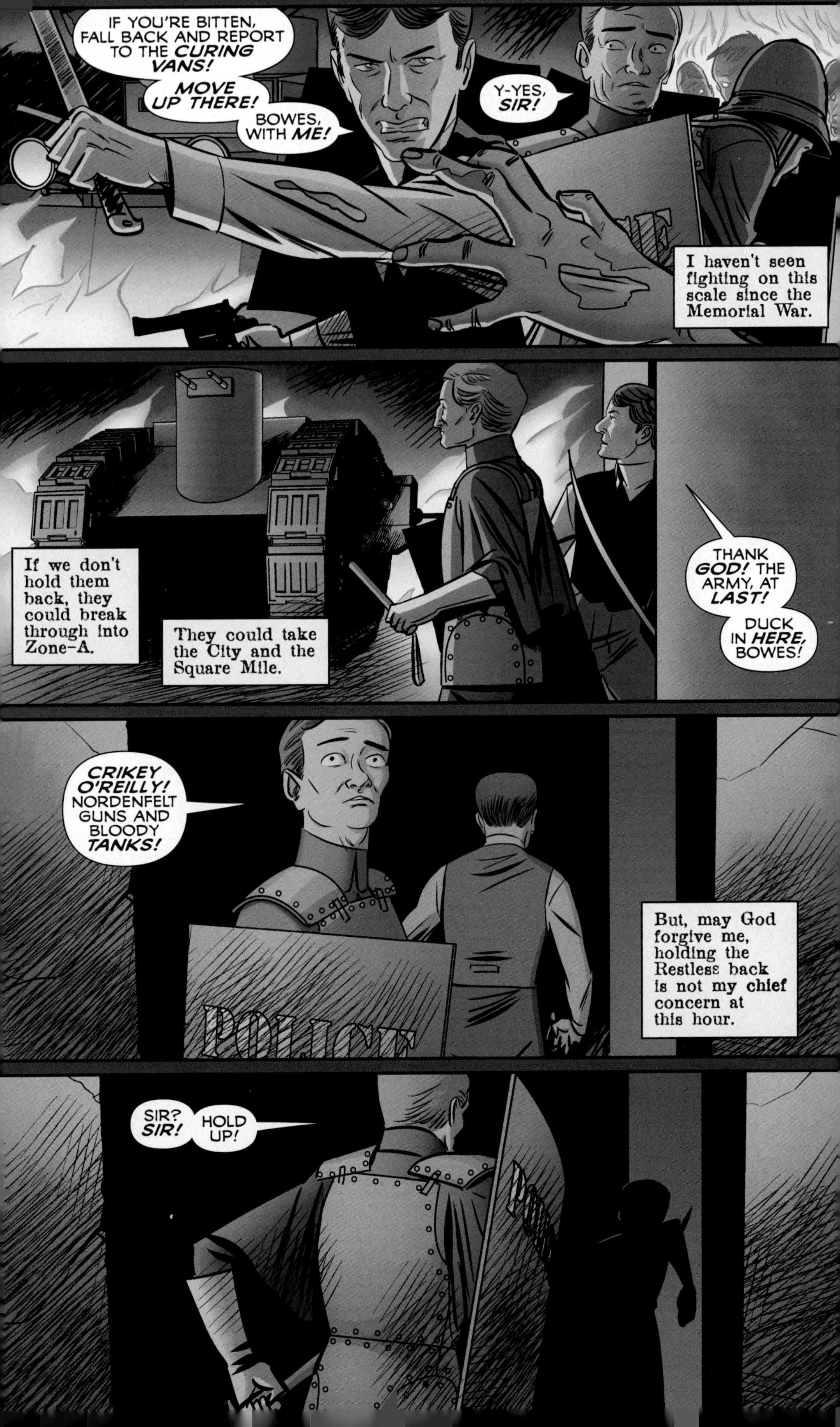

IF YOU'RE BITTEN, FALL BACK AND REPORT TO THE *CURING VANS!*
MOVE UP THERE!
BOWES, WITH *ME!*
Y-YES, *SIR!*
I haven't seen fighting on this scale since the Memorial War.
If we don't hold them back, they could break through into Zone-A.
They could take the City and the Square Mile.
THANK *GOD!* THE ARMY, AT *LAST!*
DUCK IN *HERE,* BOWES!
CRIKEY O'REILLY! NORDENFELT GUNS AND BLOODY *TANKS!*
But, may God forgive me, holding the Restless back is not my chief concern at this hour.
POLICE
SIR? *SIR!*
HOLD UP!

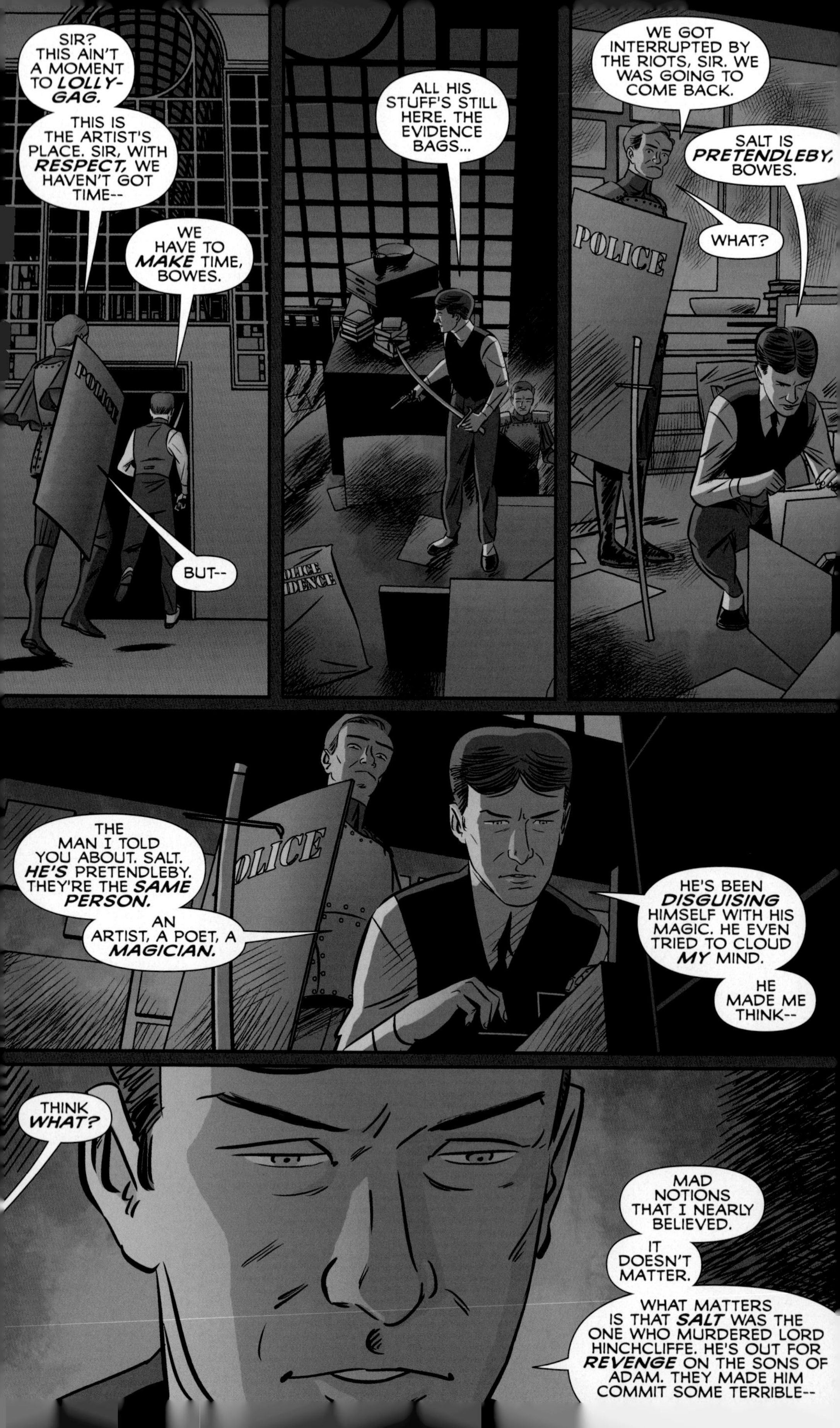
SIR? THIS AIN'T A MOMENT TO LOLLY-GAG.
THIS IS THE ARTIST'S PLACE. SIR, WITH RESPECT, WE HAVEN'T GOT TIME--
WE HAVE TO MAKE TIME, BOWES.
BUT--
POLICE
ALL HIS STUFF'S STILL HERE. THE EVIDENCE BAGS...
WE GOT INTERRUPTED BY THE RIOTS, SIR. WE WAS GOING TO COME BACK.
SALT IS PRETENDLEBY, BOWES.
WHAT?
POLICE
THE MAN I TOLD YOU ABOUT. SALT. HE'S PRETENDLEBY. THEY'RE THE SAME PERSON.
AN ARTIST, A POET, A MAGICIAN.
HE'S BEEN DISGUISING HIMSELF WITH HIS MAGIC. HE EVEN TRIED TO CLOUD MY MIND.
HE MADE ME THINK--
THINK WHAT?
MAD NOTIONS THAT I NEARLY BELIEVED.
IT DOESN'T MATTER.
WHAT MATTERS IS THAT SALT WAS THE ONE WHO MURDERED LORD HINCHCLIFFE. HE'S OUT FOR REVENGE ON THE SONS OF ADAM. THEY MADE HIM COMMIT SOME TERRIBLE--

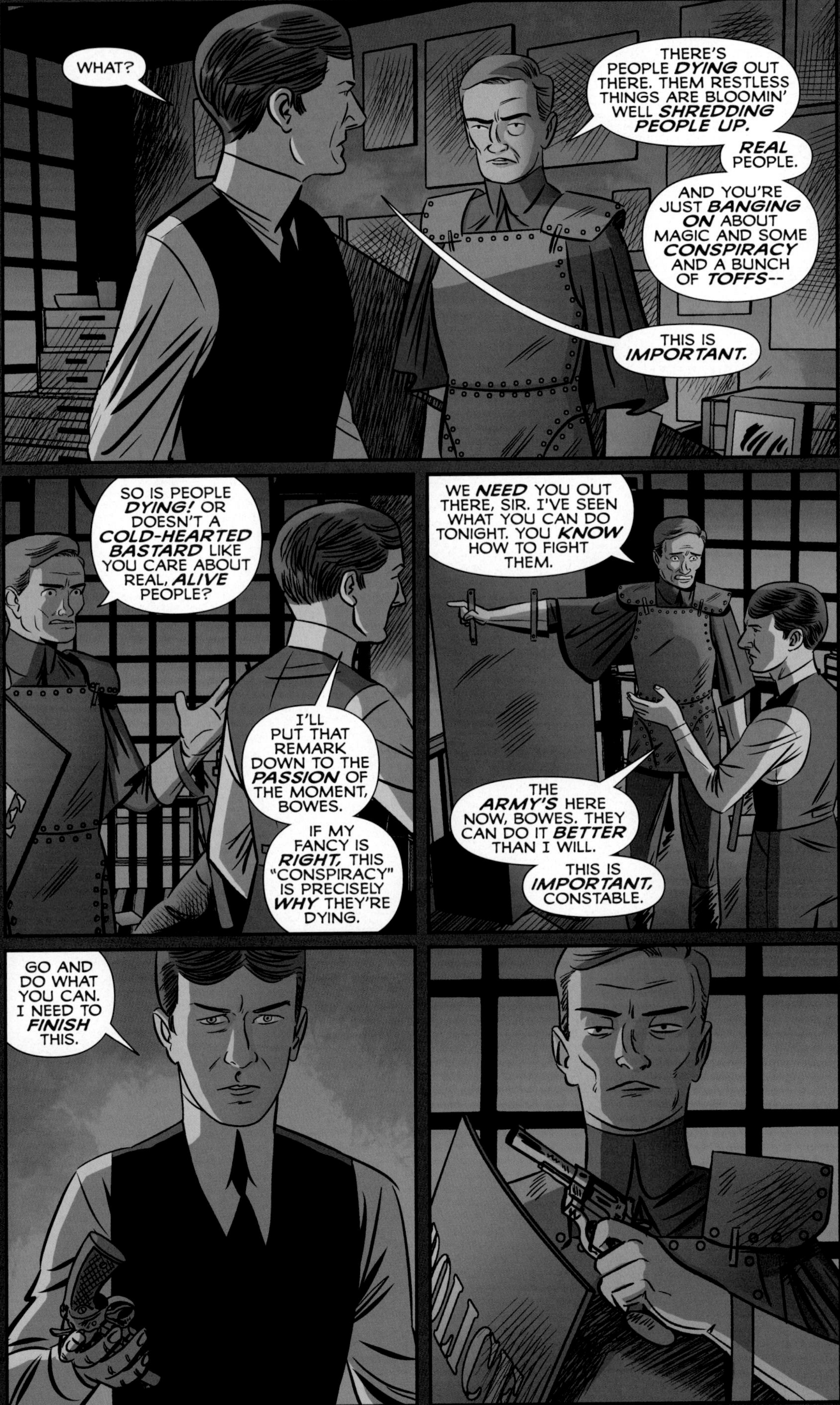
WHAT?
THERE'S PEOPLE DYING OUT THERE. THEM RESTLESS THINGS ARE BLOOMIN' WELL SHREDDING PEOPLE UP.
REAL PEOPLE.
AND YOU'RE JUST BANGING ON ABOUT MAGIC AND SOME CONSPIRACY AND A BUNCH OF TOFFS--
THIS IS IMPORTANT.
SO IS PEOPLE DYING! OR DOESN'T A COLD-HEARTED BASTARD LIKE YOU CARE ABOUT REAL, ALIVE PEOPLE?
I'LL PUT THAT REMARK DOWN TO THE PASSION OF THE MOMENT, BOWES.
IF MY FANCY IS RIGHT, THIS "CONSPIRACY" IS PRECISELY WHY THEY'RE DYING.
WE NEED YOU OUT THERE, SIR. I'VE SEEN WHAT YOU CAN DO TONIGHT. YOU KNOW HOW TO FIGHT THEM.
THE ARMY'S HERE NOW, BOWES. THEY CAN DO IT BETTER THAN I WILL.
THIS IS IMPORTANT, CONSTABLE.
GO AND DO WHAT YOU CAN. I NEED TO FINISH THIS.

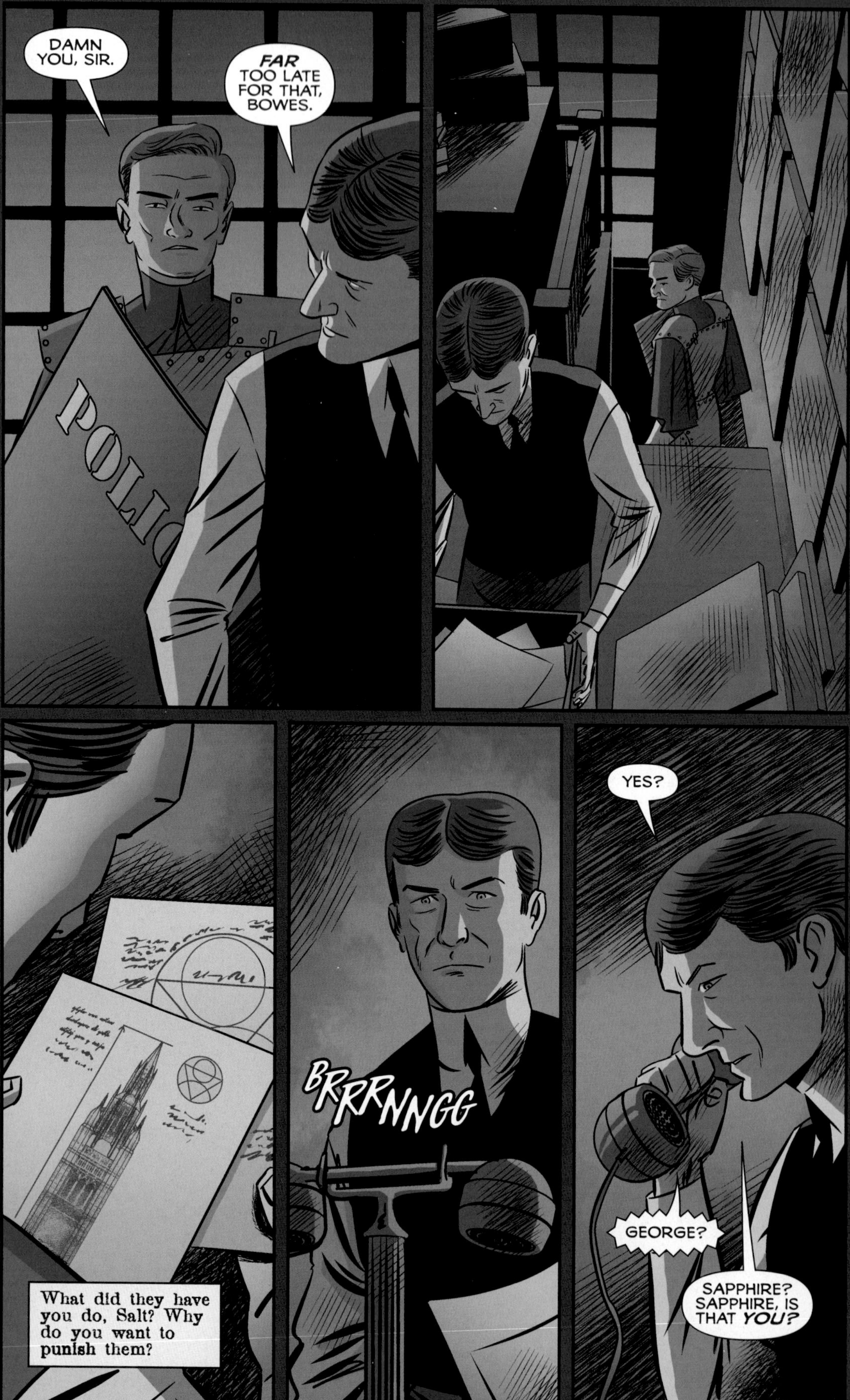
DAMN YOU, SIR.
FAR TOO LATE FOR THAT, BOWES.
What did they have you do, Salt? Why do you want to punish them?
BRRRNNGG
YES?
GEORGE?
SAPPHIRE? SAPPHIRE, IS THAT YOU?

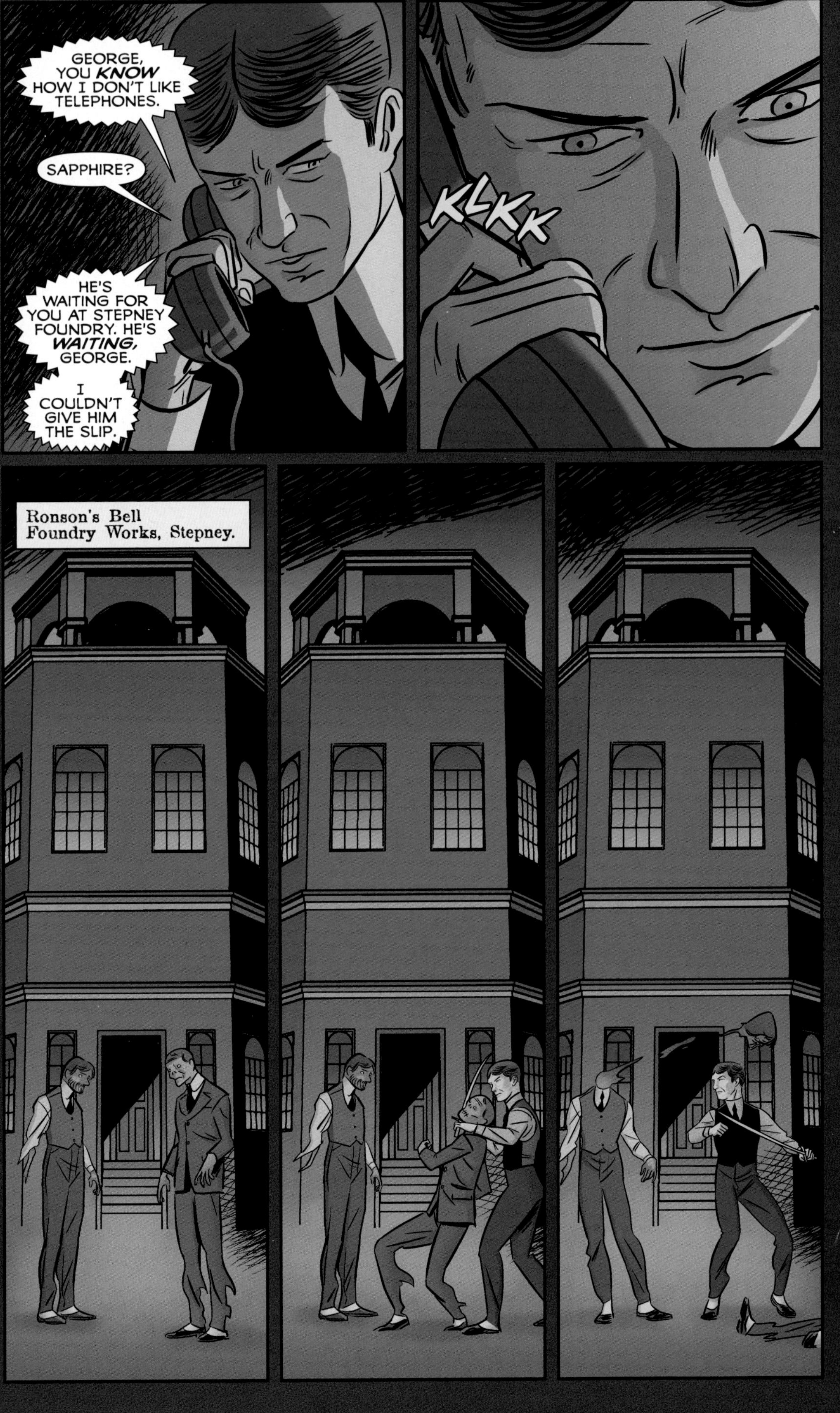
GEORGE, YOU KNOW HOW I DON'T LIKE TELEPHONES.
SAPPHIRE?
HE'S WAITING FOR YOU AT STEPNEY FOUNDRY. HE'S WAITING, GEORGE.
I COULDN'T GIVE HIM THE SLIP.
KLKK
Ronson's Bell Foundry Works, Stepney.

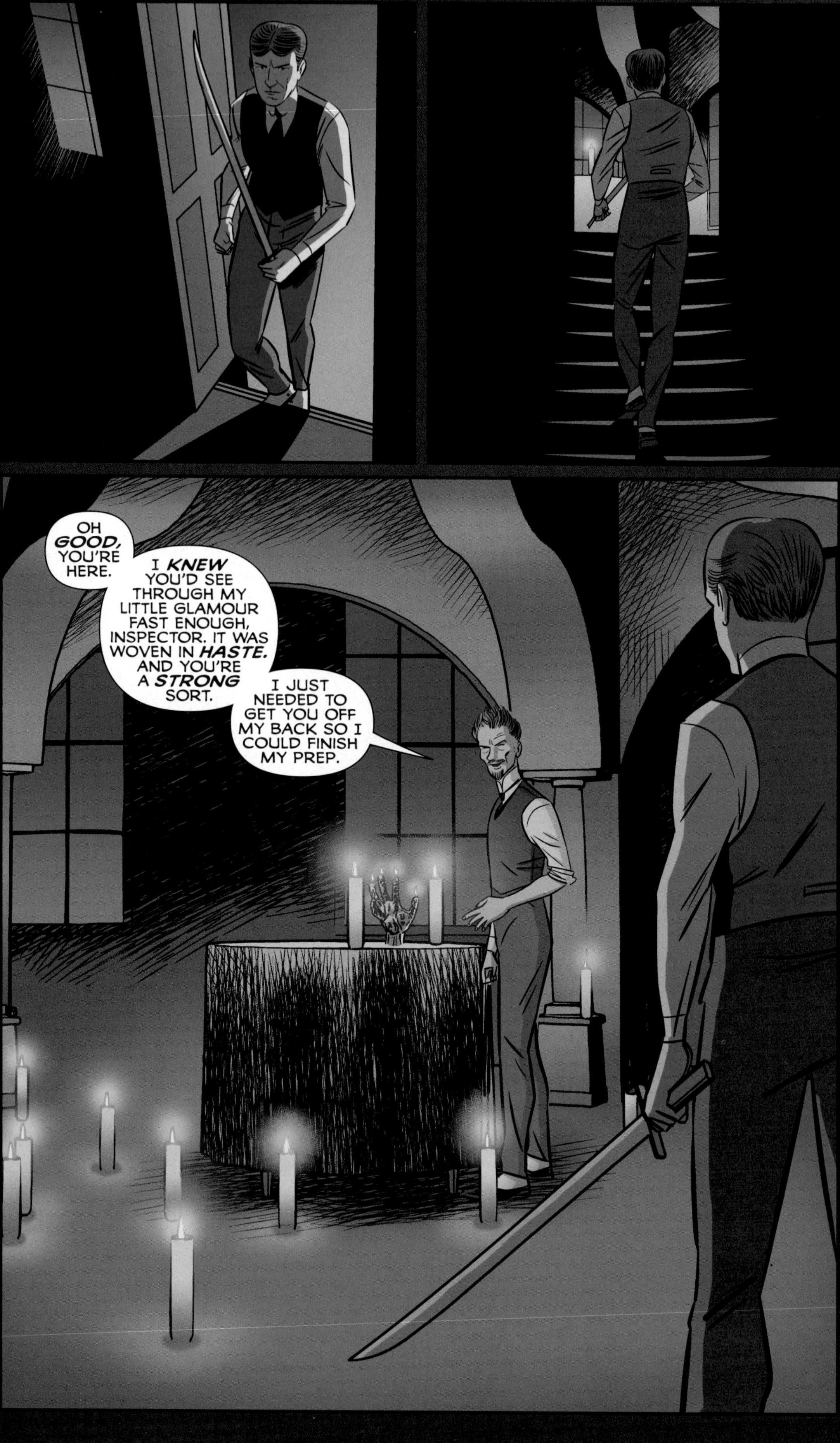
OH GOOD, YOU'RE HERE.
I KNEW YOU'D SEE THROUGH MY LITTLE GLAMOUR FAST ENOUGH, INSPECTOR. IT WAS WOVEN IN HASTE. AND YOU'RE A STRONG SORT.
I JUST NEEDED TO GET YOU OFF MY BACK SO I COULD FINISH MY PREP.

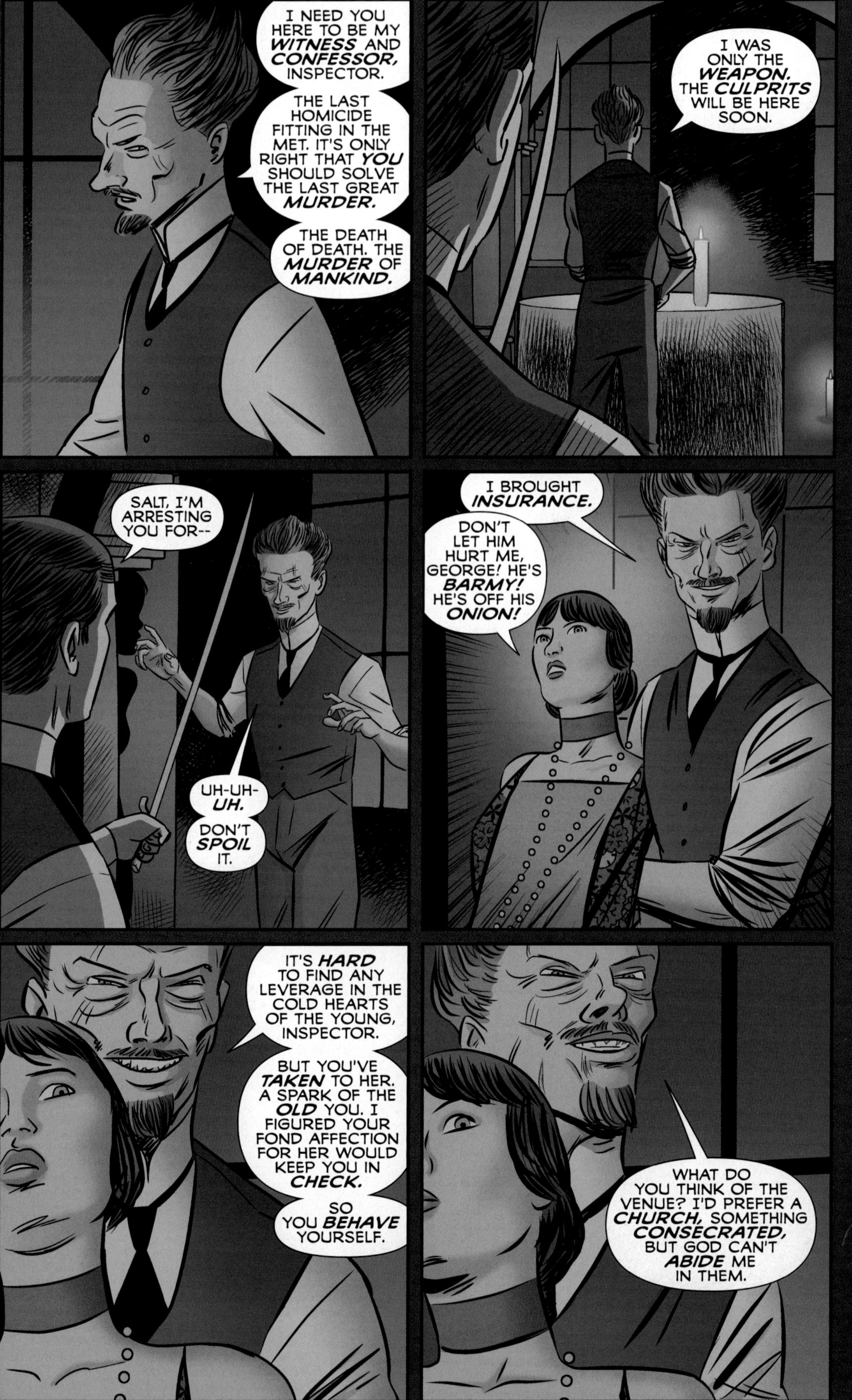
I NEED YOU HERE TO BE MY *WITNESS* AND *CONFESSOR,* INSPECTOR.
THE LAST HOMICIDE FITTING IN THE MET. IT'S ONLY RIGHT THAT *YOU* SHOULD SOLVE THE LAST GREAT *MURDER.*
THE DEATH OF DEATH. THE *MURDER* OF *MANKIND.*
I WAS ONLY THE *WEAPON.* THE *CULPRITS* WILL BE HERE SOON.
SALT, I'M ARRESTING YOU FOR--
UH-UH-*UH.*
DON'T *SPOIL* IT.
I BROUGHT *INSURANCE.*
DON'T LET HIM HURT ME, GEORGE! HE'S *BARMY!* HE'S OFF HIS *ONION!*
IT'S *HARD* TO FIND ANY LEVERAGE IN THE COLD HEARTS OF THE YOUNG, INSPECTOR.
BUT YOU'VE *TAKEN* TO HER. A SPARK OF THE *OLD* YOU. I FIGURED YOUR FOND AFFECTION FOR HER WOULD KEEP YOU IN *CHECK.*
SO YOU *BEHAVE* YOURSELF.
WHAT DO YOU THINK OF THE VENUE? I'D PREFER A *CHURCH,* SOMETHING *CONSECRATED,* BUT GOD CAN'T *ABIDE* ME IN THEM.

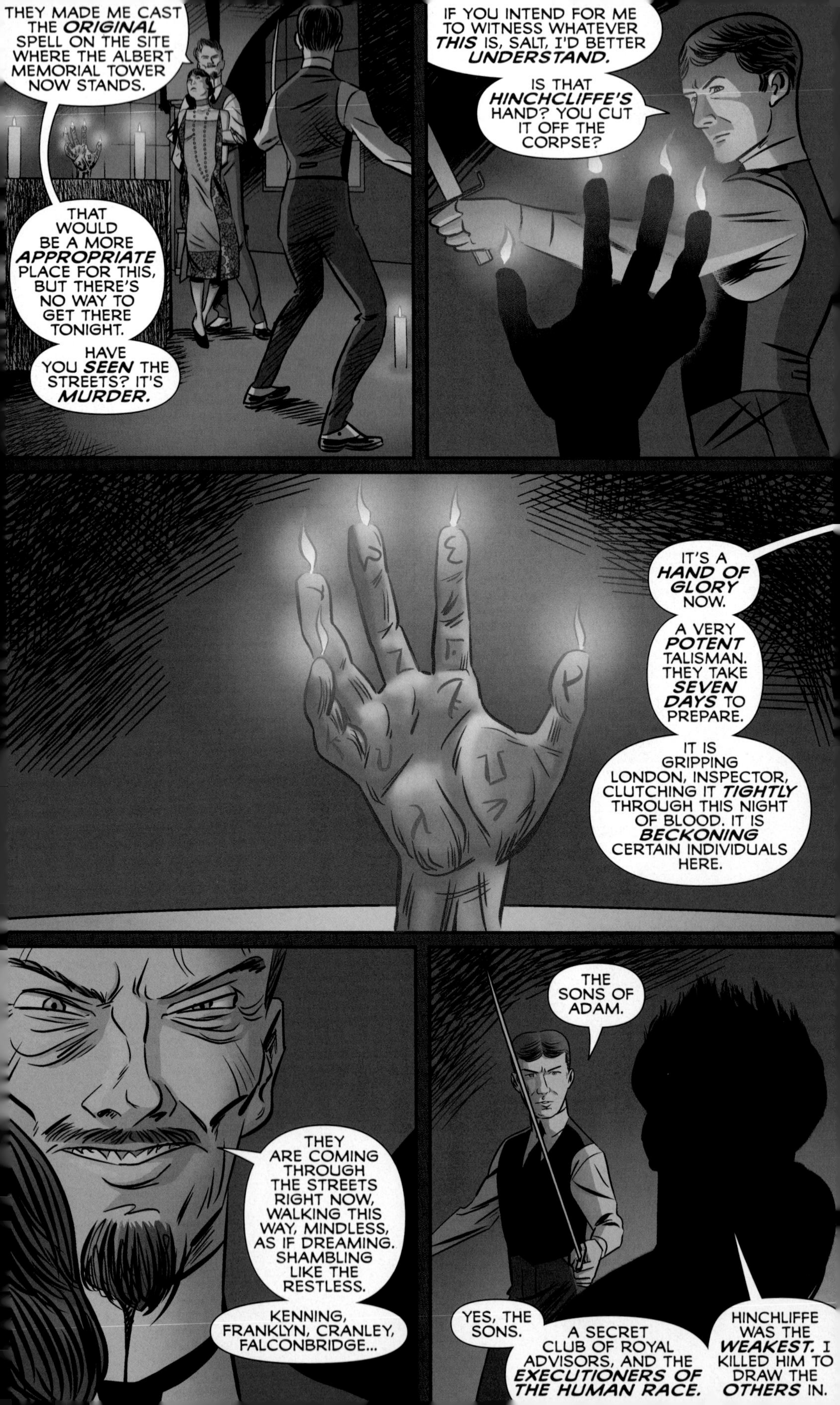
THEY MADE ME CAST THE ORIGINAL SPELL ON THE SITE WHERE THE ALBERT MEMORIAL TOWER NOW STANDS.
THAT WOULD BE A MORE APPROPRIATE PLACE FOR THIS, BUT THERE'S NO WAY TO GET THERE TONIGHT.
HAVE YOU SEEN THE STREETS? IT'S MURDER.
IF YOU INTEND FOR ME TO WITNESS WHATEVER THIS IS, SALT, I'D BETTER UNDERSTAND.
IS THAT HINCHCLIFFE'S HAND? YOU CUT IT OFF THE CORPSE?
IT'S A HAND OF GLORY NOW.
A VERY POTENT TALISMAN. THEY TAKE SEVEN DAYS TO PREPARE.
IT IS GRIPPING LONDON, INSPECTOR, CLUTCHING IT TIGHTLY THROUGH THIS NIGHT OF BLOOD. IT IS BECKONING CERTAIN INDIVIDUALS HERE.
THEY ARE COMING THROUGH THE STREETS RIGHT NOW, WALKING THIS WAY, MINDLESS, AS IF DREAMING. SHAMBLING LIKE THE RESTLESS.
KENNING, FRANKLYN, CRANLEY, FALCONBRIDGE...
THE SONS OF ADAM.
YES, THE SONS.
A SECRET CLUB OF ROYAL ADVISORS, AND THE EXECUTIONERS OF THE HUMAN RACE.
HINCHLIFFE WAS THE WEAKEST. I KILLED HIM TO DRAW THE OTHERS IN.

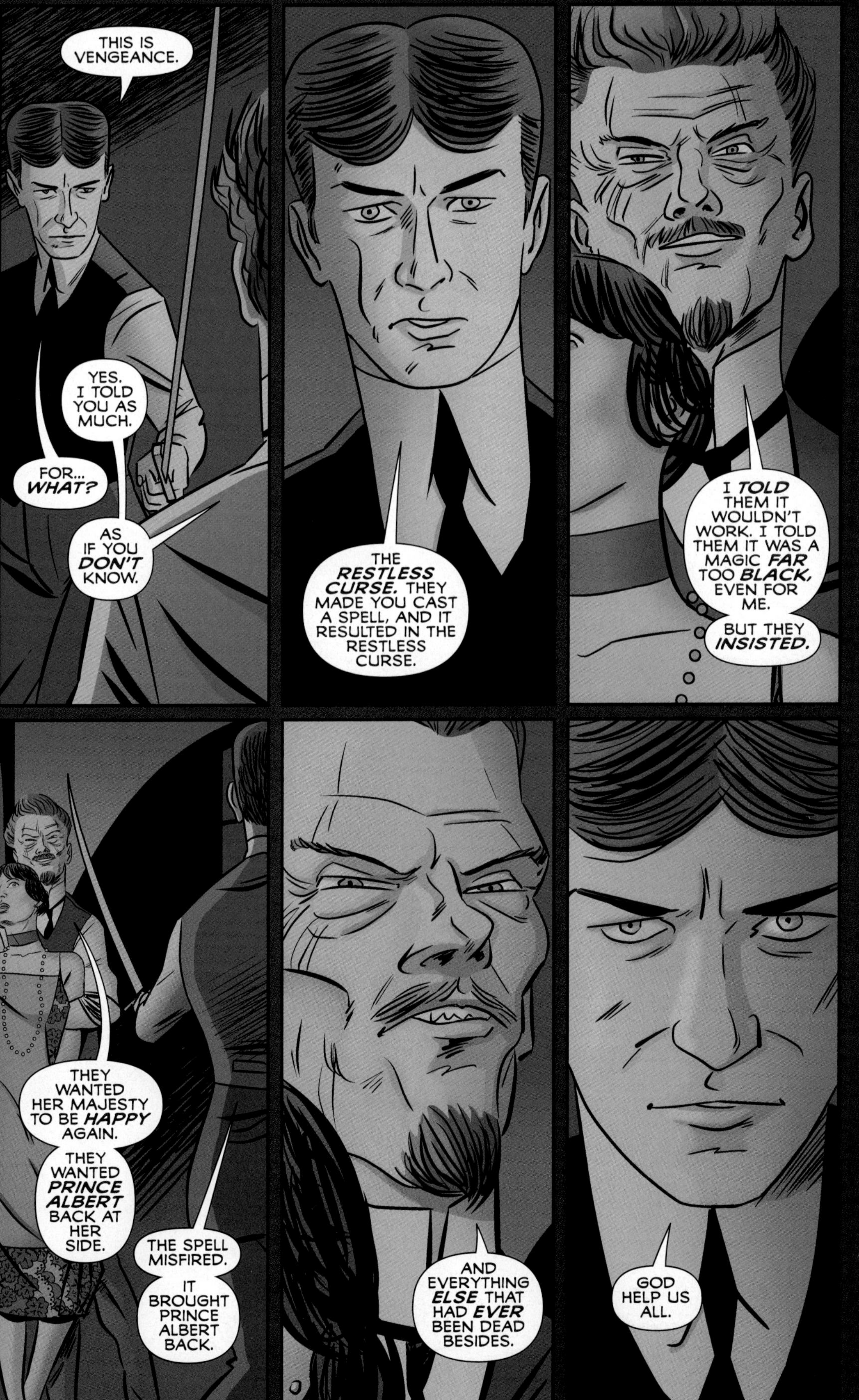
THIS IS VENGEANCE.
FOR... WHAT?
YES. I TOLD YOU AS MUCH.
AS IF YOU DON'T KNOW.
THE RESTLESS CURSE. THEY MADE YOU CAST A SPELL, AND IT RESULTED IN THE RESTLESS CURSE.
I TOLD THEM IT WOULDN'T WORK. I TOLD THEM IT WAS A MAGIC FAR TOO BLACK, EVEN FOR ME.
BUT THEY INSISTED.
THEY WANTED HER MAJESTY TO BE HAPPY AGAIN.
THEY WANTED PRINCE ALBERT BACK AT HER SIDE.
THE SPELL MISFIRED.
IT BROUGHT PRINCE ALBERT BACK.
AND EVERYTHING ELSE THAT HAD EVER BEEN DEAD BESIDES.
GOD HELP US ALL.

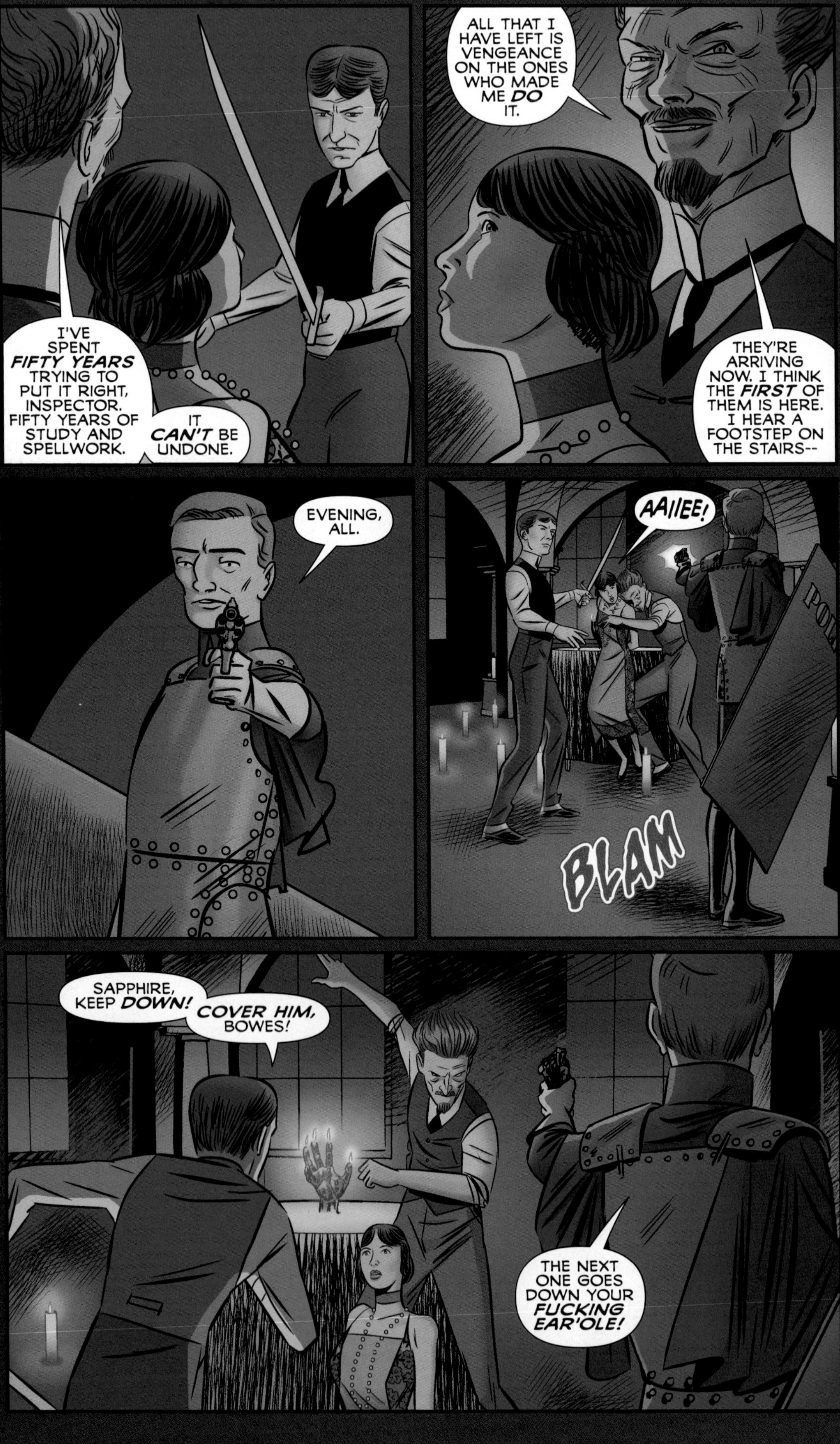
I'VE SPENT FIFTY YEARS TRYING TO PUT IT RIGHT, INSPECTOR. FIFTY YEARS OF STUDY AND SPELLWORK.
IT CAN'T BE UNDONE.
ALL THAT I HAVE LEFT IS VENGEANCE ON THE ONES WHO MADE ME DO IT.
THEY'RE ARRIVING NOW. I THINK THE FIRST OF THEM IS HERE. I HEAR A FOOTSTEP ON THE STAIRS--
EVENING, ALL.
AAIIEE!
BLAM
SAPPHIRE, KEEP DOWN!
COVER HIM, BOWES!
THE NEXT ONE GOES DOWN YOUR FUCKING EAR'OLE!

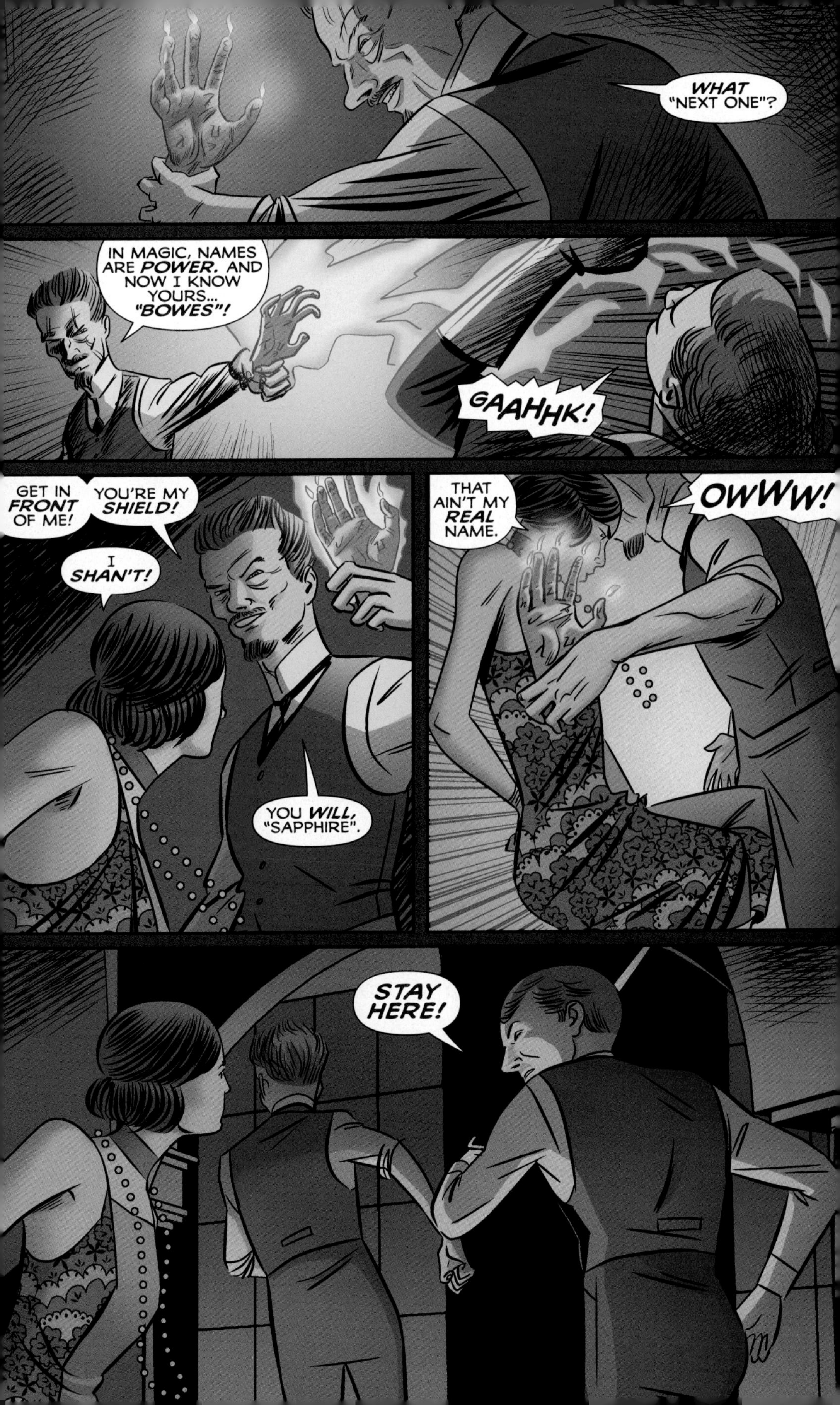
WHAT "NEXT ONE"?
IN MAGIC, NAMES ARE POWER. AND NOW I KNOW YOURS... "BOWES"!
GAAHHK!
GET IN FRONT OF ME!
YOU'RE MY SHIELD!
I SHAN'T!
YOU WILL, "SAPPHIRE".
THAT AIN'T MY REAL NAME.
OWWW!
STAY HERE!

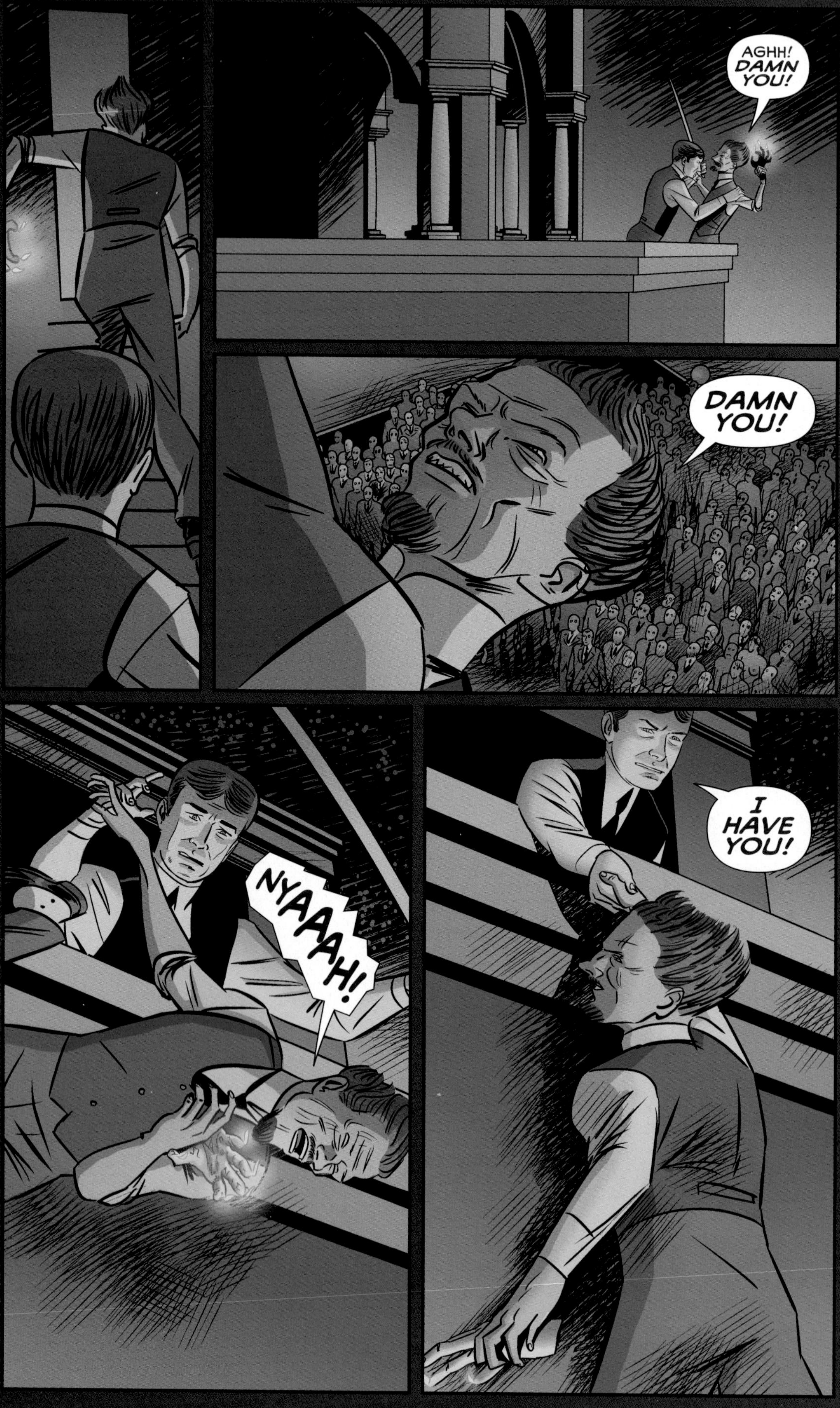
AGHH! DAMN YOU!
DAMN YOU!
NYAAAH!
I HAVE YOU!

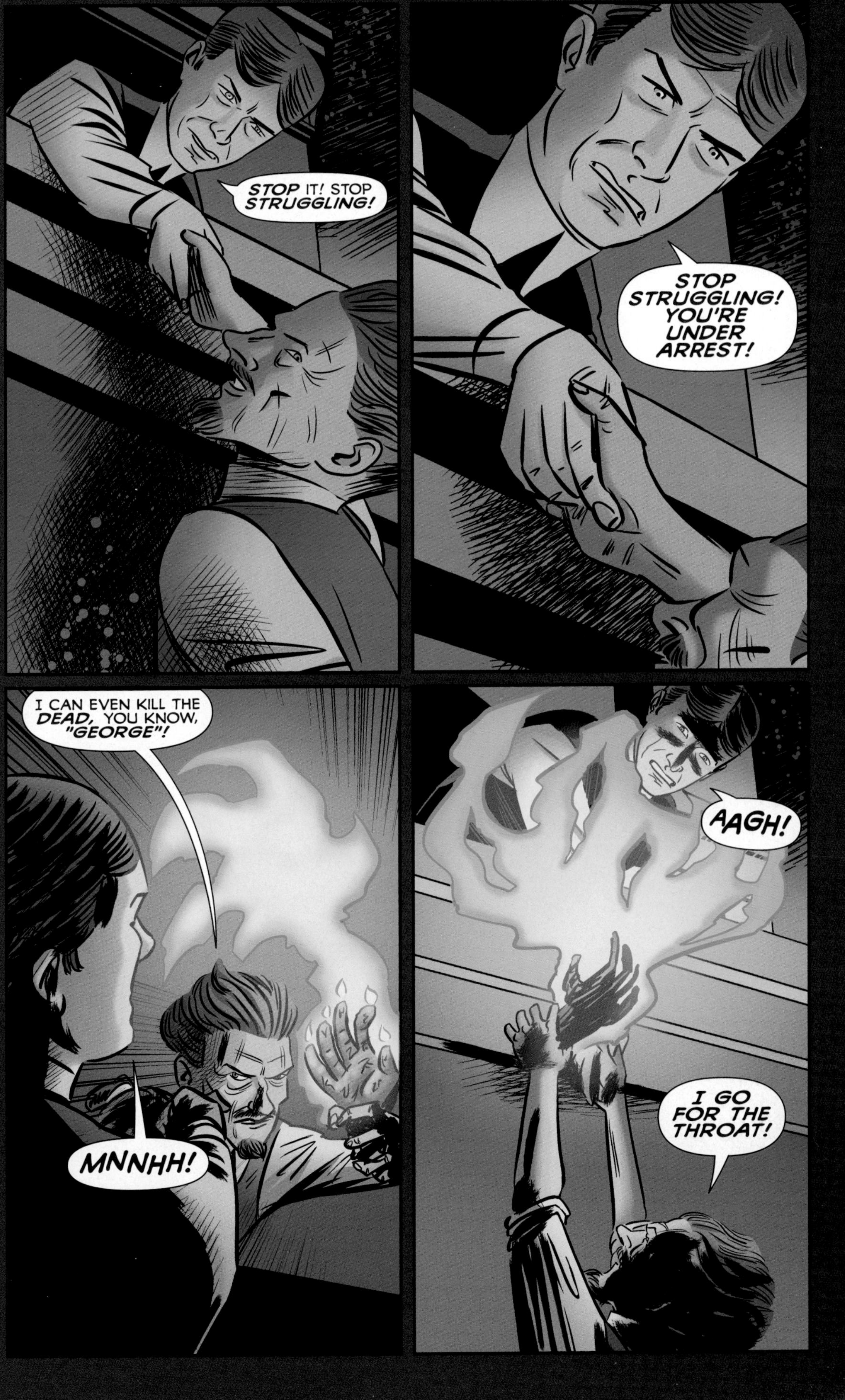

STOP IT! STOP STRUGGLING!
STOP STRUGGLING! YOU'RE UNDER ARREST!
I CAN EVEN KILL THE DEAD, YOU KNOW, "GEORGE"!
MNNHH!
AAGH!
I GO FOR THE THROAT!

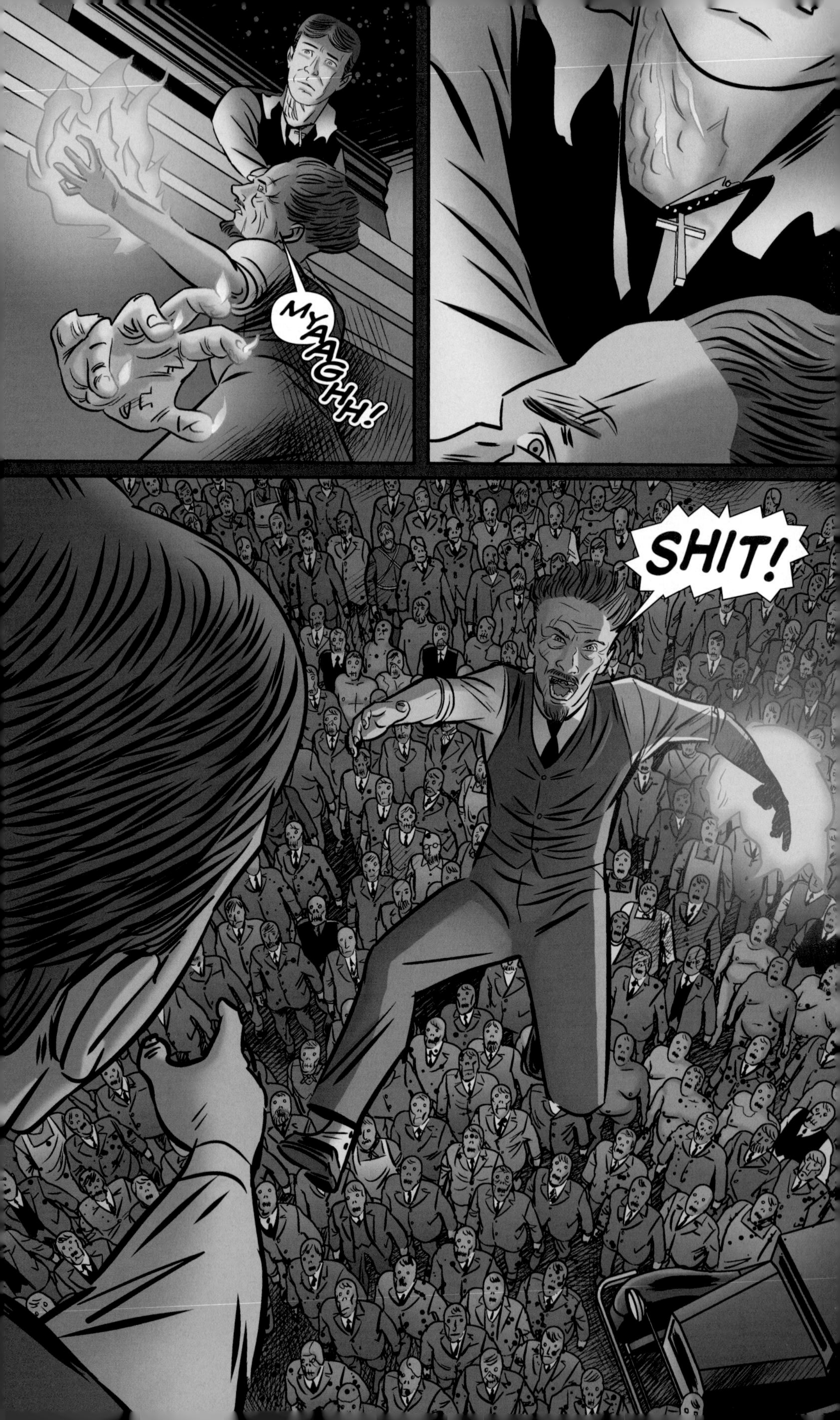
MYAAGHH!
SHIT!

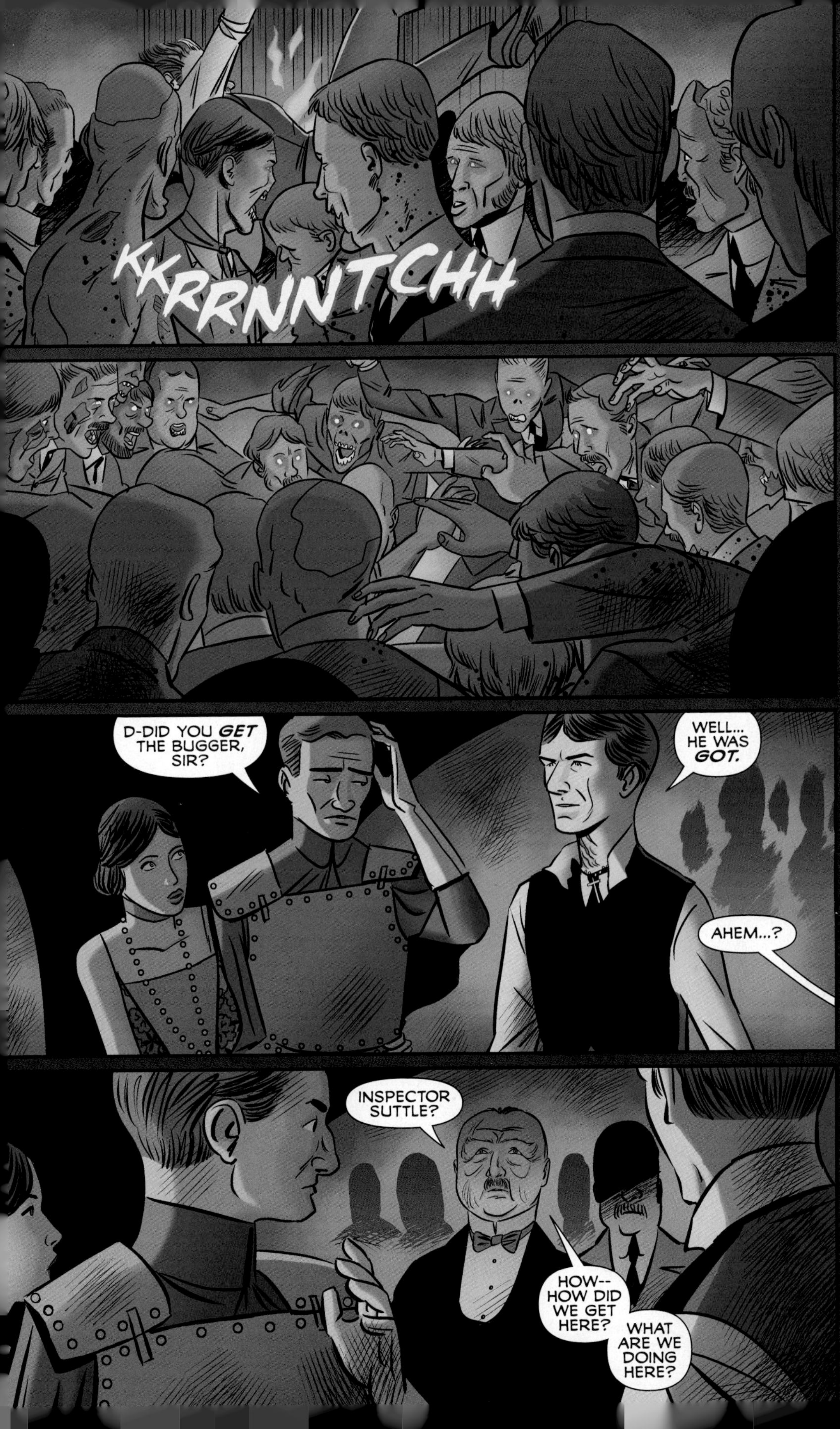
KKRRNNTCHH
D-DID YOU GET THE BUGGER, SIR?
WELL... HE WAS GOT.
AHEM...?
INSPECTOR SUTTLE?
HOW-- HOW DID WE GET HERE?
WHAT ARE WE DOING HERE?

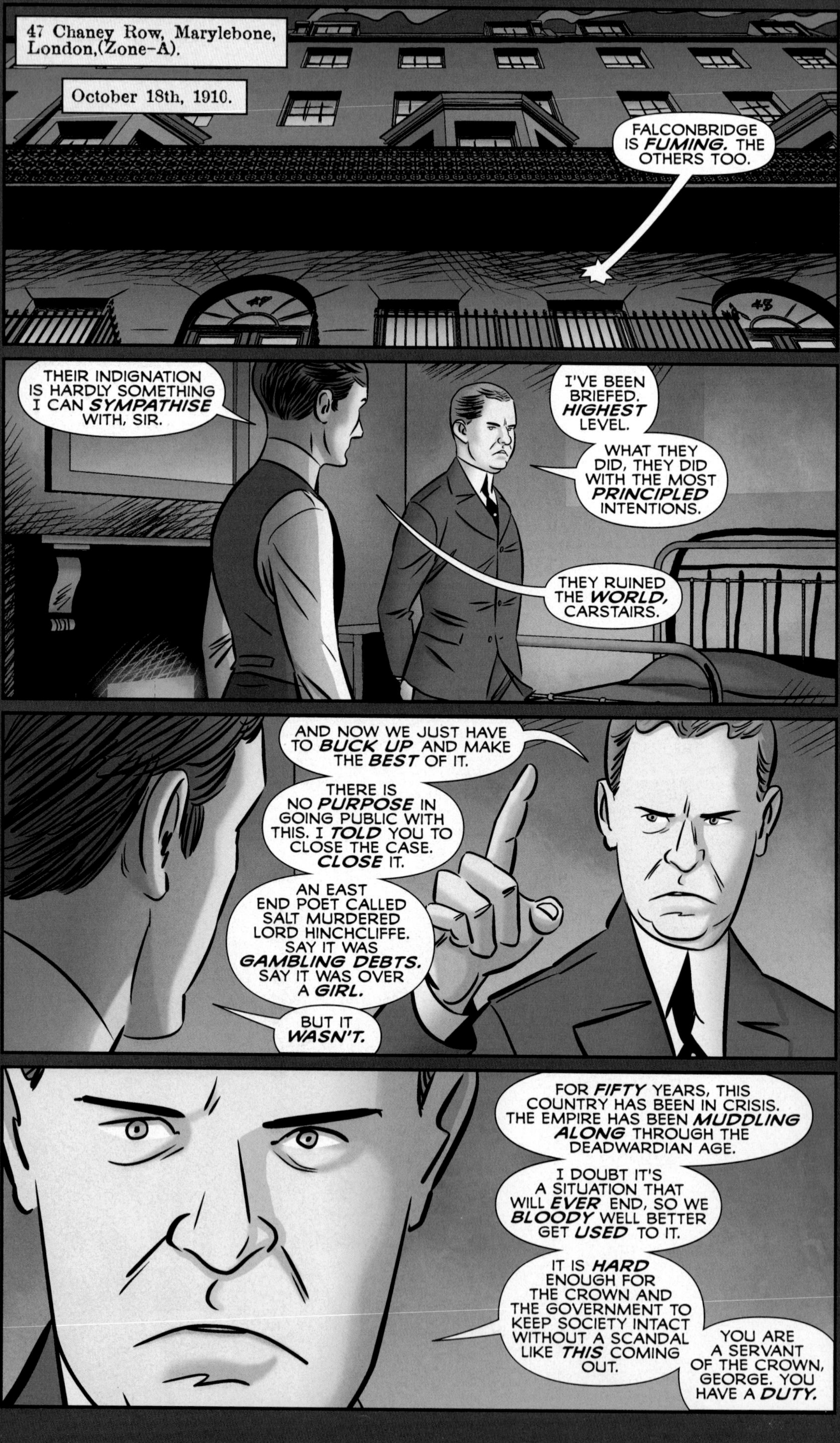
47 Chaney Row, Marylebone, London,(Zone-A).
October 18th, 1910.
FALCONBRIDGE IS FUMING. THE OTHERS TOO.
THEIR INDIGNATION IS HARDLY SOMETHING I CAN SYMPATHISE WITH, SIR.
I'VE BEEN BRIEFED. HIGHEST LEVEL.
WHAT THEY DID, THEY DID WITH THE MOST PRINCIPLED INTENTIONS.
THEY RUINED THE WORLD, CARSTAIRS.
AND NOW WE JUST HAVE TO BUCK UP AND MAKE THE BEST OF IT.
THERE IS NO PURPOSE IN GOING PUBLIC WITH THIS. I TOLD YOU TO CLOSE THE CASE. CLOSE IT.
AN EAST END POET CALLED SALT MURDERED LORD HINCHCLIFFE. SAY IT WAS GAMBLING DEBTS. SAY IT WAS OVER A GIRL.
BUT IT WASN'T.
FOR FIFTY YEARS, THIS COUNTRY HAS BEEN IN CRISIS. THE EMPIRE HAS BEEN MUDDLING ALONG THROUGH THE DEADWARDIAN AGE.
I DOUBT IT'S A SITUATION THAT WILL EVER END, SO WE BLOODY WELL BETTER GET USED TO IT.
IT IS HARD ENOUGH FOR THE CROWN AND THE GOVERNMENT TO KEEP SOCIETY INTACT WITHOUT A SCANDAL LIKE THIS COMING OUT.
YOU ARE A SERVANT OF THE CROWN, GEORGE. YOU HAVE A DUTY.

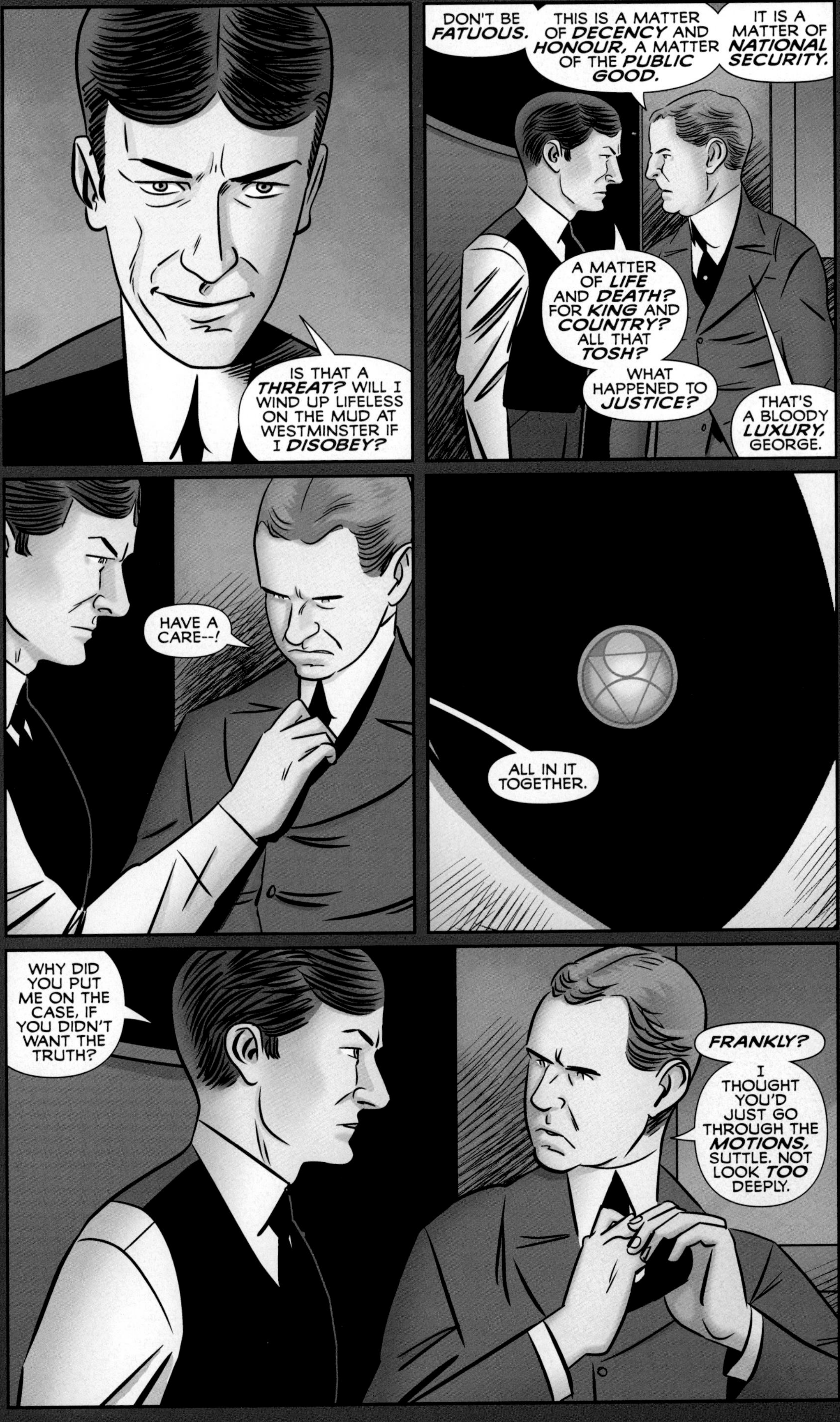
IS THAT A THREAT? WILL I WIND UP LIFELESS ON THE MUD AT WESTMINSTER IF I DISOBEY?
DON'T BE FATUOUS.
THIS IS A MATTER OF DECENCY AND HONOUR, A MATTER OF THE PUBLIC GOOD.
IT IS A MATTER OF NATIONAL SECURITY.
A MATTER OF LIFE AND DEATH? FOR KING AND COUNTRY? ALL THAT TOSH?
WHAT HAPPENED TO JUSTICE?
THAT'S A BLOODY LUXURY, GEORGE.
HAVE A CARE--!
ALL IN IT TOGETHER.
WHY DID YOU PUT ME ON THE CASE, IF YOU DIDN'T WANT THE TRUTH?
FRANKLY?
I THOUGHT YOU'D JUST GO THROUGH THE MOTIONS, SUTTLE. NOT LOOK TOO DEEPLY.

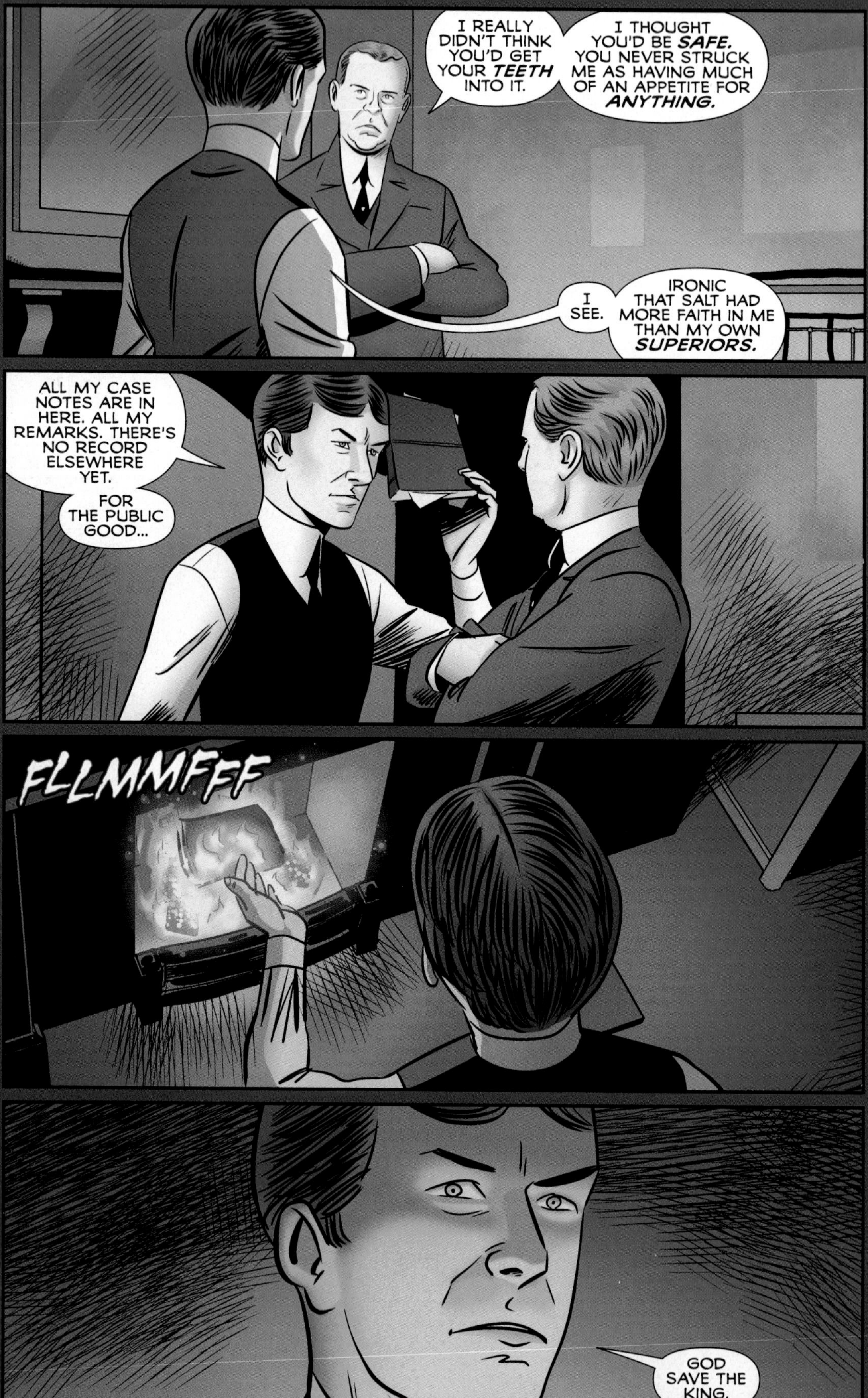
I REALLY DIDN'T THINK YOU'D GET YOUR TEETH INTO IT.
I THOUGHT YOU'D BE SAFE. YOU NEVER STRUCK ME AS HAVING MUCH OF AN APPETITE FOR ANYTHING.
I SEE.
IRONIC THAT SALT HAD MORE FAITH IN ME THAN MY OWN SUPERIORS.
ALL MY CASE NOTES ARE IN HERE. ALL MY REMARKS. THERE'S NO RECORD ELSEWHERE YET.
FOR THE PUBLIC GOOD...
FLLMMFFF
GOD SAVE THE KING.

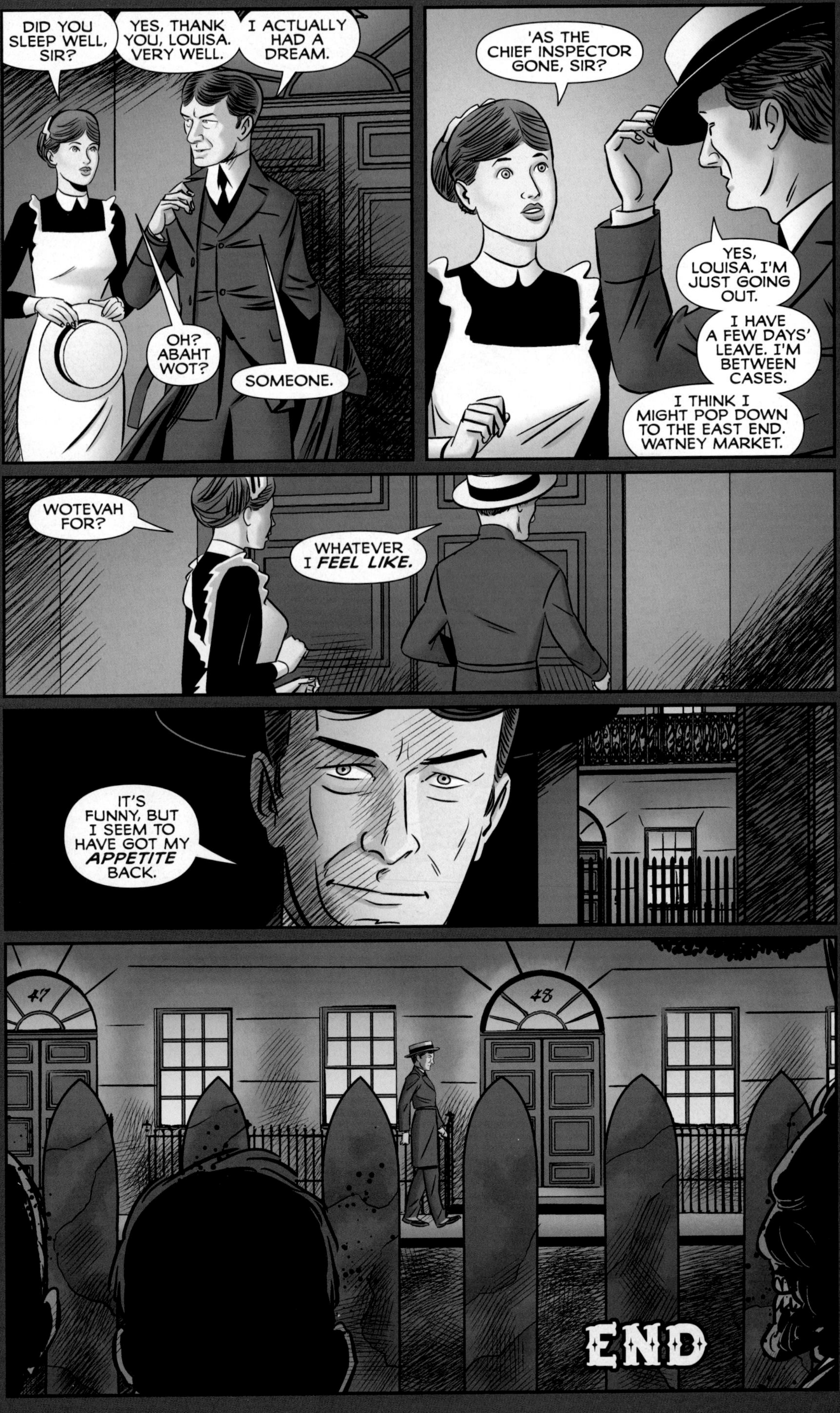
DID YOU SLEEP WELL, SIR?
YES, THANK YOU, LOUISA. VERY WELL.
I ACTUALLY HAD A DREAM.
OH? ABAHT WOT?
SOMEONE.
'AS THE CHIEF INSPECTOR GONE, SIR?
YES, LOUISA. I'M JUST GOING OUT.
I HAVE A FEW DAYS' LEAVE. I'M BETWEEN CASES.
I THINK I MIGHT POP DOWN TO THE EAST END. WATNEY MARKET.
WOTEVAH FOR?
WHATEVER I *FEEL LIKE.*
IT'S FUNNY, BUT I SEEM TO HAVE GOT MY *APPETITE* BACK.
47
48
END

THE NEW DEADWARDIANS #1 VARIANT COVER
art by Cliff Chiang

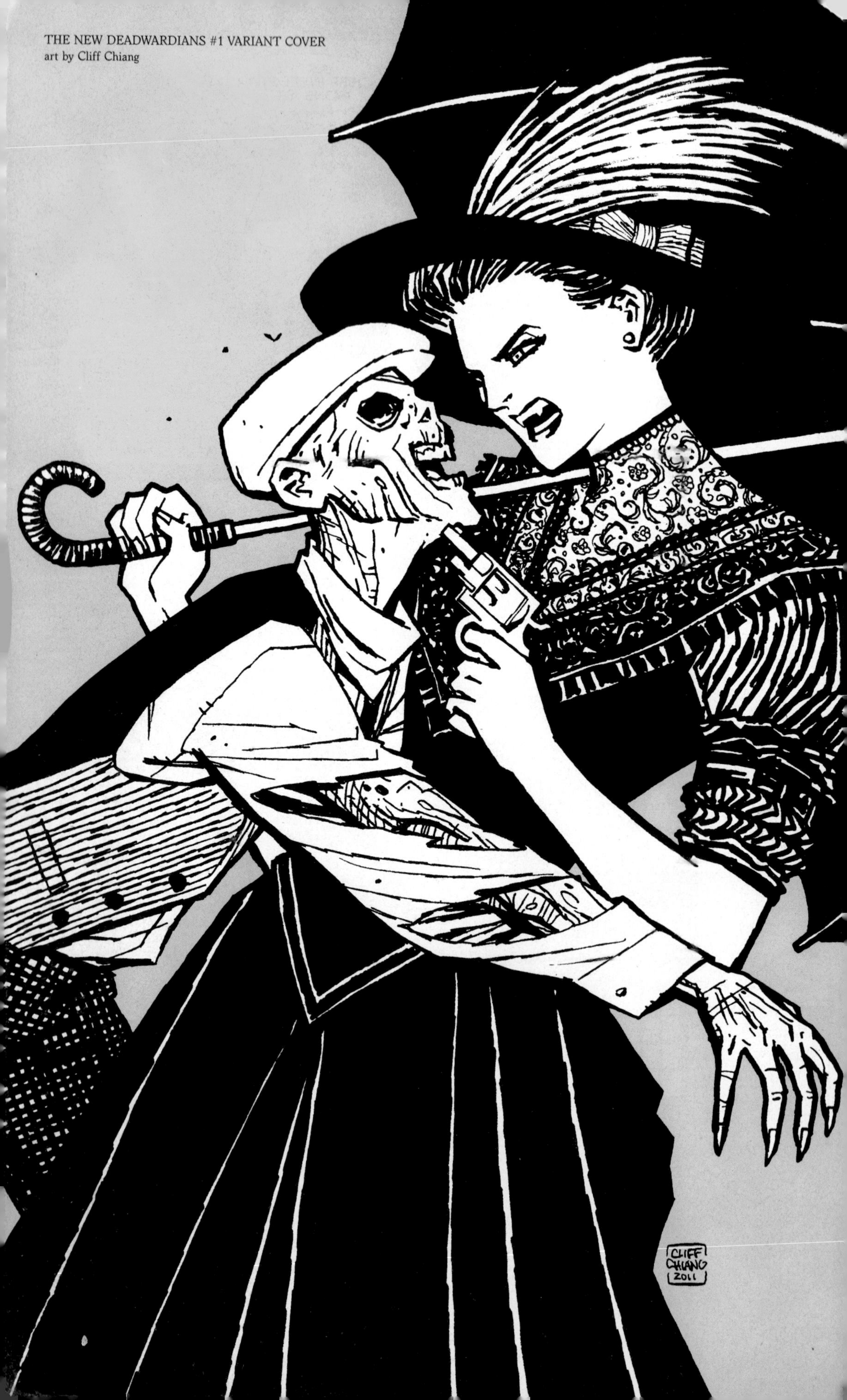
CLIFF
CHIANG
2011

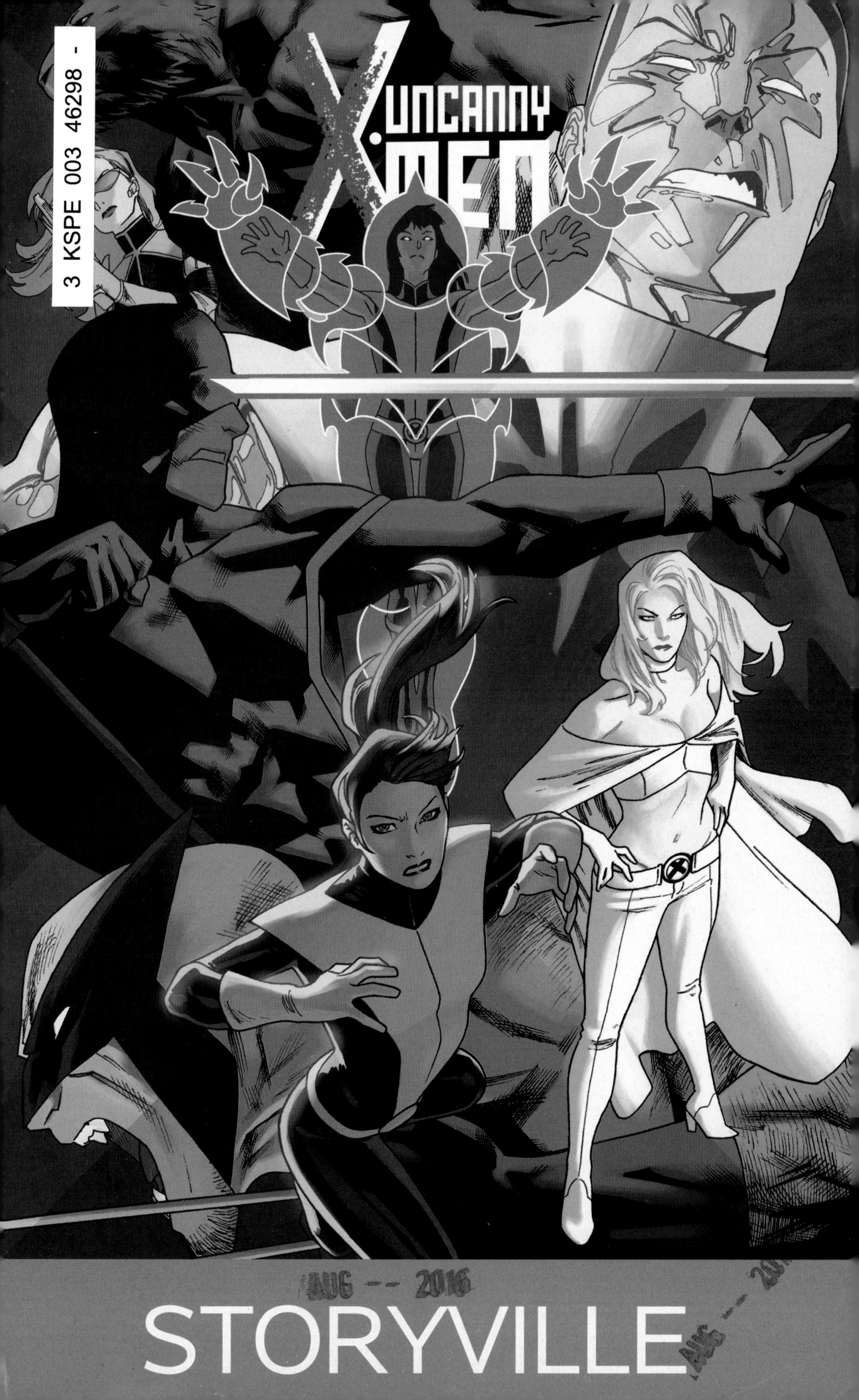
UNCANNY
X-MEN

STORYVILLE

CYCLOPS
SCOTT SUMMERS

EMMA FROST

TRIAGE
CHRISTOPHER MUSE

TEMPUS
EVA BELL

MAGNETO
ERIK LEHNSHERR

MAGIK
ILLYANA RASPUTIN

GOLDBALLS
FABIO MEDIA

BENJAMIN DEEDS

Hopkinsville Christian County Public Library

BRIAN MICHAEL
BENDIS
WRITER

CHRIS
BACHALO
PENCILER, #32

KRIS
ANKA
ARTIST, #33-34

VALERIO
SCHITI
ARTIST, #35

TIM
TOWNSEND

WAYNE
FAUCHER

MARK
IRWIN

VICTOR
OLAZABA

AL
VEY

INKERS, #32

CHRIS
BACHALO

RAIN
BEREDO

ANTONIO
FABELA

MARTE
GRACIA

RICHARD
ISANOVE

COLOR ARTISTS, #32

COLOR ARTISTS, #33-34

COLOR ARTIST, #35

ISSUE #600

PENCILERS: **SARA PICHELLI, MAHMUD ASRAR, STUART IMMONEN, KRIS ANKA,**
CHRIS BACHALO, DAVID MARQUEZ & FRAZER IRVING
INKERS: **WADE VON GRAWBADGER, TIM TOWNSEND & MARK IRWIN**
COLOR ARTISTS: **MARTE GRACIA, JASON KEITH, CHRIS BACHALO & FRAZER IRVING**

COVER ART: **CHRIS BACHALO** & **TIM TOWNSEND** (#32, #600) AND **KRIS ANKA** (#33-35)
LETTERER: **VC's JOE CARAMAGNA**   ASSISTANT EDITORS: **XANDER JAROWEY** & **CHRISTINA HARRINGTON**
EDITORS: **MIKE MARTS** & **MARK PANICCIA**

X-MEN CREATED BY **STAN LEE** & **JACK KIRBY**

COLLECTION EDITOR: **JENNIFER GRÜNWALD**   ASSOCIATE EDITOR: **SARAH BRUNSTAD**
ASSOCIATE MANAGING EDITOR: **ALEX STARBUCK**   EDITOR, SPECIAL PROJECTS: **MARK D. BEAZLEY**
VP, PRODUCTION & SPECIAL PROJECTS: **JEFF YOUNGQUIST**   SVP PRINT, SALES & MARKETING: **DAVID GABRIEL**
BOOK DESIGNER: **ADAM DEL RE**

EDITOR IN CHIEF: **AXEL ALONSO**   CHIEF CREATIVE OFFICER: **JOE QUESADA**
PUBLISHER: **DAN BUCKLEY**   EXECUTIVE PRODUCER: **ALAN FINE**

UNCANNY X-MEN VOL. 6: STORYVILLE. Contains material originally published in magazine form as UNCANNY X-MEN #32-35 and #600. First printing 2016. ISBN# 978-0-7851-9231-2. Published by MARVEL WORLDWIDE, INC., a subsidiary of MARVEL ENTERTAINMENT, LLC. OFFICE OF PUBLICATION: 135 West 50th Street, New York, NY 10020. Copyright © 2016 MARVEL No similarity between any of the names, characters, persons, and/or institutions in this magazine with those of any living or dead person or institution is intended, and any such similarity which may exist is purely coincidental. Printed in the U.S.A. ALAN FINE, President, Marvel Entertainment; DAN BUCKLEY, President, TV, Publishing & Brand Management; JOE QUESADA, Chief Creative Officer; TOM BREVOORT, SVP of Publishing; DAVID BOGART, SVP of Business Affairs & Operations, Publishing & Partnership; C.B. CEBULSKI, VP of Brand Management & Development, Asia; DAVID GABRIEL, SVP of Sales & Marketing, Publishing; JEFF YOUNGQUIST, VP of Production & Special Projects; DAN CARR, Executive Director of Publishing Technology; ALEX MORALES, Director of Publishing Operations; SUSAN CRESPI, Production Manager; STAN LEE, Chairman Emeritus. For information regarding advertising in Marvel Comics or on Marvel.com, please contact Vit DeBellis, Integrated Sales Manager, at vdebellis@marvel.com. For Marvel subscription inquiries, please call 888-511-5480. Manufactured between 6/3/2016 and 7/11/2016 by R.R. DONNELLEY, INC., SALEM, VA, USA.

10 9 8 7 6 5 4 3 2 1